Copper Mines, Company Towns, Mexicans, Indians, Mormons, Masons, Jews, Muslims, Gays, Wombs, McDonalds, and The March of Dimes: "Survival of the Fittest" in and Far Beyond the Deserts of Arizona, New Mexico, and Utah

By

Dr. Larry R. Stucki

Order this book online at www.trafford.com
or email orders@trafford.com

Most Trafford titles are also available at major online book retailers.

Note for Librarians: A cataloguing record for this book is available from Library
and Archives Canada at www.collectionscanada.ca/amicus/index-e.html

Printed in Victoria, BC, Canada.

ISBN: 978-1-4251-1334-1 (sc)

ISBN: 978-1-4251-1335-8 (dj)

Library of Congress Control Number: 2009931997

*We at Trafford believe that it is the responsibility of us all, as both individuals and corporations,
to make choices that are environmentally and socially sound. You, in turn, are supporting this
responsible conduct each time you purchase a Trafford book, or make use of our publishing services.
To find out how you are helping, please visit www.trafford.com/responsiblepublishing.html*

*Our mission is to efficiently provide the world's finest, most comprehensive book publishing
service, enabling every author to experience success. To find out how to publish your book, your
way, and have it available worldwide, visit us online at www.trafford.com*

Trafford rev. 11/03/09

 www.trafford.com

North America & international
toll-free: 1 888 232 4444 (USA & Canada)
phone: 250 383 6864 ♦ fax: 250 383 6804 ♦ email: info@trafford.com

The United Kingdom & Europe
phone: +44 (0)1865 487 395 ♦ local rate: 0845 230 9601
facsimile: +44 (0)1865 481 507 ♦ email: info.uk@trafford.com

CONTENTS

FIGURES

TABLES

Key to Tables V to XV 452

APPENDIX

PREFACE

Just as few natural species have withstood the test of ever-changing earth environments through time, relatively few human-created systems (e.g., companies, governments, religions, etc.) long survive their creation. What then is the secret of those that continue to defy these odds and what factors have led to the failure of others? This manuscript attempts to answer this question using the Phelps Dodge Corporation, its unions, its Native American and Mexican workforce, the Ajo Inter-tribal Community Council, the Mormon Church, The March of Dimes, and others as examples.

The story began in 1967 when I naively first arrived in Southern Arizona to help collect data for my dissertation and the planned creation of a Papago population registrar. Now 42 years later and hopefully much wiser, I feel that I have now collected enough additional data and insight to go much farther beyond the mere revision of my 1970 dissertation that my mentor, Robert Hackenberg, urged me then to complete.

Now, with his recent death, I deeply regret that I will not be able to personally thank him for the important suggested revisions he gave me back in 1970 that I have now incorporated into the present manuscript.

However, the long delay has enabled me to produce what, I am hoping you will agree, is a much better "product" especially with the insight I have gained through the years from thousands of Native Americans, students, fellow faculty members, members of mine and other churches, my wife and children, and the professors and other participants in the summer seminars I attended at the University of Arizona and Harvard .

CHAPTER 1:

Babies, "Black Boxes," "Tipping Points," and "Order-Maximizing" Humans

As a baby grows up, it seeks predictability and control over its own body and over its food supply and other aspects of its immediate environment. The infant early learns to use its most effective environmental control mechanism, its voice, to produce a loud cry which then almost always modifies the output of another individual in its surrounding universe (e.g., the mother or father).... At first the baby may be thought of as "an organism trying to control the output of a Black Box [in its environment], the contents of which is unknown to it" (Ashby 1960:82), but the reaction of the "Black Box" (e.g., the mother or father) to the baby's cry often becomes quite predictable.

For many decades now, behavioral scientists have been searching for a single unifying principle to unite the various disciplines. Perhaps the simplest approach to this dilemma in the past has been to construct a so-called "maximization" theory. Thus, Burling (1962:813) points out that, "the notion that human behavior is somehow oriented toward a maximization of some desired end has appeared in a great range of social science theory." And we have the "economic man" of the economists, the pleasure seeking man of Freud, and the "power-hungry man" of Leach. We even have Zipf's "man" who continually seeks to minimize effort. Burling (1962:817-819) himself introduces the concept of the "satisfaction-seeking man" but fails somewhat in his attempt to point out the usefulness of such a vague concept. Obviously all of these "men" have failed in one respect or another to survive the acid test of the real world. Therefore it is with some fear and trembling that I now seek to introduce a new maximization hypothesis which upon the basis of my Ajo data is built upon the premise that humans individually and collectively always seek to maximize the predictability and often control of certain segments of their total environment while maintaining "adequate" levels of control in all other segments.

One should be extremely careful to indicate at this point that what may be considered to be order in the environment for one individual or system of individuals may not be considered as such by another individual or system of individuals. The object of many recent studies has, in fact, been the attempt to learn how different individuals and societies "order their universe." However it is the contention of this author that, although this ordering process differs from individual to individual, and from system to system, in any given society, entropy (i.e., the perceived level of disorder or uncertainty) reduction is always the desired result.

There are two distinct ways that humans can approach the problem of attempting to gain the knowledge they feel is needed to seek this optimum level of environmental control. Thus as Singh (1966:73) states:

> ... whenever we are confronted with crowds of entities whether of men, messages or molecules, there are two ways of dealing with them. Either we specify the attribute(s) under consideration of each and every individual in the crowd, or we specify the over-all statistical average(s) of their individual attribute(s). The former is said to define the internal structure of <u>microstate</u> of the crowd and the latter its outer facade or <u>macrostate</u>[1]...

It is important to note that it is not always the desire of humans to know the microstate all portions of their environments any more than it is the wish of the average chemist to know the microstate of his molecules for most purposes. What is important to the individual is to be able to predict correctly the output of other systems which are affecting or may affect what Ashby (1960:42,43) would label the "essential" variables of the systems to which the person belongs. Thus even certain portions of the environment that are highly disordered from a molecular point of view, for the individual can appear to be quite orderly. This is apparently what Singh (1966:208) refers to when he discusses "order" arising from "disorder" "due to the stability of statistical attributes such as averages pertaining to assemblies of large numbers of microparticles." Thus, in summary, it can be stated that reduction in the entropy of certain portions of the individual's or group's environment may require a better knowledge of the microstate of those portions of the environment while in other portions, a better knowledge of the macrostate may be all that is desired.

If all men and women and systems of women and men seek to maximize the predictability of certain segments of their total environments then the question naturally arises, how do they then differ? I submit that individuals and systems of individuals differ from one another only in the level of prediction and control they seek and obtain over the different portions of their environments. Both the "slave" and the "king" seek to make their environments more predictable and both control certain aspects of their environments but the king "controls" the slave. However, this latter control is never absolute. Thus, at times, the "slave" can "control" the actions of the "king" (e.g., see Bennett 1967:450-452 or Pitt-Rivers 1961:200-201).

Humans are, by nature, curious animals seeking knowledge about and power over all aspects of his universe. Thus, even when individuals attempt to climb a mountain or explore a new canyon or see how fast their cars will run, they seek to extend their knowledge of and control over some aspect of their surrounding universe. And, even such ventures as our massive space program are more motivated by this basic curiosity and desire for "conquest" than by so-called "practical" motives. As one young spelunker said when asked why he spent his free time crawling around in caves (Petranek 1967:37):

> As corny as it sounds ..,you're conquering nature. And for some reason, even though you've come out the same place you went in, there really is a feeling of accomplishment.

As a baby grows up, it seeks predictability and control over its own body and over its food supply and other aspects of its immediate environment. The infant early learns to use its most effective environmental control mechanism, its voice, to produce a loud cry which then almost always modifies the output of another individual in its surrounding universe (e.g., the mother or father), who the baby hopes will drop whatever she or he is doing to bring food or a blanket to the baby or perhaps change a dirty diaper or just hug the baby to demonstrate her or his love for it[2]. At first the baby may be thought of as "an organism trying to control the output of a Black Box [in its environment], the contents of which is unknown to it" (Ashby 1960:82), but the reaction of the "Black Box" (e.g., the mother or father) to the baby's cry often becomes quite predictable.

As the child grows up and prediction and control become "adequate" in certain sectors of its environment then no further change occurs in the child's response to impulses (i.e., inputs) from those sectors of the environment. Thus a "habit" (i.e., stereotypic response) is established. Since an individual's knowledge and power of prediction are never absolute, due in part to constant change in the environment, the search for increased knowledge and power of prediction and control will begin anew whenever the individual feels that his or her control over some aspect of his or her environment is "inadequate" or could be improved. (Such an event frequently occurs in the contact situation and often leads to so-called cultural "innovations[11]").

This, however, doesn't mean that all humans, individually or collectively, will be equally successful in this quest. Both farmers with their insecticides and native gardeners with their magical phrases are seeking to minimize the entropy (relative to them) of the surrounding universe but the level of prediction and control actually achieved often differs.

Also, just as one can say that humans constantly experiment to see just how far their control over their own bodies and surrounding environments extend and to see how far they can further extend this control, one can also say that they cease to experiment when they are "certain" that to experiment further will cause them to lose their present level of environmental control. Thus, the native dares not climb the sacred mountain for fear of the expected wrath of the gods and the priest or priestess dares not change the sacred ceremony lest misfortune befall her or his people. In some cases these fears are justified but at other times they are not (e.g., few individuals would deliberately step in front of a speeding train or put their bare hands in a fire but most have survived Friday, the 13th, without being harmed). However, here, as in much of human behavior, it is not what will actually happen that really matters, but what is expected to happen. People act in accordance with what they believe happened in the past and what they believe will occur in the future. And, in the chapters which follow in this book, in both seeking explanations for past events and making predictions about future ones, I will often emphasize the importance of what may be called "anxiety variables"[3] which are found in all systems, human or otherwise, which have the ability to "anticipate" (i.e., make predictions about) and, at times, attempt to control the development of future systemic and environmental states.

"Anxiety" can thus be defined as the feeling that prediction and/or control in one or more areas of a system's environment are somehow inadequate. The individual usually tries to reduce this anxiety level as much as possible, but often other systems (i.e., individuals or groups) actually try to raise this anxiety level in the individual. Thus, as many of us have experienced, group leaders often deliberately try to induce stress in their group memberships so that certain resultant actions will occur.[4] In such cases the individual must either perform the requested actions or withdraw from the system before the anxiety level will fall. Unresolved anxiety may lead to mental disorders or nervous breakdowns.

The ultimate threat which such leaders utilize is expulsion from the group (i.e., system). Lesser threats include loss of rights, privileges, and rewards. All of these "punishments" will usually, however, result in a net loss of control for the individual in the system involved. On the other hand, "rewards" offered by such leaders promise the faithful follower greater control over group benefits and, often, greater control over other group members.

However, leaders usually exercise care in inducing this anxiety so that an upper "critical limit" (i.e., "tipping point" the term for this often-observed phenomenon popularized in recent years by Gladwin (2000:9)). will not be exceeded in the individual. This offers a possible explanation for the frequent appearance of comic relief in an otherwise serious religious ceremony (e.g., the clown in pueblo ceremonies and the joke in the preacher's sermon). Also, the appearance of some form of the "joking relationship" in an otherwise strained social system can possibly be explained in terms of anxiety reduction.

Finally, it should be pointed out that the absolute value that an anxiety variable assumes is functionally related to the danger that is perceived by the individual or the decision makers of a larger system to the continued survival of the system. Therefore, the value of the upper critical limit of such a variable is more or less functionally related to the upper and lower critical limits of other essential system variables such as income, food, shelter, etc. depending upon how accurately the present state and critical limits of the other essential variables are perceived. Often, however, it is the upper critical limit of the anxiety variable that is exceeded before any of the upper or lower critical limits of other essential system variables thus precipitating somewhat earlier than expected, one of the possible outcomes to be described at a later point in this book.[5]

With physical systems, elaborate testing procedures have often been employed to see how much "abuse" the system can withstand without "failing" (i.e., failing to limit essential variables within certain critical values). However, in dealing with individuals and systems of individuals, the researcher for various religious, moral, political or practical reasons is usually limited in the quality and quantity of "stress" he can impose on such systems, if any.[6] Therefore, the investigator feels fortunate indeed when on rare occasions he is able to witness massive stress being applied to individuals, groups, or societies by some outside environmental force. Such a fortunate occurrence happened during my period of field residence in Ajo, a company controlled mining town in southern Arizona--the stress in this case being induced by a prolonged copper strike beginning in 1967.

Chapter Notes

1. See also Hall and Fagan (1968:84-86) and for a related distinction see Levi-Strauss (1962:325) where he discusses the difference between a "mechanical model" and a "statistical model."

2. There are, of course, certain cross-cultural and individual differences in the behavioral responses of adults to the crying infant, so that the child may at times be punished for his crying rather than be rewarded (e.g., see Hoebel 1960:92).

3. Buckley (1968:493) and some earlier writers that he quotes would probably call these variables, "tension".

4. In a like manner, during courtship, both individuals induce stress (anxiety) in each other. This leads ultimately to an "illicit" relationship, marriage, or a rupture of the relationship.

5. Many examples of this can be found during the fall 2008 world-wide "financial melt-down."

6. See Stucki (1967) for a discussion of this problem with respect to "action anthropology."

CHAPTER 2:

The 1967 Copper Strike

"We are just being used. The high union people are not
suffering." (a quotation from L.I. 44) "Cynics might sneer
that Phelps Dodge has been extending credit in its own
self-interest to encourage key, skilled personnel to ride
out the strike." (A.R. Tues. March 5, 1968:15).

In June of 1967, little did the miners of Ajo realize just what was in
store for them less than one month later, although there were hints
that at least a brief strike was to be expected since on June 24, 1967, a
Tucson paper with many readers in Ajo reported that (A.D.S. p.A-l),
"nobody appears optimistic that a pact will be reached by the June 30
midnight contract expiration date" between "a 13-union committee and
Phelps Dodge Corporation". Many of the miners were, in fact, looking
forward to a few days off at the beginning of summer to relax from
the grueling twenty-six-day-on – two-day-off work schedule at the
mine (e.g., see F.N. February 7, 1968). They had received such a brief
vacation during the six-day strike in 1959 but at that time, as a Phoenix

paper later reported, "both the miners and Phelps Dodge Corporation people say the walkout was called "a joke or a holiday that let us get some fishing in down at Rocky Point." (a nearby Mexican village on the Gulf of California) (A.R. September 24, 1967: A-20). Therefore, although the men had kept working in the mines on a day-to-day basis after the June 30th expiration date of the contract, by July 13th, "spokesmen for the score of unions involved in joint bargaining with major copper producers disclosed that negotiations had all but collapsed" (A.R. July 13, 1967:1) and that a major "walkout" was scheduled for midnight the next day (A.R. July 15, 1967:1; July 14, 1967:19).

Both sides to the dispute stated publicly at this time that they believed that (A.R. July 13, 1967:4):

> ...a walkout will be of short duration because President Johnson will invoke the eighty-day cooling off provision of the Taft-Hartley Act.
> This the President will do ... because copper is essential to the war effort in Vietnam.

However, there were others among those closest to the negotiating tables that were not nearly as optimistic about the predicted brief nature of the strike as witnessed by the prophetic statements of one "high ranking union official" who pointed out (A.C.N. July 13, 1967:4) the fact that the nation had "more than a one-month stockpile of copper which meant that "a strike could not reasonably be immediately considered a national emergency" and of several "other informed observers" who believed that (A.C.N. July 13, 1967:4):

> ...the copper conflict scene ultimately will switch to Washington, where the administration will emphasize the vital role of copper in national defense.

...the copper industry will insist that it can not meet union demands without a price increase. With some hesitation ... the Johnson administration will approve a hike in the price of copper.

The local Ajo Copper News while not mentioning the pending strike directly, in an editorial entitled "Ajo is the Best Place to Live:" (A.C.N. July 13, 1967:2) nevertheless tried to prevent bitter feelings from developing among those to be affected by the walkout by "reminding" the people that:

> Without a doubt we are fortunate to live in a community like Ajo. ... Where we are fortunate is mostly our staid economic situation which has existed for many years. People not accustomed to our economic situation are visibly amazed to find how progressive our town is.
> How amazing it is to know how high is the average income. We have always been secretly jealous of the high standard, but Ajo has been good to us and people have been able to afford good cars, household luxuries and many of the advantages of much larger towns. It is no secret that instant credit is available in practically any city in Arizona if they learn that you are gainfully employed in Ajo.
> Even though many people in areas throughout Arizona do not know much of Ajo, the merchants do. Ajo carries a reputation of good people, stable payrolls and 7,000 to 8,000 people.

And in an editorial (A.C.N. July 20, 1967:2) a week later entitled, "It's Time to Show Our Faith" that followed the beginning of walkout that:

...The people of Ajo have always been exceptional in their endeavors to make Ajo an outstanding community. Labor, as well as management, have always been fair to each other. Today we are going through a period of adjustment which in the end will find Ajo a better place in which to live.

The people of this community are exhibiting a calm that other communities can well take as an example. We strive for stability and a better life. This is only natural.

These gentle reminders were hardly necessary though, since even before the strike had begun, representatives of both sides of the dispute in Ajo had apparently become convinced that after the formal merger of the International Union of Mine, Mill and Smelter Workers with the United Steelworkers Union on July 1, 1967 (A.C.N. June 29, 1967:1), only action on the national level would settle the differences between the two opposing sides, a view also shared by many other people in the state (e.g., see A.R. July 16, 1967:B-1). Therefore, with this somewhat fatalistic attitude the local union and company officials appear to have worked out a "gentleman's agreement" that was never publicly announced that in return for the union's "promise" to refrain from picketing the entrance to the smelter that was highly visible to tourists and others driving along the main highway through town, the company built a shack, complete with chairs and a shaded porch, by a more secluded entrance to the mine[1] to shield the pickets from the heat of the sun and even supplied electricity to the shack to heat the strikers' coffee and run a company-supplied water cooler (F.N. July 18, 1967). In fact, the local company officials had seemed so cooperative about the whole affair that one miner remarked to me while I was sitting "on the picket line" (i.e., sitting down with the strikers under the company supplied roof) just after the start of the strike that he did not know "who's on strike, us or the company" (F.N. July 18, 1967). This local cooperation continued throughout the length of the strike, even to the extent that the local union leaders continually refused to give any statements to the local paper about the strike, even though many union men and other miners privately had many pet gripes about various company policies and actions (F.N. November 13, 1967). And though the editor of the local paper told me that she had on various occasions asked the local union officials for statements concerning the strike, it is doubtful that she would have printed any statement about the strike that was too "controversial" anyway, and it was interesting to note that during the entire length of the eight month strike there were very few comments in the paper that even were remotely connected to the events taking place during the long walkout. Thus, the editor obviously felt that strict neutrality was the best policy for the local paper since it would be unwise to offend either the company who owned the press and the building in which it was housed and who rented a "special" company house to the publisher and his wife (the editor) or the striking miners who by buying the paper kept the publishers in business. Other papers, especially the most influential one in Arizona, The Arizona Republic, took a much stronger antiunion stand in most cases.

By July 27, 1967 with the "collapse" of a joint bargaining session between Kennecott Copper Corporation and the striking unions, and with the announced formation of a "national strike coordinating committee" in Denver, Colorado, it was publicly reported (A.R. July 27, 1967:B-1) that, "persons close to both sides have predicted a long strike". Therefore, it is not too surprising that a massive propaganda battle was soon launched by both sides to win support for the opposing positions from the miners, newspapers and the general public which each side hoped would force state and national elected officials to enter the dispute, either on the side of the companies or the unions, or to serve as an arbitrator between the two opponents.

The first promising result of this campaign was a quick response from the governor of Montana who announced on July 29, 1967 (A.R. July 30, 1967:C-1) that he had scheduled a meeting between himself and the governors of Arizona, New Mexico, Utah, and Nevada "to discuss action that might be taken to reach an early solution to the national copper strike", adding that:

> This western region cannot afford a prolonged strike in one of its most vital basic industries. ... Economic hardship among working families is certain to ensue, and all the states in which the copper mining industry flourishes will suffer severely....
> If the governors of our five states can focus national attention on how damaging this strike is to the economy of the Rocky Mountain region ... perhaps we can influence a more rapid solution than presently is being evidenced.

Evidently, some national recognition of the strike was soon gained by the governors and others since it was optimistically predicted by "six government officials in Washington" on August 1,1967 that "the Johnson administration will take action within the next twenty days to halt the nationwide copper strike" (A.D.S. August 2, 1967:A-1), although a union official, one of several union leaders who had been present at the meeting of the five governors, said (A.R. August 2, 1967:B-1) that the unions expected the government to intervene in the strike only "when the copper stockpiles run low", since the companies "will be ready to talk business" when they "no longer have copper".

Unfortunately for the unions, it was not long before they felt they were losing the battle for public and official sympathy, so on August 8th a co-chairman of the joint union bargaining committee charged that Kennecott Copper Company had broken a "gentleman's agreement" about "strike propaganda" (A.R. August 8, 1967:21), and a Kennecott negotiator responded a few days later (August 13, 1967) by stating in a paid television announcement (A.R. August 14, 1967:19) that "only the steelworkers union in Pittsburgh knows when the strike will end", adding that the goal of this union was to force "industrywide collective bargaining", a charge that was to be later repeated many times by others.

Tempers flared at this point, and at one location in Arizona a court injunction was sought by Magma Copper Company to prevent mass picketing which one company official thought might lead to "trouble" and physical violence (A.R. August 16, 1967:17). An ugly mood seemed to be gripping both sides in the dispute and as one newspaper stated (A.R. August 17, 1967:21), pessimism "reigned" even though both Phelps Dodge and Kennecott had by now scheduled new meetings with representatives from the striking unions (A.R. August 17, 1967:21; August 21, 1967:2).

The charges and countercharges continued to escalate on both sides as it was announced that a Utah chemical firm was forced to close down its operations because of a lack of sulfuric acid, a by-product of Kennecott's mining operations (A.R. August 21, 1967:21) and, even worse, that the United Fund drive in the Globe-Miami area of Arizona had "become a victim of the two-month-old copper strike" (A.R. September 4, 1967:25). And when Governor Williams in September (A.R. September 24, 1967:A-2l) announced that the copper strike had already cost Arizona ten million dollars in lost excise taxes, an official of the striking United Steelworkers Union countered by saying that the governor's estimate was:

> ...grossly exaggerated and a bunch of propaganda.... Like many other things the governor has said ... the statement is designed to put pressure on the unions in an attempt

to get them to agree to an unreasonable contract (A.R. September 24, 1967:A-21).

Although there was some truthfulness to the union official's countercharge, since the combined total of use and sales tax collections in 1967 for the month of August for the state of Arizona was actually $28,000 higher than for the corresponding period in the preceding year[2] (A.R. September 24, 1967:A-21), the companies' propaganda campaign was evidently having some effect on certain of Arizona's miners by this time since a rebel union had been formed by September 29th, among the striking Magma workers at San Manuel and Superior that with the aid of financial help from a rebellious local of the Steelworkers' Union in Ohio attempted, "to wrest representation at Magma from (the) steelworkers and send some 2,000 men back to work" (A.D.S. September 29, 1967 :B-1).

Part of the unions' troubles in the "battle for men's minds" during the strike came from the unions' practice of keeping the progress of negotiations during collective bargaining sessions largely secret even from their own men out on strike. As one union spokesman explained this policy (A.R. October 12, 1967:21):

> There is no value to making terms public "when parties are engaged in collective bargaining."...But if "parties are at loggerheads" and a disclosure of differences to the public can start the collective bargaining process again, then it may serve a purpose.

That any such disclosure never fully occurred was proven by the fact that all of the ordinary union members I interviewed during the strike had only vague ideas about what the unions were seeking in terms of a settlement and even the local union leaders to whom I spoke, did little to clarify the real strike issues that much later became obvious to many observers. The reason for this reticence in discussing union demands beforehand is probably due to the union leaders' fears of being accused of having "given in" to company demands. No union leader wants to admit that he has not achieved all of his planned goals in the final strike settlement package of wage increases and other benefits.

Kennecott Copper Corporation was quick to take advantage of this reticence on the part of union officials and in a full page ad placed in leading papers throughout the West (e.g., see A.R. October 12, 1967:25), officials of this company reprinted a "Special Report on the Copper Strike" prepared by the pro-company "Industrial Relations Council of Utah" which in part stated that:

> Local union leaders tell us stories that cross check closely. None of these men is willing to be quoted, but many of them deplore the strike and the reasons for it. This is what we hear:
>
> ...Local union bargaining teams have had no authority to make any settlement. They are only puppets on strings held by the men at the top. The men at the top want an industry-wide contract because this will give them greater control over future bargaining and over the smaller unions. In fact, the big union may smother out the small ones and, in time, absorb their members. Industry-wide bargaining makes it easier to service the contract. Less union agents are required. More union dues money can be used to organize new workers or for political activity.
>
> ...It is sheer nonsense to believe that any of the companies would want a strike, or that they want it extended for even one day longer than necessary. The cost to the companies is staggering. The cost to the community is staggering. The cost to the strikers is staggering. Only the Steelworker Union leaders at international levels stand to gain by this long strike.

We believe that most of these facts are well known to government officials.... You should know these facts so that you can properly evaluate this strike and the public statements that are made and the actions taken by government officials. The strikers and all who have lost because of this strike deserve our sympathy. NOBODY HAD TO LOSE...

Obviously, Kennecott hoped to drive a "wedge" between the local unions and the steelworkers by this action.

In October, a small break came in the copper strike when the relatively small (11th ranked in size) Pima Mining Company signed a new three year contract with the striking unions (A.R. October 14, 1967:19), but otherwise the strike worsened amid new accusations of satellite industries and businesses being seriously hurt by the walkout (A.R. October 12, 1967:21; October 15, 1967:6; October 17, 1967:24) and dire predictions of an increase of 2 cents per pound in the price of copper at the conclusion of the strike[3] (A.R. October 15, 1967:F-1). All hope for an early settlement dimmed as a spokesman for one of the major copper companies charged (A.R. October 25, 1967:13) that the steelworkers had "flatly refused" to say which of its issues was most important and "scored" the officials of the Pima Mining Company for agreeing to a "too fat" strike settlement.[4]

One of the main factors in the dispute that was by now becoming obvious to many strike observers was that the refined copper reserves held by the copper companies, the Federal Government, and other industries in the United States had been enormously underestimated (e.g., see A.R. October 26, 1967:A-6; October 30, 1967:3) so much so that despite the fact that ninety per cent of the United States copper industry had been shut down for many months, copper prices actually declined during the first three months of the strike. Also, vast quantities of foreign copper were by now beginning to flow into the country partly as a result of an international glut in the copper market (the result of an economic slump in Europe and greatly expanded world wide mining activities) and partly due to the fact that every major producer of copper in the United States had at least partial control over the production from certain foreign mines[5] (A.R. January 10, 1968:70).

Another very small copper company settled with the unions on October 31st (A.R. November 1, 1967:C-1) shortly after it was publicly announced that since October 2nd the unions had given up their insistence on "industry-wide bargaining", although they still wanted to achieve "company-wide bargaining" (A.R. October 30, 1967:3). However, a proposal by a major company that the strikers return to work while the negotiations continued was rejected by the steelworkers' union, even though the company said that it "would make retroactive any benefits or wage increases resulting from the end of the strike to the day the workers returned" (A.R. November 7, 1967:14).

News in November that nonfarm jobs in Arizona had actually increased, despite the copper strike (A.R. November 17, 1967:55), did little to force the White House to act, although Governor Williams continued to call for federal intervention in the dispute (e.g., see A.R. November 8, 1967:1). Also, Senator Fannin's bill that was introduced into the United States Senate on November 15th which would have allowed the striking miners a chance to vote for a return to work, although given much enthusiastic support by the influential Arizona Republic newspaper, failed to generate any federal action (A.R. November 16, 1967:21; November 17, 1967:6). Nor did emotional appeals to the companies, unions and government officials warning of a "bleak Thanksgiving and a bleaker Christmas for a good many mining families"[6] (A.R. November 18, 1967:6) have much effect toward forcing a settlement in the long dispute.

Moreover, Phelps Dodge did not even wait until the end of the strike before raising its price in mid-November on copper 4 cents a pound, twice as much as had been earlier predicted for a price rise at the end of the strike (A.R. November 18, 1967:6). Possibly this was done as a result of the alleged "higher" price of foreign copper (e.g., see A.R. December 2, 1967:7), but the actual cost of such copper is difficult to assess since many of the foreign mines supplying this copper were at least partially under the control of the strikebound American firms. Also, the fact that the two top national Phelps Dodge Corporation executives reported on February 7 in New York City that despite the five and one-half month long strike the "sales of Phelps Dodge-mined copper in 1967 totaled 157,200 tons, approximately equal to the company's mine production of 156,700 tons" (A.R. February 8, 1968:55) lends much weight to the unions' accusation that "the firms were purposely prolonging the strike to create a crisis and drive up the price of copper[7] (A.R. November 22, 1967:23), as does also the knowledge that all copper producers had enormous reserves of the red metal just prior to the beginning of the strike (A.R. January 10, 1968:70).

In a very interesting article (A.R. January 10, 1968:70) the Business and Financial Editor of The Arizona Republic said that just prior to start of the strike there was a surplus of copper in the United States "of almost shocking proportions" with enough fully refined copper in various stockpiles to equal the total output of Arizona's mines for a period of about ten months. Also, during the strike the stockpiles held by the copper fabricators continued to grow as massive amounts of European copper were "dumped" on the American market (due to a European market slump and the increasing substitution of other materials for copper (e.g., see A.R. March 19, 1968:17)) so that by November 30, 1967, four and one-half months after the start of the strike, these stockpiles were at their highest level since 1965. (In fact, as the truth about these stockpiles began to come out near the end of the strike, one news correspondent stated that "the fabrication plants of the industry's Big Four integrated corporations had over a year's supply of refined copper when the pits were struck" (A.R. March 12, 1968).)

The stalemate continued unchanged during the holiday season as both sides escalated the propaganda warfare. By now the unions had stepped up their tactics, and late in November a massive rally of "more than 3,500" persons was staged in Tucson where verbal attacks were made on the "copper barons" and on United States Senator Paul Fannin, "Arizona's antilabor senator", and Governor Williams, who was accused of being more interested in money than in the workers' rights (A.R. November 29, 1967:A-8; November 30, 1967:21). The crowd at this rally was reported to have "cheered, whistled, stomped, yelled, and applauded" while the speeches were being made and during the hanging of an effigy of Senator Fannin. As expected, Fannin struck back quickly at the strikers in a public statement the next day in which he said that "Congress must act now to curb organized labor's power if labor-management relations are to be saved" (A.R. December 2, 1967:21). Also by now, comments about the controversy were appearing regularly in newspaper editorials which in the <u>Arizona Republic</u> were becoming increasingly antiunion (e.g., see A.R. November 18, i967:6) and in the letters-to-the-editor columns of newspapers where editorial replies and other comments, both pro-company and pro-union, were allowed (e.g., see A.R. December 2, .1967:7 for a reply from a union official to a November 18, 1967 editorial).

On November 30, 1967, Senator Mike Mansfield stated that it was "too late now for a Taft-Hartley Act injunction", but he added that "President Johnson should appoint a commission to seek an end to the copper strike" (A.R. December 1, 1967:1). This plan was also endorsed by the union leaders but rejected by company spokesmen, one of whom charged that (A.R. December 8, 1967:1):

> A fact finding board ... would contribute to companywide, if not industrywide bargaining, to the imposition of identical contract expiration dates and uniform wage scales throughout the heterogeneous industry.
>
> The long-range welfare of the employees and the stockholders of the copper, lead and zinc producing enterprises would be irreparably damaged by such a solution.

A spokesman for Kennecott Copper Corporation instead suggested a plan calling for "a return to work on a voluntary basis at increased rates of pay" for a "cooling off period" (A.R. December 2, 1967:23), and Phelps Dodge offered the unions, without much success, a higher wage and benefits package (A.R. December 13, 1967:B-1). But, still the Federal Government decided against intervention in the strike (A.R. December 15, 1967:26) and the offers of both Kennecott and Phelps Dodge received a very "cool" reception[8] from the unions who by now had received money[9] and pledges of support from all the unions represented at the biennial convention of the AFL-CIO (A.R. December 18, 1967:23).

Just a few days before Christmas, in a written appeal which a union official complained was "vicious and unprincipled," officials at the Kennecott Copper Company, who by this time were obviously annoyed by statements made by union spokesmen on a local television broadcast, told the striking workers that they "should resign if they think conditions are as bad as painted by the union" (A.R. December 24, 1967:A-4; U.S. News and World Report January 8, 1968:76). The company even went so far as to include resignation forms in with the 7,500 individual letters it mailed to its striking employees. Feelings were getting quite bitter on both sides by now as the only remaining series of ongoing talks between a major producer (Phelps Dodge) and the unions was recessed until January 8th (A.R. December 30, 1967:17).

The first hints of possible federal intervention in the strike came early in January 1968 when Secretary of Labor, Willard Wirtz, announced that the government was taking "a fresh look" at the nearly six-month-old strike, although at the same time he called the failure to settle the long walkout "a default of private responsibilities" (A.R. January 4, 1968:21). However, as one newspaper headline indicated (A.R. January 8, 1968:21) federal administration officials were at this point still "split" over what action, if any, they should take in the dispute.

Meanwhile, Senator Fannin was "warning the nation" that "the six-month-old nation-wide copper strike (was) beginning seriously to affect electronic war supplies for American fighting forces in Vietnam" (A.R. January 12, 1968:1), while AFL-CIO President George Meany and Governor Williams were engaged in a verbal "free-for-all" (A.R. January 12, 1968:1; January 13, 1968:1; January 14, 1968:6; January 24, 1968:1) over what should be done to end the strike. By now it was becoming obvious to everyone (with the possible exception of Senator Fannin) that there was no shortage of copper in this country and would be none for many months to come[10] (A.R. January19, 1968:33). Therefore, things looked grim indeed at this point, despite the talk of "irresistible pressures" on the combatants in the dispute (A.R. January 15, 1968:1) and of growing "impatience" across the United States (A.R. January 20, 1968:1).

However, the antiunion forces adopted a new tactic at this point and proceeded to attempt to draw President Johnson personally into the fracas by not only suggesting that the unions' demands greatly exceeded the increase in annual productivity, which was the limit that "President Johnson said should be voluntarily accepted by labor unions" (A.R. January 16, 1968:6), but also by attacking the President personally for his inaction in the dispute. Thus, on January 18th Senator Fannin said that it was "incredible" that President Johnson did not once mention the nationwide copper strike during his "State of the Union" message on January 17th (A.R. January 19, 1968:33). He then viciously further attacked the President by saying:

> Not once did he call attention to critical labor problems facing the nation. Nor did he mention the crippling copper strike which threatens our war effort. (I wonder if) the President is unaware of the economic suffering inflicted on the families of copper workers by labor leaders grabbing for power.
> Is it possible ... for the President to be unaware of the impact on the balance of payments problem caused by having to import copper at this time?
> Is the President attempting to gloss over the fact that the American taxpayer ultimately has to bear the burden of paying the premium of imported ore currently about 50 to 70 cents over domestic prices?

This, apparently along with the other pressures being applied, forced the President to act, and on January 25th it was announced that, "The Johnson administration last night appointed a special mediation panel in an attempt to end the 193-day strike that has crippled the nation's copper industry" (A.R. January 25, 1968:1). Not everyone was happy with this action, however, and spokesmen from the companies agreed with Senator Fannin who made critical remarks about the federal panel, calling it a "kangaroo court" of "former White House associates and prolabor spokesmen" (A.R. January 26, 1968:3; February 6, 1968:12), although the chairman of the joint union negotiating committee for Arizona said that the unions would willingly "cooperate" with a "fact-finding" panel (A.R. January 24, 1968:17). Still, probably under great White House pressure, the companies all agreed along with the unions to each present its respective case before this three-member body (A.R.

January 28, 1968:D-21), although the copper industry as a group continued to complain that such a panel had no "legal standing" (A.R. January 30, 1968:19) and that the hearings "stacked the deck" against the companies (A.R. February 3, 1968:3). One company even went as far as trying to resume production immediately at a Texas refinery by sending notices to its 550 employees, telling them to report to work or be prepared to be replaced with permanent nonunion workers (i.e., strikebreakers) and threatened to take the same action at another of its plants back East (A.R. January 31, 1968:19).

Governor Williams, not to be outdone by a federal panel, also tried at this time to start his own series of talks between company and union spokesmen. Several companies accepted his offer (A.R. February 7, 1968:17), probably in the hope that any compromise worked out in his presence would be more favorable to their position than could be expected through the federal mediation efforts. However, the unions appear to have also reasoned along similar lines as these companies, for they rejected the offer as not being as "appropriate" as the talks going on in Washington (A.R. February 10, 1968:26).

Meanwhile, the idea of a federal panel was not working out as well as had been expected by the men closest to President Johnson, and on February 17th members of the panel announced their failure to achieve a settlement of the strike and blamed this lack of success on the "apparent intransigence on both sides" (A.R. February 18, 1968:B-l). However, before the panel disbanded it left a set of "guidelines", suggesting that all mining, smelting and refinery workers of a single company be covered by one contract, fabrication employees by another, and all other nonferrous metal workers by yet a third contract[11] (A.R. February 19, 1968:4).

The federal administration, still hoping to obtain a settlement based upon these compromise "guidelines", approached the unions on the subject a few days later, but representatives from the twenty-six striking unions said that the federal suggestion that they drop their demands for companywide bargaining was "unacceptable" (A.R. February 21, 1968:1), even though one union spokesman had earlier said that such a compromise might be possible (A.R. February 20, 1968:4). However, this failure did not spell complete defeat for the government's efforts since on February 28th, the National Labor Relations Board handed down a decision (on a "long-forgotten" case that had been pending before the board since November 22, 1967 (A.R. February 11, 1968:B-l)) which declared that union demands for companywide negotiations in the copper industry were "illegal" since they amounted to an unlawful "refusal-to-bargain" (February 29, 1968:1), and, on the last day in February, the Board followed up this announcement by saying that it would seek a federal court injunction against the unions striking against Kennecott Copper Company (A.R. March 1, 1968:21).

This unfavorable decision clearly indicated that the tide of official Washington opinion was turning rapidly against the unions after their rejection of the recommendations of the very same federal panel that they had originally favored.[12] At this point nothing seemed to be "going right" for the unions who were by now also losing the battle for favorable public opinion (e.g., see A.R. January 17, 1968:55) and, in many cases, for the loyalty of the striking miners, themselves as was clearly seen early in March as persistent rumors floated around Ajo that at least one mining company had cut off all credit to the strikers for rent and utilities and that Phelps Dodge had itself cut off credit for utilities at Bisbee and was also considering stopping all extensions of credit to the strikers in Ajo which had been already rumored as a possible company action as early as in late January (L.I. 32; L.I. 51; F.N. January 22, 1968). Adding weight to this rumor was another one generated by a semisecret meeting of top company officials in Ajo who, according to the rumor, were deciding whether to close down the Ajo mine completely and ship much of the heavy equipment to the new Tyrone mine being developed during the strike in New Mexico or leave the mine open (F.N. February 19, 1968). Still a third rumor was that "some white guys are talking about dropping out of the joint bargaining committee with the steelworkers' union and bargaining on their own with the company" (L.I. 37). Whether or not the company had anything to do with the creation of these rumors, they did nothing to prevent their spread, which further tended to drive a wedge between the local striking miners and their national unions. Evidence for the effectiveness of such rumors and other similar types of propaganda is seen in the statement to me by one of the striking miners at this time who said:

> We are being used. The high union people are not suffering. (Also., see A.R. January 20, 1968:1; January 22, 1968:9; January 24, 1968:6; January 27, 1968:12).

Thus, it was no surprise when an announcement that the international longshoremen would refuse to handle all imports and exports of copper in the United States and Canada (A.R. February 23, 1968:1) was rescinded a few hours later with the explanation that it had been sent out "in error" (A.R. February 24, 1968:1) and that union resistance buckled completely on March 1 when President Johnson "ordered both sides in the 231-day copper strike to the White House ... with instructions to stay there until they reach a settlement"[13] (A.R. March 2, 1968:1).

The end of the strike was now in sight, although the unions continued to make feeble attempts to show how strong they remained by initially rejecting a new Phelps Dodge wage and fringe benefit package (A.R. March 9, 1968:1) (although later accepting essentially the same offer) and by suggesting that they had the power economically to continue the strike indefinitely since each needy striker could be "adopted lock, stock and family" by one of the 60,000 local AFL-CIO unions or 1,000 city central labor councils and thus be given the equivalent of his prestrike net income (A.R. March 4, 1968:6; A.D.S. March 4, 1968:1).[14] President Johnson continued to apply pressure to both the companies and unions to follow the guidelines laid down by the three-member panel (A.R. March 13, 1968:9) while attempting to appease critics such as Senator Fannin by finally personally repeating the somewhat dubious charges that "dwindling copper supplies threaten prosperity, could jeopardize the supply of weapons for Vietnam, and that the big growth of copper imports weakens the United States dollar in foreign trade" (A.R. March 6, 1968:1).

By March 10th, there was a rumor circulating around the White House that the unions had abandoned their demands for companywide bargaining and contracts with common terms and expiration dates with the four major copper firms (A.R. March 10, 1968:A-4). Thus, an early settlement seemed near in spite of the fact that Phelps Dodge, the company coming the closest to meeting the strikers' wage and fringe benefit demands, as late as March 12, continued to resist bargaining in accord with the federal guidelines that had been suggested by the three-member panel (A.R. March 13, 1968:9). Finally on March 15th, the Phelps Dodge Corporation and twenty-five of the twenty-six striking unions agreed on a wage-fringe benefit package that was then submitted to the unions' membership for ratification (A.R. March 16, 1968:1). That this was a significant victory for the companies is seen by the fact that the steelworkers union, the supposed leader of the twenty-six-member union coalition, was reported to have been the lone union to reject the Phelps Dodge offer (A.R. March 16, 1968:1). This event seems to verify the earlier remarks of a business research specialist at the University of Arizona who said that (A.R. January 12, 1968:10):

...the copper companies deliberately are seeking a showdown with the newly merged United Steelworkers of America and the International Union of Mine, Mill and Smelter Workers. ...the firms have to show their employees the merger represents no greater worker benefits than the two unions provided separately.

The steelworkers finally bowed to the pressure of the other unions' acceptance of the new contract terms (A.R. March 17, 1968:1; March 18, 1968:2) and on March 18th the contract was voted upon by all Phelps Dodge union memberships (A.R. March 19, 1968:15) and was completely ratified on March 19th after pressure was applied to one union local in Ajo, the boilermakers, who had rejected the proposal on the first ballot but later gave in after a local dispute was partially settled (A.R. March 20, 1968:1; F.N. March 18, 1968; F.N. March 19, 1968; A.D.S. March 20, 1968:1). Thus, on March 20th, the acrid smoke again belched forth from the huge tower at Ajo as the Phelps Dodge miners finally began returning to their jobs over eight months after the start of the walkout (A.D.S. March 20, 1968:1) and by the first day of April all the other major companies and unions had settled their disputes with contracts patterned after the Phelps Dodge settlement (A.R. March 29, 1968:1, 14), thus marking the final end to one of the longest strikes in the history of the West (A.R. April 1, 1968:21).

Union leaders, including representatives from the steelworkers' union, as expected, termed the copper strike agreement "a real victory" (A.R. March 18, 1968:21), in spite of the fact that the unions had abandoned their demands for industrywide or companywide bargaining and for common expiration dates on the new contracts and had instead agreed to bargain along the lines suggested by the federal three-member panel. In explaining why they had apparently changed their goals, the leader of the twenty-six union coalition, Orville Larson representing the steelworkers, said that (A.R. March 19, 1968:1):

> In no way do we consider these concessions a defeat....
> In exchange, we're getting much more money than we otherwise would have received.

The unions had, however, experienced a real setback since they had settled for a smaller overall economic package for the metal fabricating workers than they had obtained for the mine, mill, smelter and refinery workers (A.R. March 20, 1968:4). Still, they were able in their negotiations with Phelps Dodge to narrow from seven to three months the spread in contract expiration dates between the company's different operations in Arizona, Texas, and back East (A.D.S. March 20, 1968:1; A.R. March 20, 1968:4). The real victors were, of course, the companies since on March 28, 1968, Phelps Dodge announced a permanent rise in the price of copper from its prestrike level of 38 cent to 42 cents (A.R. March 28, 1968:4) and Anaconda and Kennecott quickly followed by announcing their own 4 cent price increases, despite severe criticism of this "excessive" price increase by Arthur Okun, the chairman of the President's Council of Economic Advisers[15] (A.R. April 3, 1968:10).

It is very interesting to note that the government reportedly estimated that "a price increase of 2 cents a pound would adequately compensate for the cost of the new wage pacts" (A.R. April 3, 1968:10). Thus, not only were the companies "hurt least of all" as an editorial in The Arizona Republic suggests (A.R. March 5, 1968:6) but, in fact, they appear to have actually benefited greatly by the strike since they were not only able to reduce the tremendous United States copper surplus which by now was said to have been "over a year's supply of refined copper when the pits were struck" (A.R. March 12, 1968:6) but also were able to use the strike to justify an enormous $10^1/_2$ per cent increase in the price of copper, twice as much, according to government estimates, as the union wage-benefit packages would actually cost them. Even a staunch defender of the companies' price action calculated the increased cost of the wage-benefit packages as being equivalent to only an 8 per cent rise above the prestrike level (i.e., increasing labor costs would still be under the price hike by $2^1/_2$ per cent) (A.R. April 7, 1968:7). Also, local Ajo company officials used the high wage settlement as an excuse to remove coffee pots from several company locations and eliminate altogether the hitherto tolerated practice of allowing employees time off for "coffee breaks" (F.N. May 13, 1968).

And, as one local Ajo resident informed me (F.N. March 5, 1968), he had heard fairly reliable rumors that because of the length of the strike the companies had been relieved of the necessity of either drastically curtailing work schedules or of laying off skilled workers in 1967 or 1968 because of the tremendous glut of the red metal in mid-1967. Thus, at very little cost to the companies[16] (since all credit given the miners by the companies was to be repaid through long term payroll deductions[17]) they were able to keep almost all of their highly skilled employees bound tightly to the mining towns throughout the strike in contrast to the situation that might have prevailed had the strike not occurred.

Therefore, company executives must have secretly smiled as one newspaper columnist wrote of "How (the) Unions Tricked LBJ" (A.R. March 12, 1968:6) and Senator Fannin continued to blame the length of the strike on "the Johnson administration" and "ambitious, power-hungry union officials" (A.R. April 5, 1968:13). Also, they must have winked at each other as Governor Williams continued to speak of the loss of 171 million dollars to the state of Arizona (A.R. April 3, 1968:19) from copper which had it have been produced during that eight month period, could not have been sold.

Chapter Notes

1. Picketing was also allowed by the company at an even more "hidden" entrance to the mine.

2. Total retail sales in Arizona showed a growth in each quarter of 1967 over the 1966 figures (Valley National Bank (Arizona Progress) 1968:1).

3. The actual increase proved to be much larger than this as shall be discussed latter.

4. As shall later be indicated, the Pima Mining Company officials actually received a "bargain" settlement as compared to the major producers who settled with the unions at a much later point in time. Other small mining companies continued to settle their differences with the unions (e.g., see A.R. January 26, 1968:3; February 11, 1968:A-14; March 15, 1968:19) during the strike and one small Tucson firm even settled the dispute without a strike on April 11, 1968, despite the fact that it had been operating without a union contract since October 31, 1967 (A.R. April 11, 1968:3). However, none of these settlements had much effect on the length of the strike, although President Johnson's chief economic adviser later said that the large wage-benefit packages agreed to by the smaller companies did "(indicate) the likelihood of an excessive wage settlement for the major producers" (A.R. March 29, 1968:1).

5. There was a rumor that Phelps Dodge had no foreign source of copper and that, therefore, this company would be the one first forced to the bargaining table, but this rumor proved to be completely false (see A.R. January 28, 1968:B-1).

6. See also (A.R. December 3, 1967:A-6) where in an editorial cartoon a picketing union official is pictured as angrily blocking Santa Claus from entering the "miners' homes" while two disappointed children gaze out through a window at the scene and (A.R. December 7, 1967:41) where, in a story that was part of the series entitled "Strike

Cinches Miners' Belts," the "biggest worry" of the family being interviewed is said to have been "how to provide a decent Christmas for the kids."

7. See also, A.R. December 12, 1967:13, where a government investigation of the large copper producing "bandits" was called for by delegates to the national AFL-CIO convention. The delegates also drafted a resolution which said in part, "we condemn the cold-blooded manipulations of the copper industry which led to this strike which has been used by the industry to gain for itself higher copper prices."

8. The Kennecott offer was never even considered by the unions and the Phelps Dodge offer was rejected on December 20th (A.R. December 21, 1967:31).

9. $500,0O0 was quickly raised at this convention, including money from such diverse groups as the United Auto Workers who donated $60,000 and South Vietnam's Labor Federation which gave $50.

10. On January 19th, despite what Senator Fannin said, figures supplied by the copper industry itself showed that even after six months of strike there was still an ample supply of copper in the United States. Also, B. H. Gerwin, assistant director of the Arizona Department of Mineral Resources, said that Fannin's statements about a copper shortage that was crippling our war effort in Vietnam were false adding that, "If there is a shortage anywhere ... it's not because there isn't enough copper available, but probably because some company's purchasing agent failed to place an order far enough in advance" (A.R. January 28, 1968:B-1). However, Fannin in a letter-to-the-editor (A.R. February 4, 1968:7) defended his previous statements about the copper strike's effect on our war effort in Asia through the presentation of some rather dubious new evidence.

11. The companies had continually insisted on separate contracts for each operation and plant site within the overall corporate structure (e.g., see A.R. February 19, 1968:4).

12. See A.R. February 27, 1968:1 and A.R. February 29, 1968:1 for comments from government and company officials about this "major mistake" on the part of the unions.

13. On February 26th, Senate majority leader, Mike Mansfield, was reported as having asked President Johnson "to lock copper strike labor and management negotiators in a hotel room and throw away the key until they settle the seven-month-old strike" (A.R. February 27, 1968:23).

14. By March 5th, the local company officials were so sure that the strike would soon be settled that they began oiling their long idle machinery and told the independent firm that did all their blasting at the mine to call back its employees to Ajo (F.N. March 5, 1968).

15. He also was critical of the magnitude of the wage-benefit increases granted by the copper industry to the unions, saying that they "were larger than the public interest could justify" (A.R. March 29, 1968:1).

16. The only real cost would be the loss of interest on the credit supplied to the miners during the strike and the slightly inflated nature of the money used to repay this credit. However, even this small loss would be more than offset as the news that in Arizona the companies would probably get a 100 million dollar deduction in their assessed market value for 1968 property tax purposes as a result of the long strike (A.R. March 10, 1968:1) indicates.

17. Some miners even took out "debt consolidation" loans at the local bank to pay off the company immediately and thereby reduce their monthly payments on the debt even though they would now have to pay interest on the debt and have to pay it off over a longer time period (F.N. April 26, 1968).

CHAPTER 3:

The Indians Remained, Why?

...the machinery...is greater than the man. It operates smoothly and perfectly. It is a giant robot. ...It is a temple to engineering science. The question is whether the temple has not propounded a new code of human social behavior - has not demanded a new organization of man. ...Ajo is a mathematical formula, working to precision; and individuality and color and romance ...are unknown. (Corle 1941:81).

I first arrived there as a naive graduate student in the summer of 1967 as part of a massive effort to correct and update a very detailed Papago[1] population register[2] to be used by the scientific community for tracing genetic factors in the inheritance of such diseases as diabetes and cancer in a highly inbred population. Also, the Indian Health Service was hoping to create from the database a quick, computerized medical records retrieval system to improve the quality of the healthcare being provided to the Papago Indians both on the main reservations and in such nearby locations as Ajo.

For my own Ph.D. dissertation I was planning to use this same database to study the "push-pull" factors that were enticing many Papago men and their wives and families to move to and remain in such off reservation towns as Ajo. And in the case of Ajo, I was fully prepared to accept the conclusion of a previous researcher (Waddell 1969) who stated that the only major factor in explaining the persistence of a fairly large, mainly Papago[3] Indian community in Ajo was the relatively high paying jobs that the local copper mine and smelter provided. However, it was not long before I realized how wrong both he and I had been in making such an assumption even though most Ajo Indians were still living in the least desirable housing area of Ajo that was known as "the Indian Village", a remnant of an earlier highly segregated company housing plan.

Early during the first visits I made to Ajo although I, too, heard the popular bit of local folklore from both whites and Indians alike, that most Indian miners return to the reservation "every chance they get"[4], I began to have serious doubts about the accuracy of these statements after meeting several Ajo Indians who had either never visited the Papago reservation in their lives or who had not been there in many years. Also, since my first visits to Ajo were made just as the 1967-1968 copper strike was first beginning, I was greatly surprised to find that contrary to the predicted mass exodus of Indians from Ajo to their reservation homes that one might assume would have occurred since all mining operations had by now been shut down completely, very few Indians had actually left Ajo for the reservation even for brief summer visits. In fact, as soon as school started that fall in Ajo, most of those few families who during the summer months had gone to the reservation for short visits to their relatives living there, returned to Ajo in September so that their children could begin to attend school. Also, I later discovered that during the summer months and continuing until the end of the strike in March of the following year the only appreciable out migration of Indians from Ajo was that involving small numbers of the striking miners who worked for short periods of time doing such things as fighting forest fires, unloading ships in California, and laboring in farm labor camps or on ranches. These men usually left Ajo in small groups of friends or relatives for only one or two week periods at a time and except in rare cases left their wives and families at home in Ajo. It was also interesting to learn that in most cases of such distant employment, the majority of the Indians returned to Ajo earlier than they had originally planned and remained in Ajo despite the continuance of the strike, even though work was still available at the work location they had just left. Obviously, contrary to what one would have earlier expected from the myths that have grown up through the years about the "Nomadic Papago", Ajo, not the reservation had become the preferred "place of refuge" for the vast majority of the unemployed Indian miners and their families. Why?

To answer this question and to obtain certain types of quantitative information about the Ajo Indian community and the effects of the strike upon the individual Indian and his family, in the fall of 1967 I agreed to assist the Public Health Service personnel at the Tucson "Health Program Systems Center" in contacting all Indian families living in the Ajo area for census purposes in return for permission to use the data collected, in my dissertation work. Using two local Indian assistants this survey was begun the first week in November (1967) and was completed a few days after the new year began (1968). Unfortunately, although I was able to obtain from this census much basic data about the Indian population of Ajo, the survey form had been poorly designed[5] and was not as useful a source of information as I felt I needed. Therefore, I constructed a new survey form (see Appendix A) which I personally began using on February 5, 1968. Fifty-four in-depth interviews were obtained by me, ranging in length from two to seven hours apiece (the average length of an interview was between three to four hours) before the 20th of March when the pending strike settlement and several other minor problems that developed made it appear wise to suspend the use of this long interview form. The cooperation I received from all of the forty Indian company employees and their families that I interviewed in this manner was remarkably good, as it was also with the seven families containing ex-miners and the seven other Indian families interviewed that contained no male company employees.[6] Also, I was able to interview informally many other members of all three ethnic groups in Ajo throughout my stay of fifteen months in the Ajo area from June 1967 to September 1968, as well as participate in many community events ranging from singing in the town choir for the Easter program in 1968 to playing basketball with a group of young married Indian miners and the village priest. I was even made scoutmaster of a group of local Boy Scouts for a nine-month period.

By the end of my stay in Ajo, the answer to the question posed earlier was obvious. Through a long process of natural selection, most Indians remaining in Ajo were those who were fully committed to the "benevolent" security offered by "the company By now the social and economic integration of the Ajo Indian had proceeded to such an extent that only one Yavapai man of those Indians who were still able to work at the mine did not return to the mine at the end of the strike (F.N. April 22, 1968; April 29, 1968).[7] The extreme strength of this hold on the Indian miners is perhaps not too surprising in the case of the unskilled track laborer who, after having gotten used to the good things in life that can be purchased on an income of over $145 a week and a low monthly outlay for housing, etc., contemplates the prospect of returning to the life lived by most other Papagos lacking job skills, but it perhaps seems more unusual in the case of two highly skilled miners, one of whom who had obtained "permanent" employment in Los Angeles and had moved his whole family there during the latter part of the strike and the other who had worked on the Apache reservation during the entire strike (his wife and family remained in Ajo) and who had been offered a highly paid permanent position there after the end of the strike. Thus, not only those who felt they could not get as high wages elsewhere came back but also those who were offered equal or higher wages in other locations. Obviously, for the latter individuals, perceived benefits that could not be measured in purely economic terms were involved in their decisions to return to Ajo.

Thus, what I discovered as a result of my interviews is that in spite of much talk about the virtues of life on the reservation, very few Ajo Indian residents will ever return to remain there permanently.[8] Even, the previous researcher's (Waddell 1969) informant, in spite of his constant talk of some day returning to the reservation, died in Ajo. This explains the seeming anomaly in figure 2 where it can be seen that in spite of the fact that employment of Indians at the Ajo mine had dropped from 232 in 1936 to just 107(113[9]) in mid-1967, the total Indian population of Ajo had remained remarkably constant in Ajo since 1944. Tables V to XV illustrate dramatically the many widows, ex-miners, and unemployed Papagos who have chosen to remain in Ajo rather than return to the reservation. The situation here is not too much different than that the average white middle class American faces. For awhile the migrant makes frequent visits back to the old home town to see his parents, other relatives, and friends, but after awhile the journey back becomes more and more of a hardship and less of a pleasant experience as relatives and friends die and move away and as shared interests and experiences decrease. Finally, the children of the migrant even further removed economically, emotionally, and socially from the originally hometown often will stop making such visits entirely.

The situation among the Ajo Papagos is not really that much different from the middle class migrant described above. For example, Waddell (1969:21, 23) using the "Papago Population Register" data gathered in 1959 determined that 32 per cent of all Papago males who were residing in Ajo at that time were born in Ajo (i.e., were second and in some cases third generation Ajo Papagos). Therefore, it was not really surprising that seven out of the forty-two[10] male company employees that I interviewed said they had never gone to the Papago reservation; one said he had gone there only once during his lifetime; one said he returns less frequently than once a year; five claimed they go there only once a year; eight said they return several times a year; four said they go there every other month; and sixteen out of the forty-two gave the same answer that Waddell's informant gave him (i.e., about "once a month"). Thus, only about 38 percent of the miners interviewed said they were visiting the reservation "every chance they got". Furthermore, in addition to the nine who said they seldom, if ever, visit the reservation; twelve others said that they had visited the reservation less often in the years just prior to the strike than when they had first come to Ajo while only four said they had visited it more often in recent years than in their first years in Ajo. (Seventeen reported no change in their visiting pattern.) Even during the strike, although twenty of the forty-two miners said that they had visited the reservation "more often" than before the strike began, thirteen remarked that they had not returned there at all during the strike, and four more commented that they had gone there "fewer" times than when they had not been on strike. (Five said their visiting pattern had not changed at all during the strike.)

From all the interviews, almost without exception among those who were still visiting the reservation, although other activities were often mentioned, there were only two main types of visits undertaken: those made to talk to close relatives and/or those made to attend dances. Often both types of visits would be combined. Thus, a family could fulfill its kinship obligations and be entertained at the same time. It was also interesting to note that in many cases these miners would drive after work at night to dances in nearby Papago villages, either with their wives and sometimes their families, or with their "drinking buddies". In either case, the miner and his family or friends were apparently seeking some excitement or entertainment to relieve the relative dullness of life in Ajo. Thus, most remaining ties to the reservation are social or recreational in nature, rather than of an economic nature. This is not really surprising since I learned from many informants (e.g., see F.N. August 29, 1967) that the demanding work schedule (see footnote 4) of the mine makes it difficult, if not almost impossible, for the average Ajo Papago to effectively control any of the economic resources of the reservation while living in Ajo. Thus, I heard often of the many "cows" that the Ajo Indians "used to have" on the reservation and, in a few cases, of the land that they "used to farm". Also, in the case of one enterprising Ajo family that had planted a vegetable garden in a village on the reservation not too distant from Ajo, the miner's own parents were reported by him to me as having "stolen" most of the produce from his garden as "payment" for "watching" over the garden while he and his family were living in Ajo, and a short time later this miner's parents were even said to have tried to take full control over this newly subjugated garden plot since their own land through much abuse was by now quite infertile (F.N. August 29, 1967).

That the reservation in recent years is now being viewed mainly as a place for recreation and vacations can also be seen in the practice of many Indian miners and their families to only visit the reservation during the warmer months of the year. As one miner told me in a half-serious, joking answer to a question as to why he and his family never returned to the reservation during the winter months, "it's too cold" there; "we hardly know how to chop wood" (L.I. 26). Several other Indians also complained of the coldness and primitive discomforts associated with winter visits to the reservation and some mothers added that it was difficult to return there "while the kids are in school".[11] (e.g., see L.I. 3; L.I. 5; L.I. 20; L.I 26; L.I. 27; L.I. 42). One man said that the reservation was a good place to go "to watch Indians dance" (L.I. 20), and one wife said that she took her children there "to ride horses" that were borrowed from her husband's relatives living there (L.I. 28). Another man said that he used to return to the now-abandoned reservation village of "Hotwater" to decorate his father's grave when the roads were better, but now he just returns to areas of the reservation near Ajo once or twice a year to attend dances with his wife and to "hunt rabbits" because it is "something to do" (L.I. 48). He added, as did many others, (e.g., L.I. 12; L.I. 23; L.I. 25; L.I. 37;. LI. 52) that in recent years he has never visited anyone on the reservation because "there's nobody there" (i.e., no close friends or relatives live there any more).[12] There were several other comments from others that indicated that many Papagos now only visit those parts of the reservation that have good roads leading to them (e.g., see L.I. 31). Thus, relatives living in Sells or at some other location along the main road to Tucson are usually visited more frequently by many Ajo Indians than those relatives living at the end of a long dirt road. Also, these visits often just serve as rest stops for the "kids" and adults as they travel to such places as Sells to visit the Indian Health Service hospital or Tucson to do some shopping, etc. and are, therefore, not the prime motivation for the trip at all. This pattern is very similar to the familiar one that at one time engulfed my cousin who lives in Seattle. During the year the World's Fair was held there, every night his house was full of relatives he scarcely knew. Chain migration of the remaining relatives to Ajo has further hastened this changing relationship to the reservation in many cases (e.g., see L.I. 38). Therefore, the reservation now has become for many Ajo Indians hardly more than a rest stop or a recreation area where they can on occasion retreat to escape the pressures of life in Ajo just as do many other Americans in urban centers everywhere seeking temporary weekend relief from their workday cares.

Other evidence of this shifting allegiance from the reservation to Ajo was that only three families out of the fifty-four did not at least occasionally read the local Ajo paper (forty-six of the fifty-four bought or subscribed to the local paper every week) as compared to sixteen who said they never read a Papago newspaper. This is even more remarkable than it appears on the surface since sales of one particular Papago newspaper is actively pushed by a local village man who peddles the papers to all Indians that he meets around the village and in the downtown area of Ajo while no such salesman exists for the Ajo Copper News. Also, although there was a special social column on the Ajo Indian Village in the Ajo Copper News, which was published more or less on a continuous weekly basis from September 8, 1960 to June 3, 1965, for the almost three year period prior to my interviews very little news on the Indian village had been published in this local paper to "explain" this reading loyalty to the Ajo town paper and then only on a sporadic basis, such as an article on the election of Indian Village Council officers in 1966 (A.C.N January 27, 1966:1); and one on the tournament play in Phoenix of a girls basketball team from the Ajo Indian Village (A.C.N. March 30, 1967:2). Death notices and arrest records were also published occasionally, but none of these items appear on a regular enough basis to explain why most Ajo Indians were weekly readers of the "Copper News". Obviously, a growing awareness and involvement with the larger Ajo community is indicated here.

Further evidence for this growing involvement with the outside world is indicated by the growing numbers of Ajo Indians that subscribe to or buy at the newsstand the daily Phoenix or Tucson newspapers and many nationally distributed magazines. Also, the almost universal interest in news broadcasts[13] and the severe shock that was felt in the Indian community upon hearing of the death of John F. Kennedy (A.C.N. November 28, 1963:6; L.I. 25) demonstrate a growing involvement in state and national affairs on the part of most local Indians.

Questions about the language spoken in the home were also quite revealing since nineteen of the forty company employees interviewed said that most or all conversations were in English; eleven said that both the native language and English were used[13]; five remarked that their children spoke only English but that the language used between the miner and his wife was the native one; and only five; said that "Indian" was the language used mainly in the home. For all fifty-four Ajo families interviewed in-depth, the corresponding figures were twenty-four (English), thirteen (both languages), six (children-English, parents-"Indian"), and eleven ("Indian"). Several factors seem to be important here in "explaining" these results with the ubiquitous, ever-switched-on T.V. set being perhaps one of the most important influences on preschool age children. Among the school children it was by now "popular" to speak English and downgrading to be caught speaking Papago or some other Indian language, and in the case of intertribal or interethnic marriage, English usually served as the "lingua franca" between the marriage partners. Even one much older adult who had grown up on the reservation and still had strong ties to it when he heard that a white man at Sells (the tribal capitol town on the nearby reservation) was in the process of preparing materials to teach written Papago to reservation school children and adults said that it was "foolish to teach written Papago" (F.N. January 25, 1968), and another adult added that "if you set yourself apart, then other people will consider you as different" (L.I. 50).

During my stay in Ajo, there was only one Papago husband and wife that were attempting to teach their children any of the old Papago stories, songs, dances, and skills and this in large part was being done for commercial gain since the members of this family formed a professional dance team that often performed during various social events in Ajo, on the nearby reservations, and in neighboring towns (L.I. 30). Almost all of the parents interviewed, in fact, denied even knowing the songs or skills themselves, even though a few said that their parents had at times sung songs to the grandchildren, or in a few cases that the grandmother had tried to teach her granddaughter how to weave a basket while the young girl was vacationing on the reservation. However, it was interesting to discover that eighteen of the forty company employees (26 of the fifty-four families interviewed) had visited a Papago medicine man at least once for treatment for themselves or another family member after moving to or growing up in Ajo, and that of those Ajo Indians willing to discuss their opinion of such treatment, sixteen families thought that it was beneficial, two that it was "fair", and only nine laughed at or ridiculed the idea of going to an "Indian doctor". Still, I am not as convinced that this represents a major survival of the old Papago traditional culture as I am that it reflects the highly impersonal and, in my opinion from many hours of involuntary "participant observation", very bad medical care that one received at the local company hospital.

It was also interesting to discover that in spite of the fact that an organization to be discussed later in Chapter 7, the Ajo Village Intertribal Council, was constantly stressing the need for closer cooperation between the Indians of Ajo and the Papago reservation (e.g., see A.C.N. March 30, 1961:6; January 10, 1963:6), seventeen of the fifty-four families I interviewed in-depth said that they either did not want any closer relationship to the reservation or could see no value in having such a closer relationship; another fifteen were uncertain about the value of such a relationship; and only twenty-two said that a closer relationship would be beneficial to the Indians of Ajo, but even here not one of these people could tell me why this would be so, other than that they had a desire to know "what was happening" on the reservation. In fact, there seemed to be a growing alienation between the Indian people of the reservation and of Ajo, which I sensed from such remarks from Ajo Indians as the "people here have no business out there" (L.I. 2); there are "too many mixed people in Ajo; the company takes care of everything" (L 11); "we are now in Ajo.'" (i.e., we are not now living on the reservation; we are just like any other Americans with the same duties and rights) (L.I. 47); and "off-reservation Papagos are now learning how to get along in the state and be included in the rest of the population; if you set yourself apart, then other people will consider you as different" (L.I. 50). One man (L.I. 8) added that in previous years he and his family "used to travel all over the reservation" to attend feasts and dances on his days off from the mine, but that "for the last couple of years the Ajo villagers have been afraid that the reservation people will hurt their cars." He told of the time that "they" took the gas cap from his car in Cowlic (a reservation village) and of how other Ajo villagers have had the air let out of their tires. Also, he told me the story of the San Simon villagers who refused to feed some drunken Ajo Mexicans at a feast once. The Mexicans then threw dirt into the food pot. Another man told me about "one tribal chairman" (the Papago chairman at Sells) who "tried to keep the people (living) away (from the reservation) from coming back to the reservation if they had been away a year or more (L.I. 27) and a member of the Ajo Village Intertribal Council complained that the Indians of Ajo "get no help because we are 'behind the fence'" (i.e., we live on the wrong side of the reservation boundary) (L.I. 25). Several times I also heard stories of legal assistance that was promised but never given (e.g., see L.I. 30), and of the difficulties at times encountered by the off-reservation Indian when he tried to obtain a tribal scholarship for his son or daughter (e.g., see L.I. 52), or free medical help for himself or his family (e.g., see L.I. 21; L.I. 32). Also, the wife of the "manager" of the men's basketball team said that the Sells men are often "scared to play" the Ajo men and "don't like the Ajo Indians very much", probably because the team from Sells always gets "beaten so badly" by the Ajo team[14](L.I. 21), and another lady who is married to one of the "Sand People" (descendents of the Papago who were the original occupants of the Ajo area and the deserts to the west and south of Ajo) added that, "around here what news we have (i.e., care about) is (all) in the Copper News" when asked if she wanted to know more about what was happening on the reservation.

Nor was this dislike merely in the minds of some Ajo Indians since I vividly remember the words of a reservation man who had once been an important tribal official who remarked that while leading a fire crew from Ajo during the summer of 1967, the miners from Ajo were constantly complaining about all aspects of the work, especially the necessity of "running up and down mountains all day" (F N. Summer 1968). It was obvious that he held the Ajo miners in contempt as he concluded by saying that this crew finally was disbanded and sent home earlier than the other crews.

Another rumor (L.I. 27), that seemed to have at least some basis in fact (see A.R. March 6, 1968:A-16), was that the reservation people were being pushed out of the seasonal farm labor market by the striking miners who had been scouring the countryside looking for work at even the most menial tasks. This also, no doubt, created additional hostility toward the miners of Ajo. And, it is important to note that the two men I met in the section of Ajo that contained the Ajo Indian village who seemed to have the strongest ties to the reservation and both of whose wives and children were still living on the reservation while the men worked and lived alone in Ajo, complained the most about the unfriendliness and hostility of fellow Ajo Indian villagers toward them. The one blamed this on the fact that the other villagers felt he was "too high and mighty" for them (L.I. 14) (he had at one time attended college for several years) and the other blamed the "problem" on the parents of the teenage "hoodlums and barbarians" in the Ajo village who were always stealing things from his house while he slept or was away at work or on the reservation (L.I. 2).[16] This latter statement is especially informative since the family living just next door to this man reported that they had never had any trouble with the village teenagers (L.I. 44), and a man living a few blocks away told me that although he had once thought about moving out of the Indian Village, he had decided to stay since "this part of town is the quietest place" and there "is never any noise at night" (F.N. February 7, 1968). However, from the interview data I will present in Chapter 7, it is obvious that there were other people that were indeed having trouble with village teenagers, but it is of great importance to note that the most hostile acts of the young people were often directed against "outsiders" and "outside" institutions, such as the men from the sheriff's office and the Baptist Church in the Village. Thus, it is not really too surprising that a man who was viewed by many other villagers as being merely a "commuting" worker from the reservation and not as a permanent and "loyal" Ajo resident, had some misgivings about the protection and help he could expect and receive from his Indian Village neighbors.

Also, I was surprised to learn that very little of the miners' money actually flows back to relatives on the reservation. Only ten[17] of the fifty-four families interviewed reported that they had ever given or sent money to any friends or relatives on the reservation, although sixteen[18] of the fifty-four reported taking "groceries" to share with relatives on the reservation or in Mexico whenever they returned there for visits and a smaller number (thirteen[19] of the fifty-four) have taken clothing there at times. I also learned that thirteen[20] of the forty-two families that reported that they at least occasionally visited relatives on the reservation had never brought anything at all to their relatives there and several of the miners (three[21] out of the forty) had even borrowed money at times from their relatives on the reservation. Again, indicative of their commitment to the way of life they were beginning to imitate in Ajo was the fact that two of the Ajo families reported that the only gifts they gave their rural relatives were Christmas gifts and in the case of one of the families, a few articles of clothing. Obviously, from the data collected above, most gifts, which are today given to reservation relatives by Ajo Indians, are almost the same kind of token gifts that many of the white residents of Ajo give every year to poorer relatives and charitable organizations. It was amazing to me that, except in one case where a non-working wife was still living on the reservation, I found no evidence that any of the fifty-four families interviewed in-depth were contributing a significant amount to the support of any person on the reservation. In fact, I strongly suspect that in many cases, the Ajo Indian and his family draw more benefits from their remaining reservation ties than they give in return. This is certainly true with respect to most of those who make it a practice to return to the reservation for feast days, dances, and to use the facilities of the Public Health Service Hospital at Sells. Any significant sharing of wealth among the Ajo Indians seems to be largely confined to certain close groups of relatives often living near each other in the Ajo Indian Village

At the time of Waddell's study in 1964 (1969:138, 144), although he said he found a few "neighborhood aggregate households of kin" created through some "informal and uncondoned swapping", households that are related by kinship ties are generally dispersed throughout the village, due to company regulation of housing rental and due to the fact that turnover at the mine does not usually permit acquisition of adjacent houses by related families." However, by July 4, 1968 near the end of my field work in Ajo, the number of vacancies among the 127 houses in the Indian village had risen from the four that Waddell (1964) indicates existed when he made his survey in June of 1964 to thirty-four, thereby making the manipulation of housing in the village much easier and casting considerable doubt, in view of the evidence both economic and social that I collected, upon his statement that "the vital kinship links are still largely in terms of kinship villages, not the Ajo village" Waddell 1969:138). In fact, my evidence seems to indicate that just the opposite was true by 1968 (i.e., that social and economic links between relatives and friends in Ajo were much more important than ties to the reservation for most Ajo Indians), although a few families did continue to maintain fairly strong ties to the reservation at that time. However, it is interesting to note that almost without exception the children of the Ajo miners that do not elect to remain in Ajo migrate to the larger urban areas of Arizona and California, rather than return to the reservation. Also, in terms of mate selection, some very revealing data was collected from fifty-one of the fifty-four families interviewed concerning where the husband and wife had first met each other. In twenty-four cases it was in Ajo that the meeting first occurred, and in seventeen other cases it was in some other nonreservation location. Only in nine cases did the meeting first occur on the reservation, while in one case where information concerning a previous spouse was volunteered, the prior spouse had first been met on the reservation, but the second one was first met in Ajo.

Perhaps one of the major reasons why Waddell was misled on this point is that in Ajo, members of extended families learned to be somewhat secretive about their social and. economic interdependence when talking with outsiders, since some of them had welfare aid from the Aid-to-Dependent-Children and other programs cut off when an adult male was discovered in the house (F.N. November 26, 1967) (e.g., aid to one-half of a polygynous family was cut off in Ajo in 1967 (F.N. November 18, 1967)).

Another evidence of the growing commitment of Ajo Indians to the urban way of life is the increasing blurring of ethnic lines that is most evident in the population statistics for "Lower Mexican Town", "Integrated Ajo" and "Rural Ajo" (see tables IX, X, XI, XII, XIII, and XIV). In fact, it was quite a surprise to the company's employment agent when in verifying the job categories of Ajo's Indian miners, I inquired about several "Mexicans" and "Americans" who unbeknown to the agent, had a larger Indian heritage than Mexican or white. For rather obvious reasons, the number of "mistaken" identities was especially large among those Indians who had long been living among the town's Mexican population, and it was interesting to note that large numbers of Mexicans now participated enthusiastically in such Indian Village events as the weekly Bingo games and the St. Catherine's Day Fiesta. In fact, at the Bingo games I observed personally, the Mexicans far outnumbered the few Indians present, and I was told that by 1967 this was also true at the St. Catherine's Day celebration (F.N. November 17, 1967).

Also indicative of the increasing penetration of the modern capitalistic spirit into the Ajo Indian community were several "backyard" businesses that had been begun by local Indians. Thus, in addition to the food sales, dances, bands, and dance teams that will be discussed in chapter 7, one Indian had a flourishing car repair business; another sold Papago newspapers to everyone he could "buttonhole"; and an entire family operated a neighborhood "soda pop service" in the village, which seemed to be a quite profitable operation. Also, at one time in the past, one Indian had, for a while, taken over the operation of a downtown "snack bar" (A.C.N. September 7, 1961:4).

However, the final proof that the "Protestant Work Ethic" had finally completely engulfed at least a few of the Indians of Ajo came when I was sharply reprimanded by one Indian lady for being five minutes late for an appointment and by another family for being a half hour late. Obviously, not all Ajo Indians ran on "Indian time. Here then, at last, was the "systematized Indian" in the best company tradition. As

Aronson (1961:182) states, following his study of the degree of "labour commitment" that was found among Jamaican bauxite workers:

> It is tempting to speculate about the merit of the basic assumption with regard to the worker recruited from traditional agriculture. The gap between the earnings and employment possibilities in his new industrial employment and those open to him as a farmer or farm worker is usually wide, while at the same time, his job horizon remains relatively narrow through lack of experience and mobility. It would not be surprising, therefore, if he chose to make intensive efforts to adjust himself to the demands of the more favorable industrial situation. ...

Finally, when asked directly why they remained in Ajo during the very long 1967-1968 copper strike the most frequent responses were:

1. High pay for relatively unskilled labor requiring little or no formal education (although for all miners hired within the past few years a high school diploma is now required).
2. A high living standard (relative to the reservation).
3. Total (environmental) "security" provided by the company.
4. Good schools for the children (the necessity for children to obtain a good education was often stressed).
5. Good housing (at least relative to the reservation) at a low cost.
6. Many social and recreational activities.
7. Too many debts to quit working for the company.
8. Little discrimination against the Indian in Ajo as compared to other towns and cities in Arizona.
9. No home or social ties except in Ajo.
10. Close relatives and friends live in Ajo.

11. Sentimental attachment to Ajo (Usually this reason was given by those who grew up in Ajo).

12. Nearness to the Papago reservation.

13. Miscellaneous reasons, such as the problems created by advanced age, a lack of transportation, and the fear of going elsewhere and personal preferences, such as liking the climate or small town atmosphere of Ajo.

(No attempt has been made to order these reasons in terms of the frequency of response.)

Complaints about living in Ajo were usually minor and directed against such things as the company's employment and housing policies, the smelter smoke, "unhealthy" children, the high summer heat (a complaint usually made by the Yavapai miners who originally came from the northern part of the state), the noise and debris of blasting operations in the open pit, and various complaints against the local unions. It was also extremely interesting to discover that there were more complaints about the dullness of life in Ajo as compared to life in a bigger urban center than there were about the confinement of life in Ajo as opposed to the "freedom" found on the reservation. In fact, most people interviewed had no major complaints whatsoever about living in Ajo.

In pondering over the reasons given by the Indians themselves for their reluctance to leave Ajo during the very long copper strike, I was especially intrigued by reasons 3 and 7 and the focus of my research began to shift to an examination of the control methods used by the Phelps Dodge Corporation to not only "win" the strike but also in May of 1968 at the end of the strike, announce the final return figure for all employees, both Indian and non-Indian, as being 99 per cent (A.R. May 5, 1968:F-6), a remarkable figure considering the extreme length of the strike.

Coming to Ajo just as the strike was about to begin, "pursuing" an ethnic group (i.e., Papago Indians) into an urban environment (albeit, a simplified one since it was a tightly controlled company mining town (Stucki 1970)), I too, discovered as did Jones (1972:52) that "what is lacking in most anthropological studies of the urban poor.. is a description of the day-to-day impact of urban institutions on the life of the poor." In fact, as I look back on my own first fieldwork, I now also agree with Jones (1972:51) that "the major determinant of ghetto behavior and social organization is the relationship between the local population and higher level institutions," a suggestion which was first given to me many years ago by my dissertation advisor (Dr. Robert Hackenberg) but which was not fully appreciated until just recently when I have gone beyond focusing merely on "the company" but have also begun to reexamine the relationship between townspeople of Ajo, both Indian and non-Indian, and such powerful higher level institutions as the Catholic and Mormon Churches and the various branches of the state and federal government.

Chapter Notes

1. The name of this tribe has now been officially changed to Tohono O'~~Odum~~ odham

2. I had earlier been a "coordinator" for the on-reservation census update of the "Papago Population Register" during the summer of 1967 and later during the summer of 1968 I was "field director" for that major portion of the off-reservation census that involved the farm areas and cities north of the main Papago reservation. The tabulated results of these surveys appear in two reports published by the "Health Program Systems Center" in 1968 (Rund, Siegel, and Rumley 1968; Rund and Rumley 1968). However, the reader should be cautioned that the survey form that appears in both of these publications as an appendix was in reality only used in the latter part of the off-

reservation survey after the work on the reservation and in Ajo had been completed.

3. In addition to the migrants from the Papago reservation also living here were some Pima, Yavapai, and Yaqui Indians.

4. The men have in recent years been on a work schedule that allows them only two days off after working twenty-six days (i.e., one weekend off in every four week work period, plus a brief summer vacation period when the entire mining operation is shut down for a two week period.

5. Earlier, despite several serious objections from myself and a coworker from the University of Colorado, a much inferior survey form had been used (see Appendix D) which led to such serious errors as the figures on page 49 of the Rund and Rumley report that indicate that no Indian in Ajo uses the services of a medicine man (a grossly inaccurate statement as I later learned). Also, the figures given in this book represent a more highly refined and corrected analysis of the actual population figures for Ajo Papagos in the fall of 1967 than that appearing in the 1968 off-reservation publication.

6. The fact that I was giving the Indians a gift of either cash ($2.00) or several anthropological paperbacks about the Papago and Pima tribes seemed to win me many friends with the books being by far the most desired of the two gifts.

7. This information was supplied me by the company's employment agent. However, one Papago miner had suffered a stroke during the strike, which later proved fatal. Also, another Papago miner was fired shortly after the end of the strike for a truck accident that occurred just a few hours prior to the start of the strike and a Pima miner was fired about a month after the end of the strike for excessive absences from work. These events were, however, just part of the long selection process and were not directly related to the strike itself.

8. Hackenberg and Wilson (1969:10-11) in summarizing the results of a migration study in which I also participated in the summer of 1967 state that "more than two-thirds of all Papagos who depart from their home villages and remain away for three years or more

will never return"; after twenty years away the return probability drops to .08.

9. Although the local Indians in charge of the fall 1967 census of Ajo for the Health Program Systems Center were able to "identify" 113 of the company's employees as of July 1967 as being "Indian", the company's employment agent gave different ethnic identifications to six of these men (see Chapter 6, Chapter Note 77). Thus, the lower figure of 107 is used in an attempt to make this figure comparable to those given by Waddell as will be discussed in Chapter 6. (The figure would even be larger than 113 if one were to include such people as the many miners from Oklahoma who often said that they were part Cherokee (e.g., see F.N. May 27, 1968) and a "half Papago" unskilled miner who lived in lower Mexican town and his two "quarter Papago" sons, all three of whom were married to "full Mexican" wives and all three of whom also claimed to be "full Mexicans" and refused to be identified as being even part "Indian", even though my local Indian census worker, who knew the family's history well, verified their Papago heritage as did also a few close relatives of this particular family who somewhat reluctantly did cooperate in the 1967 Ajo Indian census. At least one additional relative of these three "Mexicans" who was also identified by the same Indian census worker as being "one-quarter Papago" also refused to identify himself as being part Indian. He, as the others, considered himself to be a "full" Mexican and had also married a "Mexican" wife. (None of these noncooperating men, nor the "one-eighth Papago" children, associated with these families are included in the census figures given in Tables V to XV.)

10. This sample includes the forty in-depth interviews with the "P.D." (Phelps Dodge) employees described earlier and two interviews which were not begun because these miners said that they had never visited the Papago reservation and had no interest in the Papagos over there, so they saw no sense in answering my questions. (They were both related and originally the family had

come from a Papago village in Mexico (i.e., they were what are locally called "Sand People").

11. Some mothers use the reservation as a place to take their children for the summer vacation period (e.g., see L.I. 24; L.I. 30; L.I. 31), although many young Ajo Indian teenagers refuse to go there because as one teenager told me, "it is too quiet" there (L.I. 16).

12. An alternative answer that I also often heard was that the miner had "no home there" (e.g., see F.N. December 8, 1967).

13. Thirty-four of the thirty-nine company employees, who were interviewed concerning their T.V. viewing habits, reported watching news broadcasts "often" (i.e., at least once a day). Two others said they sometimes view T.V. news broadcasts, while only three said that they seldom watch the news on T.V., and even one of these three reported that the other members of his family watched the T.V. news "all the time" (L.I. 11).

14. One miner with a "Mexican" wife reported that Spanish was spoken at times in addition to English and "Indian" (L.I. 51).

15. She did remark, however, that relationships between the Ajo and Sells "girls" teams had always been quite friendly.

16. Concerning his fellow villagers he said, "People here don't control their children; they (the children) are hoodlums and barbarians".

17. Two of the ten said that these gifts have now ceased to be given in the past few years, and only four of the ten sent or gave money on a regular basis to relatives or friends living on the reservation. Forty-four families reported that they never have given any money to relatives living on the reservation.

18. Of the other 38, one family said they had taken food there one time only; two more said they take food there "sometimes"; three said they used to take food there in the past but no longer; one said they "share the food bills while there"; and thirty-one said they never have taken food there.

19. One of these families took clothes to the reservation only once and another of these thirteen families reported that they used to take clothing there but no longer now. Forty-one families reported never to have taken any clothing there.

20. Two others said that only once did they take anything; three families said that they only take something "sometimes"; and two reported that they used to take something but not any longer in recent years.

21. Only one of these three had ever loaned any money to his relatives in return.

CHAPTER 4:

The Past is Often the Key to the Future

The magnets that draw trade and home seekers are
attractive business places, well-kept streets, cozy homes,
live lodges, hospitable churches, good schools, friendly
people.' We have all these .... (A.C.N. April 21, 1923:3).
We strive for stability and a better life. This is only
natural .... (A.C.N. July 20,1967:2).

It has often been stated that the "past is the key to the future". This proved
to be true in many instances during the Ajo strike for, although a strike
of this magnitude had never occurred in the history of the Ajo mine,
the key to the understanding of many of the control actions undertaken
by the various systems involved in the strike can best be understood
from a knowledge of certain events that occurred in the history of each
system. This is especially true when the control actions undertaken by
the company are examined.

Although the Phelps Dodge Company did not gain control of
the company town of Ajo until 1931 through a company merger (Ajo

Copper News October 1, 1931:1) the influence of the Phelps Dodge Company philosophy in Ajo was felt much earlier. Already by 1907, John Greenway, the manager of the Calumet and Arizona mine at Bisbee, and his chief geologist had become frequent visitors to the mine at Ajo and had even at one time held an option on the property there owned by Tom Childs, an important individual prominent in the early history of the town (Therrien 1945:72,74). In 1911, the Calumet and Arizona mining company exercised their options and took control of the most promising Ajo claims (Cleland 1952:231; Therrien 1945:80). After some initial difficulties, large-scale mining operations were begun in Ajo in the year 1917 (Therrien 1945:81-82,89). Using the open pit method developed by Daniel C. Jackling at Bingham Canyon, Utah (Cleland 1952:217-218,230), the successful development of the huge copper reserves at Ajo was made possible when Greenway and one of his associates, Dr. Ricketts, a chemist, developed a successful leaching process for the huge carbonate surface deposits at Ajo (Therrien 1945:81-82).

However even earlier, in 1916, Greenway and his associates turned their attention toward the planning and construction of a new townsite north of the old mining town of Ajo (Therrien 1945:94-95; Cleland 1952:232). Greenway in a seven page memo in November of that year to Mike Curley, his operations manager, outlined plans for the new townsite, setting forth "specifications for the kinds of buildings and homes he wanted, rents to charge (as low as $1 a month!), policies for operating businesses and utilities, and ideas for the community's development" (Lesure 1955:7). To prepare a town plan and design the required housing, Greenway hired the Minneapolis firm of Kenyon and Maine (Crawford 1995: 145). When William Kenyon arrived in Arizona, he:

> ...found that Ajo, located in a harsh and desolate area
> close to the Mexican border, consisted of a mine and a

"collection of shacks," occupied by indigenous Papago Indians and Mexican laborers. He laid out a town that reflected the new realities of copper mining, separating the area into three distinct town sites. The largest zone contained the town center and housing for the American skilled workers, administrators, and office workers, who would control production. Two smaller areas, in an adjacent canyon, housed the Mexican miners and the Indians, who survived by scavenging around the mining camp. Kenyon platted the Mexican and Indian sites in grids, but, clearly influenced by Tyrone, laid out the American site as a formal plan focused around a central plaza. (Crawford 1995: 146).

The actual construction of this model-planned community complete with a business block, individual homes, and two churches, one for the Catholics and one for the Protestants began quickly. Even the water, lighting, telephone, telegraph, gas and sewer facilities were to be completely installed before the miners would be permitted to move into the new town site. All this was supposedly done "for the comfort and care of the employees" (Ajo Copper News April 29, 1916:1). However, Allen (1966:86) quotes an interesting passage by A. T. Shurick in pointing out that "probably" western mining companies during this period provided only that housing "which was essential to keep employees working", thus casting considerable doubt upon the often repeated altruistic motives usually attributed to these companies. Thus Shurick states that:

In the well-designed mining camp today (the 1920's), recognition is taken of varying needs (of the employees) and houses built accordingly. First there will be a few substantial, well-built houses, equipped with modern conveniences throughout and comparable with the better type of modest town house, for the superintendent, clerical forces, doctor, store manager, etc. Next there is a larger group of similar houses along less pretentious lines for foremen, sub-foremen and some of the preferred class of men such as the electrician, master mechanic, etc. The balance of the houses which go to make up the bulk of the camp will be divided roughly into two general classes. The first of these will be of a fairly substantial and well-built type, usually four or five rooms and equipped with running water and possibly a bath and inside toilet facilities. This house is designed for the more permanent miners who appreciate something of a better class and it is usually plastered inside and equipped with some extras, such as a porch, that tend to lift it above the next class below. The inferior houses are designed to meet the requirements of the lower class of improvident miners who would be indifferent to anything above the crudest type of house and probably abuse anything better. These houses may be built somewhat along the lines of the next class above, but would be finished with wood ceiling inside, have outdoor toilets, and be dependent on an outside spigot for its water supply (Allen (1966:86)).[1]

In Ajo this "lower class" obviously contained the Mexican miners and their families since the initial construction activities for the model community of Cornelia consisted of "one store block", a "plaza complete with palm and other trees," a "sprinkling system and side-walks," "20 American dwelling houses," and "10 Mexican houses" in a separate townsite referred to as 'Mexican Town" which was located between the old townsite of Ajo and the new model town of Cornelia (Ajo Copper News April 29, 1916:1).

Crawford also supports Shurick stating that:

Different grades of housing underlined the company's labor policies. To encourage stability, the company encouraged American employees to purchase houses and building lots. Kenyon and Maine designed fifteen different types of four- and five-room houses. ... The company offered Mexican workers no such incentives. Kenyon and Maine ... [provided] them with a single simple type of housing, a small flat-roofed, hollow tile house with running water and an outdoor toilet, lined up in rows of repeated units. To ensure their control over the unskilled miners, company policy prohibited Mexicans from buying land or houses. Instead, they could either lease lots or rent houses, from which they could be evicted at fifteen days' notice. The Indians were left to fend for themselves. (Crawford 1995: 147).

No housing at all was provided for the Indian miners by the company until 1936 when the "first block of 10 or 15 houses was laid out" (Waddell 1969:54). Waddell further states that before 1936 "Indians were leasing small parcels of company land for one dollar a year and building their own dwellings out of anything they could manage--tin, railroad ties, scraps of lumber, or adobe" and that they also "rented houses in Mexican Town, or lived in what remained of the now defunct Rowood or Clarkston community where there was a sizable temporary settlement of Indians." (Clarkston, renamed Rowood in 1924,was almost completely destroyed by two devastating fires in 1931 (A.C.N. June 25, 1931:1)). Clotts (1915a:25, 32) mentions a small Indian settlement of five houses with 29 inhabitants in 1914 near the mine a few years before the construction of Cornelia, but other references to a separate Indian Village during the following years are not easy to find. Several of my informants verified Waddell's information and one added that Indian families lived mainly in "shacks, tents, and brush shelters" when he arrived in Ajo in 1936 (L.I. 27, February 27, 1968). Although Waddell (1966:144) feels, in spite of "sparse evidence," that "the Ajo Indian village noted by Clotts was likely the same one which now exists to the west of the open pit and flanking the eastern slope of the little Ajo Mountains just south of Ajo town (Cornelia) proper," one of my informants told also of Papago settlements and a Papago graveyard that existed at one time on the south rim of the pit before it was enlarged (S.I. 324). Several of Waddell's informants (1969:52) also confirmed this observation. Another of my informants perhaps better clarified this situation by stating that there were Indian tents and shacks scattered over the hillsides south and west of Ajo (Cornelia) at one time in the past (F.N. January 23, 1968).

The situation in Ajo for many years was apparently quite analogous to that which prevailed at Gamerco, New Mexico, where a company spokesman said that:

> The Mexicans prefer to live in more or less segregated quarters, and a Mexican village has been started somewhat apart from the main camp. The Navajos build their own "hoogans" and the solution of their housing problems does not rest on the mine owner (Allen 1966:102).

In other words, most mine owners probably felt that it would be both a waste of time and money to construct houses for Indian employees since they were used to building their own homes anyway. Also, the owners probably felt that the lure of money and perhaps such things as liquor would be enough to bind Indians to the mine, while added inducements, such as low cost but comfortable housing, would be needed to attract Anglos and Mexicans.

In contrast to the early company towns in the West which were usually haphazard in their arrangement "many of them having grown from typical mining or lumbering camps with houses located wherever the builder happened to feel like settling, and the company coming in later to take over" (Allen 1966:80), the townsite of Cornelia and other later company towns were laid out in a planned and orderly fashion. However, other promoters, sensing a quick profit, soon moved into the Ajo area and created competing townsites. Thus on May 6, 1916, the Ajo Copper News on page one stated that:

> The promoters of the different townsites were very busy men Thursday while the Phoenix boosters were here. Many automobiles were used for advertising purposes, such signs being seen as the following: "Gibson," "Underwood," "Everything Free at Clarks- ton," etc.

The "Gibson" promoters emphasized that their lots were higher and had a better view and that a "plenteous flow of fine drinking water has been struck at a depth of approximately 33 feet" (Ajo Copper News April 29, 1916:2). However, the promoters of Clarkston had a better location near the mine on the main highway and a more vigorous building and promoting program. In the same issue of the Ajo Copper News on page six they advertised the following:

> Clark's Townsite--30 substantial business houses erected in 6 weeks, all doing business. New buildings starting daily. Water, water, water. Struck large flow of good soft water at 110 feet. Fine for all purposes--on townsite. School and Post-office Applied For. Fine Residence and Business Lots Still Open. A Safe Place to Locate. Watch Us Grow.

By June 17th of that year, a Clarkston ad estimated that there were 400-500 people living on the townsite but that it still had a few vacant residence lots "for American families" (A.C.N. June 17, 1916:2). Evidently at first Clarkston was also a segregated community competing with Cornelia and the old townsite of Ajo for "American" (i.e., Anglo) families.

The total population of the Ajo area was estimated at 2500 people "without enough ice to go around" on April 29, 1916 (A.C.N., p. 1). By May 6, 1916 over 500 men were on the payroll of the New Cornelia Mine (A.C.N. May 6, 1916:1) and by July 22 of that same year there were over 750 men at work for the New Cornelia Mine plus 100 men working for a rival company, Ajo Consolidated (A.C.N. July 22, 1916:1). However, late in that year, a major copper strike paralyzed Ajo and Ajo Consolidated suspended work never to resume production again (A.C.N. December 2, 1916:1). Greenway and Curley soon began to triumph over the strikers so that by the fifteenth of December they were able to report that 626 people were again working at the mine with only about 200 (3/4 of whom were Mexican) still out on strike (A.C.N. December 16, 1916:1). These last holdouts soon afterwards gave up their losing battle with Greenway.

On the 31st of March of the following year it was announced that the new town of Cornelia was to open finally (A.C.N. March 31, 1917). Very conveniently, the old townsite of Ajo burned to the ground a few days later, forcing many businesses and people into the new townsite which was then renamed Ajo (A.C.N. April 7, 1917:1). In the following years, various company policies such as cheap rent and the use of script, the lack of development of competing mineral claims, and the steady advance of the "tailings dump" and waste rock pile aided by two disastrous fires in 1931 sealed the doom of Clarkston which was by now called Rowood[2] (A.C.N. June 25, 1931:1). In 1951, (Leonard 1954:29), the opening of the new smelter nearby added to the misery of the few remaining residents as the poisonous sulfur gases often saturated the townsite of Rowood, trapped between the towering dump and waste rock piles. As far as I could determine, only one old man still resided in Rowood at the end of 1968 and its last bar closed down during the prolonged strike of 1967-68 and has not reopened since.

To better understand why Greenway wanted to build his model community of Cornelia right at the start of the Ajo operation when $4,000,000 would be needed to be spent in developing the mine before any copper could be produced (A.C.N. May 6, 1916:1), it is necessary to examine briefly the history of a rival company, Phelps Dodge, and the history of the much wilder mining camp of Bisbee.

The origin of the gigantic present day Phelps Dodge Corporation can be traced back to an obscure saddle-making shop in the small town of Hartford, Connecticut at the beginning of the 19th Century (Cleland 1952:3). The owner and master saddler of this shop was Anson Green Phelps, a young man of rich pioneer heritage and deep religious convictions. He apparently had a tremendous talent for capitalizing on business opportunities and soon began a career as a worldwide trader and merchant exporting large quantities of iron, copper, tin, and other metals from England (Cleland 1952:6-7).

Following a long 13-year partnership with a fellow New Englander, Elisha Peck, Anson Phelps formed a partnership with two of his sons-in-law, Daniel James and William E. Dodge shortly after another potential son-in-law, Josiah Stokes, was killed in the tragic collapse of the overloaded Phelps-Peck warehouse (Cleland 1952:11, 15-17). Phelps apparently selected his sons-in-law with the same care with which he chose all of his other business employees and associates, since Cleland (1952:17) records that both Dodge and James were "closely akin to their father-in-law in ideals, convictions, and religious points of view."

Daniel James then went overseas to head the English branch of the company, which was named Phelps, James & Co., while in the United States, the partnership was called Phelps, Dodge & Co., its present name. In 1853 Anson Phelps died, and for nearly a decade after his death, a new partnership operated the business, dominated by the strong personality of William E. Dodge (Cleland 1952:34,46). The new partnership consisted of Anson G. Phelps, Jr., William B. Dodge, Daniel James, James Stokes, William B. Dodge, Jr., and D. Willis James, a son of Daniel James. James Stokes was the younger brother of Josiah Stokes, and had in 1836 married his dead brother's former fiancée, one of the daughters of Anson Phelps (Cleland 1952:27). Thus the company was still controlled by a single-family organization.

In 1881, through the efforts of James Douglas, a man in whom the Phelps Dodge partners had absolute trust, the company completed the purchase of the Atlanta claim at Bisbee, Arizona after Douglas had advised the partners against building a smelter on an island in Long Island Sound to process European ore (Cleland 1952:97,99). Douglas's faith in the rich ore deposits of the American West was soon justified when in 1884 he found a large vein of high-grade copper ore (Cleland 1952:100-101). The following year, the Phelps Dodge partners bought out the interests of the largest owners of the adjoining Copper Queen mine and began large-scale mining operations at Bisbee (Cleland 1952:102). Douglas, although not a partner of the firm and not a relative, apparently was completely sympathetic to their views at all times and came from a similar heritage (Cleland 1952:91-97,105-106).

Direction, management, and control of the parent company, however, remained in the hands of the family dynasty established by Anson Green Phelps until almost the end of the first decade of the twentieth century (Cleland 1952:151). In the later years, W. E. Dodge, Jr. and D. Willis James dominated the company. Dodge died finally in 1903 and James in 1907 (Cleland 1952:153-154). The surviving members of the family dynasty in 1908 formed a corporation, thus ending a long series of partnerships and gave up all their export-import trade to concentrate on their copper and railroad interests in the American West (Cleland 1952:154-155).

At this point James Douglas became the president of the new corporation, although the original families of the dynasty retained considerable control over the corporation (Cleland 1952:157). Cleland (1952:157) in speaking of this event states that "at the time of incorporation it (the new corporation) reputedly had fewer than two hundred stockholders, perhaps twenty of whom determined its policies".

In 1916 Douglas resigned as president and died two years later (Cleland 1952:161-162). Douglas's son, Walter, succeeded his father as president of the Phelps Dodge Corporation in 1916 (Cleland 1952:193). This leadership continued until 1929 (Cleland 1952:201). Cleveland H. Dodge was Vice-President of the Corporation from 1909 to 1924 and Chairman of the Board from 1924-1926 (Cleland 1952:201, 278). His son, Cleveland E. Dodge, became the new Vice-President in1924 and was still serving in this position in 1952 (Cleland 1952:201-202,291). Arthur Curtiss James, the only son of Daniel Willis James, served both as a director of the company from 1909-1941 and as a vice-president from 1909 to 1930 (Cleland 1952:202,278).

Finally in 1930 Walter Douglas resigned as president of the corporation and was succeeded by Louis S. Cates, a man "without previous Phelps Dodge background, training, experience, or tradition" (Cleland 1952:216). However, it is obvious from the background of Cates that he was carefully chosen to fit in with the Phelps Dodge "tradition" as were all other top management personnel.[3]

Starting in 1930 with the merger of Phelps Dodge with the Nichols Company, the corporation began to expand its operations and resources rapidly under the new leadership of Cates (Cleland 1952:219-225). A large refinery was built by the combined companies. Also, in 1930 the corporation acquired a large manufacturing and selling organization, the National Electric Products Corporation, thus accomplishing Cates' goal of "integrating" the company "in every phase of the industry from mine to market". The number of stockholders jumped from 700 in 1925 to 3,843 in 1930 in the combined corporations (Cleland 1952:304).

By the early thirties the ore reserves of Phelps Dodge in Bisbee were rapidly being depleted so its officials searched desperately for new sources of the reddish metal (Cleland 1952:227-228). Helped by the growing depression the wealthy Phelps Dodge Corporation was able to easily acquire the huge mineral assets of the nearly bankrupt Calumet and Arizona Mining Company in 1931 through a merger (A.C.N. October 1, 1931: Cleland 1952:235). Thus Phelps Dodge Company was finally in control of the New Cornelia mine at Ajo. Also, during this depression period in 1935 Phelps Dodge gained control of the once rich holdings at Jerome of the United Verde Company and a little later began development of their huge Morenci reserves that had been acquired but not developed in 1921 (Cleland 1952:240,244,248).

It is important to our analysis at this point to realize that the Calumet and Arizona Company and the Phelps Dodge Corporation had been both long-term friends and rivals at Bisbee, Arizona (Cleland 1952:227-228). Bisbee's early history is full of the local "color" that characterized many of the robust mining camps of the late 1800's in the American West. However, in 1880 the camp became officially a town, complete with its own post office and the leading citizens held a meeting during which they decided to apply to the Pima County Board of Supervisors for the appointment of local peace officers (Cox 1938:21-22).

Also in 1880, Dr. James Douglas came to Bisbee and, as stated earlier, began a long-term relationship with the Phelps Dodge Company after he had advised them of the potential wealth of the Bisbee district and they had obtained control of the Atlanta claims (Cox 1938:34-39). Douglas was immediately put in charge of exploring the newly acquired property and after many failures, in 1884 he finally, in his last desperate attempt to find rich ore, sank a shaft into the enormous Atlanta orebody (Cox

1938:40,42). Almost at the same time the engineers of the adjoining Copper Queen mine found the same new orebody (Cox 1938:42-43). They, too, were desperately seeking a new supply of the red metal since their original orebody would be depleted in the first few months of 1885. To avoid litigation over conflicting claims to this new orebody, the two companies merged under the new name, Copper Queen Consolidated Mining Company in August of the year 1885. Apparently, soon afterwards, Phelps Dodge interests secured the entire capital stock of this newly formed company that for many years afterwards was the only operating company in Bisbee (Cox 1938:96). However, unlike the situation that later developed in Ajo, Bisbee only remained a one company town until the period beginning in 1899 when other eastern interests acquired property in the district (Cox 1938:96). The most important of these companies were the Lake Superior and Southwestern, the predecessor of the Calumet and Arizona Mining Company, the Shattuck Arizona Mining Company, and the Denn Arizona Mining Company. (The latter two merged in 1925 into the Shattuck Denn Mining Corporation.) Finally in 1931, as stated previously, the Calumet and Arizona Company was merged with the Phelps Dodge Corporation.

Phelps Dodge could have easily gained control of most of Bisbee's mineral resources earlier for small sums before they were developed, but due to personal animosities and a certain hesitation on the part of local company officials, they let control of many of these valuable properties fall into the hands of their rivals (Cox 1938:105-108). However, even before their merger in 1931, both the Copper Queen Consolidated Mining Company and the Calumet and Arizona Mining Company in spite of interlacing property lines "operated in friendly competition, all disagreements being settled by conferences among the engineers" (Cox 1938:111). The consequences of this close cooperation are crucial to our understanding of the planning that later underlay the creation of the distant townsite of Cornelia and of the policies that the Calumet and Arizona Company pursued there.

Cox (1938:118) in commenting on the general character of Bisbee during the '80's states that:

> Bisbee had rapidly grown into a great industrial community, but in civic development it remained for some years a frontier town and its pioneers lived as crude a life as those who pushed into the West during the time of Daniel Boone. Not all who came to Bisbee were happy with these living conditions, however.

The officers of the Copper Queen Company were, of course, anxious that law and order be preserved so that the business of mining copper could proceed smoothly and so that they could sleep "undisturbed" at night. As Cox (1938:61,87) states, the company was "always striving to improve conditions in the camp..." since "into this mining community, rich in copper, gold, silver and lead, came not only thieves, murderers, and desperados, but gentlemen, ladies, and children

Thus it was probably not altogether pure altruism that inspired the gift of a one room adobe school building to the town by the "benevolent" company in 1883 (Cox 1938:87). It has always been the nature of elite and educated groups of people to bring or create around them a "civilized" environment when forced to dwell among "heathen" peoples. Today, for example, this tendency is often manifest in the American military base throughout the world or in the B.I.A. or Public Health Service compound on the Indian reservation.

This school building was also used for church services, a lodge room[4], a dance hall, a theater, and often as a lecture room[5] (Cox1938:90). It is interesting to note that later in 1905 when a bond issue for school expansion was proposed that (Cox 1938:95):

The bond issue was bitterly fought on all sides. The Copper Queen Mining Company had been willing to meet all expenditures of building and rebuilding the school and to sponsor all educational interests, rather than have a bond issue.

There are hints here of a power struggle between the educators and the company officials. The educators won the battle through a clever manipulation of the school children since on the election day the children themselves "paraded the streets with banners and drum corps". This last incident occurred, however, many years after the Phelps Dodge take-over of the Copper Queen Company and probably illustrates a violent reaction to the more complete environmental control desired by the men of the "Phelps Dodge tradition" than sought by the officials of most other mining companies.

The Phelps Dodge partners had had long experience with company towns before Bisbee and were well aware of the advantages to be gained by company control of most aspects of their workers' lives. Before 1835, the partners had acquired some valuable timberland in Pennsylvania as partial payment for a debt owed them (Cleland 1952:47). Dodge made an inspection tour of the property and was so impressed by the potential profit to be made harvesting the almost virgin forests that by 1837, the partners were said to own 1,800,000,000 feet of timber in Pennsylvania alone (Cleland 1952:47-48). In order to harvest this timber the company found it necessary to build both new mills and towns for its employees in the wilderness. The forest properties owned by the company continued to expand all the way from Canada to Georgia where on St. Simon's Island, near Brunswick, it is recorded that Dodge in 1868 built a company village complete with "church, store, schoolhouse, and comfortable houses for the employees" (Cleland 1952:50-51).

One of Dodge's sons later wrote about his father that (Cleland 1952:49-50):

> Probably few men, even among those exclusively engaged in the lumber trade, were more widely and practically familiar with the varied features of this great industry. Mr. Dodge took an intelligent and enthusiastic interest in every detail, from the first selection of suitable lands, the felling of trees, the driving of the logs, the sawing, piling, and the distribution of the lumber, to the final sale in the best markets.

Obviously Dodge was well aware of the human element in all his dealings and sought to regulate it also. As seen above, the worker was controlled through the mechanism of the complete company town, but Dodge also sought to control the actions of politicians and other merchants also. His great success in this endeavor was remarkably illustrated when in "recognition" of his "many contributions to the economic development and social welfare of the State of Georgia", the legislature created a new county and named it after him (Cleland 1952:51). He immediately "repaid" them for this honor by building "one of the finest and most convenient courthouses in the state" at his own expense.

All members of the Phelps Dodge dynasty and the "kindred spirits" they later adopted into the family seemed well able to blend their deep religious convictions with very shrewd business practices (Cleland 1952:21-23). They viewed themselves always as the benefactors of those with whom they dealt, although there were often practical rewards such as increased profits and increased employee loyalty to the company that resulted from their labor policies and "gifts" to the towns they controlled.

Many members of the dynasty were known as great humanitarians starting with Anson Phelps and Josiah Stokes who served together in the organization and support of numerous charities (Cleland 1952:16). The early members of this great industrial family were all "bred" in the English Puritan tradition based upon the stern, militant, uncompromising creed of John Calvin and John Knox (Cleland 1952:21). Cleland (1952:21) describes men of this tradition as being "characterized by a blend of strong individualism and an equally strong sense of social duty" and that "they submitted their own souls to the same searching scrutiny that they applied to their business ledgers."

In the following passage Cleland (1952:165-166) paints a glowing picture of the benevolence bestowed by the members of this giant industrial family on their fellow beings:

> All of these men and their families had given tangible expression to that conviction in benefactions of great magnitude and variety - churches, hospitals, educational institutions, libraries, missionary undertakings, and other organizations for human betterment, such as the Young Men's and Young Women's Christian Associations, and the development of model communities about their mills and factories. According to the best standards of their generation, they had sought to improve the condition of labor, raise the standard of living, and widen the opportunities for the cultural and spiritual welfare of their employees.
>
> In the company's mining communities in Arizona, this philosophy had been given especially wide, thoughtful, and practical expression. Schools and churches adequate to the needs of the community were a part of every town in which the Phelps Dodge company had a major interest. Hospitals with the best, most modern equipment and a highly paid medical staff were also available to the employees and their families. Free public libraries and

reading rooms were usually added. Company stores, though operated at a profit, provided foodstuffs and merchandise of superior quality at fair prices, and thus kept the cost of living in Phelps Dodge camps at a normal level. Accidents in the mines were few, chiefly because of the management's concern for the safety of the men, and no Phelps Dodge copper mine had ever suffered a major catastrophe.

Apparently early conditions in the rough wide-open town of Bisbee shocked these Easterners and were the "object of special concern" to the partners and officials of the company and their families (Cleland 1952:166). Cox (1938:77) records the story that an Eastern official of the company while on an inspection tour of the Copper Queen mine was so shocked when he saw the dead body of a Mexican swinging from the limb of a tree in Bisbee that he became convinced that "such barbarism as he had witnessed could proceed only from lack of information". Therefore, he had sent from New York a large number of well-chosen volumes of books that formed the nucleus for a new public library completed in 1887 (Cox 1938:127). Not too surprisingly, the company sent a churchman, Reverend J. G. Pritchard along with the books to "survey... the needs and desires of a reading public which, in those days, had to be developed" (Cox 138:127). Miss Grace Dodge, a social-welfare minded daughter of William E. Dodge, Jr., also entered the "battleground" of Bisbee from the East and sponsored a "company - community" Y.W.C.A. (Cox 1938:132-122; Cleland 1952:166- 167). Also Dr. James Douglas "by means of lectures, lantern slides, and other active work, caused the rough, but not unreasonable, frontiersmen to understand, and induced them to clean up the town, and to adopt the best methods of sanitation known in those days" (Cox 1938:120). His wife also assisted in this effort (Cleland 1952:).

In 1900 the company built the first hospital in Bisbee and in 1910 an employees' benefit association was organized "for the purpose of providing life, sickness, accident and disability insurance to employees" (Cox 1938:125-126).

Cox (1938:126-127) in discussing the organization of this association states that:

> Membership in the association was voluntary and was open to any employee, regardless of occupation. The finances of the association were administered by a joint board composed of officers and employees of the company. The company subscribed $15,000 annually if half the employees joined, and $25,000 if 3/4 joined, while employees contributed 2% of their monthly wages in return for industrial and life insurance. Beneficiaries received half wages in case of sickness or injury, and one year's wages in case of death by accident. By the end of the year 1910, 77% of the eligible employees were members, and by the end of 1930 the membership had grown to 91.4%.

In 1912 a "Safety First" organization was created to give "instruction in means of preventing accidents, rescue work, and first aid" (Cox 1938:127). Many safety features were also installed in the mine and laws were passed to insure the safe handling of explosives.

The Bisbee Improvement Company was incorporated in 1901 "by the same group of men who owned the mining property, financed the mining industry, built the railroad, published the newspapers, supported the churches, maintained a mercantile business, and operated the banks of the district" (Cox 1938:147-148). One look at its list of officers reveals the domination of the organization by Phelps Dodge personnel. The president was Walter Douglas, son of Dr. James Douglas. Walter was then superintendent of the Copper Queen Consolidated Mining

Company headed by his father as president. William H. Brophy, the manager of the Copper Queen company store was vice-president. S. W. French, the assistant superintendent of the Copper Queen Mine, was secretary-treasurer. Ben Williams, another Copper Queen company executive, was also one of the directors of the Bisbee Improvement Company. However, L. C. Shattuck, another of the directors, was later in 1904 one of the founders of the rival Shattuck Arizona Copper Company (Cox 1938:116).

The first project of this new "Improvement" company was to provide telephone communications between Bisbee and its smelter town of Douglas (Cox 1938:148). It next expanded into the ice manufacturing business, an important commodity in the hot arid Southwest (Cox 1938:149). A power plant for electrical production came next and in 1911 the company took over the defunct International Gas and Light Company and the independent McPherson gas plant and began to distribute household gas with complete monopoly control (Cox 1938:150). A water company was organized also by fifty Bisbee residents, many of them connected with the Copper Queen - Phelps Dodge interests (Cox 1938:150).

The first company store opened by Phelps-Dodge in Arizona was in Bisbee in the mid '80's when they took over control of an independent store managed by W. Brophy (Cleland 1952:127). Here again an altruistic motive is mentioned as being uppermost in Douglas's mind as the takeover was planned. The employees of the company were reported as being "dissatisfied" with the prices, quality, and variety of goods at the independent store. Douglas then reasoned, supposedly, that the Phelps Dodge organization with its long experience in merchandising and its ability to buy goods at lower prices in large quantities would be able to supply a wider selection of better and cheaper goods to its own employees and the other townspeople (Cleland 1952:127).

However, Cleland (1952:127) then adds the following comment:

> The assurance that the proposed plan would add a new
> source of profit to the company's operations was not the
> least of its merits.

Whatever the true motivation for this venture, with Brophy retained as store manager, the store was soon doing an enormous business in Bisbee and the surrounding area, with trade even extending into Mexico (Cox 1938:136-137;, Cleland 1952:127). A large concrete warehouse was built in 1909, and the store began supplying the wholesale business of the area. Many independent businesses bought many of their goods from the company, although they were never forced to buy anything since there were always other wholesale suppliers in the area (Cox 1938:137-138).

This initial store grew over the years into the enormous Phelps Dodge Mercantile Company (organized in 1912) with branches in every town and city in which Phelps Dodge is actively engaged in mining or smelting activities (Cleland 1952:127; Cox 1938:138).

One successful technique long employed by the company store was and still is the familiar "deduction account" about which more will be said later. The company insists, however, that no one has ever been forced to sign a deduction contract with the store or be required to trade with the store as a condition of employment with any Phelps Dodge operation (Cox 1938:138-139).

The company had also been long engaged in the railroad operations serving Bisbee. However, in 1900 legislation was passed forbidding any industrial enterprise to control its own transportation facilities if the facilities were organized as a public railroad company (Cox 1938:104-105). The Phelps Dodge directors apparently overcame this obstacle by setting up a legally separate independent corporation "entirely" divorced from the company's mining and smelting operations in 1901 under the name of the El Paso and Southwestern Railroad Company (Cox 1938:114; Cleland 1952:150). Using this legal fiction, the newly organized El Paso and Southwestern railway system was vastly expanded in the following few years with tracks stretching all the way from El Paso, Texas to Tucson by 1910 (Cleland 1952:145-150). This vast railroad empire was expanded further through the following years until in 1924, the Phelps Dodge interests sold all their railroad properties to the Southern Pacific Railroad with the interesting exception of a 50% interest in the Tucson, Cornelia and Gila Bend Railroad, a short line between Gila Bend and Ajo (Cleland 1952:214).

Although, initially the miners in Bisbee were paid in nothing but gold and silver, eventually in 1900, Brophy, the manager of the company store, and other Phelps Dodge men set up the first bank in Bisbee (Cox 1938:140). However, its monopoly status was short-lived since two years later some rival interests set up the competing Miners and Merchants Bank (Cox 1938:141).

After earlier independent attempts to publish a local newspaper failed, in 1900 the first issue of the company backed Bisbee Daily Review appeared (Cox 1938:134). Two later independent papers succeeded but Phelps Dodge interests also gained control of the larger of these, a daily evening paper leaving only one small weekly paper independent of company control (Cox 1938:135-136).

The new Presbyterian church erected in Bisbee in 1904 was a gift of several members of Phelps Dodge and Company with a member of the James family donating the pipe organ and delivering the dedicatory address (Cox 1938:131). Other churches such as the Episcopal Church were also greatly under the domination of the prominent Phelps Dodge officials and their wives as were also such social organizations as the Y.M.C.A. and Y.W.C.A. which both the Phelps Dodge personnel and the Calumet and Arizona people supported with great vigor (Cox 1938: 129,131-132; Cleland 1952:166-167). In fact, the Phelps Dodge interests even went so far as to give the house vacated in 1908 by the general manager of the Copper Queen, Walter Douglas, to the Y.W.C.A. for their exclusive use. Five years later, Miss Grace Dodge and the Phelps Dodge Company built a brand new home for the same organization with their rival, the Calumet and Arizona Mining Company donating the furnishings for one entire floor and the cafeteria (Cox 1938:133).

This close cooperation between these friendly rivals helps explain the striking parallels that existed between institutions and policy in Ajo and Bisbee even before the great merger of 1931. Among the early directors of several of these civic groups in Bisbee such as the Y.M.C.A., besides the usual Phelps Dodge officials, was a man named John Greenway, the general manager of the Calumet and Arizona Mining Company. As stated earlier, this unusually talented man together with his close associate Dr. Louis D. Ricketts, "long the friend and associate of Dr. James Douglas", began in the years between 1907 and 1911 planning the future development of the enormous low grade copper reserves in the distant Ajo mountains (Cleland 1952:231).

Through the years these leaders of the Calumet and Arizona Mining Company had participated greatly in the life of Bisbee and had had a great opportunity to profit from the mistakes as well as triumphs that they and the officials of the two rival companies had experienced in manipulating individuals, organizations, and events to further desired ends. In 1906 the directors of the Copper Queen had even cooperated with them in planning the attractive new residential section near Bisbee called Warren (Cleland 1952:126). Furthermore, the two companies operated a local city bus line under joint ownership between Warren and Bisbee in later years (Cox 1938:146). Both companies also cooperated by both building smelters near the planned Phelps Dodge townsite of Douglas between the years 1901 and 1904 (Cox 1938:112-114). Therefore, it is not surprising that Ajo, too, had its own "Improvement Company" and company store patterned after the rival store in Bisbee.[6] Many other aspects of the Phelps Dodge tradition were also transferred to Ajo from Bisbee long before the 1931 merger through the media of Greenway, Ricketts, and others as we shall see later.

Even during the time of the 1967-1968 study, many aspects of the original Phelps Dodge tradition were still quite evident in Ajo as witnessed in the company's dealings with its employees and other townsmen. However, there had been some erosion in the rigid religious attitudes held by the members of the early Phelps Dodge dynasty. Now the mines were operating on a grueling seven day schedule with most men getting only two days off in every twenty-eight.[7] In contrast, William E. Dodge in 1857 resigned from the board of directors of the New York and Erie Railroad and sold all his stock in the line when he split with the other directors over the policy of running trains on Sunday, a policy which he and the other Phelps Dodge partners vigorously opposed (Cleland 1952:40). This same opposition to Sunday work was seen much later in Bisbee when Arthur Curtiss James complained to his fellow directors about the increasing amount of work being done on Sunday by asking: "Can it be possible, that the 'absolute necessity' for Sunday work.. arises from the desire to make a larger output?" (Cleland 1952:167). James won his point, and the amount of Sunday labor was greatly reduced at that time.

During my 1967-1968 fieldwork in Ajo I became convinced that practical considerations, rather than religious motivations, perpetuated the company's continued domination of most aspects of its workers' lives. The above change in attitude toward Sunday work in recent years tends to bear this out. Cleland (1952:109) also seemed to sense that religious and humanitarian motivations alone were not the exclusive or perhaps even the major factors in explaining the continued persistence of the all-encompassing "benevolent" rule of Phelps Dodge in all of its company towns: Thus he states that:

> Nearly fifty years before the Copper Queen became a great producer, when Phelps, Dodge & Company first began its large-scale lumber operations in the forests of Pennsylvania, the company inaugurated a welfare program under which it sought to provide decent homes, adequate medical and surgical care, stores that sold goods at reasonable prices, churches, schools, libraries, and recreation centers for its many employees. The program was inspired by the religious convictions of the founders of the company and followed their interpretation of the Golden Rule. Experience also showed such humanitarian measures paid large dividends and were anything but quixotic from a business point of view.

At another point he (1952:267-268) adds in speaking of Bisbee, Jerome, Ajo, and Morenci that:

> The company, in effect, was the town. In some cases it owned the greater part of the land, houses, office buildings, and public utilities. It supported and administered the hospitals and supplied many of the services usually performed by a local government.
> In these various relations and activities, common sense and experience, as well as a very active sense of civic responsibility, played the leading role. The men who inherited the tradition of the founders of Phelps Dodge knew that it was bad business as well as bad ethics to place the company's temporary advantage above the common good.

Many of the other individuals, ethnic groups, and organizations present in Ajo at the time of the strike also have long and involved histories that are well worth detailed study if one is to gain a complete understanding of exactly what took place during the strike in Ajo. However, it would expand this book far beyond all reasonable limits to consider in detail the historical background of each of these. I will instead merely mention briefly some of the more important aspects of these histories with respect to the crisis situation that arose during the prolonged 1967-1968 strike.

While it is true that since 1934 there had been no crisis situation of a similar magnitude arise in Ajo, many of those affected were well aware of similar disruptive events occurring elsewhere in the country through newspapers, books, classrooms, TV, etc. Thus the local union leaders were well aware of many of the various strategies and maneuvers employed by both sides as they played the "strike game". This was true even though the local labor unions did not win official recognition from the company until June of 1941, long after the depression crisis was over (Therrien 1945:106).[8]

The local banker, finance company manager, or other lender was also very cognizant of the disastrous events of the late '20's and '30's, many having personally experienced living through these times.

In the case of the Indian families, most had seen a relative or friend head back to the reservation in times of personal crisis. The reservation had historically been a place of refuge for those who failed in the outside world and for those who had become sick or too old to work. This unique alternative open only to Indians will be discussed further in the next chapters.

Also it should be added that many of the organizations present in Ajo (e.g., the company, the unions, and many of the local religious organizations and social clubs) are merely part of larger national systems. Therefore, the local leaders of these sub-systems did not always have the necessary authority or power to manipulate variables within their subsystems as they saw fit during the strike. Indeed, as shall be discussed later, many of the local residents of Ajo harbored a very fatalistic attitude toward the strike. This was especially true during the post-Christmas period when most people with whom I talked felt that only action on the national level could end the great impasse that had developed between the various giant copper firms and the striking unions.

Chapter Notes

1. In Ajo during the strike there were still different types of houses for people of differing social status. Thus, the newly arriving local newspaper editor told me (F.N. November 13, 1967) that the house she and her husband were moving into had lain vacant for a year because "no one of a suitable social status or character had needed such a house during the past year." Others receiving special houses, besides high company officials, included, among others, the priests and ministers of the two downtown churches, and the doctors at the local company hospital.

2. The developer of Clarkston, Sam Clark, ran into trouble with his planned townsite development, as certain government officials, spurred on by several local people who refused to pay rent to Clark, tried to reduce Clark's land holdings to just his actual mineral property and instead of his townsite, establish a government townsite, to be called Rowood, on the east portion of Clark's larger claim (A.C.N June 4, 1921:1; November 10, 1923:1; November 17, 1923:2; December 8, 1923:6). Clark lost the court case that developed over this dispute, and Judge Gerald Jones was appointed Trustee over the land, which he then proceeded to auction off to the highest bidders as Rowood came into existence (A.C.N. March 1, 1924:1; April 5, 1924:5; May 9, 1925:1; May 16, 1925:1).

3. My own personal association with one of the top Phelps Dodge men in Ajo and several other lesser but still important local officials of the company, convinced me that even today top company officials are chosen with the greatest of care to fit in with the Phelps Dodge "tradition". Therefore, even though there were over thirty thousand

share-owners in the company by 1950 (Cleland 1952:267) and even more today, control of the company's policies seems to have remained tightly in the hands of a top management group which although not remaining a single family dynasty, still is very selective in its membership.

4. The first lodge started was the Ancient Order of United Workmen. They stored their ceremonial "paraphernalia" in a lean-to built on the side of the main building (Cox 1938:91).

5. Apparently Dr. James Douglas liked to give frequent lectures to the people about various subjects (Cox 1938:93). See also the remarks about the contents of these lectures to follow later in this study.

6. To illustrate how closely parallel these institutions were to each other in both towns, the following quotation from a letter in 1917 from John Greenway to M. Curley is very revealing. He states that (Johnson n.d.:21-22):

> I have long wished to make trial of a cooperative store for the benefit of our employees working for the New Cornelia Copper Company at Ajo. I put the matter up to our Directors and they have willingly consented to give the plan a trial.
>
> I now desire that you employ a competent Manager and start the store at Ajo, and charge prices for goods sold which will be comparable with prices charged in other mining camps in the State.
>
> No employee will be forced in any way to trade in this store and the store will be run as economically as possible. At the end of each year it is planned to deduct the actual operating cost of the business from the income for the year and divide the balance among the employees in the proportion in which they have made purchases in the store during the year. There will be a reasonable rental charge for the building and an interest charge of 6 percent will be made upon the amount of money borrowed by the Mercantile Company from the Copper Company for the conduct of the business.

The men will not be asked to assume any obligation or risk in the operating of the Mercantile Company, we will simply give them the profits on their business and the Company intends to make no money out of the transactions whatever.

Thus, only in the matter of the return of most of the store's profits to the company employees did the Ajo store differ from the Bisbee store. This, however, was a significant difference the importance of which we shall later discuss.

7.   In the midst of World War II, the government desired that the production of vital raw materials be speeded up, so in April 1942 the Ajo mine first began operating on a seven-day basis (Therrien 1945:106-107). However, during the last few years economic factors rather than patriotism motivated the reintroduction of this practice. The true feelings of many people in Ajo concerning Sunday work were hinted at as early as in 1922 when the local paper stated that (A.C.M. August 12, 1922:1):

Most workmen are eager for Sunday work because it increases the pay-check. As there is more Sunday work and as the force is added in the fall (as it will be) the workmen will be better off. So will the businessmen.

8.   In June 1941, the National Labor Relations Board ordered the company to disband its own "Ajo Association of Copper Mine Employees" and recognize employee membership and activity in other unions.

CHAPTER 5:

The New Paradigm

No substantial part of the universe is so simple that it can be grasped and controlled without abstraction. Abstraction consists in replacing the part of the universe under consideration by a model of similar but simpler structure. Models, formal or intellectual on the one hand, or material on the other, are thus a central necessity of scientific procedure (Rosenblueth and Wiener 1945:316). ...Models are especially useful when there is some understanding of the problem, but ideas about how to analyze the data are limited. They help to (1) define the problem, (2) organize thought about it, (3) understand data, (4) test the understanding, and (5) make further predictions. In effect, they are heuristic tools that discipline our attempts to work from general premises to concrete and testable illustrations of them. (Winterholder and Smith 1992: 13)

In my own attempt to find a suitable model to deal with the massive "hodgepodge" of information I had collected during my long stay in Ajo and the nearby Papago reservation I came upon the following passage:

> Since early times men have tended to order their thoughts in terms of pictorial models. The model itself was usually drawn from something in their immediate experience, available from their technology, and acceptable to their society and culture. Once adopted it served more or less efficiently, to order and correlate men's acquired habits and experiences, and perhaps to suggest a selection of new guesses and behavior patterns for unfamiliar situations. (Deutsch 1951:732)

Thus we had early models based upon such natural observations as the cyclic nature of the day, the seasons or point on a wheel, the flow of a river or of sand in an hourglass, the balance, and the thread taken from the spinning wheel. However, even more influential in anthropology, were models based on the web, the clock, and the organism (Deutsch 1951: 233-236) leading otherwise rational scientists to make the mistake of equating change in human societies to "breakdown" or "death" as if human societies were perfect "webs," "clocks," or "living beings." The "never-never" land of the "ethnographic present" that was often used in the past in ethnographic accounts also furthered this illusion.

All of these models continue to be used by many analysts often leading to false predictions about future events. Thus, in trying to use these traditional models, I quickly began to fully agree with Ashby (1970:94) who states that:

> ...the basic fact [is] that every model of a real system is in one sense second-rate. Nothing can exceed, or even equal, the truth and accuracy of the real system itself. Every model is inferior, a distortion, a lie...

However, some scientists have sought new models, this time derived from technological advances. Thus, from the development of the vacuum tube, the thermostat, and the governor on the steam engine, came the notion of "feedback" which along with other advances in "the science of control and communication" led to a new theoretical approach named "cybernetics" (Ashby 1956:1), which in turn inspired Ashby (1960) in his book, Design for a Brain, to introduce the important concept of "ultrastability" which he defined as:

> Two systems of continuous variables ...[the] "environment" and [the] "reacting part" ...[which] interact, so that a primary feedback (through complex sensory and motor channels) exists between them. Another feedback, working intermittently and at a much slower order of speed, goes from the environment to certain continuous variables which in their turn affect some step-mechanisms, the effect being that the step-mechanisms change value when and only when these variables pass outside given limits. The step-mechanisms affect the reacting part; by acting as parameters to it they determine how it shall react to the environment. (page 98)

And, just as Einstein tried to achieve in his search for a "unified field theory" after deriving important relationships between energy, mass, the speed of light, space, and time, I feel that a more universal model of human behavior will enable us to achieve the analytical/predictive power we seek in any new model.

Additional clues to aid us in the construction of such a universal paradigm are already found in the literature. Thus Levi-Strauss in 1953 (p. 539), obviously influenced by the same intellectual environment that in 1956 gave birth to the Journal of the Society for the Advancement of General Systems Theory, stated that the main contribution that had come out of such pioneering studies as Shannon and Weaver's book, The Mathematical Theory of Communication (1949) "was to provide anthropology with a unifying concept--communication--enabling it to consolidate widely differing types of inquiry into one, and at the same time providing the theoretical and methodological tools to further knowledge in that direction." A society is thus defined by Levi-Strauss (1953:536) as "individuals and groups which communicate with one another" who then added that:

> In any society, communication operates on three different levels: communication of women, communication of goods and services, communication of messages. Therefore kinship studies, economics, and linguistics approach the same kinds of problems on different strategic levels and really pertain to the same field. Theoretically at least, it might be said that kinship and marriage rules regulate a fourth type of communication, that of genes between phenotypes. Therefore, it should be kept in mind that culture does not consist exclusively of forms of communication, like language, but also (and perhaps mostly) of rules stating how the "games of communication" should be played both on the natural and on the cultural level. (Levi-Strauss 1953:536)

Other researchers since this time have tried to keep alive this idea of a single unified communications-based societal theory. Thus Rubinstein in 1975 (p. 252) stated that:

> ...since people in all societies in all places at all times exchange (both goods and services), the ethnological problem is to devise a model which will adequately deal with exchange in both complex and primitive societies. It is to be hoped then, that a model which seems to provide an adequate description of exchange in a particular type

of society, be it primitive or complex, might profitably be generalized to describe exchange in societies of all types.

And Leeds in 1979 (p. 229) added that:

> ...at a most general level, all human nucleations, from the smallest "tribal" villages to the largest megalopolises, have the same functions with respect to an inclusive society; facilitation of all forms of exchange, transfer, and communications, while linking the nucleation or locality both with other localities and with the society at large.

However, as Moran points out (1990: 17-18) many scientists in the 60's and 70's were "obsessed with calories" as they studied the flow and magnitude of energy in human societies while failing to "give sufficient attention to the numerous decisions made which control those same flows." Thus, in my own work beginning in the late '60's, I realized that any truly universal theory of human behavior should be based not only upon this broadened definition of communication but also upon such other crucial scientific concepts as the second law of thermodynamics, Ashby's notions of "ultrastability" and the "black box," White's observation that "culture is an organization of things in motion, a process of energy transformations" (White 1959:38), and the importance of "critical limits" (i.e., "tipping points") in determining how systems react to changing environmental parameters. And, to avoid the ambiguity that often characterizes new theoretical constructs, it would be wise at this point to give fairly precise but simplified definitions to certain key portions of the terminology I shall be employing in the construction of this new, "universal" model of human behavior. Thus I shall begin by defining a system as a region in the space/time continuum that is characterized by direct, intense, and highly predictable (i.e., redundant) reciprocal communication links between its component parts (i.e., subsystems), which has the overall "transducing" power to change the entropy and/or direction and/or form of any communicated item passing through its sphere of influence in predictable, nonrandom ways. In turn, each component part or subsystem can be defined in a like manner in terms of its own component parts (i.e., sub-subsystems of the original system) and overall transducing powers.

Such a breakdown of larger systems into smaller ones (or the reverse process of combining smaller systems into larger ones) can usually be continued almost indefinitely but, as we shall soon see, for most analytical purposes it is often not necessary to carry this process too far.

The "items" being communicated are themselves nonrandom (i.e., organized) arrangements of matter/energy but instead of the three categories of such items proposed by Levi-Strauss (1953:536) (i.e., "information," "goods and services," and "women"), I will separate these items into the categories -- "information;" "organized matter/energy;" "bound transducers;" and "money" as defined thusly:

1. Information--a description about the state of organization (i.e., the degree of negentropy (order) or entropy (disorder)[1]) of energy/matter and/or systems in one or more portions of the space/time continuum. (This description may or may not reflect actual perceived "reality" by the originating or any modifying system and is often withheld or distorted to gain an advantage over other systems.)

2. Organized matter/energy--any nonrandom arrangement of energy and/or matter.

3. "Bound" Transducers--whole systems, each of which has the power to change the entropy and/or direction and/or form of any communicated item passing through its sphere of influence in predictable nonrandom ways. (Thus besides women entering into new or leaving old structural positions in "family" systems,

this category would include such items as employees, machines, horses, pigs, children, sports players, soldiers, slaves, etc. whenever the control of movement of the given transducer into or out of the system's sphere of influence resides not in the transducer being communicated itself but at some other point in the system although such "bound" transducers can occasionally be "stolen" or escape from the system's sphere of influence on their own.

4. Money--a symbolic "laundering" credit invented by humans, given in exchange for the transfer of one of the above items from one human system to another. However, as Odum (1971:174) points out it is wrong to equate money directly to energy (or other item being communicated) since the two flow in opposite directions and the two have no intrinsic equivalence. Furthermore, the symbolic "token" which we call money can just as easily be a piece of printed paper or an entry in a computer data bank as a more solid item such as a gold or silver coin. However, at any given point, in the space/time continuum, for any given transaction, a current "market value" equivalence in terms of organized energy and/or matter or transducers can often be calculated although this is subject to rapid change especially when there is a loss of faith in the government issuing it or of those in debt having the ability to repay such debts. And, as seen often in this book, when anxiety motivates the decisions humans make in dealing with the real or falsely perceived oversupply or shortage of such items as copper or skilled workers.

Money is frequently used as a powerful controlling weapon by systems to gain control over other systems in their environment. Thus, in Ajo, keeping miners in perpetual debt to the company store and providing housing and utility credit during strikes did much to weaken the power of the copper unions.

To avoid the trap of being blinded by the "web," "clock," or "organism" analogy, it should be pointed out that the individual component "transducing" parts (hereafter called "transducers") that comprise any given system at a particular point in the space/time continuum often retain a considerable amount of "freedom" to enter or leave the system at certain points in the space/time continuum, an observation hinted at by Buechler who in her study of the dynamics of a Bolivian market states:

> Urban markets like the one in La Paz, Bolivia should not be studied as places fixed in space and time but as nodes in a fluid system of distribution entailing the movement of goods and persons over time. Such markets are not bounded entities, defined spatially, temporally, or in terms of social structure. They must be viewed as parts of larger systems, which evolved through time and which change in response to migration from the countryside... (Buechler 1978:356)

(This mobility of individual transducers into and out of the overall system is especially characteristic of human socioeconomic systems whether they be simple or complex.)

Furthermore, while recognizing that there is no such thing as a truly "closed" system in the real universe (at least not for very long)[2], I shall define a system's boundary as that collection of points in the space/time continuum beyond which no "direct" control exists over items being imported from or exported to other systems even though the system may be able to "indirectly" increase, modify, and/or decrease certain outputs of one or more other systems in its environment by increases, decreases, and/or modification of communicated items to these outside systems.

Also, it is important to realize that despite the fact that many systems have key "control" centers (i.e., transducing sets), often these centers have no "direct" control over the inner structure and/or items communicated between many (or at times, any) of "their own" component transducers. This is especially true in human socioeconomic systems where as Ashby (1956:86) states, "In our daily lives we are confronted at every turn with systems whose internal mechanisms are not fully open to inspection, and which must be treated by the methods appropriate to the Black Box."

Thus many of the typical system's "very own" component transducers must also be consigned to the "environment" of the system using our above boundary definition.[3]

The response of a system to the fluctuating output of such internal "black boxes" may take the form of an attempt to directly or indirectly manipulate the outputs of these "incorporated" or nearby transducers (i.e., "aggressive" control) to produce more "favorable" environmental parameters or the control attempt may take the form of boundary and/or internal defense measures to block, limit, or transform "unfavorable" incoming communication (i.e., "defensive" control).

There are three different types of transducers (keeping in mind that the boundaries between these types are not always absolute):

1. Those with a "fixed" internal structure and "fixed" transduction "programming." Living plants of all types and most machines fall into this category. The outputs of such transducers are often extremely predictable, given certain inputs, as long as there is no internal component failure. However, this very predictability is often viewed as a being a "liability" by nearby systems attempting to exert "aggressive" control over such transducers since major changes of the "hardware"[4] type will often be needed before the "aggressive" systems seeking such control will be satisfied with the given output. Thus it is frequently easier, in terms of energy expenditure by systems seeking such control to replace transducers with both fixed internal structure and fixed transduction programming with "newer" models than to try to modify the "older" ones.

2. Those with a fixed internal structure but with "variable" transduction "programming." Assembly line "robots," the human body, animals, etc. fall into this category. While the outputs of such transducers are less predictable than the outputs of the first type of transducer, "desired" changes in output can often be achieved by nearby systems attempting "aggressive" control through changes of the "software" type since a certain range of differing transduction capabilities is already resident in this type of transducer. The stored "patterns" for

producing these differing transducing behaviors I shall call "cultural genes," borrowing terminology from the biological sciences to avoid the ambiguity and imprecision that surrounds the use of such traditional concepts as the "cultural trait" or more recent ones as the "meme" (Dawkins 1976:206). These, in turn, may be further broken down into "dominant cultural genes" (i.e., the usually chosen behavioral pattern(s) for transductions when the transducer is faced with a "normal" set of environmental parameters) or "recessive cultural genes" which are the patterns for transducing behavior that are only chosen when one or more essential system variable(s) has exceeded or is in danger of exceeding (a) critical limit(s)[5]. Thus, I fully agree with Kunkel (1985:82) when he states:

> Instead of analyzing cultural evolution in terms of culture traits ... why not go all the way and begin with the fact that the basic elements of culture are behaviors and their material manifestations? ...
> ... Thus, a person adapts to the environment through various behaviors, which ... are largely determined by (quoting Bandura 1969:132) "anticipated outcomes based on previous consequences that were directly encountered, vicariously experienced, or self administered."....
> ... Actions change when they no longer produce the old outcomes, perhaps because the environment has changed. Random behaviors and variations occur quite frequently, but they are usually not reinforced and therefore are not repeated. Some "new" activities do lead to positive outcomes, perhaps because the context has changed or simply because the action is more effective (i.e., adaptive), and these tend to be maintained. Through modeling they are transmitted to other individuals, but not necessarily perfectly....

The concept of a "superorganic" (i.e., socially-transmitted) "cultural gene," would thus provide the missing logical link that Kaplan (1965) felt would be needed to connect the "science of culture" to that of psychology as well as the foundation for the new "paradigm" which according to Keesing (1972:325) anthropologists "need to develop ... within which a cognitive model of culture can be systematically related to sociological, biological, ecological, and other realms, not simply abstracted from them."

3. Those with a variable internal structure as well as variable transduction "programming." Most human socioeconomic systems are of this type. However, for analytical purposes it is important to note that all such systems are in a constant state of structural flux. For as Deutsch (1951:251) stated:

> ...we can tell a society from an organism or a machine [by]...the freedom of its parts to regroup themselves; and [by] the nature of the regroupings, which must imply new coherent patterns of activity--in contrast to the mere wearing of a machine or the aging of an organism, which are marked by relatively few degrees of freedom and by the gradual disappearance of coherent patterns of activity.
> ...The difference between organisms and societies rests, then, in the degree of freedom of their parts, and the degree of effectiveness of their recombinations to new coherent patterns of activity. ...This in turn may rest on specific properties of their members; their capacity for readjustment to new configurations with renewed complementarity and sustained or removed communications.

However, it is also imperative that we avoid the mistake of many scientists who still build models of this type of transducer upon such structurally fixed analogies as the network, web, clock, or organism. Instead, the most characteristic feature of such transducers is not the "stability" emphasized by many proposed models but rather "adaptability." Thus, as Moran(1990: 16, 17) states,

> ...[there is] a tendency for models to ignore time and structural change, thereby overemphasizing stability in ecosystems. ...studies have over-emphasized the self-regulatory features of ecosystems to the neglect of processes by which systems transform themselves in response to either external or internal dynamics.

Therefore, borrowing from Ashby's earlier concept of "ultrastability" (1960:98), I will now introduce the concept of "ultra-adaptability" which I will define as the capacity of a system to persist in time through structural or behavioral modification whenever an essential system variable has exceeded or is in danger of exceeding a critical limit or "tipping point."

Such ultra-adaptable social systems usually contain one or more transducing subsets whose occupants attempt to regulate the level and type of environmental control both sought and achieved by the system as a whole. Failure in the attempt to minimize any resulting discrepancy between the type and quantity of control sought and that actually achieved usually triggers conscious structural and/or behavioral modification efforts (i.e., "control actions") before complete loss of internally generated environmental control occurs.

Focusing now on human socioeconomic systems, we usually find individuals occupying active structural positions (i.e., transducing statuses) in more than one larger ultra-adaptable system. And as he/she moves from one system to another throughout the day, week, month, or year, some degree of structural change occurs in the system being "entered" or "left." However, it is important to note that in many human socioeconomic systems it is not essential for the system's survival that the new occupant of any given transducing status set be precisely the old occupant returning after a predictable absence to his/her previous position although in many systems such predictable, periodic migrations to and from a given transducing status set in a larger system are commonplace. Thus the factory or office worker usually shows up on Monday morning in the workplace; family members almost always return to their home in the afternoon or evening; etc. However, such systems as the family, factory, etc. usually have ways of coping with not only occasional unexpected absences on the part of individual systemic status set occupants but also with permanent changes due to such factors as death, divorce, change of occupation or residence, etc. And, especially in the modern urban setting, many "controlling" systems do not really care who occupies certain given "systemic status sets" (systemic status set = set of one or more transducers performing similar transducing functions in any given system) at any one point in the space/time continuum, as long as a critical minimum number of new or returning "black boxes" enter the system each day. For example, it is not essential to the survival of a local store that exactly the same customers return day after day to make their purchases as long the critical minimum number do.

Ultra-adaptable organizations can be classified according to their ability to remain ultra-adaptable through time as systemic status set memberships change. Here, we can pick out three types. (It should be stressed that the boundaries between the three types are not absolute):

(1) Those that persist without major structural change or loss of ultra-adaptability <u>only as long</u> as membership in each systemic status set does not change (e.g., a business partnership, a family consisting of only a husband and wife).

(2) Those that persist without major structural change or loss of ultra-adaptability <u>only as long</u> as membership in the "higher" (i.e., more powerful) systemic status sets in the group hierarchy does not change (Change may occur in the membership of lower systemic

status sets) (e.g., children in a family consisting of husband, wife, and children).

(3)   Those that persist without major structural change or loss of ultra-adaptability in spite of changes in membership in all systemic status sets (e.g., many large companies and bureaucracies).

This classification scheme reflects the observation that in a newly formed system, systemic status sets lower in the hierarchy tend to become standardized faster and the role behavior of occupants of these systemic status sets tends to become more predictable more rapidly than the role behavior of systemic status set occupants higher in the hierarchy. Therefore turnover in systemic status set membership tends to affect the average input-output of systemic status sets lower in the group hierarchy less than the average input-output of systemic status sets higher in the hierarchy. This degree of systemic status set standardization can be referred to as the degree of institutionalization of that systemic status set. One fairly accurate way to measure the degree of institutionalization of any systemic status set would be to measure the redundancy of messages and actions originating from the successive occupants of that systemic status set.

As Henry Ford demonstrated with his Model "T," greater interchangeability of parts makes it possible to repair mechanical systems more cheaply and efficiently and without noticeable change in the "behavior" of the repaired machine. One can generalize this observation to human systems as well. Thus the following general argument can be proposed:

(1)   Greater interchangeability of parts tends to permit greater stability in both mechanical and human systems.

(2)   Ultra-adaptable systems are usually characterized by a large percentage of interchangeable parts.

(3) Change occurs in an ultra-adaptable system when the parts interchanged are not completely identical.

(4) Since in any system, the identity of parts interchanged can never be absolute, change is always occurring in every system as parts are interchanged.

Therefore another way to measure the degree of institutionalization of any ultra-adaptable system might be to measure the degree of component interchangeability. And, in human systems, greater interchangeability of "common" men and women usually precedes much interchangeability in those filling leadership roles in any newly formed system. However, in our country today, many ultra-adaptable organizations have arisen where not only are the people at the bottom of a system's role pyramid interchangeable, but also often those at the top of the pyramid[6] (e.g., Robert McNamara's journey from the presidency of Ford Motor Company to become Secretary of Defense and his movement later to become Head of the World Bank vividly illustrate this growing interchangeability of occupants of the upper management systemic set status in many modern systems. George Romney's move from American Motors to the governorship of Michigan and later to the Cabinet level in the Nixon administration is another good example of this growing interchangeability as is also his son's rise from being the rescuer of the Utah Olympics to become the Governor of Massachusetts and later prove to be a strong Presidential contender.)

One important difference remains in all organizations between the occupants of higher occupants of the lower systemic status sets than of the higher. This difference is that statistical laws can usually be utilized with a higher degree of probability to predict the average behavior of the numerous occupants of the lower systemic status sets in a system than to predict the actions of the individual or small group of individuals occupying the higher systemic status sets.

In other words, the statistics of the individual or small group of individuals must be known for accurate prediction of role behavior if only one or several individuals occupy a single systemic status set (often one of the highest systemic status sets) in a system (e.g., the CEO of a large corporation). One must therefore seek a knowledge of the microstate of such systemic status sets through time.

On the other hand, average statistics may be all that are needed for accurate prediction of role behavior if many individuals occupy a single systemic status set in a system. Such systemic status sets are usually (but not always) found at the lower levels in most systems (e.g., students in a large classroom, track laborers at the Ajo Mine). In this case all that is usually needed for an accurate prediction is a knowledge of the macrostate of such systemic status sets through time.

It is always difficult for one man, even the most dynamic one, to control the actions of any large group to any great extent. The larger the group, the fewer group decisions he is likely to control and the more his suggestions are likely to be modified even if accepted by the group. However, this does not mean that all individual decisions have equal weight in determining group actions. The relative weight of a person's individual decision can be measured by its effects on the parameters of other individuals and groups (i.e., on the parameters of other ultra-adaptable systems). Thus, an action by the President of the United States usually (but not always) has more weight in changing the parameters of other ultra-adaptable systems than a decision by a Mexican laborer in Tucson. (However, the Mexican's decision to rob a bank would be more important than the President's decision to brush his teeth before retiring for the night.)

Obviously as the number of individuals occupying a systemic status set increases in number, probabilities based upon an analysis of the macrostate through time tend to become increasingly more reliable. Furthermore, as the number of occupants of a single systemic status set increases, the power of the individual to shape the action of the total systemic status set is likely to decrease since the other members of the systemic status set can "band together" to overrule even the most powerful individual. Also, if the occupants of lesser systemic status sets unite, they can often modify or even nullify the decisions of occupants of higher systemic status sets (e.g., Congress can overrule the President, mine workers by going on strike can modify or nullify the decisions of mine management personnel.)

In fact, it can even be proposed that in any system when the occupants of lesser systemic status sets in the system collectively gain more organized (in the vector sense to be discussed later) power than the occupants of higher systemic status sets in the system, that structural change has already occurred in the system.

Also, in human affairs, a man or woman who is a member of two systems establishes a synaptic link between the two systems and is likely to try to control variables in one system to provide favorable inputs to the other system and vice versa. Often such an individual may occasionally add or subtract bits of information from the message being transmitted from one system to another to further his or her own ends.

In contrast to a mechanical or many organic systems where each component has a fixed degree of power and control ability, human systems are composed of individuals who can either gain or lose power and the ability to control, individually or collectively. In organic systems a similar shift in power and the ability to control occurs with the growth of cancer cells in the body. The cancer cells increase their relative power in the system at the expense of other components of the system thus producing a structural reorganization. However in this case, this type of transformation often brings about total systemic collapse (i.e., the death of the organism).

Perhaps a coefficient of parameter control could be assigned to each output of an ultra-adaptable system dependent upon the change that this output effects in the parameters of other systems. Such an output would therefore not necessarily always have the same coefficient of parameter control. For example, the act of tossing a lighted cigarette out of a car window would almost always have a parameter control coefficient near zero, but if, on one occasion, a forest fire were to be started by this cigarette, the coefficient of parameter control for that particular act (system output) would quickly rise to a high value. It is important to note, however, that the coefficient of parameter control as defined above is only a measure of the effect of a system's output on one or more parameters of other systems. This parameter change may or may not be reflected in modified outputs from the system or systems faced with the altered parameters as inputs. Perhaps a coefficient of output control could be assigned to a system's output to indicate the effect of this output on the output of another system. These coefficients would apply only to the relationship between the controlling system and one system being controlled. If several systems were being affected by the output of the controlling system, then separate coefficients of output control would have to be calculated for each pair of relationships.

Carneiro (1967:240-241) has suggested that population growth is the key (i.e., "essential") variable in explaining the structural reorganization that occurs when certain "elastic limits" (i.e., "critical limits") are exceeded as human numbers increase in any given sociocultural system. He bases this conclusion upon the argument that growth in any organization while appearing externally as an increase in size "manifests itself internally as an increase in units" which "leads inevitably to a critical point at which the system must either fission or advance to new levels of organization by undergoing a qualitative transformation," adding that (1967:241):

> One further qualification remains to be made. It is that the units whose increase brings about structural change in a society are not so much human organisms in and of themselves as they are individuals embodying cultural roles.

However, while independently developing a similar model for my own dissertation research at about this same time, I went one step beyond Carneiro, arguing that just knowing the total population change in any given system through time is not as useful in the analysis of social change as is a knowledge of the change in the population of each systemic status set in the system through time, an idea that had, also unbeknown to me at the time, earlier been partially recognized by Broom et al. (1954:980) who state that, "the integrity of the role network within each culture is seriously affected by the selective removal or addition or personnel in certain age-sex categories." Thus each systemic status set population variable can be considered to be an "essential" system variable with both an upper and a lower "critical" limit, the exceeding of either of which will produce either a general loss of ultra-adaptability in the total system or a restructuring of the system.

Each systemic status set in an ultra-adaptable organization demands a certain minimum input from each occupant of that systemic status set if that individual is to remain in "good standing" (i.e., to avoid being replaced) even though these minimum inputs vary both in quantity and quality from one individual to another even within any given systemic status set. In return, each occupant of a systemic status set seeks a certain minimum system output to help maintain his/her physiological and psychological variables within their critical limits. Such outputs may take either a physical form such as food or a psychological one such as the promise of a reward in the afterlife.

Therefore each social organization in order to achieve ultra-adaptability must have some sort of mechanism for maintaining overall systemic status set inputs and outputs above certain minimum values or some mechanism to insure an increase in input or output in some other part of the system or its environment when the input or output decreases by a corresponding amount in a given systemic status set. (This latter possibility will lead to structural or behavioral change, however, if any certain critical limit for the input-output of any systemic status set is passed.) Failure of such a mechanism will lead to a loss of ultra-adaptability and perhaps irreversible systemic collapse.

No two individuals are ever completely alike so that no two people will ever seek exactly the same quality and quantity of output from any given system nor can they supply the same quality and quantity of input to the system. Therefore if the system fails to provide the minimum output needed or desired by the occupant of a systemic status set he/she will often withdraw from the system or if the occupant of a systemic status set fails to provide the input needed by the system he/she may be rejected by "stronger" members of the system and "cast out." This selection process tends through time to reduce the amount of variation occurring in the input-output of each of the system's systemic status sets.

There are always a smaller number of individuals that attempt to control certain responses and outputs of a larger system of individuals (e.g., adults attempt to control the family, management personnel attempt to control the company). However, it is usually difficult[7] for one person, even the most dynamic one, to control the actions of any large group to any great extent. The larger the group, the fewer group decisions he/she is likely to control and the more his/her suggestions are likely to be modified even if accepted by the group. But, this does not mean that all individual decisions have equal weight in determining group actions.[8] And, collectively, the occupants of certain systemic status sets are often able to gain relatively greater control over other systemic status sets and overall system inputs/outputs than others. Thus, controlling individuals and/or systemic status sets can be identified by their abilities to "fix" certain environmental parameters within which subordinate individuals and/or systemic status sets are not free to self-determine the priority order of completing transducing assignments and/or how they should be done.

Furthermore, the occupants of the "controlling" systemic status set(s) of most social systems have set up elaborate control mechanisms (i.e., transducing subsystems) to try to prevent losses in lower systemic status set populations but many of these same people actually try to suppress the operation of control mechanisms that would tend to keep systemic status set population variables from exceeding their upper critical limits. Instead, such individuals often seek to maximize certain systemic status set population variables lower in the control hierarchy even though continual structural reorganization is necessary if loss of control or systemic fission is to be avoided (e.g., the conversion efforts of the occupants of the controlling systemic status sets of the Mormon Church by its large force of young missionaries and encouragement of larger than average families is an example of this latter type (see Chapter 10),)

All ultra-adaptable systems have "interface" transducers that extract more organized energy/matter from their environment than these systems return to it as well as "control" centers whose outputs are designed to maximize the prediction and control of certain environmental parameters which are the outputs of other systems. The most basic purpose of such attempted control is the maintenance of certain essential system variables within their "critical limits," but often the control is such as to maximize other system variables such that the entropy of the controlling system will actually decrease.

Any decrease in entropy in a system must, of course, come at the expense of one or more of the surrounding systems and the weapon used to accomplish this task can be any carefully chosen communicated export. Such items which I will label "control vectors"[9] (using terminology derived from the field of physics) are designed to promote the continued plentiful input of "desired" items from the environment while suppressing "undesired" items. It should by now be obvious that in theory to keep any essential variable from exceeding either of its critical limits an ultra-adaptable system must be capable of generating such control vectors or persuading a "helping" system to generate them. These must have maximum force outputs equal to or greater than any possible "hostile" incoming force vector. In practice, however, certain systems can retain their ultra-adaptable states for long time intervals even though they or a "helping" system are capable of only generating a control vector for preventing an essential variable from exceeding an upper critical limit but not a lower one or vice versa (e.g., an architect designing a house for hot climates would include an air conditioning unit in his or her plans but not, normally, the installation of a furnace in the house.).

Control vectors can operate at any of three levels:

(1)   Within the system
(2)   At the system's boundaries
(3)   Outside of the system (in the environment of the system) We can label these internal, boundary, and external control vectors.

And they may be divided into two ideal types:

(1).   "Focused control vectors"--these are aimed specifically at certain systems in the environment in an attempt to directly control certain outputs of such systems.

(2). "Diffused control vectors"--these are used to create or alter key environmental parameters to encourage the in- or out-migration of certain kinds of "black boxes" to or from the immediate environment of the system (e.g., customers to a retail store, or as was discussed earlier, workers to the mines of Ajo, etc.).

The most important limitations on the usefulness of this second approach to the control of certain environmental parameters are that:

(1)   few systems have the power to either completely control or cast out all of the other systems in their nearby universe

(2)   given a certain set of control vectors, there may be an "insufficient" supply of the "proper" type of black box that can be "enticed" to begin "communicating" (i.e., trading inputs and outputs) with the system (e.g., the possible shortage of trained workers at the end of a long strike).

Most of the control potential inherent in an item being communicated resides in the belief[10] by the receiving system that it must supply certain outputs, accept certain inputs, or undergo certain structural modifications to continue receiving desired inputs or avoid receiving undesired ones. However, the control achieved either qualitatively or quantitatively may not always be that desired by the exporting system.

Any such exchange between systems is inherently unequal and the "winning" or controlling system can be defined as the system that profits most from such an exchange in terms of having expended the least amount of organized energy. Thus in the modern world the highest level of control is often achieved by those systems whose output is mostly in the form of communication of information and/or money rather than organized matter/energy and/or transducers unless the latter are in unusually scarce supply for either natural or "artificial"[11] reasons. Or using the terminology of the new model being developed in this chapter, the major identifying feature of "controlling" systems is that internal structural or behavioral change often precedes and actually induces "favorable" (to the controlling system) change in environmental parameters in contrast to controlled systems where such internal structural or behavioral change is the result of changing environmental parameters induced by (an) outside "controlling" system(s).

For analytical purposes, I shall define the creation of a new systemic status set (or any other "transducing set") as a +1 structural transformation and the disbandment of such a systemic status set (or any other transducing set) as a -1 structural transformation. However, though such transformations can give clues as to whether or not any given system is "winning" or "losing" in its struggle for environmental control, the key to creating a quantitative, predictive general systems model of human behavior is to calculate the before and after organized-energy-in / organized-energy-out ratio after a system executes one or more control actions in an attempt to increase its level of control over some portion of the surrounding environment or to counter a perceived threat to its present level of environmental control. Thus if any control action (e.g., a +1 or -1 structural transformation or a change in the behavioral option chosen) is followed by an increase in this ratio to a point above what the ratio was before the control action was attempted then the system has increased its control over its surrounding environment in a manner that can be quantified. And if not, the system has lost some of its control over its surrounding environment (in a manner that can also be quantified) to competing systems although it may still be able to achieve a lower level of ultra-adaptability as long as the organized-energy-in / organized-energy-out ratio remains greater than zero or does not fall below zero for a period of time beyond which the system no longer retains sufficient transducers and organized energy to complete any further "successful" control actions.

In order to build a better predictive model for the outcome when two or more systems attempt, each in its own fashion, to "order their environments" in the same portion or portions of the space/time continuum, it is useful to borrow terminology from the science of ecology. Thus by substituting the words "system" for "population," "systems" for "populations" or "populations of two species," "obligate mutualism" (See Addicott 1984:438) for "mutualism," and "facultative mutualism" (See Addicott 1984:438) for "protocooperation" -- the following quotation from Odum (1953:165) can be modified to read:

> Theoretically, (systems) may interact in six basic ways corresponding to the six combinations of 0, +, and -, as follows: 00, --, ++, +0, -0, and +-... These...are as follows: (1) neutralism, in which neither (system) is affected by association with the other; (2) competition, in which each (system) adversely affects the other in the struggle for food, nutrients, living space, or other common need; (3) (obligate mutualism), in which growth and survival of both (systems) is benefited and neither can survive under natural conditions without the other; (4) (facultative mutualism), in which both (systems) benefit by the association but relations are not obligatory; (5) commensalism, in which one (system) is benefited but the other is not affected; (6) amensalism, in which one (system) is inhibited and the other not affected; (7) parasitism and (8) predation, in which one (system) affects the other by direct attack but is dependent on the other,... (The terms "obligate mutualism" and "facultative mutualism" come from Addicott (1984:438))

And Odum's table 10 (1953:166) can likewise be modified for our use in a similar manner to read:

Table I

Analysis of the Interaction Between Two Systems (Systems A and B) where:

"+" indicates environmental control is increased,

"-" indicates environmental control is decreased

"0" indicates environmental control is not affected

Type of Interaction	When Not Interacting A B	When Interacting A B	General Result of Interaction
1. Neutralism (A and B independent)	0 0	0 0	Neither system affects the other
2. Competition (A and B competitors)	0 0	- -	System most affected is eliminated from niche
3. (Obligate Mutualism) (A and B are partners or symbionts)	- -	+ +	Interaction is obligatory for both
4. (Facultative Mutualism) (A and B cooperators)	0 0	+ +	Interaction favorable to both, but not obligatory
5. Commensalism (A commensal; B host)	- 0	+ 0	Obligatory for A; B not affected
6. Amensalism (A amensal; B inhibitor)	0 0	- 0	A inhibited; B not affected
7. Parasitism - (A parasite; B host)	- 0 -	+ -	Obligatory for A; B inhibited
8. Predation (A predator; B prey)	- 0	+ -	Obligatory for A; B inhibited .

In human affairs, a person who is a member of two systems establishes a synaptic link between the two systems and is likely to try to control variables in one system to provide favorable inputs to the other system and, at times, vice-versa. Often such an individual may occasionally add or subtract bits of information from the message being transmitted from one system to another to further his/her own ends or those of one of the systems to which he/she belongs over the other(s). The biological analogy of this latter process is called "nuclear invasion" (Lewin 1984:427) and in such cases the person and his/her transducing activities really function as "viral vectors" (i.e., control vectors that are designed to induce temporary or "permanent" mutations in extant "cultural genes" or insert entirely new "genetic" material). And though the system being "attacked" by such vectors is often able to initially resist the importation or creation of new "dominant cultural genes," it is usually much more difficult to block the importation or creation of new "recessive cultural genes", one or more of which may lay dormant for long periods of time until possibly being activated when the system is faced with a "crisis" for which none of the other stored "dominant" or "recessive" cultural "genetic material" provides a satisfactory transducing pattern. And, it should be noted, as Kroeber has done (Steward 1955:13), that usually this "process of cultural development" (i.e., the addition of "new cultural genes" to the total set of those already stored in the receiving system) "is an additive and therefore accumulative one, whereas the process of organic evolution is a substitutive one."

Let us now for a moment examine systems facing the loss of ultra-adaptability or systemic collapse due to "unfavorable" changing environmental parameters. In such cases we can predict three possible outcomes:

(1) A falling domino-type chain reaction may occur with one -1 structural transformation triggering others, leading to an irreversible systemic collapse as illustrated during the strike by the death of several of the miners, including the leader of the local Indian village's "Intertribal Council". Although one would have a difficult time proving that these men would have lived had the strike not occurred, still, the prolonged lack of exercise for men often heavily overweight and probably somewhat depressed by the strike may

have been the crucial factor that "tipped the scales" (i.e., forced an essential variable past a critical limit) against several of these idle strikers.

(2) Systemic collapse or loss of ultra-adaptability may only be temporary so that the system may again revive itself or be revived by an outside system after the removal of (a) disruptive input(s) that has (have) driven one or more essential system variables past (a) critical limit(s) as seen during the strike when organizations in the Indian village, such as the Village Council[12] and the Catholic Church choir, suffered a temporary loss of ultrastability during the latter part of the strike as the population of certain key systemic status set sets dropped from one to zero. Thus, although the Village Intertribal Council had survived one threat to its continued maintenance of the ultra-adaptable state when the chairman of the organization died shortly after the beginning of the strike, (the vice-chairman had at that time been elevated first in practice and then later in name to the office of chairman), it ceased to function altogether after the replacement chairman started working in a distant location and was, therefore, absent from Ajo much of the time during the latter part of the strike. In the case of the church choir, the organist during the strike spent most of her time on the nearby Papago reservation. Thus, with no one to play the organ the group ceased to practice and perform during the latter part of the strike.

(3) Systemic collapse or loss of ultra-adaptability may be prevented by control actions initiated by one or more transducing sets either acting independently or in cooperation with each other. (The locus of each of these transducing sets need not be within the system being threatened.)

Control actions that transducing sets use to increase their control over other transducing sets or to counteract incoming "hostile" control vectors include the following:

(1)   Moving a system to a new and "more benevolent" environment as observed during the strike when several Indian and white families simply moved to other locations during the strike. In all cases about which I have personal records, this involved living with or near relatives either on the reservation or in distant urban centers. In most of these cases the miner and/or his wife did not entirely rely on the resources of their relatives but instead found part or full-time jobs to help buy food, etc. This option was, however, never too popular and even in the case of the approximately ten families who spent the two summer months of July and August on the Papago reservation almost all returned to Ajo when it was time for their children to begin school as stated previously.

(2)   Moving part of a system to a new and "more benevolent" environment. (e.g., the manufacturing facilities of a U.S. company being moved to a foreign country. Also, although several miners were able to obtain new local sources of income (e.g., several began working at local gas stations), many others were forced to commute to fairly distant locations such as Phoenix to find employment, staying there during the week in a rented room or apartment and coming home on weekends. Several additional miners working in distant areas seldom returned to Ajo during the strike, although they in contrast to the few miners previously described continued to send money and messages to their families in Ajo.

(3)   Splitting a system into two or more smaller, more viable systems as observed during the strike when a small number of Indian families split almost completely during the strike. In one case four out of seven children were sent to a reservation school and in a few other instances the wife and children stayed in Ajo and lived on credit and occasional part time jobs, such as housecleaning, while the husband was away in some distant location working and supporting himself there. In at least one such case the wife heard nothing from her husband for over one month.

(4)   Abandoning certain portions of the surrounding universe formerly under at least partial control (e.g., Countries that have given up

land to more powerful neighbors; companies closing stores in certain communities).

(5) Reducing the level of control over other systems or transducers in the surrounding universe as seen during the strike when by giving each miner a small amount of credit instead of the usual large paycheck, the company was able to hold many, but not all, of the miners in Ajo. Thus, this action led to a greater uncertainty in its "control" over even those who chose to remain in Ajo during the strike.

(6) Changing the absolute value of either the upper or lower "critical limit" of one or more essential variables as seen during the strike when individuals and families "tightened their belts". Most people were able to lower their "minimal" needs and wants thresholds (i.e., they were able to establish lower critical limits for certain essential variables) during the strike. As the Arizona Republic newspaper reported, Ajo's bars remained full, but the customers "preferred beer to hard liquor" (A.R. September 24, 1967:A-20) and Ajo housewives bought "chicken or hamburger instead of the better cuts of meat" (A.R. December 10, 1967:C-3). On a larger scale the planners of the community Christmas program were also able to hold the annual event during the strike by such measures as reducing the value of the gifts to be given to each of the local children by the town "Santa Claus". Also, the planners of the annual St. Catherine's Day Fiesta (to be discussed later) in the Indian village limited the amount of free food to be given out at the celebration in 1968 and completely eliminated the traditional dance band from the program. This was by far the most common type of "outcome" since near the end of the strike only about 17 of the 113 Indian miners were out of town and very few of these 17 had taken school-age children with them to other locations.

(7) Substituting a new behavioral option (i.e., "cultural gene") for an old one (e.g., as will later be discussed, the abandonment of "polygamy" by the Mormons).

(8) Eliminating one or more systemic status sets (e.g., the elimination of certain middle management positions in a large corporation).

(9) Expelling an unproductive or disruptive "black box" from his/her systemic status set or from the total system (e.g., the firing or demotion of a worker or the excommunication of a church member).

(10) Attempting to "contain" or eliminate other transducing sets that are potential internal rivals for the structural position in the system occupied by the "threatened" transducing set. However, when this action is taken against occupants of certain higher (in terms of control over the flow of communicated items both within the system and to and from its environment) systemic status sets there is always the possibility that this will result in a splitting of the system into two or more competing ones (e.g., the splitting of a church, political party, or nation) which may often (but not always) weaken the ability of one or more of the resultant systems to continue to survive. (e.g., see chapter 10's discussion of the fight for leadership and the subsequent split that occurred in the Mormon church after the death of Joseph Smith)

(11) Implementing a qualitative or quantitative change in the control vectors aimed either directly or diffusely at one or more structurally bound systemic status sets (e.g. the setting of new production goals, the raising of wages paid, etc.).

(12) Blocking or controlling of the flow of certain forms of communicated items (e.g., "viral vectors") to or from one internal transducer to another or from the outside environment to one or more of the internal transducers (e.g., parents "locking out" certain cable TV channels or internet sites that they wish to prevent their children watching).

(13) Implementing a greater standardization of the selection process for each systemic status set in the system so that leaving "black boxes" are replaced by almost identical incoming "black boxes." (Non-standardized replacement procedures for the occupant(s) of the highest (in terms of control potential) systemic status set(s), in particular, have often contributed heavily to periods of system instability or collapse.) (e.g., hundreds of new American religions

arose in the 19th century but only a few survived the death of their founders)

(14) Implementing a qualitative or quantitative change in the internal communication linkage network between one or more of the structurally bound systemic status sets (e.g., a change in the routing of memos, etc. through a large office).

(15) Creating new systemic status sets to eliminate growth inhibiting restrictions in the flow of communicated items either internally within the overall system or to the surrounding environment (e.g., the insertion of a new management systemic status set in the command structure of a growing organization).

(16) Using focused or diffused control vectors that are deliberately designed to entice "more compatible" "black boxes" into joining the system while discouraging more "potentially disruptive" ones from joining or remaining in the system. (e.g., see chapter 10's discussion of the Mormon church's public condemnation of homosexuality and of giving the priesthood to women while heavily promoting the virtues of the traditional family)

(17) Creating better legal or physical "traps" to prevent the escape of "black boxes" from the system and its controlled surrounding universe (e.g., keeping miners in debt to the company store)

(18) Creating better legal or physical barriers to prevent the entry of "hostile black boxes" into the system and its controlled surrounding universe (e.g., the issuing of restraining orders; the employment of security guards; the building of border fences)

(19) Creating better psychological "traps" (i.e., not knowing when to cut their losses many people continue to pour more effort, time, or money into failing relationships, careers, aging cars, telephone calls on hold, etc. (Rubin 1981)) Thus in chapter 2, the company by the giving of credit for food and housing during the long 1967-68 strike persuaded its best "black box" employees that they had too much to lose if they left the system.

(20) Using physical punishment to control "deviant" "black box" behavior (e.g., spanking a child; arresting and jailing criminals)

(21) Using psychological punishment to control "deviant" "black box" behavior (e.g., as discussed in chapter 10, the taking away of a Mormon temple recommend)

(22) Using physical rewards to channel "black box" behavior (e.g., a parent giving candy to a child to quiet it; a bonus or a better office given to better performing employees)

(23) Using psychological rewards to channel "black box" behavior (e.g., praising an employee for his/her good work)

(24) Creating new patterns of speech, clothing, food avoidances, marriage, rituals, etc. that serve to increase in-group solidarity and identify and isolate "insiders" from "outsiders" (e.g., see chapter 10)

(25) Censoring, "correcting," "enhancing" or perhaps even falsifying certain types of information being released internally or to competing systems. (This is perhaps the most used control action by all interacting human systems sometimes but not always for what most would consider "selfish" or "evil"" reasons. See Chapter 11 for a fuller discussion of what are often viewed as being "altruistic" reasons for the ubiquitous use of this control action by all human systems.)

(26) Using focused or diffused control vectors that are deliberately designed to limit or inhibit the control options open to a competing system (e.g., the state lawsuits filed against the tobacco industry)

(27) Using focused or diffused control vectors to deliberately drain negentropy from other systems in the surrounding universe whether or not these systems are in open competition with the exporting system. (i.e., parasitism) (e.g., the mafia's "protection" racket)

(28) Using focused or diffused control vectors to deliberately destroy a competing system. (i.e., predation) (e.g., lowering the price of the items that you sell below the cost of production of similar items produced by a competitor)

(29) Becoming more of a "black box" through the erection of better psychological/physical barriers to decrease the flow of certain microstate information to outside systems (e.g., Firing or threatening

to fire "whistle blowers"; blocking access to information previously publicly available).

(30) Maximizing the delay time between when a communicated item is received from another system and when a return item (e.g., money, etc.) is sent back to the other system or forwarded on to a third system.

(31) Maximizing the output of low energy consuming items (e.g., information) while minimizing the output of high energy consuming items (e.g., manufactured goods).

(32) Entering into a amensal relationship with another system. (e.g., a teenager deciding to stay at home with his or her parents rather than engaging in gang activities)

(33) Entering into a commensal relationship with another system. (e.g., an individual deciding against committing suicide after attending a church service in a large congregation where his or her absence would not be missed by those in charge of the service)

(34) Entering into a facultative mutual relationship with another system. (e.g., two companies agree not to sell similar products below a certain price. Also, see chapter 10 about the relationship between the Mormon church and other powerful systems in Utah.)

(35) Entering into an obligate mutual relationship with another system. (i.e., each system needs access to something the other system possesses or produces for its very survival)

(36) Merging the system with one or more other systems.(e.g., the merging of two competing banks to eliminate the need for redundant facilities and staff in various city locations)

(37) Attempting the nuclear "conversion" of surrounding systems to control actions that will result in inputs/outputs favorable to the exporting system through the use of various types of "viral vectors" (e.g., as will later be discussed in chapter 10, the large scale missionary efforts of the Mormon Church).

(38) Allowing and encouraging the nuclear invasion of surrounding systems by exporting "viral vectors" in the form of individual

preprogrammed "black box" transducers whose primary loyalty (often covertly) continues to reside with the exporting system. (e.g., elected officials in Utah, most of whom are active members of the Mormon church (see chapter 10))

(39) Using any of the above control actions to pit two or more systems against each other. (i.e., the old divide and conquer strategy used by military forces in warfare and by companies in negotiations with labor unions.)

(40) Threatening to use any of the above control actions. (e.g., the threat to close the Ajo smelter if it didn't receive an exemption from new air pollution control government standards.)

In introducing ecological terminology into this general systems model, it is critical to point out that there has been much recent debate in the anthropological literature about the precise meaning and usefulness of such long accepted terms as "adaptation" and "selection." Thus, as Bargatzky (1984:400) points out:

> Even in biology, fundamental problems arise from the use of "adaptation" as a conceptual tool. "Adaptation" implies a preexisting world that poses a "problem" to which adaptation is the solution.... The "mechanism" of adaptation is natural selection operating upon a mutant, a gene, or an organism that has undergone a heritable change. Yet this is where the problems begin. Adaptation can now be described as the process of niche occupation by an organism. However, there is no natural way of subdividing the world into niches pre-dating organisms, because organisms themselves are active in creating their niches... Hence, we should expect coevolution of a species and its niche rather than the empty niche waiting to be occupied by a species.... There is one further problem with "adaptation" as a conceptual tool in biology. It is maintained that without change, or "stress,"

in the environment there is no adaptive change in the organism... The organism, however, is not just a slave of its environment; it actively modifies it, even without external stimuli... Moreover, the immense diversification of organisms in evolution cannot be accounted for by "passive" adaptation alone... What is true for the organismic level, in this respect will surely be true for the higher levels too--for example, for society or "culture"...

And while in biology almost all scientists have abandoned earlier Lamarckian teleological notions except when discussing human cultural change (e.g., see Gould 1997:2210), the debate begun by Kroeber (1917) rages on about how much conscious control humans can exercise over their ultimate social and cultural destinies. Thus Rindos (1984:6) states:

The idea that we as a culture, a nation, or a species are in conscious control of our environment and thus of our destiny is one part truth, one part rhetoric, and two parts wishful thinking. The various controls of society are often inward-directed and are generally more efficient at rationalizing the status quo than at bringing about directed long-term change. It is all very well to speak of social or cultural goals if these are restricted to the realizable or if this is simply a shorthand way of describing change that has occurred over time; to use the goals or problem-solving abilities of people as an explanation for long-term historical change is another matter entirely. The danger of this approach is that we may attribute powers to people or to culture that they do not have...

He (1984:6) then goes on to agree with Darwin who was also reluctant to attribute to humans "any great deal of awareness of the ultimate effects of their selection" from among the variation that confronts them in the real biological world and in a heated debate with many other scholars in the pages of Current Anthropology (1985:65-88) Rindos asks:

Why do so many anthropologists get upset when intentionality is reduced to an irrelevant variable?... (p. 84) I have not, as the commentators suggest, ignored the directed, problem-solving conscious, purposeful, goal-seeking, guided, designed, in a word "intentional" aspects of human culture; I have consciously and purposefully excluded them.

These elements are useless for problem solving...(p. 84) By providing the illusion of an answer, they get in the way of important new questions --- questions that not only cannot be answered by invoking intentionality but cannot even be asked... (p. 84) ...a trait may well have originally arisen by means of planning, intent, problem solving, limitation, etc., but so what? It was successful over time, and it became established in a culture not because it was "guided" but because it was fit and hence selected. In the same way, I never held that because the original variation was random some of it couldn't be adaptive. Some of the variants were adaptive--the adaptive ones spread because they increased the fitness of the carriers... (p. 85) ...I am claiming that "directed" in an evolutionary sense is not the same as "directed" in a psychological sense. I do not deny the belief in intent, direction, etc.; this belief is amply demonstrated by the anthropological record. Rain dances, ritual purification, and supply-side economics are undeniably motivated actions. All are performed by individuals who believe in the efficacy of their behavior. Yet this is not enough to guarantee success. We have not explained the impact of an invention by naming the inventor. Nor have we explained why certain inventions are successful while others fail... Consciously performed rituals are occasionally followed by success.

Does the belief in the instrumentality of an act mean that the belief exists? Of course. But does it mean that the belief is "true," that, in fact, the act is efficacious? Of course not. We must separate the belief structure from the material consequences of acts generated by that belief structure. Barring omniscience, no necessary correlation exists between them. Consciousness, intent, and design are not meant to explain; they are what we need to explain (pp. 85-86). ...Few, I am sure, would dare claim that the increasing possibility of nuclear holocaust is a result of logical, conscious adaptation on the part of human culture. If war is designed for population control, it has functioned poorly of late (or should we embrace a coming disaster as the inevitable expression of good design?)... (p. 86)

Thus, in the construction of a new general systems model of human behavior, it is important to keep in mind that the control vectors "consciously" generated by a system seeking to alter certain environmental parameters do not always produce the "desired" quality or quantity of increased environmental control even on a short-term basis. And often in those cases where the system does appear to gain the desired temporary advantage, cause and effect events may be set in motion that will ultimately have unforeseen positive or negative consequences for the system. Also, it should be noted that many times the true source and/or nature of the "benevolent" control vectors in a system's environment are not really "consciously" perceived by the system's "controllers" (e.g., the "power" of a "lucky" object or a religious ritual may be given false credit for a beneficial change in one of the system's environmental parameters as Rindos clearly pointed out in the above quoted passage). Still, despite these objections let us now see how, starting with Ajo, this new paradigm can not only help us understand the "true" sources and nature of the most important control vectors found in human societies but also help us predict the future fate of "controlling" systems in general as they attempt to maximize and expand their power over all other nearby systems.

Let us now examine several of the systems involved in the strike and the "stability" threatened in each system by the prolonged shutdown,

The essential variables of "the company" whose "stability" were most threatened by the strike were the net income variable (i.e., one of the "communications" variables) and many of the systemic status set population variables (i.e., the threatened loss of men "selected" over a period of many years for their desirable personal characteristics and often well trained for highly specialized and skilled jobs at company expense.)[13] Ajo's relative isolation from "civilization" made the possible loss of skilled "Anglo" employees an especially serious problem since they would be hard to readily replace at the end of the strike.[14] However, even the close proximity of the Papago reservation and the Mexican border would not guarantee an easy replenishment of the supply of Indians and Mexicans possessing the desired personal characteristics and skills.[15]

Thus the directors of the company faced a vexing dilemma at this point. By exercising "destructive control"[16] over the system of workers attached to it at Ajo, the net income variable of the Company could be protected from exceeding its lower critical limit during the strike but only at the cost of increased entropy in the overall universe of company plus workers. Instead, the company chose the technique of "manipulative control"[17] to preserve as much as possible the state of low entropy that existed within the closely associated system of workers, even though the danger to the company's net income variable was thereby increased.

The main mechanism of manipulative control used by the company was the extension of credit to the strikers so that most of the necessities of life (e.g., food, clothing, housing and utilities) could be provided for as well as a few of the "luxuries."[18] This gamble proved to be a highly successful one, although at times, to try to force a settlement, the company threatened to change its control method to the destructive variety by shutting off the credit. This threat was also an attempt at manipulative control (i.e., an attempt to raise the level of certain "anxiety" variables) but was aimed ultimately at the union leadership rather than at the individual workers of Ajo. This attempted control of the content of information flow between systems proved to be not only an important manipulative "tool" in the hands of the company, but also in the hands of the unions as well as was seen in Chapter 2.

The various unions represented at the Ajo mine also were concerned about the "disruptive force vectors"[19] operating on their net income and systemic status set population variables during the strike. Even before the strike had begun, a fairly large number of men had already withdrawn from the unions, usually because they felt that the benefits derived from belonging were not worth the trouble or money involved (i.e., in terms of the "entropy" model, the individual either deemed his prediction and control of the work environment to be adequate or at least felt that no improvement could be obtained through union membership)

Faced with a possible loss in membership that had been gained gradually through the years by means of the mechanism of "creative control"[20], the unions also chose manipulative control measures rather than destructive ones during the strike (e.g., they supplied cash or credit to the strikers). Loss in membership would not only have meant reduction in dues paid and in relative power, but if enough men had deserted their ranks so that a lower critical limit was passed, the unions would no longer be recognized as the official bargaining agents for the men on strike. [21]

Local business men and creditors were also concerned about "disruptive force vectors" threatening to drive net income variables beyond their lower critical limits. These individuals were threatened by the possibility of massive defaults on loans and other debts (e.g., the filing of bankruptcy or flight to avoid debt payment). The seizure of homes, furniture, cars, etc., on such a large scale would also have been unprofitable, especially since the market for such items was already depressed in Ajo because of the strike.[22] Business men and creditors in more distant centers (e.g., Phoenix and Tucson) were not faced with the same type of problem, however, and were generally much less "sympathetic" to the strikers.

Other systems affected by the strike included schools, fraternal and civic organizations) and church groups. Here again, "disruptive force vectors" threatened systemic status set population variables and in many cases, net income variables.

Finally the "stability" of the net income variable was threatened on the family level. The needs and wants of the individual family members all had certain lower critical limits, although these varied from individual to individual. Most family heads also became skilled "manipulators" of available "resources" (i.e., the outputs of other systems) in their attempts at maintaining a low degree of entropy, both within the family system and in the surrounding social and material environments. In particular, many members of the Indian minority in Ajo became especially skilled in manipulating the "resources" of the nearby Papago reservation in maintaining a state of low entropy in the family unit and its environment.[23] Thus through the interaction of all the systems involved, a truly remarkable degree of "stability" in what I have called "essential variables" was maintained throughout the entire length of the strike, thereby holding the entropy of each affected system, with but very few exceptions, (to be discussed later in this and later chapters) at an extremely low level.[24]

At this point in the development of this chapter, it is profitable to examine certain aspects of the entropy model as illustrated in the previous pages by the Ajo data.

Systemic status set population, in particular, is an interesting variable that should be examined in more detail at this time since each systemic status set in an ultra-adaptable organization demands a certain minimum input from the occupant of that systemic status set if that member is to remain in "good standing" (i.e., receive the maximum output of the system when needed). These minimum inputs vary both in quantity and quality from status to status in any given system (e.g., the expected role behavior of father, mother, and child in the family). Each member of a system also seeks certain minimum system outputs that will be of use in maintaining his physiological and psychological variables within their critical limits. Such outputs may take either a physical form such as food or a psychological one, such as the promise of a reward in the afterlife.

Therefore, each social organization in order to achieve ultra-adaptability must have some sort of mechanism for maintaining these inputs and outputs above certain minimum values or some mechanism to insure an increase in input or output in one part of the system when the input or output decreases by a corresponding amount in another portion of the system. (This latter possibility will lead to structural change, however, if certain critical limits for the input-output of each systemic status set are passed.) Failure of such a mechanism will lead either to structural change or to a loss of ultra-adaptability and perhaps systemic collapse.

No two individuals are ever completely alike so that no two people will ever seek exactly the same quality and quantity of output from any given system with which they interact, nor can they supply the same quality and quantity of input to the outside system. Therefore, if the system fails to provide the minimum output needed or desired by the occupant of a systemic status set, he or she will usually withdraw from the system or if the occupant of a systemic status set fails to provide the input needed by the system, she or he will be rejected by the other members of the system and "cast out". Thus, a selection process occurs among the membership of any given system. (The "weeding-out" of habitual drunkards among the Indian miners of Ajo by the company is a good example of such a process in operation.)

Most social systems have set up elaborate control mechanisms to try to prevent losses in systemic status set populations, but many of these same systems actually try to suppress the operation of control mechanisms that would tend to keep role population variables from exceeding their upper critical limits. Such systems often seek to maximize certain systemic status set population variables, even though continual structural reorganization is necessary. One nationally known church, "The Church of Jesus Christ of Latter-day Saints," that is represented in Ajo, as will be examined in later chapters, is typical of such organizations. It has a large, aggressive missionary program and encourages its members to have many children. Nationally, with a rapid increase in membership, continual splitting of small congregations is occurring. However, since centralized control of all members is still desired by the highest authorities of this church, this fission of small congregations is never complete. This has led to many major structural reorganizations in the church hierarchy, often culminating in the creation of new systemic status sets at the intermediate and highest levels in the overall system.

Other systems, while also seeking to maximize the population variable manage to do so only to a certain critical point after which complete fission occurs, resulting in two relatively independent systems. Still other systems maintain rigid population controls and try to keep the numbers of occupants in each systemic status set within rather narrow limits. The company in Ajo is a good example of this type of system, although the value ranges of the various systemic status set variables have been subject to many discreet shifts during the history of the Ajo Corporation. Thus, the value ranges for systemic status set variables lower in the company hierarchy were drastically shifted downward (i.e., the absolute values of both critical limits for these variables were lowered) during the depression years and again recently, due in large part to the automation of many menial jobs. However, these same value ranges were shifted upwards during and immediately following World War II when the demand for copper was very high. Also, recently the value range for the skilled-labor systemic status set variable has been shifted upwards year after year as more new and complicated machinery has been installed in the mine and smelter.

Many other social systems also from time to time shift the value range of certain systemic status set variables, each in an attempt to deliberately alter the structure of the system, occasionally for economic motives, but often also for other reasons (e.g., some companies now set minimum quotas for selected "minority group" members. In Ajo, the Indian rather than the Negro is the "official" minority group receiving special treatment from the mining company (Waddell 1969:54-55, 57). Such minimum quotas are usually set up for political and social reasons rather than economic ones.).

Ultra-adaptable organizations can be classified according to stability through time as role memberships change. Here, we can pick out three types. (It should be stressed that these are merely three points along a continuum):

(1)   Those that persist without major structural change or loss of ultra-adaptability only as long as membership in each systemic status set does not change (e.g. a business partnership, a family consisting of only a husband and wife).

(2)   Those that persist without major structural change or loss of ultra-adaptability only as long as membership in the higher systemic status set in the group hierarchy does not change. (Change may occur in the membership of lower systemic status set.) (e.g., a family

consisting of husband, wife, and children, France under DeGaulle, Haiti under Duvalier, Hitler's Germany, many Boy Scout troops, the Indian Village Intertribal Council in Ajo. See Chapter 7.)

(3) Those that persist without major structural change or loss of ultra-adaptability in spite of changes in membership in all roles (e.g., the Telephone Company, the "Company" in Ajo since the 30's, National and State Governments in the United States).

This classification scheme reflects our earlier observation that in a newly formed system, the average behavior of occupants of systemic status sets lower in the system's hierarchy tend to become more predictable more rapidly than the average behavior of occupants of systemic status sets higher in the group hierarchy. Therefore, turnover in lower systemic status set memberships is less likely than turnover in higher systemic status set memberships to alter either qualitatively or quantitatively the inputs and outputs of the overall system. (One fairly accurate way to measure the degree of such role standardization (i.e., institutionalization) of any systemic status set would be to measure the redundancy of messages and actions originating from the successive occupants of that systemic status set.)

Finally, a few statements can be made regarding the entropy of social systems in general at this point. It is clear that the entropy of a system decreases as either the membership of certain systemic status set sets in the system increases or as the interaction rate per unit time among and between members of certain systemic status set sets increases and increases as either of these two measurements falls. Therefore, it can be postulated that at different "levels" of entropy, different types of group structures are possible (e.g., the so-called "state level" of social organization would require a certain minimum interaction rate and level of membership). Thus a general classificatory scheme of social systems based upon the entropy concept may be possible.

Obviously, the continued future existence of an absolute control potential by an ultras table system over all of its essential variables is impossible to predict since it is impossible to know with complete certainty the maximum value of all possible future "disruptive force vectors."

Therefore, as has been shown, using these few examples, the model of human behavior developed in this chapter is adequate to "explain" the qualitative changes that occurred in the affected Ajo systems during the strike, but what about its power as a quantitative predictive instrument?

As Singh (1966:74) points out, the "sheer bulk of numbers in a crowd" of molecules forced the chemist and physicist to turn to statistical mechanics to bring order out of chaos in their calculations of molecular energy. Other scientists also have found the statistical method to be the only practical way to deal with large masses of data. Modern sociology and psychology are to a large extent based upon the use of statistics to "explain" and predict human behavior. Even the countless ethnographies of the traditional anthropologist are merely descriptions of the "average" behavior of the groups studied. (However, the traditional anthropologist has seldom used precise statistical techniques for obtaining these averages so they are often quite misleading.)

Most descriptions of human behavior have in general tended to emphasize the macrostate of social groups and societies rather than the microstate. This is perhaps one of the major reasons why most anthropologists and sociologists have tended to stress the unity of the members of a given society and the assumption that all members of a particular society share common values and aspirations and act with common motives in mind. Any behavior observed by the ethnologist not fitting into this average pattern in former times was usually dismissed as being deviate or anti-social behavior.

Furthermore, probably the key underlying reason why there have been so many pseudo-macrostate descriptions of cultures in anthropology rather than microstate ones is that until now we have lacked sufficiently powerful methods to handle the large quantities of both quantitative and qualitative data that are present when we study even the simplest of human societies. This is true in spite of our increasing use of such sophisticated, mathematical techniques as multiple regression analysis and lately factor analysis (e.g., Robins et al. (1969) and Benfer (1967).

At this point I would like to suggest that perhaps the answer to this problem lies not in finding increasingly more sophisticated statistical techniques and in using bigger and faster computers but instead in applying the model I have proposed in this chapter where only those variables which are "essential" to the maintenance of ultra-adaptability in a system need be quantified and their corresponding critical limits determined. In fact, in the Ajo examples described previously, only two classes of variables and one set of upper critical limits would have needed quantification before the researcher would have had enough information to have made reasonably correct "microstate" predictions about change and "stability" in the affected systems in response to outside "disruptive force vectors" during the recent copper strike. These are:

(a)   The systemic status set population variables

(b)   The net income variables

(c)   The upper critical limits of the anxiety about (a) and/or (b) variables

Both (a) and (b) would have needed to have been quantified initially and throughout the strike while the upper critical limits, (c), although perhaps proving to have been more difficult to quantify could have at least in theory been estimated through an examination of the history of conflicts involving each of the affected Ajo systems using the method of "frequency interpretation" (Erasmus 1961:22-23) or perhaps through the use of some form of psychological testing. Next, using the estimates of these upper critical limits, (c), the critical limits of (a) and (b) could have perhaps been also estimated by deriving a functional relationship between these limits, (c), and those of variables (a) and (b) again using historical data or actual psychological testing procedures.

Also, even if it may have proven to have been impossible or impractical to collect sufficient data on the critical limits of the anxiety variables of some of the individuals and groups involved directly or indirectly in the strike or perhaps even sufficient data on the net income variables of certain of the affected systems, it would still have been possible to make certain "macrostate" predictions about the behavior of most of the affected systems in Ajo under the stress of the strike.[25] Thus, using only membership data, it can be postulated that ultra-adaptable organizations must undergo structural change or face loss of ultrastability as the membership occupying any systemic status set-set increases or decreases past certain critical values)[26] or using only interaction data that structural change or loss of ultrastability must occur as the frequency of interaction (acts of communication) between occupants of different systemic status set sets increases or decreases past certain critical values. (It should also be noted that change in one of these essential variables often is correlated with change in the others.)

Although I was not present in Ajo in time to make such a predictive analysis before the strike began, I have now become convinced after a lengthy historical analysis of the systems involved in the strike that such quantification of the model presented in this chapter is indeed possible. What I have, in essence, proposed in the preceding pages is, therefore, not as much a new data reduction technique as it is a new method of selecting the data to be collected and analyzed since the problem the anthropologist usually faces today is not one of possessing a lack of data but, instead, a problem of having too much data. Essentially then, I have suggested that by a careful selection of the variables to be quantified, the problem of eliminating relatively irrelevant and redundant data can be often handled prior to the collection (or at least the analysis) of the data, rather than afterwards, when even the most highly complex statistical techniques we possess today may be inadequate to make any sense out of the "hodgepodge" of measurements, categories, and random thoughts in the possession of most anthropologists after even the most modest field experience. By thus setting up a hierarchy of variables beginning with those most essential to the survival of the system under study at any given time, it should be often possible to reach high levels of social prediction with relatively small quantities of carefully selected data. However, here, as with many other analytical techniques, it is easier to use this model to "explain" past events than to predict future ones. And, when one attempts to increase the probability of a prediction's accuracy even slightly higher, the variables that must be taken into account multiply greatly and are, therefore, often impossible to analyze let alone to collect. This is perhaps the main reason why so many approaches to systems analysis in the past in terms of the analysis of communications networks have proved to be so sterile. The total flow of information, of matter and energy, and of systems capable of organizing matter and energy in even the simplest of communications networks during a brief span of time usually overwhelms our puny efforts to collect and analyze.

Chapter Notes

1. See Depew and Weber (1995: 459-462) and Schrodinger (1944) for a clear explanation of the second law of thermodynamics and the meaning of these two terms as they are used in this book.

2. See Moran (1990: 7) for a discussion of the problem of boundary definition

3. Anderson (19 84: 126) in his discussion of White's final book (1975) also states that, "I believe that White's thermodynamic system would be served better by positioning humans as an aspect of the environment with which culture interacts..."

4. Such words as "hardware" and "software" are obviously being borrowed from modern computer "jargon."

5. A critical limit is the maximum (or minimum) value that an essential variable can assume if the system is to remain in an "ultra-stable" state without change (e.g., see Hardin 1963:66 or Ashby 1960:58,98).

6. In reality, use of the simple pyramidal structure to represent any social system is never really valid.

7. But not impossible (e.g., see the example of certain decisions of Mormon Prophets in Chapter 10.)

8. The relative weight of a person's individual decision can be measured by its effects on the parameters of other individuals and groups (i.e., on the parameters of other systems).

9. This definition is similar to but not quite identical to the one given by White (1975:59-60) who uses the term to apply to the total set of outputs of entire systems.

10. See Rubin (1981) for a good description of how such beliefs (i.e., "psychological traps") are created.

11. A good example of this is the control of most of the world's gem quality diamonds by the De Beers monopoly.

12. See Chapter 7 for more details concerning the "rise and fall" of this very interesting organization.

13. See Bennett (1967:451) for a description of a similar selective process in occupation.

14. As one mining camp resident put it (A.R. January 15, 1968:10): 'What's worrying me now is that some of our best people, the kind who want steady work, who want security, are moving away permanently." (See also A.R. March 4, 1968: 1,15; May 10, 1968:18).

15. Migration from the reservation to Ajo in recent years had apparently almost entirely ceased, despite the fact that after a two-year slowdown in hiring activity, men were again being recruited for jobs at the mine, beginning in mid-October, 1966 (A.C.N. Oct. 13, 1966:1). An important factor in this nearly absolute cessation of new migration from the reservation to Ajo is, without a doubt, the much higher employment standards now in force at the mine for even the simplest of jobs (e.g., now a common unskilled laborer must be a high school graduate). (See Chapter 6).

However, an even more important factor is probably that connected with the phenomenon known as "chain migration." Hackenberg and Wilson (1969:28) in commenting on such migration patterns report on the basis of the data which they (and I) collected that:

> … destinations where there are no relatives are seldom considered. This kind of chain migration is … common among groups with high migration rates.

It is interesting to note that on the basis of the long interviews I held with 40 Indian company employees (see Chapter 3), only one man said that he didn't have relatives or friends living in Ajo before he came here (10 of the 40 were born in Ajo) and only one other of the 40 reported having friends but no relatives in Ajo before coming here (See also F.N. July 25, 1967). Obviously, then, the migration pattern to Ajo appears to have been largely kinship-oriented. Thus, as the gap widens between those relatives left on the reservation and those now living in Ajo (19 of the 40 were either born in Ajo or moved to Ajo as young children with their family), fewer close relatives remain on the reservation to form a potential pool of new migrants to the Ajo mines.

16. As stated previously, all human behavior, both social and antisocial, may be said to be based upon prediction and control. This control may, however, take any of three forms:

    (1) Destructive control

By such control the entropy of some system in the environment is actually increased (i.e., the "order" of this system is decreased).

(2) Creative control

By such control the entropy of some system in the environment is actually decreased (i.e., the "order" of this system is increased).

(3) Manipulative control

By such control the output of another ultras table system is either changed or modified quantitatively. This type of control does not change the structural entropy of the ultra-adaptable system being controlled although entropy changes will occur in the total universe (i.e., system plus environment).

Various combinations of these three basic forms of control are also possible.

17. See Chapter Note 16

18. 18. Thirty-five dollars a week credit at the company store was given to married strikers in the form of coupon books plus an additional twenty-five dollars a child credit, up to a maximum of one hundred twenty-five dollars on "back-to-school" specials at the company store (F.N. July 18, 1967; September 11, 1967). However, no credit at all was given to the few single miners still living in Ajo. (The company has never really tried to hold single men in Ajo and, as shall be shown in later chapters, the control mechanisms that are used by the company in Ajo to control its physical and social environment are largely geared to behavioral control of the more stable and, from the company's viewpoint, more desirable married miner. The older unmarried man is often viewed as a possible threat to the social and moral order that prevails in the community.

19. i.e., an entropy increasing input to a system designed to weaken or destroy it

20. See Chapter Note 16

21. The number of union members in Arizona had already declined by 9,000 (11 percent) between 1964 and 1966 (i.e., 81,000 in 1964 as compared to 72,000 in 1966) (A.R. December 18,1967:15).

22. Thus in Morenci, a spokesman for the Valley National Bank, which had branches in several mining towns, including Ajo, said that the bank had been "carrying families which have been hard pressed to meet payments, here and in all mining communities" (A.R. March 23, 1968:24) and that the bank was "dropping all customary late charges and is undertaking the enormous bookkeeping involved … at our own expense." Also, the manager of the local finance company in Ajo said that his firm would renegotiate loans to the striking miners, adding that (A.R. September 24, 1967:A-20): "We have to go along with the people … we won't foreclose.

This is not the time to get hardnosed." That he felt compelled to be "generous" is evident in his next statement, in which he said that Ajo miners were "not especially good risks" because the majority lived in company houses and were therefore "not tied down" by owning property in Ajo. However, as I will attempt to demonstrate in the following pages, his company's money was much more secure than he mistakenly believed at this time.

23. At least ten Indian families lived on the nearby Papago reservation during the first two months of the strike, although most of these families returned to Ajo in September to put their children in school there. Also, some Ajo men borrowed money from relatives on the reservation and others used the free health service offered at Sells (the Public Health Service Indian Hospital on the main Papago reservation).

24. Evidence of this "more-than-expected stability" was given in December 1967 when it was reported (A.R. December 10, 1967:C-l) that although the miners had been on strike since the middle of the summer, enrollment at the local high school was down only 12 students from the preceding year (586 students on October 31, 1966 as compared to 574 students on October 31, 1967) and elementary school enrollment had only dropped from 1,211 to 1,083 for the corresponding dates. Later, in early March 1968, the enrollment at

the elementary school had risen to about 1,200 ("off about 100 pupils from the normal 1,300 student body") (A.R. March 3, 1968:A-4), despite the fact that at this point there was no real evidence that a strike settlement was near.

Also, although some small businesses had closed their doors shortly after the strike had begun and business was down greatly for a few others, many reported that their sales were much better than they had originally anticipated (A.R. December 10, 1967:C-1, 3; March 3, 1968:A-1, 4) so that after September 1967 no more small businesses closed in Ajo, although most continued to operate "on abbreviated hours with abbreviated payrolls and abbreviated stocks" (A.D.S. March 4, 1968:1). However, the owner of one local newsstand and liquor store reported that in February 1968 business was actually 7 to 10 percent higher than in the corresponding month in 1967 (F.N. March 5, 1968).

25. Although by using only such data the investigator will not be able to predict exactly which individuals will enter or leave a given role set, he can still predict how certain fluctuations in the population of this role set will affect the system as a whole. Indeed, it may prove impossible as some authors suggest (e.g., Bock 1969:115-116) to ever predict exactly what an individual will do.

26. Several actual examples from the Ajo strike to illustrate the operation of this postulate have already been given earlier in this chapter and more will be forthcoming in later chapters, including many other examples from the strike and pre-strike periods, including a very important application of the entropy model as an explanatory tool in understanding the growth and decline of racial segregation in the school system of Ajo through the years (see Chapter 6).

CHAPTER 6:

Crisis and Calm: Perfecting Ways to Attract, Retain and Control "Good" Workers

Ajo is an anachronism in many ways; a survival of the hundreds of old one-industry communities that at one time dotted the American countryside in the more rugged frontier days. As in the classic company town of yesteryear, control over the workers' lives extends far beyond the mere place of work. In fact it is safe to say that there is no aspect of Ajo life, from religion to recreation, that is not dominated by "the company." nothing is done in Ajo even by such outside agents as the county sheriff without the prior approval, either tacit or official, of "the company." (Stucki 1969:1)

The Indian, though usually ignored in most recent writings about Ajo, has always been an integral part of the Ajo mining scene. Waddell (1969:51-53) summarizes the evidence that has been presented through the years by several authors regarding the facts and legends that surround the discovery and early development of the Ajo mineral deposits and concludes that although the Papagos probably visited the mine site often in the early years and perhaps mined some of the minerals there, they had no permanent settlement there until at least 1884. This also corresponds to the conclusions reached by Hackenberg (1964:IV-41, 45) following an earlier synthesis of much of the same material[1]. However, this does not mean that Papagos were not important in the early history of the site since a great deal of the early written and oral history of the area surrounds their activities there.

Let me now demonstrate how the new model developed in the last chapter can help us better analyze some of the events that occurred in Ajo through the years. Thus, from the first short-lived association of an Anglo mining firm and the "nomadic" Papagos, comes our first recorded attempt at "parasitic" system manipulation in Ajo when Rose (1936:28-29) records the following amusing incident:

> Horse thieves were at Ajo at this time too. Some reckless Papagoes were none too honest; for they devised a covetous trick that placed them in the class of horse thieves. But it was done so naively that they escaped severe punishment. Strange Papagoes would drive the camp's stock into the rocky hills where their trail could not be easily followed, leave them there and beat it.
> In a day or so, the go-between would approach Peter Brady and in a patronizing manner say, "I see um caballos."
> "Where?" he would be asked.
> Then with a sweep of his hand he would indicate the direction
> "You catch 'em?"
> "Si, Senor, me ketchum. How much dinero?"
> "Five dollars."
> Then the Papago would shake his head and reply, "Me show um five pesos. Me fetch um here ten pesos."

"All right. You bring them here to camp, ten pesos."
Then the Papago would amble off with two or three others and in a short while the animals would be safe in camp again. The scheme worked smoothly a few times hut when the outfit caught on to the guile of the innocent Papago, he was given a good or bad, whichever way it looks, flogging and was run out of camp.

In terms of the theory now presented in the last chapter, the clever Papagos were trying to manipulate variables in another system (i.e., the mining company) to achieve a certain output (i.e., pesos) by deliberately inducing an element of uncertainty into the system (i.e., the company's decision maker was now unsure of the location or fate of the company's horses). In turn, the company's decision maker was seeking to lessen his uncertainty through manipulation of the go-between. Through the use of pesos (i.e., providing input to the outside transducing system) he was attempting to produce the desired output from that system (i.e., the act of finding and bringing back of the "lost" horses). However, this form of communication between the systems continued only until the company's decision maker discovered a simpler and more permanent way of reducing his uncertainty about the fate and location of the horses after finally realizing the real source of the uncertainty was a "hostile" control vector.[2] Thus by changing his output from pesos to a "good ... flogging" the source of this particular uncertainty was permanently removed from his company's environment.

In contrast to this short lived scheme, when the first American mining company, under the direction of Peter R. Brady in 1854, began developing the Ajo mineral deposits, Dan Rose (1936:23) records that:

Papagoes urged by Mr. Brady's friend Juan Largo soon began to come to the camp and from among them Mr. Brady selected the huskiest and most willing, and put them to work clearing surface ground where the richest ore was exposed. While the white men drilled and blasted the ore the natives packed it to the dumps...

Some time shortly after the opening of the mine in 1854 sixty[3] "self-styled Mexican patriots" tried to raid the mining camp but they were "defeated" by the miners (Rose 1936:26-28). In speaking of the composition of the mining camp during this encounter, Rose (1936:26) states that "there was (sic) about thirty men in camp, sixteen whites and the rest Papagoes." Thus, at this point, there were about fourteen Papago males working for the company. These Papagos apparently maintained their homes in "rancherias" near the mine, according to Rose (1936:23), but it is uncertain just where these were located, or if the Indian miners continued living in them after the mining operation was shut down in 1856.[4]

By 1855 one of the early pioneers at the mine reported that there were about "a hundred peons, most of them Indians from Sonora tribes" working for the "American" (i.e., Anglo) miners (Therrien 1945:35). Probably many of these were Papagos, but this is not certain.

Skilled labor was brought in, roads were opened, and water tanks, buildings, mills and furnaces were built during the 1855-56 period as much money poured into Ajo from San Francisco (Therrien 1945:38). However, by the end of 1856 (1859, according to Rose), the operation was abandoned, due most likely to a combination of factors (Therrien 1945:39; Rose 1936:25). Among these were listed such difficulties as, "the isolated position of the mine", "the distance from a source of supplies", "the slow, laborious method of producing the ore", "the uncertainty of its reaching the smelting plant at Swansea (Wales)", "the long waiting for returns", "a scarcity of water" and "poor administration."

Therrien (1945:41) in further discussing this failure of the first American venture at Ajo describes an additional crucial factor missing in the total systemic network present in Ajo at that time when she remarks that:

> These early residents of Ajo were not interested in establishing a town; their chief ambition was to get as much ore as possible from the mines and convert it into cash. Had they realized the extent of the deposits, doubtless they would have planned for better and more permanent living conditions. The community was not made up of families, but largely of men who came alone or in groups, prospected for a time, became discouraged or restless, and left.

(The importance of this factor was not lost on later mine officials when they created their version of Ajo built around the family man, which has weathered several serious crisis situations since its creation without any general systemic collapse occurring.)

Shortly after this first American failure, an English corporation tried to reopen the mine using Mexican miners (Therrien 1945:41-42). However the neighboring Indians became hostile and the price of copper fell. Also the Civil War prompted the withdrawal of military protection from Arizona. These new difficulties combined with the old led first to a slackening of operations and then to complete closure in 1870 (Therrien 1945:42-43).

A few years later in 1872, a man from Gila Bend tried to build a smelter at Ajo but failed so it was not until April, 1878 that the mines were reopened with a workforce of eight which was expanded to twelve by May of that year (Therrien 1945:43). However in spite of the presence of large quantities of rich ore, the various claims were worked only on a sporadic basis and changed hands frequently in the next few years until 1884 when Tom Childs appeared on the scene.

It was fortunate for Childs that in 1879, just a few years prior to his arrival, a very crucial event in the history of the area had occurred--the Southern Pacific Railroad had finally been finished as far west as Yuma (Rose 1936:33). This meant that the Ajo claims were only 45 miles over "good road" from the railroad station at Gila Bend, thus making almost certain for the first time in Ajo's history, the marketing of the high grade ores at a profit (Therrien 1945:44-45).

When Tom Childs, Sr., and his son together with W. M. Jacobs arrived to inspect the Ajo mining property in 1884 they reported that "not a soul was in camp" (Rose 1936:43). However in contrast to those who had come before, Childs and his son had a dual purpose in coming to the Ajo area. Thus, Tom Childs, Jr. is recorded as having said (Vanvalkenburgh 1945:4):

> It was after Mother died that Father and I moved down here. He had wandered by here in 1850 while looking for the copper deposits that the Mexicans in Sonora had told him about. We came down here to get a start in the cattle business. But neither of us ever got very far away from mining. We were always looking for a good prospect.

Therefore, although times were often very rough for these men during the next 28 years, by not relying entirely upon income from the sale of copper ore for daily sustenance, they were able to retain ownership of their claims until they finally sold out their interests to the Calumet and Arizona Mining Company in 1912 for $100,000, cash. (Brady 1941; Vanvalkenburgh 1945:5). Tom Childs and his son were also apparently quite successful at raising cattle as the following story illustrates (Weekly Phoenix Herald, December 18, 1890, 4:2):

Uncle Tom Childs, at Ajo Copper Mines fifty miles south of Gila Bend, is a typical pioneer.

Two or three years ago a partner sold most of the fat beeves the firm had grazing about Ajo and left Uncle Tom in the lurch. Uncomplainingly that weatherbeaten old man gathered together his few remaining head of cattle and began once more to raise a new herd. He has about 100 sleek kine again, and seems contented.

Also benefiting from this new subsistence strategy were the nearby Papagos whom these partners and a man named Rube Daniels incorporated into this new mine-labor, cattle-raising system, first as workmen and their families but later through marriage ties as actual kinsmen. Thus Therrien (1945:47) reports that:

> Tom Childs and Rube Daniels were leaders of the group. They tried to set a good example by pasturing cattle among the mesquite to help feed the families of their Papago workmen....

And Tom Childs, Jr., adds that:

> It was about this time that I began to take an interest in our Papago neighbors. Then I married one of their girls. Not counting the adopted children, I now have 13 living children and 35 grandchildren. While at times I have lived at Quitovaquita and Bates Well down near the border, I have always called this place on Ten-Mile Wash, home.[5] (Vanvalkenburgh 1945:5).

This last passage indicates yet another subsistence strategy introduced into the original system. Thus, in times of trouble Tom Childs, Jr. could, through his kinship ties, now share in the resources of his newly acquired kinsmen in the nearby villages in obtaining daily sustenance. And, even after Tom became wealthy enough that he no longer needed to fear the lack of "daily bread" he apparently perceived an advantage in continuing this relationship since Brady (1941) in speaking about Tom Childs, Sr., records that:

> His son Tom, who was born in Arizona and raised at Ajo, sold the claims to the Calumet and Arizona Mining Company for $100,000 cash. Tom had married a Papago Indian girl and they had a lot of children. Everyone predicted, after he got his money, that he would leave her but he stuck. He is an easy going sort of man and his wife is really a fine woman.

Many of the descendants of this union are still living in Ajo. but having no direct ties to the present Papago reservations, these so-called "Sand" people form a very distinct population among the Ajo Indians. Since these people have had no reservation to return to in times of distress, they have through the years been the most permanent of the Indian populations in Ajo. Tom's Papago wife, as stated earlier, was supposedly a descendent of the "Sand" people. Members of this racially mixed group are even today not considered to be "true" Papago Indians (e.g., see F.N. October 30, 1967) by many local Indians originally from the area of the main Papago reservation. And many "Sand" people have now joined the Assembly of God Church in the Indian Village (and one family, the integrated Mormon Church), which further tends to isolate them from other Ajo Indians. The 1967-68 high crime rate among many young members of this group was probably at least in part the indirect result of this rejection by both the Indian as well as the white communities in Ajo. Thus, it is somewhat ironic that the oldest residents of Ajo, in terms of ancestry in the immediate area, were in 1967-68 without a doubt the most marginal of all the ethnic groups there in terms of social acceptance.

Daniels, also, as stated earlier, married a Papago woman and was reported by Clotts (1915a:l) as living with her and four children at Bates Well in Growler Pass (14 miles south of Ajo) in the year 1914. Thus both Childs and Daniels through the creation of this type of control mechanism were better equipped to continue to remain in the Ajo region despite the constant fluctuations in the highly unpredictable copper market that had driven many miners before them out of the region.

The period between 1884 and 1911 was an interesting one complete with all the local color that made the West famous. Tom Childs, Jr. apparently at one time also became interested in Mexican girls as well as Papago ones, as is related in the following incident that took place in 1901 (Arizona Daily Citizen February 1, 1901, 4:2):

> A young man from Ajo Mining Camp, south of Gila Bend, brought the news of a killing at the camp several days ago. It appears that Thomas Childs, Jr., and a Mexican by the name of Miguel Lasado had become enemies through their mutual regard for a Mexican girl. They met in the store of a man named John Hovey and began shooting at each other. The result was a funeral in which Lasado played the leading part. No further particulars of the trouble were learned, but from the fact that Childs was not arrested it is presumed that public sentiment justified his conduct.

Mining during this period continued to be done on a sporadic basis although much money was poured into several fantastic schemes that involved much fraudulent activity (Rose 1936:45-50; Therrien 1945:49-71; Leonard 1954:10-14). Tom Childs, Jr. gives the briefest summary of the period by stating simply that (Van Valkenburgh 1945:5):

> We located our first mines at Ajo in 1887. At first we were in partnership with the Shotwell-Calado company,

but their money soon gave out. After another try with the St. Louis Copper company we decided to handle it ourselves. We made some money that way. In 1912 we sold out our holdings to the Calumet and Arizona company.

There are several brief statements about the ethnic composition of the Ajo camp during this period that are quite interesting. For example, Therrien(1945:48) reports that in 1894:

> What few people were there lived in tents or rude shacks built of rock and clay. With the future of the mine so uncertain there was no incentive for building permanently. ... The few women residents were wives of Mexican and Indian laborers... ...herds of horses supposedly owned by Indians ran wild...

And in 1900 she (1945:57-58) states that:

> The camp (Ajo) consisted of only a few men, mostly Mexicans and Papagos, who worked for Shotwell. There was a small grocery store owned by Colonel Hovey who was somewhat of a boss in that section. Through him miners employed laborers under contract at so much a day in currency while Hovey settled with the laborers in groceries and whiskey.[6]

Here, several control mechanisms are obviously at work (See Figure 1). Hovey and his store represent a system that is attempting to manipulate the output of two other categories of systems so that an essential system variable (i.e., net income) will not fall below a certain lower critical limit. One of the key controlling mechanisms that Hovey was able to use most effectively was his knowledge of Papago and Spanish as well as English (A.C.N. July 4, 1919:1). This apparently was the most important factor in maintaining Col. Hovey's position as a middleman between the miners and their Mexican and Indian laborers, thus preventing a system transformation in which the miners might be tempted to pay the native workers directly. However, the extension of store credit to each common laborer would also be an important additional control mechanism in maintaining Hovey's structural position. By supplying a certain amount of whiskey and groceries (i.e., controlled system inputs) to the Mexican and Papago laborers if they would work a certain number of hours (i.e., a controlled system output) for the miners, Hovey hoped to obtain a certain controlled system input (i.e., money) from the miners.

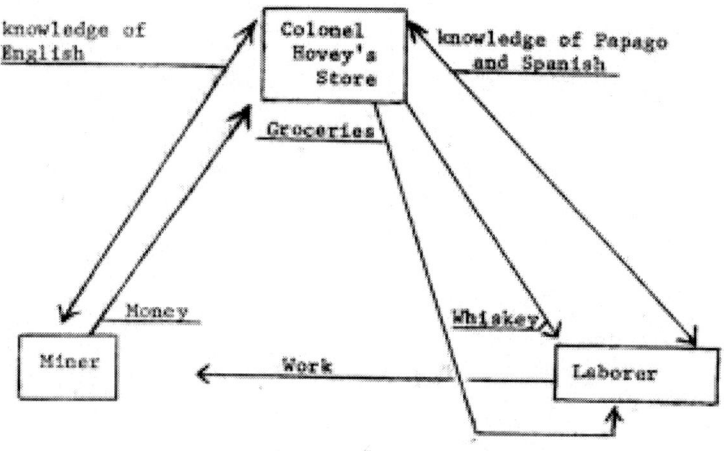

Colonel Hovey's Store

Although one might argue that this systems-model is really equivalent to one in which the miner would pay the laborer directly for his work and in turn the laborer would then spend his money on whiskey and groceries at Colonel Hovey's store, this is not necessarily so. The laborer when he received his money might not spend it all at Colonel Hovey's store. Instead he might buy whiskey from a Mexican peddler and meat from a local rancher or competing store. The laborer might even decide that he wants to save some of his money to spend at some later time and place. Therefore it is easy to see why Colonel Hovey preferred the previous arrangement better than one in which he would actively have had to compete for the laborer's dollars.

In 1907 when Sam Clark, the founder of Clarkston, first arrived in Ajo, he found only three white men in the camp, "the rest being Mexicans and Papago Indians" (A.C.N. October 5, 1933:4), but a few years later the census of 1910 lists Ajo as having a population of fifty consisting of "twelve or fifteen Americans, and a larger number of Mexicans and Indians" (Therrien 1945:77-78). However, the 1909-10 economic boom soon cooled down to the point where the mining of copper was no longer profitable, thus ending, temporarily, the life of the mining operations at Ajo (Waddell 1969:53). Lumholtz(1912:336), visiting the camp at the end of this boom, probably in late May or early June of 1910, speaks of Ajo as being "the name of an apparently great copper mine, on which work had been temporarily abandoned" but fails to mention how many people were still living near the mine at that time. However, Barnes (1960:257) confirms the census figure of fifty, and seems to indicate that the people enumerated during the census were merely those individuals who had survived the collapse of the mining operation and had remained in Ajo, when he states that:

> In 1910 the population - including Mexicans, Indians and American citizens - was fifty people. The main business among these people was grazing cattle. Lack of water was a serious problem and poverty rampant.

By 1911, the year Greenway first arrived in Ajo, an early pioneer records that "of the twenty five people living here, only eight were white" (Ekman 1926:5).[7] By this time most of the extremely rich ore had been taken from the Ajo claims leaving mainly one or two percent ore behind (Leonard 1954:ll).[8] However, as stated earlier, the new method of open pit mining developed in Utah plus the new leaching process developed by Ricketts, brought new money and life into the Ajo mines just a few years later and by 1916 a full scale development program for the Ajo mine had been begun.

A teenager, in describing her first impression of Ajo in 1916 states that(Ekman 1926:5):

> ...All people lived in tents then. There were only two places then that really looked like houses....There seemed to be only Chinese, Mexicans and Papagoes everywhere....I was the second white girl living here, the other one was older than I. For a school building there were only two small tents...

Between January and June of 1916, the population of the popular new townsite of Clarkston rose from 6 to about 500 people (A.C.N. June 24, 1916:4). With this rapid increase in population came an important shift in the ethnic balance of the work force at the mine. Seventy-five "American" families now lived in Clarkston, as opposed to only fifty-eight Mexican families.[9]

Clotts (1915b:25,32), as previously stated, in 1914 locates what he calls "Ajo Indian Village" or "Moivajea" ("Soft Well")[10], 43 miles southwest of Gila Bend and 70 miles northwest of Indian Oasis (Sells). He (1915b:94) also locates the Ajo Mine at the exact same location, indicating that the Indian village was in close proximity to the mine.

The Indian village in 1914 is described by him as having 5 houses, 29 people, 1 well, 4 horses but no charcos, corrals, fields, or cattle. Furthermore, Clotts states that "some of the men (living in the village) work at the mine." In his figures for the mining camp of Ajo he lists a post office, 4 stores, a school and about 90 houses with a population of 150 of whom about 50 are employed "about the mine". However, it is not clear whether or not these latter figures include the Indian village which was physically separate from the remainder of the old camp.

Clotts(1915b:41), also in 1914, locates Tom Childs, his Papago wife and 4 children at Childs Ranch, 6 miles east of Ajo in the Ajo Valley "6 miles north of the divide." At this site were "62 acres of fields," and "two buildings, a well and a wind pump." And as stated earlier (Clotts 1915a:l) in 1914, Daniels with his Papago wife and 4 children lived 14 miles south of Ajo, at Bates Well.

Also, apparently in two other nearby locations lived Papagos at least some of whom were probably related to Tom Childs' wife. These were the sites of Batamote "10 miles north of Ajo) and Quitovaquito "19 miles south of Bates Well" and "just north of Mexican line." Clotts (1915a:l), in discussing these locations, records that "there are a few families at Batamote" and that at Quitovaquito there were "4 families" who:

> ...represent the remnants of about 150 families of Arenenos or sand Papagoes, who used to inhabit the country farther west toward Yuma in the sand dunes, and were devastated by some disease about 40 years ago, the survivors moving to Quitovaquito.

Clotts(1915b:37) also describes in greater detail the site of Batamote or "Childs Well" by stating that yet another white man, John Merrill, was living there. He also had "an Indian wife and 4 children" as well as one well, a house, one corral, and 30 head of cattle (Clotts 1915b:25). Quitovaquito is listed as having a total population of 25 with a reservoir, 8 acres of fields, 50 head of cattle and 8 horses (Clotts 1915b:27). Three small springs provided water for the small lake and the fields which lay mostly in Mexico. Seven miles north of here, near a well dug by Capriano

Ortega, were "5 wickings" where the Quitovaquito Indians also lived part of the time.

From this small beginning, the Indian population of the Ajo area grew until in the late 1930's, a level of 800 to 900 Papagos was reached (Waddell 1969:54). However, the Ajo Indian was often so totally ignored in such local news sources as the Ajo Copper News that it is almost impossible to document accurately the periods of growth and decline of the Indian population through the time interval from 1914 to 1936. Waddell (1969:54) on the basis of an interview with the local Phelps Dodge employment agent even describes a period when "the Indian community must have been abandoned." However on the basis of other evidence to be presented shortly the validity of this assumption is highly questionable.

Tom Childs, on the other hand) is easy to trace through the years. In May of 1916 he is listed as being one of the members of the local school board (A.C.N. May 6, 1916:4). Also in May of that year an ad appeared in the local newspaper advertising Childs Market and Cold Storage in the Ajo camp (A.C.N. May 27, 1916:8). And by September, Childs had opened up a second store in Clarkston as a branch of Childs Market and Cold Storage (A.C.N. September 23, 1916:7).

Near the end of 1916 the number of miners had grown to about 1200 men[11] (A.C.N. November 25, 1916:1) and the continued prosperity of the camp seemed to be assured. Among these new workers were apparently enough Indians to attract a full time missionary effort by the Presbyterian Church for an extended period of at least "several months" and probably longer (A.C.N. October 7, 1916:6).

However, late in the same year (1916), union organizers fomented labor strife at the mine which culminated in a strike of brief duration (A.C.N. November 25, 1916:1; January 20, 1917:1). The main issue used by the organizers to stir up the miners against the Company was the fact that although the price of copper had risen recently from 22¢/lb. to over 30¢/lb. there had been no corresponding increase in wages to meet the rapidly rising cost of living (A.C.N: November 25, 1916:1). Company resistance to such an increase was probably based on the general belief that the high price of copper was just a temporary phenomenon and that when the European war ended the price would probably decline rapidly (A.C.N. December 2, 1916:1).

Initially, about 1130 of 1200 men were out on strike including both "organized and unorganized labor" (A.C.N. November 25, 1916:1). Apparently, the unions were preparing for a long battle since it was reported on November 25th that, "if the strike continues, an eating house for the strikers will, it is expected, be provided." (A.C.N. November 25, 1916:1) and on the 9th of December that (A.C.N. December 9, 1916:1):

> The strikers are prepared to continue the strike indefinitely, it is said, since the reported coming now of financial help from out of town. They have a complete system, including picketing, parades, benefits, and relief. The men receive two meals a day and there are daily baskets for the families.

Although the declared motto of the strikers was "no violence, and no drinking" (A.C.N. November 25, 1916:1) apparently some management personnel felt that the "sinister" "Industrial Workers of the World" (I.W.W.) organization somehow lay behind the series of walkouts now beginning to plague the western mining camps (A.C.N. July 6, 1917:1; Cox 1938:175-176). This organization was alleged to be composed of members who were "anarchistic pacifists who had in mind a conspiracy to overthrow the government of the United States and to bring about a defeat of the United States in the World War ..." (Cox 1938:176).

However in contrast to the infamous Bisbee strike that began a half year later there was remarkably little violence at Ajo during the entire strike period. In fact, it was reported by the Ajo Copper News (Jan. 27, 1917:2) that both Capt. John Greenway, the C. & A. general manager, and Supt. Curly "mingled freely with the strikers, talking, laughing and joking with them as never before heard of in a strike in Arizona or elsewhere."

Apparently this management technique was quite successful, especially with the "American" miners since less than a month after this method had first been attempted in Ajo, it was reported that the strike was almost over with 626 men again working and only about 200 strikers remaining out on strike - three-fourths of whom were Mexican (A.C.N. December 16, 1916:1). Also, the Ajo Copper News (January 27, 1917:2) reported that no drastic measures such as the importation of outside workmen, the hiring of a lawyer, evictions from rooms, houses or apartments, or the arrest of strikers were apparently tried by the company during the strike although the paper earlier had stated (A.C.N. December 9, 1916:1) that during the height of the strike the company had been hiring "additional" men, thus casting some doubt on these later assertions to the contrary.

By January 20, 1917, over 1,000 men were back at work at the mine and the Western Federation of Miners had finally called off its strike although the union organizers said that one of their officials would stay around to supervise the "free soup" that was to be "dispensed for several days in order that the strikers left here may have a chance to shift for themselves..." (A.C.N. January 20, 1917).

It is interesting to note that at this early date, it was the unions, not the company, who took the responsibility for feeding the men out on strike, thus easing the economic stress on the individual worker that might otherwise tempt him to return to work on company, not union, terms. Perhaps one could speculate that the very control mechanisms employed by the company only a few years later in response to an entirely different type of environmental crisis, would, when utilized again in 1967, actually help prolong a strike unintentionally. This was, however, not true of those control mechanisms activated by the company during this initial strike in Ajo.

One of these early control mechanisms has already been mentioned, i.e., the hiring of "additional" men. Although not in name hired to replace those out on strike, these men were undoubtedly considered to be "scabs" (strikebreakers) by those workers still out on strike.

Also it is very likely that one of the most effective of these early company attempts to control the strikers[12] in Ajo was the appeal to each worker's "patriotism" made by Greenway, Curley and others. After all, this was wartime and the U.S. was on the verge of entering the fracas. It is interesting to compare the use of this particular control mechanism at Ajo with its use at Bisbee about six months later in another attempt to end a strike.

The Bisbee strike also began peacefully, even though an investigation of the situation by a regular army officer was requested by local and state officials. Still, after carefully surveying the troubled area, this officer reported to the governor of Arizona that "troops were neither needed nor warranted under existing conditions." (Cox 1938:178). Therefore, as in Ajo earlier, a peaceful settlement of the dispute seemed assured. However, one key variable had changed in the 6-month period between the Ajo and Bisbee strikes, the U.S.A. had formally declared war on Germany and its allies (Cox 1938:173) and in the following pages the drastic effects of this altered variable upon the sequence of events that occurred in Bisbee at this time, will be shown.

The initial demands of the strikers in Bisbee were listed by Cox (1938:174-175) as being:

...abolition of a regular physical examination, to which every man was obliged to submit before obtaining a job and which they claimed had been used as a basis of blacklist; two men on all machines, a custom which the strikers claimed was the practice in most mining districts; abolition of blasting during working shifts; abolition of all bonus and contract work; abolition of the sliding scale of wages and the substitution of a flat minimum wage of $6 per shift underground and $5.50 per shift above ground; and no discrimination against members of labor organizations.

It is interesting that Cox (1938:174-175) also states that:

$6 had no more purchasing power at that time than $3.50 had when miners received that sum and copper was selling at fourteen and fifteen cents a pound. In 1917, the price of copper was twice that amount.

Greenway (Cox 1938:174) responded to these demands by commenting that "Bisbee was the highest paid mining camp in the world." He and the other company officials represented at Bisbee refused to grant any of the miners' demands by claiming that they were "inimical to good government in time of peace, and treasonable in time of war" (Cox 1938:175).

It was soon being rumored that "the strikers had brought in weapons and dynamite and intended to destroy the mines" and that "the majority of the strikers seemed foreign; and the whole thing appeared pro-German and anti-American" (Cox 1938:177).

Finally at a meeting of concerned "citizens" on the night of July 11, 1917, plans for the infamous Bisbee deportation were formally decided upon (Cox 1938:179). One of the first to address the "citizens" was an important official of the Copper Queen Branch of the Phelps

Dodge Corporation, who denounced the strikers in the western mining camps as being of "pro-German origin" and advised that the strikers be deported by force if necessary as a "patriotic remedy" (Cox 1938:179). Later, Greenway, who was then a reserve officer in the U. S. Army, gave the impression to the people present at the meeting that the deportation would be carried out with the full knowledge and consent of the United States Government (Bruere 1918:203). However, in reality, to avoid possible government interference, nothing concerning the planned deportation had ever been told "to the officers of the United States Army who were stationed near Bisbee, to the United States Attorney in Arizona, or to the officers of the state or county" (Cox 1938:180) with the exception of the local sheriff, who was also a leader in the planned conspiracy.

Probably most of the "citizens" present at this secret meeting were members of the "Miners' Loyalty League." Almost 1,600 miners had joined this anti-I.W.W. organization and on the 4th of July they had staged a gigantic parade down the streets of Bisbee, each man carrying an American flag (A.C.N. July 6, 1917:1). The local chapter of I.W.W. had urged the miners to stay away from the parade route, but apparently this advice was not heeded by all of the I.W.W. sympathizers, since the Ajo Copper News reported that.

> When a spectator made slurring remarks about the flag, half a dozen miners and citizens attacked him. He was removed to a hospital when officers got him out of the crowd which quickly gathered. Another was compelled to kneel and kiss the flag. (A.C.N. July 6, 1917:1):

Thus, the mining companies had apparently rather cleverly twisted the perceived major issue behind the strike from the basic economic dissatisfaction of the miners in a period of inflation to a question of whether or not one was loyal to the U. S. government in time of warfare. The economic woes of the laborer could therefore be dismissed as being a necessary sacrifice for one's country.

Striking quickly the next morning before news of the secret meeting could leak out, the local sheriff with 2,000 newly deputized "citizens" (i.e., largely company officers and the loyal employees of the "League") overpowered 1,186 strikers and their alleged sympathizers and corralled them in the ball park in Warren about three miles away from Bisbee (Cox 1938:182-183). People were forcibly taken from their homes and from the streets. Only those men who agreed to tie a white handkerchief on their arms and join the mob were spared. Even many prominent townspeople who had taken no part in the strike were not spared unless they agreed to join in the mob action (Cox 1938:183). To suppress the news of what had happened, one mob leader tried to use his reserve officer's title to cut off all communication between Bisbee and the outside world (Cox 1938:181-182). He successfully seized by force of arms the local Western Union Telegraph office and prevented the dispatch of an Associated Press bulletin about the mob action. However, he failed in his attempt to force the manager of the local Bell Telephone Company to obey him, since the manager knew that this man was not a regular army officer.

The rounded-up "traitors", "under the muzzles of rifles, revolvers and machine guns" were loaded into a train of cattle and box cars provided especially for the occasion by the El Paso and Southwestern Railroad[13] (Cox 1938:183). Those responsible for the deportation attempted to take the captives to Columbus, New Mexico, but when the Columbus authorities refused to accept the prisoners, the guards took them to the nearby desert town of Hermanas, where they released the men under threat of great bodily harm, or even death, should they ever return to Bisbee (Cox 1938:183-184). After they had been left without "adequate food, water, and shelter for three days" (Cox 1938:184) the deported men were taken by the U. S. Government to the stockades in Columbus built for Mexican refugees during border raids. Here the Government fed and housed the men until the middle of September (Cox 1938:184).

Both the state and federal governments hesitated to act for a period of almost two months after this monstrous deed had been performed (Cox 1938:185). In the meantime Bisbee was governed by a "kangaroo court" which forcibly deported many additional men and threw others in prison or forced them to work on the convict road repairing gang (Cox 1938:185). Although "order" had been finally restored to this "chaotic" situation, the perpetrators of this, by now, infamous deportation were never convicted of having committed any crime, although several state and federal trials were held (Cox 1938:187-190).

In the above paragraph, the words "order" and "chaotic" were put in quotation marks, since, after the deportation, the situation at Bisbee was only disordered (i.e., incapable of being controlled) from the point of view of state and federal officials and the deported or imprisoned men. However, the copper companies themselves probably felt that a higher state of order now existed in their local universe after the deportation had occurred. In terms of the theory presented in the last chapter, chaos resulting from the strike situation was the "hostile" control vector (as viewed by the company officers) threatening to drive certain essential system variables beyond their critical limits. The control mechanism utilized (i.e., deportation) succeeded in restoring order in the system's immediate environment (i.e., the remaining workers were again mining and processing copper ore), but there was a net gain in structural entropy since the larger system (i.e., companies plus workers) was now reduced in size.

Probably to escape the "heat" from the growing scandal, several of the important company officials including Greenway chose as a personal control mechanism, volunteering for active duty in the armed forces[14] (A.C.N. October 12, 1917:1; Cox 1938:188). However, for the reader of the Ajo Copper News, Greenway's decision to join the war effort was presented as being motivated purely by his patriotic love for his country and his desire to lead our boys to victory.

Just before the 4th of July, 1917, when the labor trouble in Bisbee threatened to spill over into Ajo, two very important Anti-I.W.W. organizations were created in Ajo (A.C.N. July 6, 1917:1). The first of these was called the "Property Holders Protective Association of the Ajo Mining District" and included mainly mine officials and local business men in its membership. The second was known as the "Workmen's Loyalty League" and included as members mostly company employees. The members of this "League" promised under oath to "support the Government of the United States to the protection of men in this district who desire to work and to the protection of their homes from any unlawful acts". Here again, the worker was urged to forget about his falling standard of living but instead "work for and fight for" his country and the "rights" (i.e., right to work) and "homes" of his fellow workers - the villain, of course, being the "seditious" I.W.W. organization. To further mask the real intent of the "League", the secretary of the group stated that "the movement is decidedly not against unionism, but ... it is opposed to disloyalty and to anything savoring of lack of patriotism, and is opposed to action by a small minority[15] that would bind the majority in that which they did not desire" (A.C.N. July 6, 1917:1).

In contrast to Bisbee, labor trouble at this point in time in Ajo was thoroughly suppressed by the group social pressure thus generated rather than by physical violence.[16] Both of these newly formed organizations created in Ajo to avoid a repetition of the trouble that had developed in Bisbee had thus proven their effectiveness as control mechanisms.

However, as mentioned earlier, certain other mechanisms for the control of the Ajo worker were in the process of development by the company even before the Ajo and Bisbee strikes began. These strikes had merely helped speed up the development of these control devices. Furthermore, not only had the strike in Ajo helped strengthen the control of the company over the lives of its workers in the manner already discussed, but it had also eliminated the only major rival employer of men in Ajo, the Ajo Consolidated Mining Company, which had suspended development work because of the strike and had never resumed operations again (A.C.N. December 2, 1916:1). Thus, men wanting to remain in Ajo had little in the way of choice of employers anymore, the choice in most cases now being either to work for the company or to leave town.

This control was further strengthened when a short time after the Ajo strike had ended, the company announced that the American and Mexican sections of the new, planned town of Cornelia would soon be opened "to provide a suitable and healthy location to accommodate its employees..." (A.C.N. February 17, 1917:1). As stated earlier, the creation of the tightly regulated company town had already been proven in the past to be a most effective control technique.

Also, a letter to M. Curley dated June 13, 1917 in both English and Spanish versions authorizing the creation of a cooperative, rebate giving, company store (A.C.N. July 6, 1917:6) was another important step in achieving the level of control over the workers' lives desired by the company officials. The rate of the annual store rebate was often higher than the average profit on total sales throughout the year, but this was usually offset by the fact that many of the store's customers were not eligible for the rebate since only full time employees who had worked at least the preceding four month period for the company were eligible to receive the payment (A.C.N. October 21, 1922:4; Johnson n.d.:21-

22). However, in 1921 a $7^1/_2$ per cent rebate was given, despite the fact that the store had lost money during the preceding twelve month period (A.C.N. December 3, 1921:1), thus proving that the primary purpose of the store was in its power of control over the lives of the mine workers and their families rather than in its ability to feed profits directly back into company coffers.

One important additional control mechanism should be mentioned at this point, the Ajo Copper News. This local paper, although not an official company paper, has always mirrored the official company line.[17] Thus, during the brief winter strike of 1916-17, Greenway and Curley were said to have "(met) and mingle(d) with the strikers with good feelings on both sides, because they are upright men who have nothing to keep back and are frank" (A.C.N. December 23, 1916:2). Later after the labor troubles began to develop in Bisbee, several vicious attacks on the I.W.W. were launched by the paper in which the I.W.W. was described as being disloyal to the United States Government and possibly connected to the German war effort (A.C.N. July 22, 1917:4; September 21, 1917:8). Therefore, anyone wishing to know what the official company position was on any controversial matter merely had to read the weekly editorial or front-page story. Furthermore, although there were other sources of news available to Ajoites such as an outside newspaper or local gossip, most townspeople probably did not dare question the official line, at least not in public where it might reach the ears of a company official.

Thus, on September 21, 1917 (A.C.N. pg. 8) was printed one of the most important editorials ever to appear in the Ajo Copper News. Obviously top company officials had been deeply disturbed by what had transpired in the previous months at Bisbee. After discussing the "traitorous" nature of the I.W.W. labor organization, the members of which are "in reality Socialists who believe in direct action rather than political and educational efforts to win," the editorial goes on to state:

And why are they? Surely something is wrong. We do not have at hand figures as to their nationality. Probably a majority of them are foreign born.[18]

The trouble is, such men have no conscience. A conscience must be developed and fed. Almost the complete answer, then, is in three words. Home, school, church. To cure I.W.W.'ism you must have all three - HOME, SCHOOL, CHURCH. One day, every day; year in and year out - a child must be taught the right from the wrong. A good home is of course the principal thing, but it isn't enough, as we see. If all homes and all schools were ideal there would not be so many I.W.W.'s, but there would still be some. Religion furnishes an incentive, an ideal, material help in uprightness. You'll find it out some day if you won't admit it now. Every president this nation has ever had admits it. That churches are for women and children only is a fallacy and an expensive one.

With education comes a help and a stimulation for industry. The industrious boy never becomes an I.W.W.; it is the idle. Teach the boys to try, all of them, to reach the top; to master a calling and so to be worth more money to their employers.

Another thing: You notice very few Industrial Workers of the World have families - as a rule they do not, as we have said, believe in marriage.[19] There are too many single men.

This problem should receive attention, particularly in the West. There should be more gatherings where worthy young men and good girls can meet and mingle, and in general, a systematic plan should be formulated and worked out. The subject is receiving attention already in the larger cities and towns. Our churches and higher institutions of learning can be of greater help along this line...."

Therefore, it is not too surprising that from this time forward the company has pursued with increased vigor, policies designed to strengthen the "HOME", "SCHOOL" and "CHURCH". Not only have large amounts of money been donated toward implementing these policies, but also much time and personal effort has been expended by local company officials in voluntary community service.

Typical of this intensification of effort toward the strengthening of these three basic institutions was the insertion of an additional ritual event, a public Christmas ceremony, into the yearly community holiday cycle. (The Fourth of July celebration had already been established as an officially sponsored annual community event early in the history of the company's development of Ajo.[20] (A.C.N. July 1, 1916:1; July 7, 1916:1). Therefore, on November 2, 1917 (A.C.N. Pg.4) it was announced that:

> Superintendent Curley is arranging to have a District Christmas Tree in the park Christmas eve. The tree will come from Williams ... and will be a fine large one, bearing presents for all the children.
> To the project of having a masquerade dance, and possibly a carnival on New Year's eve Superintendent Curley is also lending his aid.

Thus was born the annual Christmas ritual which survives in a much elaborated form to this very day.[21]

Christmas was the ideal holiday from the company's standpoint to add to the official ritual calendar. What other holiday fuses so perfectly the ideals of "HOME", "SCHOOL", and "CHURCH": To further insure that this would be a major yearly "rite of intensification", the annual rebate payment date on purchases made at the company store was set for December 20, just five days prior to the holiday. Also, in spite of the initial suggestion by Curley to include New Year's Eve in this officially sponsored annual, end of the year ritual event, Christmas has always received the major emphasis in company planning. Christmas because of its religious overtones and emphasis on love, friendship, the home, and children is a much better symbol of the ideals that the company officials have always been trying to foster than a New Year's Eve party with its often drunken participants. Always, the thought has been that God-fearing men with happy well-fed and educated families make the best workers.

This emphasis on seeing that the families of the worker were kept well-fed and happy proved to be an extremely valuable control mechanism in stabilizing the work force and holding down the number of complaints from the individual workmen. Thus, although one of the main purposes of encouraging parents to send their children to the new Ajo public school at least through the eighth grade was so that "I.W.W.'ism" would "practically vanish" (A.C.N. October 19, 1917:5), the school itself soon began to bind the parents tightly to Ajo.

Other acts of kindness toward the children also helped strengthen the ties holding the parents to Ajo. Examples of these included the giving of gifts to the children at Christmas time and the throwing of pennies to the children by Superintendent Curley at the annual 4th of July celebration (A.C.N. July 6, 1917:1). Later, a community swimming pool was built using company funds (A.C.N. May 29, 1920:1; August 14, 1920:1) and the Boy Scout Movement was introduced by company officials (A.C.N. April 28, 1923:1).

Although racial prejudice ran high in Ajo as witnessed by the cheering that greeted the appearance of the "onrushing Ku Klux Klan" in the movie "Birth of a Nation" (A.C.N. April 12, 1918:1) and such headlines as "Chink Patriotic - Bread from 'Lice Flour'" appearing in the local paper (A.C.N. April 12, 1918:5), compliments were often given to members of the various minority groups in Ajo. Typical of these kinder remarks are those found in an editorial in the Ajo Copper News (May

23, 1919:8) describing what constitutes a "good company" and a "good camp" in which it is stated that Ajo has a "good intelligent class of people - this applies to Mexicans and Indians, as well as to whites".

Through the years the same mechanisms of control used to bind the "American" miner to Ajo were extended to the Mexican miner and usually somewhat later to the Indian miner.[22] A very interesting editorial describes vividly just what the company hoped to achieve with its fairly complete environmental control policy with respect to the Mexicans (A.C.N. October 10, 1919:5):

> As is well known by Ajo residents and all others familiar with this camp, New Cornelia treats its employees considerately, appreciatively, generously. The Americans expect this, though not all are accustomed to it. The Mexicans as a rule, do not expect it, because unaccustomed to such treatment.
>
> All are appreciative but none are more so than the Mexicans. Any kind of deference to Mexican labor - or perhaps we should say due deference to them for good service and as human beings - is not common and is deserving of more than passing notice.
>
> In the case of the Mexican, the first result of good treatment is surprise. When he sees it is not sporadic, but continued - a permanent policy - his roving disposition fades; he settles down in contentment and proceeds to make a good, loyal employee and citizen, ever ready to show his appreciation.
>
> There is a very desirable class of Mexicans in Ajo. Most of them have families; many of them have worked for New Cornelia for a long time; quite a number have bank accounts and are the possessors of Liberty Bonds. There are those who own their homes.
>
> Mexicans love music. They appreciate cleanliness. They love flowers and trees and grass, and proceed to beautify

their homes to every extent possible. ... The Mexicans are encouraged and helped by General Superintendent Curley, who proposes further to give them a chance to secure paint at cost, so that they may paint the buildings and fences, which will be the finishing touch, adding wonderfully to the result.

Cleanliness of premises is insisted upon and it has been found that the Mexicans respond fully as readily as the Americans. In the case of buildings owned by the company and rented, as well as in every other respect affecting sanitation, there are monthly visits of inspection by the Medical Department, in addition to frequent inspection of yards by the foreman in charge of that department.

In winning the respect and confidence of the Mexicans within the brief space of two and one-half years, so that they are more contented here than in any other mining camp, perhaps, in the Southwest, General Superintendent Curley and the company deserve much credit. Results are already beginning to show, and will be more apparent in the years to come.

The Mexicans were further encouraged by the company to buy or build a house of their own with construction materials being furnished by the company store on the installment plan (A.C.N. November 21, 1919:3). Ownership of a home was viewed as "one remedy for the present general unrest and dissatisfaction of American workingmen". In addition individual home ownership was viewed by the company as having the following advantages for the Mexicans (and often itself) (AC.N. November 21, 1919:3):

It saves them the useless expense of paying a monthly rent for the house they live in. It makes them take more interest in the upbuilding of the town they live in. It makes them more contented and more steady in their work. It makes them more interested in making improvements to the place, being their own property. It makes them consider the town they live in their HOME.

It is interesting that no mention is made of the Indian miners' housing during this early period. In the 1918 Papago Reservation survey (McCormick 1919:1), the population of the Ajo Indian village was only listed as being twenty-eight, or one less than Clotts (1915b:25) found there in 1914. However, other Indians were apparently living at various locations on the nearby Childs Ranch and other nearby ranches and probably also in Mexican town and the Mexican section of Clarkston (Waddell 1969:53; A.C.N. December 27, 1918:4). Still, the total number of Indians in Ajo during this early period must have remained rather small in comparison with the larger Mexican minority. Also, many of the Indians living near Ajo were in the employ of Tom Childs as "cowboys" for his thriving cattle industry and meat market or worked for other ranchers and were therefore not miners (A.C.M. December 27, 1918:4). Apparently even those Papagos who were miners were, as Indians in other mining camps of the Old West, assumed to be perfectly capable of solving their own housing problems (Allen 1966:102). This situation continued until 1936 when the company laid out the first block of ten or fifteen company-owned houses in the Indian village, although some Indians had previously been "leasing small parcels of company land for one dollar a year and building their own dwellings out of anything they could manage - tin, railroad ties, scraps of lumber, or adobe" (Waddell 1969:54).

The control mechanism of the school as a method of binding the miner to Ajo, at first, was more effective with the "American" element of the camp than with either the Mexican or Papago segment of the population. However, some Mexican parents, even in this early period, considered the school an important reason to remain in Ajo as did also some Indian families whose children probably as early as 1919 attended a school being maintained at Childs' Ranch[23] (A.C.N. April 25, 1919:3).

In January, 1921, the Ajo Copper News (January 1, 1921:5) reported that "of the school attendance here 62 per cent are Mexicans, which includes the Indians and mixed bloods" (the total enrollment then was 447 pupils) and although by Match of that year a serious depression in the copper industry had already resulted in the laying off of large numbers of men in Ajo, the Ajo Copper News (March 5, 1921:1) stated that:

> The dullness of the camp (as in all other mining camps) is not reflected in any great falling off of (school) attendance. Very few families in which there were children of school age have gone away, and on the other hand several new pupils have been registered recently.

Obviously, such a control mechanism operates most effectively during the school year so that after further cuts in the work force were announced (A.C.N. April 16, 1921:1) and the summer came, some families began to migrate out of Ajo (A.C.N. June 4, 1921:1).

By that fall only 287 students were still enrolled in the school system (A.C.N. September 30, 1922:1) and probably because their fathers were the last to be laid off, the ethnic balance had shifted toward a majority of "American" (i.e., white, non-Hispanic) students.

In the middle of the next summer (1922), with the copper crisis passed, Greenway ordered Curley to resume full production at the mine (A.C.N. July 8, 1922:1) and soon it was reported that, "The Mexican force is about complete, but more white men could be used". (A.C.N. July 15, 1922:1). However, when the schools again reopened that fall, at the end of the month of September, only 312 students had enrolled (an increase of only 25 students over the previous year) (A.C.N. September

30, 1922:1) despite the fact that hundreds of miners had been added to the payroll again. Adding to this mystery was the fact that apparently many of these new miners were married with large families since on December 30th of that year (1922) gifts were given to 1,700 children as opposed to 700 the previous year (A.C.N. December 31, 1921:1; A.C.N. December 30, 1922:4). Johnson (n.d. :47-48) writing about this apparent paradox (probably later in 1927 or 1928) states concerning the ethnic makeup of this newly expanded workforce that "a considerable number of the employees of the mine are Papago Indians, very few whom are literate or at all interested in schools"[24]. Then when, average school attendance showed a rise from 243 in 1924 to 425 in 1925 and to 534 in 1926 [25], Johnson attributes the great growth in school attendance in 1925 and 1926 to "the increase in attendance of the Mexicans" adding that "few Mexicans had attended school up to this time". He further adds that among the Indians and Mexicans, "there seems to be a very rapidly growing sentiment in favor of the schools and school attendance" (Johnson n.d.:47-48). Thus by 1967 this interest on the part of the parents had increased to the point where it became one of the most important control mechanisms binding the Indian miner and, to an even greater degree, his family to Ajo during the 1967-68 prolonged copper strike.

An unknown variable in this discussion is the extent to which the slowly developing pattern of racial segregation in the school system affected the attitude of the Mexican and Indian parents toward the education of their children. Initially, the "American" and the Mexican children were separated only in the first grade and then probably only because of the difficulty the incoming Spanish-speaking children had with the English language (A.C.N. November 23, 1917:3). In fact, one older Mexican lady who could speak English and who had attended school during this early period remarked that she was always in a racially "mixed class" including "even a Negro"[26] during her years as a student in Ajo (L.I. 47). However, by 1925, a rigid pattern of racial segregation in the local school system was developing that apparently was based upon more than just language difficulties (A.C.N. November 7, 1925:3; A.C.N. November 14, 1925:3; A.C.M. December 12, 1925:6). At first only the lowest grades were segregated, but by 1925 fairly rigid segregation extended through the fourth grade (A.C.N. December 12, 1925:6) and by 1928, a special sixth grade class was created for the Mexican children (A.C.N. September 22, 1928:1). According to the Ajo Copper News (September 22, 1928:1) such a class was not "necessary" before since so few Mexican children in the history of the school" had ever advanced so far. In discussing this event, the school superintendent explained that "where formerly it took a Mexican child three years to complete the first grade work, the new methods of teaching are so efficient that the Mexican child is now able to move forward and enter the higher grades much younger than under the old methods" (A.C.M. September 22, 1928:1). Therefore, in 1928 there were about 100 fewer Mexican students in the lower three grades than there had been during the preceding year, due to these more rapid promotions.

In terms of the systems model presented in the last chapter, one can consider the number of Mexican students in a particular grade level (usually one classroom) as being an essential variable whose upper tolerated limit was determined by what we would today call the racist attitudes of not only the local school administration but also of company officials and most if not all other local "Americans." As this critical limit (i.e., "tipping point") was exceeded at each grade level, a segregated fission restructuring of the local school system occurred.

The number of Indian children in a particular grade level can also be viewed as being an essential variable of that "racist" subsystem. Here, too, there was an upper critical limit beyond which the Indian student was no longer treated as if he were a Mexican child but instead was placed in a separate classroom (i.e., below this critical limit Mexican and Indian children were in a sense "interchangeable"). That this critical limit was being approached in the spring of 1926 can be seen from the statement (A.C.N. May 1, 1926:1) that "to the present teaching force of twelve grade teachers and five high school teachers, the proposed plans would add four more teachers, viz., one for manual training, one for Mexican children, one for overflow, and one, possibly for Indian children."

However, according to a reliable informant (F.N. December 4, 1967), a new development occurred just a few years later which helped lower the value of one of these essential variables, the number of Indian students per grade level, to a point near zero. Apparently, sometime shortly after 1927, an Indian agent had come to town and offered to give parents of Indian children a five dollar per head payment for each child they would allow to be sent to a distant boarding school.[27] This informant told of the great bitterness her mother, who was one of the children "sold" at this time, still holds toward her grandfather, who was a white man, for this act. Many, if not most, of the school-age Papagos of Ajo were evidently deported at this time and not allowed to return to Ajo for many years. The onset of the depression probably also helped decrease the numbers of Mexican as well as Indian students in the Ajo school system during much of the 1930's, thus further reducing the role population variables associated with these two minority groups to values far below their upper critical limits. Therefore, it is not too surprising that two of the few Papago children who remained in Ajo during this period and who attended school remarked that "all students were mixed in all grades" (L.I.41; L.I.52).

After this first and apparently last major roundup of school-age Indian children to occur in Ajo, by at least September, 1938, a "special teacher" for the Indian students of Ajo was finally hired (A.C.N.

September 16, 1938:1; L.I.30)[28] as the number of Indian students per grade level finally exceeded a critical limit in some of the lower grade levels and in 1939 or 1940, one miner remembered being in an all Indian class in the second or third grade presided over by a lady who "liked to teach Indians" (L.I.31). But, he then added that after a few months he was put into a mixed class of whites and Indians, indicating that perhaps by the late 1930's segregation by race in the Ajo school system was not yet complete.[29] However, it is certain that by the beginning of World War II, the segregation by race was absolute (F.N. December 3, 1967).

Throughout most of the forties the three "races" were rigidly kept separate "up to the 6th grade" with the Indian children spending the first five grades of their school career in one classroom with each grade level occupying one row in the room (L.I. 30; L.I. 38; L.I. 50). Many bitter memories concerning this discouraging five-year period spent in one classroom filled the mind of one informant (L.I. 30) who entered the school system in about 1941. Promotion to the next grade merely meant for her and her companions a shift to the next row of seats in the same room. If the child survived this first five year period (a relatively rare occurrence), then in the sixth grade, he would be mixed with Mexican students and in the seventh grade, the few Mexican and Indian survivors would be mixed with the majority "Americans" occupying this grade level (A.C.N. September 16, 1938:1). (Using the theory presented in the last chapter, the upper critical limit for Indian students had evidently not been exceeded at this time in that subsystem associated with the sixth grade level in terms of their "equation" with the Mexican students. Apparently, also at this time, in that subsystem associated with the seventh grade level, the upper critical limit for the combined dark-skinned minority group living in Ajo had not been exceeded.

A schoolteacher who had come to Ajo in 1943 also recalled the strict segregation of races that was rigidly enforced in the schools during the war years (F. N. February 25, 1968). However, after the war ended, the brighter Mexican and Indian students in the 4th and 5th grades were gradually introduced into white classes[30] and by at least 1947 or 1948 all races were, in theory, mixed after the first grade although grouping students by ability was retained, thereby continuing a pattern of partial separation of the "American" students from the darker races[31] (L.I.28; L.I.30; L.I.35; L.I.44; L.I.48; L.I.50; F.N. December 3, 1967; F.N. February 25, 1968). Finally, in 1966 the last special first grade teacher for Indian children retired and since then all Ajo students have been mixed, at least in theory, even as early as in the first grade (L.I.30; F.N. February 25, 1968).

Several important factors seem to be involved in explaining this final collapse of the segregated school system in Ajo in the last few years in addition to the obvious drop in the number of "specially trained teachers for Indian students" from one to zero. Clearly the local school administrators felt no urgent need to replenish the supply of such "specially trained" teachers so that the final collapse of the racially segregated first grade could have been predicted much earlier. Therefore, one must look elsewhere for explanations, probably the most important of these being the increasing exposure of young Indian children to the English language in their homes via the ubiquitous T.V. set and the conversations in English of second generation Ajo Papagos. In addition, in recent years, large numbers of Ajo Indian children have begun attending a special Indian kindergarten held at the local Indian Village Catholic Church before enrolling in the first grade at either the local public or private Catholic grade school. As one miner said when asked why the Indian students no longer had a need for a special Indian-oriented first grade program, "Now they have kindergarten to take care of this." (i.e., the lack of English skills, etc.) (L.I.37).

From the above discussion it should not be inferred that the school system was a particularly conservative institution in Ajo town life. On the contrary, desegregation in the schoolroom occurred long before a partial desegregation in housing was even suggested and several important individuals have stated that both school officials and teachers have always formed the "most progressive" element of Ajo society (F.N. February 25, 1968). Apparently, Ajo school personnel, until it was no longer a popular philosophy, were merely going along with the rest of the country in practicing the separate-but-equal (at least theoretically)-- treatment-of-the-different-races doctrine.

Whether or not the Indian child in the late 60's actually received a better education in an integrated classroom can perhaps be debated, but the important fact remains that most Indian parents at that time strongly believed that their children received a better education in such a racially-mixed environment[32] (e.g., L.I. 30; L.I. 50). This belief was by this time coupled to a strong positive commitment to the value of an education in obtaining a good job, an attitude probably developed in response to the increasing shortage of jobs for the unskilled and uneducated laborer. Therefore, during the long 1967-68 copper strike, the school was equally important as a control mechanism in binding the Indian worker and his family to Ajo as it was in binding the Mexican or "American" worker and his family to the town.

In 1918 near the close of the year, a major influenza epidemic swept over Ajo apparently threatening the lives of many company employees (A.C.N. December 13, 1918:1). The local company officials responded quickly to this crisis as the following quotation from the Ajo Copper News (December 13, 1918:1) indicates:

> That many lives among the Mexicans and Indians of the camp were saved by nourishing soup served to employees and their families by the New Cornelia

Copper Company during the recent influenza epidemic, is the belief here.

The epidemic came so suddenly and in such proportions, attacking several hundred almost at once, that it found New Cornelia unprepared. But preparations were at once started to combat it and to render relief. When the situation among the Mexicans and Indians of the camp was explained to Superintendent Curley, he gave orders to secure a suitable building and a good cook and serve hot, nourishing soup to them and their families. The same day the plan was being carried out, Superintendent Curley said it was wonderful to see how rapidly the condition of these people improved. Their strength and ambition seemed to return almost instantly - they got up on their feet and took an interest in life; in fact the transformation in some cases seemed almost miraculous, those apparently almost in the grave a few moments ago, now laughing and joking, moving around, jumping about - as these happy peoples are wont to do when in good health.

Relief was rendered these and American families in other ways, a house-to-house canvass being ordered by Superintendent Curley. Bedding was furnished at some homes. The canvass disclosed the fact that some of the Mexicans are not provided with the means of getting and keeping warm as they should in winter - they are receiving good pay, but in some instances are spending money in other ways that should keep them and their children warm and better fed. The result will be, no doubt, that New Cornelia will keep a closer watch on them in their homes in the future.

In addition to the obvious suggestion that the company needs to do whatever is necessary to prevent "some of the Mexican" workers from making "unwise" personal spending decisions, especially those that affected the health of themselves and their children, the psychological and physiological effects of the flu outbreak are the "hostile" vectors, while the production and distribution of soup is the company's control vector. This "act of kindness" on the part of company officials can perhaps be viewed cynically as being merely an attempt to prevent an increase in entropy in the total system of workers plus management since the loss of workers either temporarily or permanently (i.e., in this case through death or a permanent move out of Ajo) was threatening to both systemic status set population and net income essential variables, but it is not easy to rule out other perhaps more altruistic motives also. Humans are in one sense unique systems since they often attempt to control variables in other systems, even though no clearly defined benefits to their own systems are perceived other than perhaps a psychological "boost" from the very act of being able to control these outside variables. Another way of stating this is that some humans seem to have an "innate" desire (i.e., a psychological need) to order any system within which they detect what to them appears to be disorder.

By January of 1919 the company had acquired the property of the defunct Ajo Consolidated Mining Company thus insuring that this property would never be developed by a competitor (A.C.N. January 31, 1919:1). At this point nearly everyone was optimistic about the long-range future of the mine and the camp, but ominous danger signs began appearing in February of that year when it was announced that production at New Cornelia would be cut by 40 per cent and that roughly 40 per cent of the work force would be laid off (A.C.N. February 7, 1919:1). Further gloom settled over the camp when a member of the executive board of the International Union of Mine, Mill, and Smelter Workers stated after a Washington, D.C., visit that "the copper market is dead" (A.C.N. February 28, 1919:1). Now that the war was over almost one billion pounds of copper remained unsold.

As mentioned earlier when discussing the Ajo school system, a very severe crisis developed in Ajo shortly after these announcements were first heard. By March 21 the number of men on the company payroll had been cut back to 680 men (A.C.N. March 21, 1919:1,8) and even these 680 survivors had to each accept a wage cut to remain on the job as copper production at the mine was curtailed by the announced 40 per cent. In November, there was a further 25 per cent cut in the production of copper at the mine, although nothing was mentioned about any additional layoffs, that probably occurred at this time (A.C.N. November 28, 1919:1).

In letting men go, the company pursued a predictable pattern as reported in the Ajo Copper News (March 21, 1919:1,8):

> The policy in letting out men in effecting curtailment has been first, staying preference to married men having homes here; second, preference to married men without property in the camp; and third to those single men who have been longest in the employ of the company. In employing men, preference is given, first, to soldiers who were formerly in the employ of the company; and second, to other soldiers to the extent of their qualifications and the openings for them. ...

This emphasis on the employment of soldiers before others was probably a result of the events that had earlier transpired in Bisbee and of the power that certain war veterans held in company affairs. Greenway, the most important of these men, was later that year among the founders of the powerful local chapter of the American Legion (A.C.N. July 11, 1919:5; August 29, 1919:1). However, initially, in this troubled period, many members of the Mexican, Indian, and black minority groups who were married and had built their own homes in Ajo or had in some other way given some sign of their commitment to Ajo were apparently permitted to retain their jobs in spite of the fact that large numbers of these people were not war veterans (A.C.N. May 23, 1919:8; October 10, 1919:4; November 21, 1919:3; July 3, 1920:2; April 30, 1921:1; January 1, 1921:5; January 8, 1921:5). The dilemma faced by the company and other copper producers at this time is well stated in an article in the Ajo Copper News May 23, 1919:4):

> Without a doubt many of the copper producers in the country would make money by closing down; this however, would cause great hardship among the men who have been in their employ for a long time, who have been encouraged to build their own homes, and would throw a large number of men out of employment, thus greatly disturbing the industrial situation of the country at large.
>
> With the curtailed production, it has not been possible to keep on production all of the men who have been in their employ a sufficient time to have established their homes in the community, and in some cases ... development work is being done to give these men employment, which from a financial and economic point of view, is not justified under the present conditions.
>
> The companies all over the country have agreed to curtail production in order that the world surplus may not become top heavy, and to allow for the demand to catch up to the supply.
>
> How long an organization can keep men employed upon development work and other operations merely for the purpose of giving employment to old employees and returning soldiers, is problematical; in some cases operations are being maintained where the cost of producing the copper is greater than the present selling price.
>
> The faith of the Arizona producers in the future copper market, upon which so much of the prosperity of

Arizona depends, is clearly shown by their attitude in preventing insofar as it is possible, unemployment.

In many respects, with too much unsold copper, the company was experiencing the same dilemma it again faced in 1967 at the beginning of that prolonged copper strike (i.e., the problem of maintaining the net income essential variable above a certain lower critical limit while at the same time trying to keep certain systemic status set population essential variables from also exceeding lower critical limits). In both cases, initially the company chose to protect the systemic status set population variables at the risk of increasing the danger to the net income variable. However, the major control mechanism employed by the company to achieve this goal differed greatly in the two instances. In the earlier period, new jobs in "development work and other operations" were created to provide for the basic needs of the workmen but in the 1967-68 period of crisis, the main mechanism of control employed by the company in supplying these basic necessities was the liberal extension of credit to the strikers.

An additional mechanism of control during this period aimed at eliminating the underlying danger to all of the essential variables threatened by the copper crisis is of interest in attempting to understand the decisions that were later made by the company during the 1967-68 strike period. Apparently, the company had entered into either a verbal or perhaps written agreement with the other major American copper producers and the United States Government to limit the production of copper "in order that the world surplus may not become top heavy, and to allow for the demand to catch up to the supply." This voluntary cooperation between major copper producers was also quite evident during the 1967-68 copper strike as was demonstrated in Chapter 2.

Although there were temporary small increases in the market price of copper, such as that occurring in the fall of 1919 (A.C.N. September

12, 1919:1) things progressively became worse in the Arizona copper camps during 1919, 1920 and the first half of 1921. To further add to the misery of the Ajo camp, the postwar era had been a period of inflation and on the 25th of July, the company store announced a number of drastic price increases (A.C.N. July 25, 1919:3).

By February of the following year, soon after the November cutback in production, officials of the local chapter of the American Legion launched a vicious attack on the "aliens" working in Ajo in an article in the Ajo Copper News (February 20, 1920:1) headlined "Deportation of Aliens Sought".[33] Mr. Gibson and other members of the Legion were resentful of the fact that many aliens were accepting "American" protection and getting "American" high-paying jobs while "so many Real Americans were suffering and while many others were making the Great Sacrifice that Our Democracy should survive" (A.C.N. February 20, 1920:1). The American Legion members wanted these undesirable aliens deported by an act of Congress while requiring the "American employer ... to give precedence to Americans, native born or naturalized, without regard to race or creed over and in preference to alien residents" (A.C.N. February 20, 1920:1). However, in spite of this last statement, the Legionnaires were even concerned about Ajo's "naturalized citizens" since they also proposed a resolution at this time supporting the establishment of an "Americanization" school in Ajo to teach "our foreign population ... at least: American History, Reading, Writing and Civil Government ..." (A.C.N. February 20, 1920:1).

Here, deportation of "aliens" is being promoted as the best control mechanism to counteract the unemployment problems generated by this depression in the market demand for copper (A.C.N. February 20, 1920:1). Compare this deportation recommendation to the earlier similar strategy in Bisbee to deport all workers who were believed to be part of an international union conspiracy. In both cases, the company was able to shift the blame for the financial problems "Real American" workers were experiencing, from the company to these "outsiders". But, fortunately for the "alien" population of Ajo, massive deportations were never carried out as they had been for the union supporters earlier at Bisbee.

Beginning in March, 1920, with an editorial stressing that living costs were as cheap or cheaper in Ajo than elsewhere "thanks" to New Cornelia, the company began a campaign of projects and propaganda to entice the worker to remain loyal to the camp throughout this difficult period (A.C.N. March 26, 1920:4). In April, a crusade was mounted to build a "HOME" for the "brave boys" that fought "our wars" (i.e., a meeting house for the American Legion) (A.C.N. April 9, 1920:4). On May 8 it was announced that the Moose were also to have a "home of their own" (A.C.N. May 8, 1920:3) and on May 15 the Ajo Copper News (1920:2) stated that the local hospital was currently losing about $1,200 per month, but that it paid off in:

> ... health, appreciation, and in the efficiency of men. Any other policy would not be a New Cornelia policy.

On May 29 it was announced that the company planned to build a 60 by 40 foot swimming pool in Ajo (A.C.N. May 29, 1920:1) and in July that the July 4th celebration was to be the biggest ever held in Ajo (A.C.N. July 3, 1920:1).

Opposition to the ethnic intolerance of many of the American Legion members also began to surface at this time. For example, when Superintendent Curley in July, 1920, was asked "if he didn't think Ajo would have to 'go some' next year to put on a Fourth celebration to excel this one," he replied (A.C.N. July 10, 1920:1):

No, I don't think so. Next year we will put on a new number and have a motion picture taken of it. It will feature the Papago Indians on horseback.

Also, on July 4th, a local minister giving the "oration of the day" emphasized that (A.C.N. July 10, 1920:1):

> ... the Papago Indians present were the purest of all the American blood, and ... the American citizenship we prize so highly is made up in Ajo and elsewhere of a number of different nationalities blended into one. ... among our good American citizens are people from many different countries.

Whether or not this appeal for tolerance and brotherhood represented an attack on the "deportation of aliens" campaign of the American Legion or merely represents a moderate view officially endorsed by company officials, is uncertain but it is also interesting to note that on July 3rd, it was announced that the company had donated a building site to the local Catholic congregation so that a new church could be built just to the north of the mine for the exclusive use of the Indians living in the camp (A.C.N. July 3, 1920:1).

In August the new swimming pool was opened (A.C.N. August 14, 1920:1). However, in the water, despite the noble 4th of July speech, the different nationalities were not "blended into one". Instead, an article on the new swimming pool ends by saying that (A.C.N. August 21, 1920:1):

> On account of the limits of the pool, and the large number of those desiring to enjoy it, decision has been made to divide the patronage as follows: Americans - Tuesdays, Thursdays, Saturdays and Sundays. Mexicans - Mondays, Wednesdays, and Fridays.[34]

Other recreational activities also expanded as witnessed by the organization of the town's third baseball team near the end of August (A.C.N. August 28, 1920:1). Even the youth of Ajo were forming baseball teams by now. These apparently were organized along ethnic lines since earlier in the year there was an article in the Ajo Copper News describing how "the American boys beat the Mexican boys in a game of baseball on the school diamond" (A.C.N. May 8, 1920:1).

Finally, although deportation laws were never enacted for the purpose of getting rid of "alien slackers", the Legionnaires did apparently succeed in seeing that an "Americanization" class was established in October of the same year in Ajo (A.C.N. October 23, 1920:8). The local paper in describing this new class commented in glowing terms that:

> ... Unless The News is lacking in ability to predict correctly, Spanish-speaking people of the camp will avail themselves of the opportunity to learn English, thus proving their loyalty to the country of their adoption; and will make excellent citizens. There will be a certain enrollment from purely voluntary action, no doubt; but this should be supplemented by encouragement on the part of those in a position to advise the Mexicans for their good....

To the "American" living in Ajo, conversations that he overheard that were in a "foreign" language such as Spanish or "Indian" would always be somewhat suspect. Not being able to understand the conversation would introduce an element of uncertainty into a portion of the "American's" environment. Therefore, an easy way to decrease this uncertainty relative to the "loyal American" would be for him to insist that all non-English speakers be required to both learn and use the English language in their daily conversations.[35]

In November 1920, the new Catholic church for the Indian population of Ajo became a reality, although instead of erecting a completely new building on the promised site near the new town of Ajo it was decided to remodel an old company building in old Ajo[36] for use as the new church (A.C.N. November 13, 1920:1). Both Catholic and Protestant "Americans" were praised for raising a $260 sum toward the new Papago church, and it was stressed that both groups had contributed "equally liberally" to this cause, thereby proving the "broadmindedness and nobility of mind of the Protestant people of Ajo" (A.C.N. November 13, 1920:6). The local Catholic priest also stressed that he wished "to extend his heartfelt gratitude to Mr. M. Curley, the nobleminded and big-hearted general superintendent of the New Cornelia Company for having been instrumental in securing this fine vacant building from the company for the purpose of converting it into a church for the Papago Indians" (A.C.N. November 13, 1920:6). It is quite obvious that by now the company was actively seeking to extend its control over the environment of the Papago laborer as it had earlier done with the Mexican and Anglo mine worker.

However, the very next week a new shockwave spread over the town of Ajo as an additional 25 per cent reduction in copper production was announced, (the first reduction since the previous November) with a corresponding reduction in the number of employees retained by the company (A.C.N. November 20, 1920:1). On page six of the same issue of "The News" was an editorial telling people not to worry about this new curtailment in production, stating that it would probably not last long and is "not great" (A.C.N. November 20, 1920:6). In the end New Cornelia would, of course, emerge from this period of crisis, "triumphant".

However, in spite of this plea for optimism on the part of the Ajo population, things did get worse as the wages of the remaining employees were cut 15 to 20 per cent just before Christmas (A.C.M. December 18, 1920:1). Apparently, in an attempt to partially ease the pain of this unpopular action, the company decided to pay its employees the regular 15 per cent store rebate as a "Christmas present" on December 20, even though this percentage was far more than could be justified from the store's earnings that year (A.C.N. December 11, 1920:1; December 25, 1920:1). Also, on Christmas day it was announced that the prices on meat at the Co-operative store would be reduced (A.C.N. December 25, 1920:6). This time in contrast to a previously announced so-called "price reduction"[37], the price cuts although on many items rather small, seemed to represent genuine reductions.

A "support your local merchant" editorial also appeared in the paper on December 25th urging the worker to be loyal to his local merchants who were "taking losses to help out their customers" during this difficult period (A.C.N. December 25, 1920:8) and soon afterwards landlords were urged by the paper to cut their rents to correspond to the reduced pay the miners now were bringing home (A.C.N. January 1, 1921:6). Further cuts in the prices of "all lines of merchandise" were announced by the company store a short time later although the company officials added that, "please understand, by this action we are retailing some commodities considerably under actual cost" (A.C.N. January 8, 1921:6).

By now, even officials of the major copper producers were becoming very pessimistic about the chances for a speedy recovery from the copper industry's depressed status. One observer even went as far as stating that he believed that the copper situation would remain bad for "six months or a year, at the end of which time improvement would come slowly" (A.C.N. January 8, 1921:1). Near the end of March rumors were rampant that "a complete shut-down" of the New Cornelia property was "contemplated", but the editor of The Ajo

Copper News tried to quell these rumors by stating that (A.C.N. March 26, 1921:3):

> The rumors are without basis in fact, The News is reliably informed. There is no foundation for the story. New Cornelia is one of the two lowest of the low-cost producers of the state and would naturally be one of the last to discontinue operations should shut-downs be general. As a matter of fact, only one of the main copper producers in Arizona has shut down, and it is one of those known to produce at a high cost.

However, by just two weeks later, every copper mine in the state had shut down except New Cornelia and Miami Copper Company, and even New Cornelia announced that they were having a directors' meeting on April 11 to decide whether or not it too would completely close down operations (A.C.N. April 9, 1921:1). But, the Ajo Copper News in a page one editorial, tried to calm some of the townsmen's fears by stating that (A.C.N. April 9, 1921:1):

> Employees of New Cornelia and other Ajoites may rest assured that the directors and officials of the company will do everything possible for the camp. For they have the welfare of Ajo at heart. If there be any way to avoid a complete shutdown, it will not be ordered, the News feels sure.

However, this editorial then went on to state that

> ...there might be circumstances over which they have no control, or various reasons why they might think it best. (i.e., to shut down completely) ...

Finally on April 16, 1921 came the momentous news that New Cornelia would not close completely, although production would be cut by another one-third and an estimated additional 180 to 200 men would be laid off (A.C.N. April 16, 1921:1).

An interesting editorial in this same issue reveals very clearly that the welfare of the individual worker and his family was a matter of only secondary importance in the minds of the company's directors in reaching their decision to keep the Ajo mine open with a reduced labor force (A.C.N. April 16, 1921:6). This editorial begins by speculating that if a complete shutdown had occurred that, "the company would no doubt in such case have taken care of employees and their families desiring to stay, but many would have gone away and there would have been very little money in circulation", but it then goes on to state that:

> The decision of the directors, The News should observe in all fairness and to relieve the above observations from any semblance of camp braggadocio is due almost entirely to peculiar local conditions, chief among which is the leaching process which is such that a shut-down would have been almost fatal. Fatal to the plant and fatal to the organization. ... It would have been practically impossible to gather the force together again - impossible without keeping the men on the payroll while idle - and to break in new men would have taken time. The city is dependent upon the company for water, electric lights and power. To continue pumping at the well would have necessitated running the power house almost as usual. It would have been necessary to haul water by train in cars from Gila on the S.P....
>
> There are not in the copper game directors and officials more loyal to the best interests of the industry and to their fellow producers than those of New Cornelia, but all familiar with the situation here must admit that any other course than that taken would have been suicidal. To fully

protect the interests of the stockholders, they no doubt felt - and justly so - that their decision was necessary.

...a slight loss, while the plant is kept in operation and repair, is far preferable to a shutdown which would have resulted in considerable deterioration and thus, in the end, a far greater loss.

While the directors cannot be expected to act solely for the benefit of the business interests of the camp, it is safe to say that they are very glad thus to be able to make a decision that will be so well received here.

Another editorial on the same page (A.C.N. April 16, 1921:6) urged the laid-off workers to:

...not be too hasty about leaving Ajo if employed here. Practically all copper camps are worse off than this, and there are not many localities in the west where extra labor is required just now. At least (if you have a family) be reasonably sure of a position before you depart. For things are quieter than one imagines who has not been away from Ajo for the past few months and is not posted on the real conditions on the outside.

If you are prepared to stay in the camp until the copper market improves sufficiently to warrant increasing metal production, it might be wise to do so.

Here, the critical limits of two main classes of essential variables that were under threat were the net income variables of stockholders, local business men, and miners and the systemic status set population variables of company related systems and again the company had to choose between protecting these systemic status set population variables and protecting the net income variable to the stockholders. However, the choice was not quite this simple since closing the mine would have apparently resulted in a very large deterioration in the leaching equipment.

Thus, the company was faced with a certain loss of income no matter which alternative it chose. The problem now became one of minimizing cash outflow while retaining as large a supply of those workers most difficult to replace as possible.

Most modern companies faced with such a problem would probably set up a pair of simultaneous equations based upon certain assumptions and solve them for the optimum values for both variables. New Cornelia, on the other hand, probably relied more on managerial "skills" and "talents" and less on formal mathematics to achieve similar optimizations of these variables. Therefore, the company chose, as could be predicted, to keep the most difficult to replace workers operating the equipment most likely to deteriorate if left idle. Other workers more easily replaced and other machinery not as subject to deterioration were no longer functioning parts of the shrunken system. In terms of our model, the scale of the system had been decreased (i.e., the entropy of the system had been increased) in an attempt to protect essential system variables from exceeding lower critical limits.

And to the dismay of other American copper producers, this continued production of copper would prolong the basic problem of the oversupply that was plaguing the industry. From the point of view of the other copper producers, the cessation of all activity in Ajo would have been optimum. However, business men and other groups dependent upon money spent by the worker would have preferred to have seen the company retain all of its workers since this would have kept their net income variables at the optimum values. The company's actions did however tend to stabilize these net income variables but at a new and lower level. In some cases this lower level might be below a particular critical limit in one or more of the many systems present, thus leading to at least a temporary loss of ultra-adaptability in the system affected (e.g., the closure of a shop for the duration of the crisis only, would illustrate such a temporary loss of ultra-adaptability). Of course, loss of ultra-adaptability in many systems probably was prevented by one or more of the transformations described in the last chapter (i.e., this might include changes in the size of the system or in the structure of the system or in the value range of the essential variable being threatened).

For the worker who had been laid off, the company's decision was of course far from optimum as far as the effect it would have on his net income variable. To prevent loss of ultra-adaptability within his own personal system and his larger family system, alternate ways of either obtaining income or the "necessities" usually obtained in trade for income were needed.

Thus, in this period of crisis it seems clear that the decisions made by the company seemed more aimed at optimizing certain essential variables vital to the inner systems of the company than at optimizing variables in other more peripheral systems. In other words, the region of space under effective company control had diminished as well as the number of systems and system variables under effective company control (i.e., there had therefore been a general increase in entropy in the company's universe so that a relatively low state of entropy could be maintained within the central and, from the company's[38] viewpoint, more vital systems. The analogy to the shutting down of the blood supply to the body's extremities under stress from cold weather to protect the temperature of its central core from exceeding a lower critical limit should be obvious.).

Unfortunately there exist no figures on the ethnic composition of those workers laid off shortly after these announcements were published, but from later data it seems reasonably certain that most of the Indian miners and perhaps many if not most of the Mexican miners would hardly be considered to be in the category of those workers most difficult to replace. Most of the men in both of these ethnic groups have until just recently dominated the ranks of those in the lowest job categories at the mine, doing work that required a strong back but little skill or training. However, even these manual laborers had survived a long selection process because of their superior work habits and thus would be somewhat difficult to readily replace. But a choice had to be made, so many of these workers were probably the first to be laid off as the work force was slashed from 650 to 300 workers by May 7, 1921 (A.C.N. May 7, 1921:2; A.C.N. June 11,1921:1)[39], an even more drastic reduction in the work force than had previously been announced. And even those workers remaining on the payroll were forced to take another pay reduction on the first of May (A.C.N. April 30, 1921:1) and received only a 7-1/2 per cent rebate on store purchases that following December instead of the usual 15 per cent[40] (A.C.N. December 3, 1921:1).

The work force, as expected, was also reduced in other areas of company activity (e.g., the company store) not directly related to the fundamental business of mining ore (A.C.N. April 16, 1921:3). However, as mentioned previously, there is evidence that many of the "American" workers and possibly quite a few Mexican miners did not leave Ajo until their children were out of school for the summer[41], (e.g., A. C .N. April 30, 1921:1; June 4, 1921:1) but apparently by late summer the population decrease in Ajo had become noticeable (A.C.N. July 30, 1921:4).

As earlier stated, an indication of this population decline during 1921 can be seen from the number of children attending the annual town Christmas celebration in 1921 as opposed to the more normal number attending the celebration in 1922 (i.e., 700 as opposed to 1,700). However, despite this decline in town population the two traditional company sponsored town rituals (i.e., the 4th of July and Christmas celebrations) were held as usual, but this year no contributions were solicited from the miners themselves to support the Christmas program (A.C.N. July 9, 1921:1; December 10, 1921:1).

Finally, by late summer and continuing through the fall and winter, encouraging news from the international copper market began appearing on the front pages of the Ajo Copper News[42] (e.g., A.C.N. July 30, 1921:1; August 13, 1921:1; August 20, 1921:1; September 24, 1921:1; October 8, 1921:1; November 26, 1921:1; December 3, 1921:1). Then on December 10, 1921 New Cornelia again resumed shipments of copper out of Ajo but without increasing the level of production at the mine (A.C.N. December 10, 1921:1). However, finally after several other mines in Arizona had reopened (A.C.N. January 28, 1922:1; February 25, 1922:1) New Cornelia was ordered by Greenway to begin full production "as soon as possible" (A.C.N. July 8, 1922:1) despite some lingering softness in the price of copper in the market place (A.C.N. July 1, 1922:3).

By November, the work force had been built back up to 815 men, the highest number in many years (A.C.N. November 18, 1922:1) and in December, 850 employees received a 15 per cent rebate on purchases made during the preceding year at the company store (A.C.N. December 22, 1923:1). Of these 850 men, 487 (57.3%) were "Americans", 353 (41.5%) were Mexicans and Indians, and 10 (1.2%) were "American Negroes". It is interesting to compare these figures to those of December, 1920, when 535 workers received rebates, 314 (58.7%) of whom were "Americans" and 221 (41.3%) of whom were Mexicans (A.C.N. December 25, 1920:1; April 30, 1921:1).[43] The exact meaning of these latter, earlier figures is unclear since no mention of either Indians or blacks is made although, as we saw earlier, the company at that time employed members from both of these ethnic groups. Perhaps, some of the Indians were merely "conveniently" combined with Mexicans in the "Mexican" category in the December, 1920, article. However, without more evidence this would be difficult to prove as would also the alternative that no Indians or blacks received a rebate that year.

The remarkable stability in the ratio of "American" workers to "Mexican" ones both before the crisis and after as indicated by the December rebate figures in 1920 and 1922 might be difficult to explain were it not for an article appearing in the Ajo Copper News on July 15, 1922 (p.1) one week after the mine had been ordered to resume normal production by Greenway. This article states that:

> At a plant like this operated on a leaching process, a little time is required in which to increase production to desired figures. For this reason, development at the mine and additions at the crushers can not be too rapid, even if labor were plentiful. The Mexican force is about complete, but more white men could be used. However, things are moving along satisfactory, it is understood.

Thus, the stability of the ratio of "white" to "non-white" workers seems to be more a product of some quota system in operation at the mine than the ease of acquiring workers from the different ethnic groups represented at Ajo and the surrounding areas.[44] Probably at this time, from evidence to be presented later, many of the higher paying, more desirable jobs were restricted in practice if not also in theory to "Americans" only.

It would be interesting to know just how many Mexicans, Indians, and blacks remained in Ajo during the worst part of the crisis, but the evidence is very sparse for this period. One brief article in the Ajo Copper News on March 18, 1922 (p.4) seems to indicate that at least the Mexican community was not completely deserted during the height of the crisis. Probably a few especially favored Mexicans were still employed at the mine. Also it is probable that at least some of the Papago Indians found employment at Childs Ranch or at other ranches in the vicinity of Ajo while others obtained food, etc. from relatives living nearby, including those employed by Tom Childs and other ranchers near Ajo. Thus, the sharing of economic resources was probably important in enabling both the Ajo Indian and Mexican communities to survive this difficult period (i.e., ultra-adaptability was preserved in both cases, although there was a reduction in the size of both systems).

The differential retention of workers by race during this crisis period also had a tremendous impact on the relative power of several important voluntary associations in Ajo. Thus, on March 18, 1922 (A.C.N. March 18, 1922:4) spokesmen for the Ajo Mexican community announced that they were abandoning plans to celebrate their most important annual ritual activity, the 5th of May celebration, in order to support the "American" dominated Legion's proposed carnival. Also, an editorial in the Ajo Copper News (June 24, 1922:4) near the end of the partial shutdown stressed the loyalty of Ajo workers to the celebration of "American" traditions (i.e., the annual company sponsored 4th of July and Christmas celebrations) and emphasized that the "camp stands for Americanism" and that English is not only spoken in "the school", "the plant", and "the mine" but that "provision" was also made for "foreign adults to learn our language". Finally, on July 29 (A.C.N. July 29, 1922:1), the local paper announced that New Cornelia had given the American Legion a new concrete building in the center of Ajo. The symbolic meaning of this gesture is obvious, the "white" dominated American Legion had by now reached a new peak of power in Ajo affairs and the centrally located, solid new building stood as a highly visible monument to the supreme status held by this organization among the voluntary associations of Ajo.

Wages were raised 10 per cent in September 1922 (A.C.M. September 9, 1922:1) and again by 10 per cent in March of the following year (A.C.N. March 17, 1923:1) as an era of prosperity began in Ajo for all people living there. By April, 1923, employment figures for the Ajo mine had almost reached 1,000 (Therrien 1945:101), and it was stated that every house was occupied from the "eastern confines of Clarkston a mile and a half to the western limits of Gibson"[45] (A.C.M. March 24, 1923:1). Good times had indeed come to Ajo again and would remain until 1930. However, it was not long before a new peril threatened to destroy one of the company's most effective worker control mechanisms, the Company Cooperative Store.

In the election campaign of the fall of 1922, a state representative from Clarkston launched a bitter attack on company stores in general and the New Cornelia store in particular and promised to introduce legislation to prevent mining companies from operating company stores if elected (A.C.N. October 21, 1922:4; January 20, 1923:6). The Ajo Copper News, as expected, in an editorial (October 21, 1922:4) urged the voters of the Ajo district not to elect this man, but this attempt to control the actions of the local voters, failed. Thus, early in the following year this state representative from Clarkston, John W. Mayes, introduced two bills into the state legislature, the first of which "would prevent mining companies from engaging in the mercantile business, or from having any interest in any mercantile business whatsoever", and the second of which "would make it a misdemeanor for any mining company to deduct from the wages of any employee, the amount of any claim against him" (A.C.N. January 20, 1923:6).

The editor of the Ajo Copper News responded quickly in righteous indignation to what he apparently felt was a vicious personal attack upon the benevolent company (A.C.N. January 20, 1923:6). In a very revealing editorial he states that:

> The two bills were fathered in the last mining camp in the State that one should expect them to be - the camp in Arizona where there is the least justification for any criticism or change....

... there is no company store here but a co-operative store for the sole benefit of the employees of New Cornelia and affiliated companies. It is co-operative in that employees each December receive rebates on purchases of the twelve months preceeding....

... one would not expect objection here because of the high character, motives and practice of New Cornelia. Employees are not dismissed for spite or without cause. They can buy supplies where they choose - in the camp or outside - without fear of losing their jobs. "New Cornelia is a good company to work for" is what every employee says.

One would not expect objection on the part of business houses of the camp. When we business men came to the camp, New Cornelia laid all its cards on the table saying: "It is our ground, our store rooms. You pay us ground or room rent. We protect you from competition until the camp grows sufficiently. We think it best for the employees that there should be conducted for them a co-operative store - we believe this a good plan, though new, and we are going to see it tried out. You will have (in some, not all cases) competition from this co-operative store, but most of you will have no competition whatever from the co-operative store. The directors thought these plans best. If any mistake has been made by New Cornelia, it has been made on the side of too great leniency, rather than on the other side; New Cornelia has been more fraternal than paternal - lenient almost to a fault.

We business men all want to enjoy good business. But you can not legislate business. The only way to increase business is to be sticking around when the industry gets back on its feet and copper brings 16 cents or such a matter with plenty of sales. ...

The editorial also goes on to state that many newly hired miners needed credit at the company store because when they reached Ajo "ninety per cent" of them were "broke". Therefore, it was argued that the company store was forced to protect its investment through payroll deductions (i.e., a control mechanism to protect the net income variable). Herein, probably lies the key to the trouble that now threatened the company store because this was a period when a great number of miners had recently been hired by the company. Since each of these men was initially given credit at the company store "to get started", probably most of the new worker's money, at least for a while, ended up in the cash registers of the New Cornelia store. Apparently one or, more likely, several of the Clarkston merchants seeing this huge influx of new miners became dissatisfied with their share of the total Ajo economic "pie" and were unwilling to wait for the promised time when there would be "plenty of sales" of copper so that additional money would be available in the camp to fill everyone's coffers.

The promise to "protect" the business man "from competition" also must have seemed rather ludicrous to these objectors who really wanted protection from what seemed to be unfair competition from the company store. They probably felt that even having the lowest prices on goods would not draw the miner caught in the familiar credit-payroll deduction "trap" and quite possibly this was true despite the company's repeated denial that it ever forced anyone to trade with the company store. Thus blocked from most direct forms of action on the local level, the Clarkston business men were, however, apparently successful in helping to elect a representative from Clarkston who would carry on the battle at the state level for them.

This animosity between the merchants of Clarkston and the company had deep roots going back to at least 1916 when the company refused to sell water to the residents of Clarkston so that they had to develop their own well (Barnes 1960:263). Clarkston and Gibson not being completely under the company's domination were probably always "thorns in the side" of the company and at times such as this were capable of introducing much uncertainty into the company's environment. Contrary to the inferences made in the editorial, the independent merchants of these two communities were not integral parts of the non-competitive system of businesses set up by the company in the area of the Ajo camp under its direct control but instead were often in fierce competition with the company store for the miner's dollar.

However, these merchants lost this battle at the state level, one probable factor in this defeat being that New Cornelia and the other mining interests of the state undoubtedly had powerful friends among the state legislators. Another possible factor in this loss was that although the Clarkston merchants represented themselves as being the saviors of the poor working man who was being exploited through the mechanism of the payroll deduction plan, the company was able to obtain a statement from "a spokesman representing the Employee's committee of the Ajo district" supporting the company's stand (A.C.N. March 7) 1925:5).

In terms of the theoretical model developed previously, no control vector of sufficient magnitude could be generated on the local level by the Clarkston business men to overpower the "hostile" control vector generated by the company store-credit-payroll deduction system. Therefore, they gambled that a suitable control vector could be created in the state legislature - a gamble that they lost.[46]

This crisis having been overcome, the company officials then turned their attention to strengthening their control over the lives of the youth of Ajo. Thus, in April it was announced that a local Boy Scout troop had been formed under the direction of Superintendent Curley with the support of the American Legion and the Trustees of the local school board (A.C.N. April 28, 1923:1) and in December an editorial in the local paper in discussing the Christmas and 4th of July celebrations urged "Ajoites" to put "more life and vim in these semi-annual community festivities" since "they certainly are for the good of all the 'kiddies' for this place and miles around" (A.C.N. December 1, 1923:1).

With the return of prosperity to Ajo, tolerance toward members of the various minority groups in Ajo apparently increased. Evidence for this increase with respect to the Papago Indians can be seen in the pages of the Ajo Copper News when, for example, in describing the semi-annual community holidays the paper states that (A.C.N. December 15, 1923:5):

> ... Both events are not without local color to make them attractive to people hundreds of miles away - the presence of a host of Papago Indians - men, women and children of splendid physique, almost majestic of mien, proud as if in full knowledge of traditions of the first and purest American race.

However, part of this praise may have had certain economic motivations since just a few weeks previously it had been reported that recent rains on the nearby reservation had produced:

> ... good ranges for the cattle in this vicinity throughout the winter and early spring, and fine crops of winter wheat on the reservation. Thus the Papago Indians are expected to have a prosperous season, which will mean added trade for the local merchants. ... (A.C.N. November 24, 1923:6).

Just as not all control mechanisms employed by system decision makers to minimize fluctuations in essential variables succeed in accomplishing this objective, often, as was discussed in chapter five of this book, success is achieved in meeting this desired goal, even though the control mechanism involved can not be scientifically demonstrated to be capable of producing a suitable control vector. Such is the case with the Papago "tiswin" ceremony, a control mechanism evolved by the Papago Indians to bring summer rains for their crops and pasture. As a control mechanism to bring rain, the wine ceremony appeared to the early Papagos to be quite successful, although a modern weather expert would almost certainly say that the southern Arizona summer cloudbursts would usually arrive even if the "tiswin" ceremony didn't take place at all.[47] However, in the summer of 1924 the rains didn't come and as the Ajo Copper News (August 23, 1924:3) reports:

> The white man and his diligent enforcement of the prohibition laws, which have prevented Papago Indians from making "tiswin", is blamed by members of the tribe for the absence of rain this year...
> By making the intoxicating drink the Indians believe that their gods will favor them with rain for their crops. Yearly the authorities have trouble with the "tiswin" manufacturers, and this year several offenders have been arrested by the Indian police.

The Indians finally even sought a favorable court decision to save this valuable (to them) control mechanism (A.C.N. August 30, 1924:4).

The Mexican Independence Day Celebration also was reported that year with glowing terminology on the front page of the Ajo Copper News (A.C.N. September 22, 1923:1) and a special continuing newspaper column in Spanish was begun the following February (A.C.N. February 2, 1924:1). Nor were the local blacks neglected in this rising spirit of brotherly love. No longer were they called "Negroes." Instead they were now referred to as "colored people" in a favorable article that told Ajoites that "the colored Baptists have a church of their own in the Mexican town, with Sunday school, young people's union and ladies' aid"[48] (A.C.N. February 24, 1923:3).

However, the following year an unfortunate incident occurred that apparently reinforced the half-forgotten prejudices of many Southern-born Ajoites toward blacks.[49] On June 7, 1924, an editorial appeared in the local paper stating that, "Ajo had a close call the other day - a Negro charged with attempt to commit the unpardonable offense against a white woman, almost got away with it without having to answer in a court of justice" (A.C.N. June 7, 1924:4). The local black community apparently felt somewhat differently about this alleged offense and probably began receiving threats from the aroused Ajoites for it was soon reported that, "A meeting was called July 10 by Attorney Robert L. Fortune to be held at Greenleaf Baptist Church, for the purpose of organizing a Negro Constitutional and Political League" (A.C.N. July 19, 1924:1).

Feelings were evidently running high on both sides when the accused man was brought to trial in Tucson (A.C.N. August 9, 1924:1) and although he pleaded guilty to the charge, many Ajoites were apparently greatly angered when he received a fairly light sentence for his deed as witnessed by the following editorial in the Ajo Copper News (A.C.N. August 9, 1924:1):

> In the superior court last Wednesday at Tucson, before Judge George Darnell, Paul Honoto, of this place, plead guilty to a charge of simple assault, and was sentenced to thirty days in the county jail.
> This is the case that occurred in Gibson about a month ago, when the above Negro in an intoxicated condition, committed an assault on Mrs. Bert Adgate, a resident there, and tried to commit a beastly criminal action on her. The above sentence is not justice to the people of Ajo. What county official is at fault we do not know, but there is a "screw loose" somewhere.

The above puts the question right to our eyes, "Are we FIT for Statehood?" We all know what would happen to this Negro if this offense were committed in Texas, and why dont (sic) our proper county officials give us JUSTICE so these necessary human thoughts will not have to enter our minds? Such is life in Pima County.

Whether this was the major incident leading to the rapid decline of the black population of Ajo in the following years or not, it illustrates the extreme dislike for members of this race that was strongly expressed to me in the late 1960's by many Ajoites including a few local company officials who told me that large numbers of Negro workers in Ajo would only increase racial tensions in the town and might precipitate riots (F.N. June 18, 1967; F.N. January 11, 1968). Thus I heard from many different sources that outside "Negroes" were "not welcome" in Ajo and at the nearby radar base. And one important local Indian said that he and several other men had gotten two "Negroes" jobs with the company, one as a janitor in the local hospital and one as an employee of the company store, but that company officials had refused to put a "Negro" in the mine complex itself, except for one "part-Papago, part-Negro" male which they had reluctantly let work there after much pressure had been applied to them by local Indian leaders (F.N. November 3, 1967; November 15, 1967). Therefore, by the late 60's, only a handful of blacks still resided in Ajo and the latest available figures from the 2000 census list still only 9 Black or African Americans in a total town population of 3,705 (i.e., 0.24%) (local census.com 2008).

In contrast to an act of discrimination that at this time was disturbing the Papagos' nearby relatives, the Pimas at Sacaton, who were being denied the right to vote in Pinal County, voting rights apparently were not a burning issue among the Indians of Ajo since the Ajo Copper News (A.C.N. September 6, 1924:6) reported that:

While we have no report on the Indian (voter) registration, Indians having recently been declared citizens, by Federal order, and registering to some extent throughout the country, it is not likely that the figures include very many Indians of this precinct. For Indians, as a rule, register republican and the republican registration has fallen off, while the number registering as democrats is almost doubled.(Later - the registration officer asked the approximate Indian registration (said) not very many Indians probably not over a dozen - registered here. She is under the impression that the majority of Papagos living in this precinct are unable to read - and write).

However, the Papagos on the main reservation east of Ajo did cast 92 votes in the primary election held that September (A.C.N. September 13, 1924:1), although this was still a very small percentage of the total reservation population.

By the late 60's in Ajo there was a significant Pima minority in the resident Indian population. These people, as will be shown later in greater detail, on an average differed in many important ways from their Papago cousins. Among these differences was the degree to which the two groups participated in the institutions of the dominant cultural group (i.e., "white" society) with the Pimas apparently in 1924 as well as in the 1960s, being the more eager of the two to participate in such institutions and the more rewarded for this participation.[50] More will be said about this later.

An interesting description of the Ajo Papago population in 1925 is given by a person identified only as an "Editor of Michigan Paper"[51] in the Ajo Copper News (January 31, 1925:1):

There are still to be seen a considerable number of Papago Indians about the mine and mill, they proving to be excellent workers. They come from an Indian reservation distant twenty or more miles. They are inured to the heat of the sun, and welcome the change their jobs permit, it being a great variance from their home conditions where their fare consists of beans and bread for the greater part. They spend their earnings freely for the best local stores can provide in the way of meats, fruits, etc. They are very fond of bright-colored clothing and have a mania for the movies which they visit on Sundays as well as week days. They are also fond of riding in an automobile and will wait an hour after the show to ride a half mile to their local village.[52] They would think nothing of a twenty-mile walk to or from their reservation, but in town they demand the very latest in locomotion as well as in neckwear.

It is obvious from the above passage that several important control mechanisms were already by this early date proving to be quite effective in binding the Indian worker to the mine (e.g., the movie theater, the bright-colored clothing, the greater variety of food available, the automobile and the increased supply of cash to purchase other goods and services). It is interesting to note that most of these listed inducements to continued residence in Ajo while of importance to the resident "American" population also, would be things that the "American" worker could easily find in other towns or cities but which the Indian could not find on the reservation. Therefore, one might suspect that this type of control mechanism in the 1920's might have been more effective in holding Indians and rural Mexicans in Ajo than their Anglo co-workers.

Later, when added control mechanisms, such as the building of company houses for Indians were introduced, the vast differences in what was available on the reservation and what was available in Ajo, resulted in even stronger bonds being forged between the mine and the Indian worker, the enormous strength of these bonds being very evident during the 1967-68 strike as already discussed in chapter two.

In May of 1925 the company created a new control mechanism in Ajo, the so-called "Employees' Benefit Association" to provide "benefits" in case of sickness, accident, or death, patterned after the C. and A. Employees' Benefit Association of Bisbee (A.C.N. June 6, 1925:1). Approximately 60 per cent of New Cornelia's employees signed up for this new group insurance plan by the end of May, although there was no breakdown of membership by ethnic group.

Natural disasters such as flood and fire which on many occasions, through the years, plagued the company and the residents of the various areas of the Ajo camp (e.g., A.C.N. July 18, 1925:1) on at least one occasion added to the prosperity of the community by eliminating competition for about a year's time from a major South American copper producing firm suffering from its own natural disaster (A.C.N. April 18, 1925:5). Thus, fluctuations in variables in the company's environment that were somewhat unpredictable did not always pose a threat to the survival of the company but instead at times, as in the example above, tended to stabilize or actually improve its stability.

It is also interesting to note that at least some of the Ajo Indians after prosperity had again returned to the mine were not putting their complete trust in the company for the basic necessities of life since in July, 1926, the Ajo Copper News (A.C.N. July 17, 1926:1) reported that:

> Ajo Indians having planted wheat are leaving the district
> for the reservation to harvest their crops, it is stated.
> There will be a fairly good crop.

The article then added a story about the Pisinimo trader who was planning to buy a flour mill to process the grain raised near Pisinimo.

Unfortunately, it is not stated whether or not most of the grain raised by the Ajo Indians was in the vicinity of Pisinimo, although at least some of it probably was, if not most.

Greenway resigned his leadership of the company in 1925 (A.C.N. May 30, 1925:1) for reasons that were not too clearly stated and then died unexpectedly less than a year later during a minor operation (A.C.N. January 23, 1926:1). Important to the theory discussed in Chapter 5 is the fact that his will specified that $100,000 of his vast fortune be distributed to about 700 employees of New Cornelia (A.C.N. April 7, 1928:1). This last act of Greenway's completed the myth of omnipresent goodness that surrounded the company and its leaders and elevated Greenway to near-sainthood in Ajo. Symbolic of the reverence paid Greenway by Ajoites was "the Greenway Cross" erected on the highest mountain near Ajo, on which Easter Sunrise services were often held after this time (A.C.N. March 27, 1926:1). Much of the Greenway mythology persisted even in the late 60's in Ajo.

As the year 1929 began, the era of prosperity in the copper industry appeared never ending (e.g., See A.C.N. July 4, 1929:1). Although, the races were still segregated into different classrooms at the local school until they reached the seventh grade (A.C.N. April 11, 1929:1) and rather rigid segregation persisted at the local movie house, swimming pool, and in the various social organizations and churches, all racial groups in Ajo seemed to be living in relative peace and harmony as the "Americanization" of Mexicans and Indians apparently was proceeding nicely (A.C.N. January 26, 1929:1). Indicative of this spirit of brotherhood and good will that existed in Ajo at this time was the formation in April of the "Ajo Community Council", the stated purpose of which was: "to serve as a clearing house and inter-club advisory committee; to encourage cooperation among member clubs in the discussion and promotion of matters of common interest and betterment to Ajo, to the end that concerted effort on their part may be effectuated" (A.C.N. April 4, 1929:1).

In March of 1929 the miners had received their third pay raise since the preceding September. (Their wages had thus been increased by 20 per cent in less than six months' time.) Therefore, such a buoyant atmosphere filled the camp that even the news that the new Tucson-Casa Grande-Gila Bend road (bypassing Ajo) had been completed failed to dampen this optimism[53] (A.C.N. September 26, 1929:2), nor did the supposedly humorous rumor that Indians were moving to higher ground in anticipation of a disastrous flood (A.C.N. July 25, 1929:1).

The flood didn't come, but something more disruptive for the Ajo camp did although when the infamous stock market crash occurred near the end of October, few Ajoites seemed to feel greatly alarmed about it and business went on as usual. Even an editorial published almost a month later (A.C.N. November 28, 1929:2) while condemning the fact that people were beginning to sell their stocks in fear and that certain companies were engaging in questionable practices with regard to their own stock, showed little pessimism about the future of American industry. Furthermore, Christmas of 1929 was described as being the "best ever" (A.C.N. December 26, 1929:1) and the annual pre-Christmas rebate, that year again 15 per cent, was paid to a record 1,250[54] employees, an increase of 280 men over the previous year (A.C.N. December 5, 1929:1).

The first local hints that all was not well in the copper industry did not appear until early the next year when a very brief announcement was made in the Ajo Copper News that there would be a small cut in production and that a few men would be temporarily laid off (A.C.N. January 23, 1930:1). However, by March the price of copper remained at a still high 17.75 cents per pound and it was reported that the demand for copper had "improved" (A.C.N. March 13, 1930:2). Thus, the rumor that the Phelps Dodge Corporation was planning to merge with the Calumet and Arizona Mining Company (A.C.N. April 17, 1930:1) probably did not initially seem very ominous to the Ajoites.

These two firms had long been the "friendliest" of rivals in Bisbee as was discussed earlier in this book and apparently signs of this close relationship were very much in evidence in Ajo as well since Walter Douglas, the head of the Phelps-Dodge Corporation, had once made a special trip to Ajo to visit Mrs. Greenway just after the death of her husband (A.C.N. February 20, 1926:1) and the Phelps-Dodge Corporation had "for some time" acted as selling agent for C. & A. Copper (A.C.N. May 8, 1930:2). An editorial in the Ajo Copper News (May 8, 1930:2) in discussing the proposed merger spoke of this friendship in the following terms:

> ... the two companies have for many years been on the friendliest of terms, acting as nearly a unit as would seem possible with two separate mining companies. They are understood to have consulted each other a great deal and to have refrained each from committing itself to any act or policy that would seem to the other unfriendly.

However, friendship alone would not be reason enough for a merger of this magnitude to occur. That both companies were approaching crises can easily be inferred from the above editorial which goes on to state that:

> ...a merger like this would tend to give the combined company more power in the copper world. With more and keener competition, resulting from the development of large ore bodies in foreign countries, it is clear that there is strength in the union of United States copper producers. And mergers not only bring about larger influence--they also result in savings in the various items

that go to make up the cost in production, administration and marketing.

It is believed that each of the two, for various reasons, would naturally desire a union with the other--if the examination now being made should prove favorable. Phelps Dodge is strong; with many large interests; and has exceptional financial backing. The C. & A., strong, successful, has a wonderful ore body in the Campbell, on its property adjoining the Copper Queen of Phelps Dodge. And in New Cornelia Mines, Calumet and Arizona has a large, low cost copper mine that any ambitious company would be glad to have an interest in.

Calumet and Arizona is perfectly capable of holding her own in the copper world--perhaps as capable as any one company. Yet for the reasons stated above, mining men would no doubt agree with the statement that the right kind of merger would be a good thing for the C. & A., New Cornelia Mines, and Ajo, as well as for United States copper mining as a whole. It would make this camp (if possible) more safe and sure and solid, assisting in stabilizing copper prices, production, employment and wages.

However, as noted earlier,[55] both companies were not quite as capable of independent survival in this period of rapidly worsening conditions in the world copper market as this editorial theorizes. The one company desperately needed a reserve supply of money to keep its operations going although it still had tremendous ore reserves while the other had plenty of money but few large reserves of copper ore left (Cleland 1952:227-228,235; Leonard 1954:17).

There was probably little doubt by this time in the minds of the directors of these two companies that all signs pointed to a very difficult period ahead since they undoubtedly had access to "inside" information about the true state of the American copper producer's "environment" that was not yet available to the ordinary resident of Ajo (e.g., See (Cox 1938:194)). However, by May 1st when the price of copper dropped to 13.775 cents per pound with wage cuts expected to follow (A.C.N. May 1, 1930:3), the ordinary miner probably began to worry a little about the future and when the price of copper declined further to an historic low of less than 4 cents[56] a pound later in 1930 (Cox 1938:194) no one could harbor any more doubts about the seriousness of the enormous disaster that threatened the very survival of the American copper industry.

Finally, near the end of the following January, another sign of the impending doom that seemed to be hovering over all American copper producers, appeared in the local paper when it was reported that the Clarkdale smelter had been ordered to close, thus throwing 450 men, out of a total force of 1,000, out of work (A.C.N. January 22, 1931:1). Two great natural disasters also seemed to testify that the year 1931 was to be the beginning of a very difficult era in the history of Ajo. In January, the west end of Rowood-Clarkston was destroyed by fire and then fire again returned in June--this time to completely level the east end of that town (A.C.N. June 25, 1931:1).

The real blow to most Ajoites, however, came shortly after the merger of the Phelps Dodge Corporation and the C. & A. Mining Company was completed that fall (A.C.N. October 1, 1931:1). On the fifth of November, in another small article "hidden" on page four of the Ajo Copper News (A.C.N. November 5, 1931:4), it was announced that due to the depressed state of the copper industry that further layoffs at the mine would be necessary. Although there is no mention of the exact number of men laid off at this time, apparently it was a large enough group that the local Company officials, and persons representing the various "fraternal, social, civic and religious organizations" of Ajo got together and organized a relief organization (i.e., a "collective" control mechanism), the stated purpose of which being to "concentrate all activities for the relief of distress among persons living in our community" (A.C.N. November 12, 1931; March 17, 1932:1).

This newly created "Ajo Relief Committee" immediately set up subcommittees "to canvass the town and obtain donations and pledges of money and items of food and clothing to be used in this (relief) work" (A.C.N. March 17, 1932:1; December 3, 1931:1). 291 persons and business firms responded positively to this appeal for aid and food was distributed to 9 needy families on the 14th of November, just nine days after the layoffs were first announced (A.C.N. December 3, 1931:1; March 17, 1932:1). From early November until the following June, other distributions of food and clothing (and toys at Christmas time (A.C.N. December 3, 1931:4)) were made to the men and their families out of work in Ajo although the committee probably suffered from a lack of funds after the 24th of March, 1932, for reasons that shall be given shortly (A.C.N. May 26, 1932:1; March 17, 1932:1).

It is interesting to examine the meager data given on the recipients of this welfare aid and see that help was given to 49 Mexican families[57] but only 33 American ones[58] (A.C.N. March 17, 1932:1). This again confirms my previous supposition that in times of crisis there were differential layoff rates for the different ethnic groups represented at the Ajo mine. Also it is of interest to note that the type of assistance given to an estimated 9 of the 49 Mexican families was not in the form of food and clothing but rather, as stated in the Ajo Relief Committee Report (A.C.N. March 17, 1932:1), "Assistance has also been rendered to families returning to Mexico, consisting of 19 adults and 26 children--a total of 45 persons, who otherwise would have been a burden on the community."

The question of what happened to the Papago Indians who undoubtedly were also laid off in fairly large numbers in November 1931 perhaps can best be answered at least in part by the following article in the Ajo Copper News (February 4, 1932:1):

> That Uncle Sam is not neglecting "Poor Lo, the Papago, during the present depression when he is unable to secure work or sell his cattle and produce at a fair price, is the statement of those in Ajo who are in touch with the Sells Reservation.
>
> It is stated that the men of the reservation are wearing good, warm overcoats, and the women and girls, good warm dresses--all provided by the Indian Department of the Federal Government. The Department is also furnishing the Papagoes, in some cases, with tractors and other farm implements, and taking steps to provide increased water supplies for cattle and horses and for such farming as can be done close to such supply. The water provisions include the digging of a large water tank at Sweet Water (Agua Dulce, as it is known on the reservation). Another help is a fence that is being built from the reservation near Sells to the Menager ranch.

However, as pointed out earlier, there were many of the "Sand" People who had no close ties to the reservation and therefore could not return there to partake of the Government's seductive cornucopia although it was true that some of these people had married into reservation families and would therefore be accepted on the reservation. Still, all was not hopeless for the Indian blocked from access to reservation resources, however, since in most cases, as noted earlier, such an Indian often had a white kinsman[59] (e.g., Tom Childs) who could provide temporary work or assistance for the Indian on the cattle ranches that surrounded Ajo. Also the sharing of resources between relatives was probably an important mechanism in the maintenance of "order" in the Indian's universe during this trying period.

On the 24th of March came the final devastating announcement to the residents of Ajo -- New Cornelia was to be closed completely for an indefinite period beginning April 24, 1932 (A.C.N. March 24, 1932:1). 495 men were to be laid off--practically the entire labor force still remaining on the job except for a few management people and a few men to guard the company's property.[60] Furthermore, as one might suspect, the Ajo Relief Committee announced that it would "close its books and go out of business June 15th ..." (A.C.N. May 26, 1932:1).

Many men, or at least their families, probably remained in Ajo until the end of the school year and then left. Life in the copper camp ebbed greatly that summer but the town probably never was "almost deserted" as one outside report had stated in a "slight" exaggeration of the true situation in the camp (A.C.N. July 14, 1932:4).

In terms of the theory presented earlier, ultra-adaptability had not been maintained in the overall Ajo copper mining complex of systems since the lower limits for most of the systemic status set population variables had been exceeded so that the Company's net income variable could be protected from exceeding its lower critical limit. This temporarily large increase in system entropy could be, at least in theory, reversed once the company's directors decided to again rehire enough employees to increase each essential systemic status set population variable above its lower critical limit although for the reasons previously stated, this replacement process would probably take a fairly long period of time especially in filling those systemic status sets formerly occupied largely by skilled "American" employees.

Initially during this crisis when only a portion of the labor force had been laid off, the company and the "group representing the various fraternal, social, civic, and religious organizations in Ajo" had, as previously stated, formed a new organization to create control mechanisms to protect systemic status set population variables by providing enough income in the form of food and clothing to the individual workers and their families who had been laid off so that each family's net income variable would not fall below its lower critical limit.

In terms of the systems theory developed in the last chapter, this relief organization also had several essential system variables, again both a net income variable and several systemic status set population variables. Furthermore, some of these variables were functionally related (e.g., the more workers that were unemployed, the fewer men there would be to donate funds to the organization). Loss of ultra-adaptability occurred in this case when the population of the systemic status set containing the unemployed worker and his family exceeded an upper critical limit while both the net income variable and the population of the systemic status set of donators[61] fell below their lower critical limits. Because of the functional relationship between the number of men in the systemic status set of unemployed workers and the population of the systemic status set of men donating to this relief organization, shifts in the absolute values of the critical limits of both of these essential variables as well as of associated variables such as the net income variable took place as the ratio of the number of men in the first set to the number of men in the second set changed through time.

Loss of ultra-adaptability would have also occurred for this newly created organization if the company had been able, by some unknown fortune, to resume normal operations again, thereby reducing the population of the systemic status set containing unemployed workers to a value below a certain lower critical limit. Such a fortunate occurrence did not take place, however.

Although the directors of the company had a greater degree of control over the population of the systemic status set containing unemployed workers in Ajo than did the directors of the semi-independent Ajo Relief Committee, the latter group was able to reduce the ranks of the unemployed and their families by 45 persons, as stated previously, (i.e., the people they helped send back to Mexico.). Other outside forces such as the lure of the reservation for the Indians and jobs in other towns and cities for the "Americans" and possibly also some Mexicans and Indians also tended to reduce the population of this systemic status set.

Returning now to the question of why the directors of New Cornelia decided this time to close down this mine when in the crisis of 1921 they had decided to "shrink" their system but prevent even a temporary loss of ultra-adaptability in the shrunken system—several changes in key system variables can be seen. One of these changes was that the oxidized ore that had required the apparently difficult-to-shut-down leaching process was largely depleted by 1930 (Leonard 1954:16). Another change was, of course, one of management. As was pointed out earlier, the Phelps Dodge Corporation had acquired New Cornelia not so much for its present output but for its reserves (Cleland 1952:227-228,235; Leonard 1954:17). Therefore, the loss of a few skilled miners in Ajo due to a decision to shut down this mine completely would not really be much of a hardship for the enlarged company since when the Ajo mine reopened the company could easily afford to wait until the ranks of skilled "American" workers could again be filled. The newly merged company's main center of immediate concern was, of course, its very large operating mines at Bisbee, not the Ajo pit. Also the company had in December, 1931, closed down its Bisbee Copper Queen Smelter shortly after the merger had taken place and all smelting activity was transferred to the Bisbee Calumet and Arizona plant (Cox 1938:195). Thus "Phelps Dodge" workers were laid off in large numbers as well as "C. and A." workers, although the impact of the decision to keep Bisbee partially open while closing down Ajo was probably not regarded by most Ajoites as being a particularly fair and impartial decision.

A third change that had occurred in the intervening years since the crisis of 1921 was that several extremely large copper mines with very low costs of production had by this time been opened in South Africa and Chile (Cox 1938:194; Leonard 1954:17). Thus, although the price of copper which had dropped from a high of 24 cents a pound in 1929 to a low of less than 4 cents a pound in 1930 (Cox 1938:194) had started to recover in price by 1931, in 1932 the price per pound had only risen to 5.67 cents (Leonard 1954:17) and in January 1933 the price dropped to as low as 4.88 cents per pound (Cox 1938:195). Here again, as in 1921, an overabundance of mined copper was the key variable in holding prices down, but this time in contrast to 1921 the oversupply of copper was not just a temporary phenomenon that could easily be corrected, but a permanent problem that would require, eventually, the drastic limitation of imports of foreign copper if the American industry was to survive. Therefore, the company directors, when deciding whether or not the New Cornelia mine should remain open in 1932, had little to be optimistic about at least in the immediate future.

However, early in June 1932 came the first ray of hope to begin to dispel the gloom that had long settled over the copper camps of the West - the much hoped-for Copper Tariff Bill had now become a law of the land (A.C.N. June 9, 1932:1). No longer would foreign producers of copper be able to undersell the American copper firms. The manipulation of variables in high places by the American copper producers had apparently met with success as evidenced by this new, powerful control mechanism to drastically reduce the influx of foreign copper to the already glutted domestic copper market.

Also that summer the newly created Reconstruction Finance Corporation began to accept applications for loans to the states for their long awaited relief programs (A.C.N. July 28, 1932:1) and by the end of September, Ajo was promised $25,000 in relief money for road construction (A.C.N. September 29, 1932:1). Now in September, in contrast to a previous report that we have already cited that said that in July Ajo was "almost deserted" (A.C.N. July 14, 1932:4), it was stated that an estimated 400 unemployed miners were still in Ajo (A.C.N. September 29, 1932:1). Whether or not there had been a large exodus of miners that summer who then returned in the fall to Ajo can be debated, but it is more probable from evidence in the pages of the Ajo Copper News that many miners had remained in or about Ajo both in the summer and early fall.

Of these estimated 400 men, 200 had signed up for work on the road crews by the 13th of October (A.C.N. October 13, 1932:1). Sixty-two of the 200 were said to have been Mexicans with no reference being made to any Papagos at all, thus appearing to give partial support to the statement given to Waddell (1969:54) that the Indian Village "must have been" deserted during this long shutdown. (However, evidence to be presented shortly will refute this statement).

Not all of the 200 who signed up for roadwork were given anything to do immediately. In fact, only fifty-four of these men were called out for road crew assignments the first week and eighty the second week[62] (A.C.N. October 13, 1932:1). The men who were fortunate enough to be chosen were paid $3.50 per day plus transportation to and from the job. Nothing is said about the method of choosing which of the 200 men obtained employment in any given week or whether or not the same men were hired two or more weeks in succession, but there is some indication that the selection committee did try to take individual need into account in making these decisions and tried to spread the work equally among those most in need (A.C.N. March 16, 1933:1). However, as illustrated by evidence to be presented shortly, the "race" of the applicant may also have had, at least in the initial stages of this relief program, some effect on this selection process, although this is not certain.

It is interesting to note that, as possibly suspected, M. Curley, the mine superintendent was the chairman of the local committee in charge of the R.F.C. road funds (A.C.N. March 16, 1933:1) while his wife became an important leader in another charity endeavor created in the fall of 1932, the local Red Cross clothing relief program (A.C.N. October 13, 1932:1). In the latter program, fabrics were supplied by the regional office of the Red Cross to the local members of the organization who then made simple clothes out of this material for distribution to the needy. Here, there is some evidence that in keeping with the company's earlier policy of trying to keep "Americans" from leaving Ajo, this form of aid was first given to "worthy" "American" families before being given to Mexican ones since on the 13th of October, 1932 (A.C.N. p.1) it was recorded that, "Mrs. Curley is anxious that American families who wish clothing register right away ..." while on the 16th of March, 1933 (A.C.N. p.6) the local paper in describing why clothing relief figures rose somewhat in February over the January figures states that, "This gain in total figures for February is due in part ... to the fact that not until the month of February were a number of Mexicans aware of the fact that clothing relief was available".

Although there seems to be something more to this delay than a mere breakdown of communication between the clothing committee members and the Mexican population of Ajo, I doubt seriously that Mrs. Curley and the "investigating" committee members were really trying to deny aid to the Mexicans, especially since twenty-two Mexican women were among those Red Cross Volunteers sewing clothes for this relief work (A.C.N. November 10, 1932:1) but rather that they probably set up a system of priorities with the needs of most "Americans" coming first. Evidence for this are the great pains Mrs. Curley took to convince the "American" ladies that this clothing was not really charity and that the dress patterns would be varied to retain their originality (A.C.N.

October 13, 1932:1). Thus, the priority of this relief program seemed to revolve more around satisfying the needs and desires of the typical "American" woman than those of the Mexican or Indian lady as is clearly shown in Table II.

Other forms of aid were also available to the people of Ajo during the winter of 1932-1933 and by March an extremely intricate communications network had evolved in Ajo to insure the speedy delivery of goods and services to those in need. The nature of this highly complex system that had by now replaced the company as the supplier of most of the basic needs of the people of Ajo (i.e, the supplier of those inputs necessary for the maintenance of the essential variables of the unemployed worker and his family within certain critical limits) is clearly discussed in an article that appeared in the Ajo Copper News in March, 1933 (A.C.N. March 16, 1933:1,6) that states among other things that:

> Local relief is divided into two general classes - work and direct relief; and the latter is divided into two classes, food from the commissary and clothing from the Red Cross committee.
> Clothes are furnished mostly through the Red Cross, though some of the clothes that are needed and are not furnished by the Red Cross are paid for with R.F.C. money. A certain portion of the county indigent fund is used at times - mostly for shoes.
> The local commissary is fully supplied at all times with staple foods, bought through the Organized Charities in Tucson and sold at exact cost without any charge for overhead added. It is not often that the local committee is obliged to buy any kind of supplies, direct, but when this is necessary (due to inability to buy through the Organized Charities, or to not being furnished by the Red Cross) the purchase is made in the cheapest market outside of Ajo, with R.F.C. funds.

In all cases, there is no charge for transportation as this item is borne by Pima County, county trucks bringing in the supplies without expense to the local committee.

And as the Organized Charities C.E. Goyette, chairman, purchases in large lots at reduced prices and ships goods into Tucson in carload lots, it will be understood that those who are assisted here get wonderful bargains that go a long way toward taking the sting out of the depression.

In addition, the local committee has at times received for free distribution some Red Cross flour that was manufactured from U.S. Government wheat. There is none on hand now, but while it lasted it was distributed - according to Red Gross rules - at the rate of ten pounds per month per person. ...

The Relief work is done on upkeep and widening of the Tucson highway between Ajo and the point about thirty-seven miles east of Ajo where the old portion of the highway ends and the new portion begins.

Those seeking work sign a questionnaire application in which they answer a number of questions asked. As with the Red Cross relief, applications are personal. Whether the work is one day or four days, each man working signs a receipt for the full amount of the check, stating that the work has been performed. He may take all, none or a portion of the amount in commissary goods - as he chooses; and no money is handled at the commissary - no supplies may be secured at the commissary otherwise. Each transaction is completed when check and commissary supplies (or check or commissary supplies) are received for the work period of one to four days. For pay is by check on the Valley Bank and Trust Company signed by the local committee. The committee pays out money only as received.

There is a similar strictness, of course, as between the local committee and the Organized Charities, for every shipment received must be checked, receipted for and accounted for.

Thus it will be seen that Ajo relief is both a big business and a strict business institution. Every committee is made aware of its responsibilities. This must be so if there is to be proper functioning. Relief is a Federal business as necessary and as thorough as any Government-controlled, Nation-wide act in war time; and those who are engaged in this distribution of relief without pay are serving their country just as much and well as if this country were engaged in war. Similarly, those who cooperate with the committee in this emergency are just as much entitled to credit and thanks as though it were a war emergency.

This highly organized system of relief, in contrast to the earlier Ajo Relief Committee, had obviously by now become more than a simple control mechanism serving the interests of other more complex systems. It was now by far the most complex social system (i.e., the one having the most negentropy[63]) in existence in Ajo and in many respects represented a mere transformation of the company since it was staffed by company personnel and pursued company goals (i.e., the maintenance of essential company system variables within their critical limits). Thus, although the major physical portion of the environment handled by the system became government money and other government supplied goods and services rather than copper, this new relief organization functioned to protect both the net income variables and systemic status set population variables of the company and related systems while outwardly accomplishing the Federal Government's announced "patriotic" goal of protecting the net income variable of the individual unemployed worker. This manipulation of the resources (i.e., output) of a larger system by a smaller one to further the ends of the smaller system is an apparently almost universal phenomenon (e.g., see Bennett 1967:450-452 or Pitt-Rivers 1961:200-201). Several other examples of this type of manipulation will be given in the following chapters.

It is extremely interesting to examine the statistical breakdown of the aid received by the different ethnic group members of Ajo during this difficult winter period. Table II is a summary of data published in the Ajo Copper News on March 9, 1933 (p.1) while Table III is a summary of data published on March 16, 1933 (A.C.N. p.6). Here, there is definite evidence that "Americans" were favored over the other two ethnic groups in obtaining items of clothing and the much more desirable (in terms of financial benefits) work relief. Also because of the relatively smaller average family size associated with the "American" worker, the gap between the amount of aid received by the average "American" family and the amount received by the average Mexican or Indian family was even wider than it appears at first glance at these two tables. This was true in spite of the fact that those people who were "better off" as decided by the local Relief Committee had supposedly been dropped from the list of road crew workers. However, a further tightening of eligibility requirements for this form of aid was to be imposed in March (A.C.N. March 16, 1933:1) but nothing indicates whether or not this action changed the ethnic balance of those qualifying for work on the road crews. It should also be added in all fairness to the local Relief Committee that each man on the work relief rolls was limited to four days of work a month, if he headed a family or three days a month if he did not[64] (A.C.N. March 16, 1933:1).

TABLE II

CLOTHING RELIEF (OCTOBER 22, 1932 - MARCH 1, 1933)

	Americans	Mexicans	Papagos
Number of families assisted	99	103	27
Number of individuals assisted	332	475	111
Average family size	3.35	4.61	4.11
Number of clothes donated by Red Cross	1188	981	244
Number of clothes donated by Direct Relief	1379	1604	236
Total number of clothes donated	2567	2585	480
Average number of clothes per person	7.73	5.44	4.32

TABLE III

RELIEF STATISTICS (FEBRUARY 1933)

Number of men working	Americans	Mexicans	Papagos	Total
on relief projects	230 (59.3%)	117 (30.2%)	41 (10.6%)	388

(Total wages paid in February = $4,802.00 or $12.38 per man average but no breakdown by ethnic group) (361 men were working in January but again no breakdown by ethnic group)

Number of persons	Americans	Mexicans	Papagos	Total
receiving direct relief	630 (46.1%)	559 (40.9%)	178 (13.0%)	1367

(This would include most if not all the men working on relief projects also)

	Americans	Mexicans	Papagos	Total
Amount of direct relief	$603.25	$548.15	$132.44	$1,283.84
Average per person	$.96	$.98	$.74	$.94
Total number of persons	Americans	Mexicans	Papagos	Total
receiving work, food or	716 (48.9%)	567 (38.7%)	181 (12.4%)	1464
clothing relief				

(A total of 1317 persons received either work, food, or clothing in January, but there is no statistical breakdown by ethnic group) (Total value of this three-way assistance in February was $4.13 per person as opposed to $4.56 in January, but again there is no breakdown of figures by ethnic group)

One curious aspect of these reports is the fact that 181 Papagos had been aided during the month of February, including at least forty-one adult male unemployed workers (i.e., those signed up for work relief) when the previous October, no Papagos were mentioned as having signed up for work on the road crews (A.C.N. March 16, 1933:1; October 13, 1932:1). The explanation for this discrepancy is not at all clear. Perhaps the paper in October did not give a complete ethnic breakdown of those signing up for road work since only Mexicans were specifically mentioned by name, although the implication seemed to be that the other 138 men were "Americans". Or, maybe most of the Papago males were away during the summer working on ranches or farms or living with relatives on the reservation, since almost no aid was available during this period. A third possibility might be that the Indians were not allowed or "encouraged" to sign up for the work relief at first. Finally, a fourth possibility is that the Indians present in October were perhaps included in the Mexican category of unemployed workers.

Very few of the 1967-68 Indian residents of Ajo had arrived in Ajo before the depression began, but I was fortunate to find one man who had come to Ajo in 1916 to work for Tom Childs and who seemed to have a fairly good knowledge of what had happened to the Indians of Ajo since that time. Although he was not living permanently in Ajo during the 1926-1936 period, he said that he was sure that about thirty families of Papagos remained in Ajo throughout the depression shutdown, although almost all of these families later went back to the reservation as they retired or were laid off (L.I.45). He, himself, worked as a truck driver for a reservation work relief program (C.C.C.) during the depression with a Papago crew installing fences between the reservation districts.

Only a few other Papago miners or their wives were still alive in 1967-68 who were working in Ajo during the 1930's since death strikes down the average Ajo Papago long before he or she reaches the retirement age. Unfortunately, one Indian (L.I. 52) who did live in Ajo all during the depression shutdown said that he was "born and raised with (the local) Mexicans" and "never had much to do with the Indians" here in Ajo, but still he estimated that only "about half (of the Ajo Indians) left" town. Giving a different version of this time period, a miner (L.I. 27) who came to Ajo in 1936 said that before he had arrived in Ajo the only Indians living in the town were the "local people" (i.e., the sand people who had intermarried with Tom Childs and the other early white miners) and those from "Gunsight" and other "close-by places". Finally, one lady (L.I. 41) who was born in Ajo in 1930 said that she and her family remained in Ajo all during the depression years while two other miners told me that their families had left Ajo during the depression, one family going to the farm areas of the state to work (L.I.43) and the other family returning to the village of "Hotwater" on the reservation until the crisis was over (L.I.48). Unfortunately, even though the fathers of all three of these individuals were miners and thus directly affected by the shutdown, they themselves were too young to remember much about this period of time.

Data of a more definite nature proved to be difficult to locate although from the relief figures quoted above, obviously a large number of Papago families had either remained in Ajo after the depression shutdown had begun or had returned to Ajo right in the midst of the shutdown. Therefore, these figures together with my interview statements cast great doubt upon the validity of the previously mentioned secondhand statement given Waddell (1969:54) that "the Indian community must have been abandoned" during the depression shutdown.

Although no breakdown is given by ethnic group, it is also possible to obtain some idea of the depopulation and repopulation of Ajo during the depression shutdown through the use of the school enrollment figures contained in Table III (Leonard 1954:82). For example, since the total population of Ajo and the surrounding area in 1930 was 4,570 (A.C.N. May 15, 1930:1) and the total number of students enrolled in the Ajo school system for the school year 1930- 1931 was 815, we can make the very rough estimate that for every student in the Ajo camp there were 5.61 people in the Ajo population. Assuming that this same ratio is valid[65] during the entire 1932-1934 shutdown then we can calculate that in September, 1932, there were 1,402 individuals still living in Ajo, that at the beginning of March, 1933, there were 1,974 people there, and that by January, 1934, there were 2,226 persons in Ajo. The 1974 figure in March agrees fairly well with the 1,464 figure representing those receiving welfare aid for the month of February (A.C.N. March 16, 1933:6), especially when it is remembered that 28 men were still on the regular company payroll (Therrien 1945:104) and others were deriving income from other sources such as cattle (e.g., Tom Childs and his relatives) and store income[66] while still others were probably working in other areas of the state and sending their pay back to Ajo to support their families.[67] Thus, all evidence seems to indicate that the low point in Ajo population during the long shutdown occurred near the end of the summer in 1932 and that beginning that fall the relief mechanisms funded by the Federal Government but controlled on the local level by company officials succeeded in drawing back large numbers of unemployed miners to Ajo.[68]

TABLE IV

SCHOOL ENROLLMENT FIGURES (LEONARD 1954:82)

School Year	Enrollment		
	Grades 1-8[69]	Grades 9-12	Total
1930-31	712	103	815
1931-32	744	107	851
1932-33	340	62	402[70]
1933-34	444	68	512[71]
1934-35	581	102	683
1935-36	792	125	917
1936-37	825	146	971
1937-38	842	165	1007
1938-39	759	171	930

Throughout the year of 1933, additional programs of work relief became available to the unemployed of Ajo. For example, in April, it was announced that twenty-five Ajo youths would be employed in government forest camps (A.C.N. April 27, 1933:1) and a second group was solicited in September (A.C.N. September 7, 1933:1). Also, in September, eight men were called to work on a natural gas pipeline from Douglas to Phoenix and a request was sent to Ajo to supply at least part of a seventy-five man crew needed for work in the forests near Tucson (A.C.N. September 14, 1933:1). Later that fall, it was announced that more work would be available for teachers to teach unemployed workers English and other basic "American" subjects and skills (A.C.N. November 16, 1933:1) while the main government work program was to be expanded to employ about two-thirds of the Ajo jobless for thirty hours per week at 37-1/2 cents per hour throughout the entire winter (A.C.N. November 9, 1933:1). Much of this work was to be done on civic improvement projects in or near Ajo, beginning first with the improvement of an aviation field north of town and then proceeding to the building of a town recreation park, new storm drainage systems, and other projects of a similar nature (A.C.N. November 23, 1933:1; November 30, 1933:1). This new program was an instant success with the local unemployed miners and by early December, the weekly payroll was over $3,000 with more money and an expanded program to include also the direct distribution of eggs and fresh beef to needy Arizona families, promised shortly by government officials (A.C.N. December 7, 1933:1; December 14, 1933:1). This C.W.A. (Civil Works Administration) program was scheduled to continue until May 1, 1934 with a slow tapering off of the program from March 1 to May 1 as C.W.A. workers would be gradually incorporated into an enlarged public works program (A.C.N. December 14, 1933:1).

Finally on April 19, 1934 (A.C.N. p.1), the most comprehensive work relief plan of all was announced. One person from each of the 21,000 needy families in the state of Arizona was to be employed for forty-two hours a month at 50 cents per hour (i.e., $21 per month of work aid would be available to each needy family). However, even this important news was far overshadowed by the surprise announcement on March 29, 1934 (A.C.N. p.1) that the New Cornelia mine would be reopening in July of that year.

In retrospect, one interesting aspect of this long shutdown period was the continued performance of the community rituals on the 4th of July and Christmas Eve. In fact at Christmas time, the children were even able to each receive a small gift of an orange, an apple, and a small box of candy and nuts, thanks to donations from several individuals and clubs (A.C.N. December 8, 1932:1; December 28, 1933:1). In addition, other ritual events such as the Mexican Independence Day were also celebrated during this period (A.C.N. September 14, 1933:1). All such events helped strengthen the somewhat weakened bonds that tied people to Ajo by creating warm feelings for the town and the company in the minds of the workers and their families. Evidence for the strength of this "affection" that many people demonstrated for Ajo is seen in the statement by the local paper that very few subscribers had stopped their subscriptions to the Ajo Copper News during the shutdown, even those who had left town (A.C.N. February 16, 1933:1). In fact, many Ajoites in desperate need, even traded such things as chickens, eggs, and wood to the local paper to insure that their subscriptions would not be cancelled.

It is difficult to describe in rational terms, the exact nature of this "affection" for Ajo but it is obvious both from that which is recorded in the literature and from my own personal research, that through the years the carefully chosen control actions (including the community ritual activities) generated or strongly supported by the company have been largely responsible for creating many of these feelings of "affection" for Ajo. But it is even more difficult to assess the true motives that lay behind the actions of company officials and their wives during the 1930's crisis. Thus when the visiting Mrs. Briggs donated $100 to the Ajo Relief fund (A.C.N. January 5, 1933:1), was she doing this to raise her relative standing in the eyes of the community members or did she really have a genuine concern for the welfare of the unemployed? Such questions are difficult to answer, but in either case the entropy model that was presented in Chapter 5 still applies since she was trying to extend her powers of control over the events that were taking place and increase the order and predictability of her environment. Also when Therrien (1945:104) states that, "Manager Curley found his ingenuity hard pressed to keep miners and their families from undue suffering", she assumes that his acts were motivated purely for the benefit of the workers, not himself nor the company. Is this a safe assumption? No definite answer can be given, but the question can also be asked, does it really matter since obviously all systems involved "benefited" from his actions. Therefore, it can be argued that for analytical purposes so-called personal "motives" are not really of concern to us since, as was earlier stated, individual or collective acts are only of importance to the study of change in a society if they weaken or strengthen the ability of any individual, system, or systems to be able to predict and/or order its (their) environment(s). Furthermore, it is also clear that often the effect of an individual or collective act on the system directly involved or on other associated systems is not that which was originally intended.

In anticipation of the announced resumption of activity at the mine, two local businesses, an independent drugstore and the local movie theater that had closed their doors (i.e., suffered a temporary systemic collapse during the shutdown) announced plans to reopen (A.C.N. April 19, 1934:1). One important factor in this decision was that the company had already begun to rehire men to begin the repair and maintenance work necessary for the grand reopening day (A.C.N. April 19, 1934:4). In fact, by May 31, 1934 (A.C.N. p.1) about 750 men were back on the payroll. Thus, money was again becoming readily available to fill the coffers of both the "loyal" local business man and the fair-weather "out-of-town" opportunist salesmen who were again beginning to descend upon the unsuspecting townsmen according to an editorial in the local paper (A.C.N. April 19, 1934:4).

Three important steps, by now, had been taken on the national level by top officials in both the Government and the copper industry to insure that the price of U.S. copper would again begin to rise to at least a level where a minimal profit could be realized. The first of these, the imposition of a tariff on all copper imports has already been discussed. The second was that each copper company was to be given a production quota by President Roosevelt which initially was to be equal to about 20 per cent of each one's capacity to produce (A.C.N. April 19, 1934:supplement p.2) while the third was that the huge eighteen month reserve stockpile of copper held by the various companies was to be "frozen" for an indefinite period of time, thus allowing only newly mined copper to be sold to consumers on the prescribed strict quota basis (A.C.N. April 26, 1934:1-2). All of these actions were designed to raise the price of copper quickly to at least 9 cents a pound (A.C.N. April 19, 1934:supplement p.2).

The mine did open in July, in fact on the very first day although this was a Sunday[72] (A.C.N. June 28, 1934:1). However, at first, employment must not have been complete due to the production quota system since on August 9 (A.C.N. 1934:1) it was reported that 72 families were still on relief in Ajo including 42 "American" families, 20 Mexican families and 10 Papago families.[73] More road work employment relief was being considered for the heads of these families until production again rose at the mine. Still, by November, it was reported (A.C.N. November 15, 1934:1) that all the estimated 800 to 1,000 houses in the camp were occupied, leaving no vacancies for new arrivals. That at least some Papagos had been rehired by this time is confirmed by the report on October 4 (A.C.N. 1934:1) that one of two men killed in a mine accident was a Papago Indian.

By September, 1935 (A.C.N. September 20, 1935:1) it was announced that slightly over 1,000 men were by now employed at the mine and although a sign saying, "No Men Needed" was displayed prominently at the employment office, a 25 per cent production increase in copper output was announced by Phelps Dodge to begin that month. The beneficial effects of such national relief mechanisms as the copper tariff and the quota system were finally reaching the local level (A.C.N. September 27, 1935:1).

With prosperity assured, a new crushing plant was installed at the mine in 1936 and a natural gas line to Ajo was completed, using funds borrowed by the El Paso Natural Gas Company from the Phelps Dodge Corporation (Therrien 1945:105). Also, one hundred new company homes were constructed in the "American" residential section of town as well as "the first block of ten or fifteen (company) houses" for the Indian population of Ajo (Therrien 1945:105; Waddell 1969:54).

However this relatively small number of new houses for the Indians was apparently far from being adequate to meet the needs of the 232 Papagos (representing 18.8 per cent of the total Ajo workforce) that Waddell (1969:55), using company employment figures, states were on the payroll in 1936. This large figure was not altogether surprising since, through such programs as the C.C.C. fence-building and the road work relief crews on the reservation, many Indians had by now "committed" themselves to a wage labor pattern of work habits. Therefore, as the government relief programs were cut back, many nearby Papagos were probably more than willing to hop on the company recruiting trucks bound for Ajo.[74]

However, it was not long before the increasing number of "uncontrolled" Indians in Ajo living under what must have seemed to company officials as being chaotic and extremely unsanitary conditions, could not be tolerated. This rising number of Indian employees was probably equated by company officials with an increasing state of disorder in the formerly smoothly functioning giant system they had created. To "solve" this "problem", company officials felt they must either attempt to control the lives of their Indian employees as fully as they had controlled the lives of their "American" and Mexican workers in the past or replace them with "Real Americans." The latter option was apparently chosen to take advantage of the large depression-era pool of unemployed "Real Americans," since it was reported that by the end of 1941 only 100 Indians remained in Ajo (A.C.N. September 23, 1943:1).

But despite this initial large decline in the number of Indian miners employed by the company after 1936, the bombing of Pearl Harbor changed everything. Thus, as the large pool of unemployed "Real Americans" quickly vanished and the total number of employed miners in the wartime years, 1944 and 1945, drastically declined (See figure 2), (due apparently to the result of an acute labor shortage due to the manpower requirements of the Military rather than of a lessened demand for copper[75]) (Leonard 1954:28), the number of Indian workers and their families in Ajo climbed from 100 in late1941 to "over 700" in November 1942 (A.C.N. November 5, 1942:1) and to 800 by September 1943 (A.C.N. September 23, 1943:1), forcing company officials to again examine ways to decrease the anticipated rising degree of systemic and environmental disorder by more fully integrating these workers into the overall highly controlled company town[76].

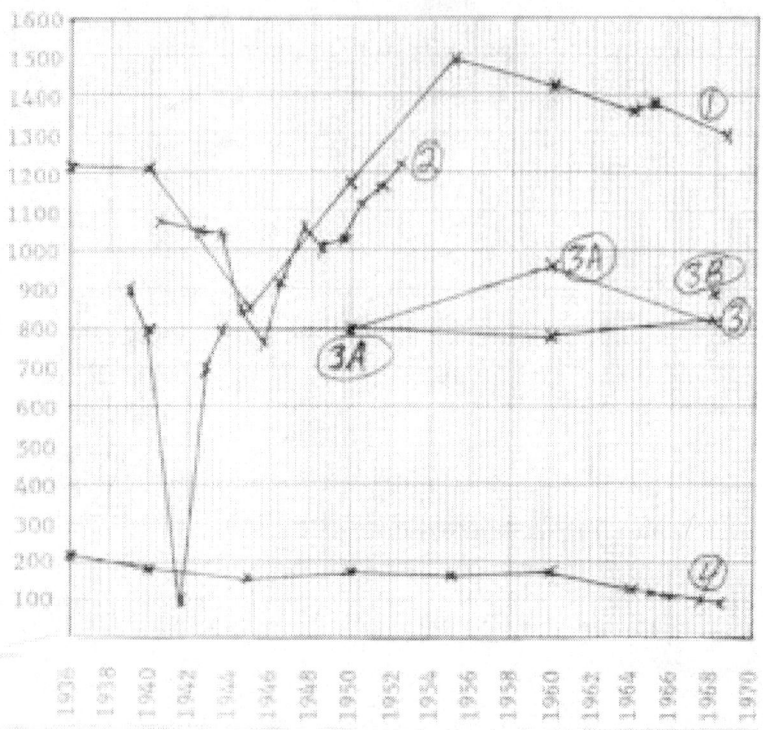

Employment and Indian Population Trends from 1936 through Mid-1968

1. Total Mine Employment for years 1936, 40,45,50,55,60,64,65 calculated from (Waddell 1969:55); for July 1968(F.N. July 16, 1968))

2. Total Mine Employment (for Aug. 1, 1940 (Therrien 1945:106); for years 1942-1952 (Leonard 1954:38);

3. Total Ajo Indian Population (for 1939, 1940 estimates (Waddell 1969: 54); for 1960 (Waddell 1969:55); for 1968(3B) (includes Indians away in boarding schools) and 1968, see Table XV); for late 1941 to November 1942 (A.C.N. November 5, 1942:1); for September 1943 (A.C.N. September 23, 1943:1).

3A. Total Ajo Indian Population for 1950, 1960 (U.S. Census "others"). In Ajo in the 50s and 60s, "others" would be almost entirely composed of those claiming Indian ancestry.

4. Number of Indians on Mine Payroll (for years 1936, 40,45,50,55, 60,64,65 (Waddell 1969:55); for late 1965 (F.N. Oct. 30, 1967); for July 1968 see Chapter Note 77, Chapter 6). **The straight-line extrapolation for the years from 1940 to 1945 is probably highly inaccurate given the extreme fluctuation in the numbers of Indians resident in Ajo during those years as reported in the local newspaper.**

Thus, the Indian miner from this point on began to be treated by the company as an integral part of the functioning whole Ajo company complex of systems. No longer would he be regarded as a temporary migrant worker from a nearby reservation but rather as a stable permanent working resident in the greater Ajo community. In terms of the theoretical model developed earlier, one increasingly important systemic status set population variable in the greater Ajo complex of systems at this time was the number of Indian workers within the system. Apparently, an upper critical limit (i.e., "tipping point") had been exceeded by this variable during World War II, thus precipitating a major structural transformation in the overall system so that ultra-adaptability could be maintained.

Why then did the number of Papago miners increase during the war years and achieve a period of remarkable stability in this number until about the year 1960 and not suffer a similar wartime "Real American" worker decline? The answer can be found in the following January 1, 1942 (p.1) article in the <u>Ajo Copper News</u> entitled "Papagos of Sells invest $7500 in Defense Bonds":

> If they can't serve in the armed forces of the United States, they can at least buy Defense Bonds....

There are 6500 Papagos, but only 48 of them are in military service. This is not their fault; far more than that have offered to enlist but were turned down because of educational requirements. Since day schools were established on the reservation only a few years ago, a great majority of the men of military age can not read or write.

Thus, Papago men during this period were more likely to escape the draft than "Americans" and more easily replaced if drafted due to the oversupply of unemployed men on the nearby reservation. Nor could the company now count on its Mexican workers being allowed to return after crossing over the border for their customary visits with friends and relatives since in the aftermath of the attack on Pearl Harbor, "to accomplish a more effective control of border crossing" only "Mexican citizens lawfully domiciled in the United States" would be allowed to leave the United States without a permit but they would not be allowed to re-enter without one (A.C.N. December 11, 1941:1). Also implied, but not stated, in this article would be the difficulty in recruiting and gaining entry permits for new Mexican workers.

However, as also seen in figure 2, this Papago employment stability did not last after the Korean war years when the number of Indians employed at the mine continually declined from 174 in 1960 to about 102 in 1968. At first glance, this decline in the number of Indian workers after 1960 may not seem to be too significant given the general decline in the total number of workers at the mine beginning even earlier than 1960, due largely to automation, until the percentage of the total work force that was Indian is calculated for the years 1960 to 1968. In 1960 12.2 per cent of the total labor force was Indian, but by 1964 this percentage had dropped to 10 per cent and further to 9 per cent in 1965 (Waddell 1969:55). And, by mid- 1968 it had dropped to 7.8 per cent[77], and there was every indication that it would continue to drop rapidly in the foreseeable future.[78] This decline, on the surface, seemed even more remarkable since the company had in recent years discouraged the keeping of ethnic records and, "officially holds to the current emphasis on equal opportunity for all" (Waddell 1969:55). Also, they had by the late 60's attempted to stabilize the ethnic composition of the labor force "at a controlled 65 per cent Anglo, 25 per cent Mexican, and 10 per cent Indian proportion" (Waddell 1969:55) or approximately the same percentage each ethnic group occupied in the total population of the Ajo area (Waddell 1969:57, 1974: 178-179). Obviously they were failing in this attempt, but why?

To understand what happened in Ajo, one must go back to 1957 when strong "civil rights" sentiments were sweeping the country. The company, despite a long history of rather rigid segregation policies, perhaps out of fear of Government intervention or perhaps with "nobler" motives, suddenly decided in 1957 to prove that they were being fair to all job applicants regardless of race, religion or cultural background by giving each applicant a battery of equally graded tests[79] (Waddell 1969:54). However, much to their surprise only ten percent of the Indian applicants passed the test, even though they were often given a second chance to take it (this second chance was denied to Anglos and Mexicans) (Waddell 1969:57). For the first few years after the test was initiated, exceptions were even made for some of the Indians failing the test both times but after 1960, the interpretation of the test results gradually became more rigid in the determination of a person's employment fate, "in order to achieve the equality of treatment ideal" (Waddell 1969: 54,55). Thus, as occurring also in other similar cases throughout the country, a well-intentioned action originally set up to give minority group members equal rights in the larger society had just the opposite effect of actually barring many minority group members from jobs they could otherwise perform in a satisfactory manner. The Indians, in particular, failed to comprehend how the ability to read and write well could be of much importance to one's ability to lay track, sweep a floor, or drive a truck.

However, the Indian worker who either joined the Company's labor force before these tests were given or who did succeed in passing the test was often given preferential opportunities to advance if he knew the right rules of the advancement "game" and obeyed them.

Such an Indian is praised by almost all of the local whites who know him. These few "successful" Indians were pointed to with pride as examples of the fairness of the company to minority group members and the potential that all Indians had if they would only "apply themselves" to their work and adopt the proper set of corresponding habits needed for "success" in life.[80]

By 1968, very few Indians complained of overt on-the-job discrimination, even from fellow workers of different ethnic backgrounds. However, the employment tests and especially the man who gave them, were the object of many sarcastic and often bitter remarks, and the employment agent, in particular, was occasionally accused of outright discrimination against the average Indian.[81]

Following the 1936 reopening, several Pima families moved to Ajo, beginning at least as early as in 1940, and possibly as early as 1937 (L.I. 47; L.I. 51). In contrast to most Papago Indians, these people interact much more with the "Americans" and Mexicans of Ajo, as stated earlier, and are generally held in high regard by all who know them. Although the Pimas of Ajo form only a small minority of the total Indian population of the town, their impact on certain aspects of the Indian "community" in recent years has been quite large, as shall be shown in the following chapter.

In 1950, when the new smelter was opened in Ajo, four Yavapai and one Apache families and a few single Yavapai men were transferred to

Ajo from Clarkdale as Phelps Dodge closed the smelter there (L.I. 9; L.I. 19; L.I. 21). However, of these original transferees, the single men have all quit, while one family head has died and another has retired and moved back to Northern Arizona, thus drastically reducing the surviving Yavapai population of Ajo since only one son of these original miners had in the intervening years become a miner himself, and no further Yavapai recruits from the Clarkdale area had come to Ajo by 1968 (L.I. 9; L.I. 19).

Except for these few Indians[82], most of the workers at the new smelter were and continue to be Mexicans (Waddell 1969:54). As expected, this employment policy has greatly increased the Mexican population of Ajo, which had been drastically depleted during the depression shutdown.

Finally, it should be mentioned at this point that World War II with its acute labor shortage apparently helped change the attitudes of the local townspeople toward the Indian. Thus, in 1942 (A.C.N. July 16, 1942:4), an editorial appeared in the local paper, praising the local Papago Indians for their progressive attitudes and improvements in reading and writing skills and in 1943 (A.C.N. June 24, 1943:2) a long article appeared in the Ajo Copper News recounting the noble deeds of various Indian War Heroes. These were followed in 1944 (A.C.N. May 11, 1944:4) by an ad placed by the Southern Pacific railroad in the local paper praising America's Indians for their great contributions to the war effort, both on the battlefield and on the home front.

The War also affected other aspects of the "culture" of Ajo. In December 1941 (A.C.N. December 18, 1941:1), Phelps Dodge and another copper producer declared that they would be patriotic and begin to operate the mine 7 days a week rather than the usual 6 so that copper production could be "speeded-up" for the war effort. No longer would Sunday work be considered sinful.

Also during the war years, 1942, 1943, and 1944, no 4th of July celebrations were held. [83] This may seem strange occurring right in the midst of a war where patriotism was being stressed everywhere in the country, but possibly the war itself was probably acting as a "substitute" for the celebration in arousing patriotic feelings in the people of Ajo. Also, the number of those most active in planning the event (e.g., the members of the American Legion) seemed to have passed a lower critical limit (i.e., "tipping point") during these war years since in 1945, after many men had returned from Europe, the celebration was again held despite the fact that fireworks were still not available, and the war against Japan had not yet entered its final stages[84] (A.C.N. July 5, 1945:1).

One final paragraph on labor relations between the company and the various national unions of mine, mill and smelter workers during the '40's, '50's, and early '60's, should be written at this point since in June, 1941 the company was ordered to "disband the Ajo Association of Copper Mine Employees[85] and to reinstate with back pay six workers who had been dismissed because of membership and activity in other unions" (Therrien 1945:106).

As discussed earlier, company officials had often, previous to this time, voiced their disapproval of union organizing activities in Ajo, but after this Board ruling was laid down, perhaps also due initially in large part to the increasing demand for copper in military production, the wartime federalization of the mines, and shortages of wartime workers (Rosenblum 1995: 30), cooperation between the local chapters of the national unions and the company until the bitter 1983 strike[86] was extremely high even during the long 1967-68 strike. As a consequence of this high degree of mutual cooperation, Ajo escaped most of the labor strife that closed down much of the copper industry after World War II ended (Leonard 1954:28) and hardly noticed a brief shutdown of 6 days in 1960 because of a railroad workers union strike (A.C.N. February 11,

1960:1; February 18, 1960:1). Therefore few Ajoites were prepared for the shock of the extremely long 1967-68 strike.

Chapter Notes

1. Rose (1936:3,5) quoting John D. Mitchel, speaks of the establishment of the village called Moivavi (which he translates as "many wells") at the Ajo mineral deposits long before the arrival of the Americans into the area, but during the Apache raiding period. However, this legend has not been verified.

2. Thus, although the company decision maker initially believed that this system interaction was a facultative mutual one he later learned that instead it was a parastic one.

3. Therrien (1945:33) using another source reports that there were only 42 Mexicans. Her figure is probably closer to the true number. Many other aspects of the story also differ in her account which she feels may be more reliable than Rose's account, especially those aspects concerning the details of the "battle" scene.

4. Waddell (1969:53) seems convinced that the Papago miners "attached themselves to the mining camp temporarily but maintained their homes in surrounding rancherias and returned there whenever the mining operations came to a halt." However, I tend to be somewhat skeptical of the suggestion that these miners after an initial exposure to the concept of wage labor would be willing to sit idly by during the 1859-1884 period waiting for the mine to reopen. I rather suspect that many of them could be found in road crews working on the new Southern Pacific railroad or in other similar endeavors during this period. In fact, the Sand Papago that began to move into the Gila River Valley after the Civil War "probably in connection with the Southern Pacific Railroad" (Hackenberg 1964:IV-54,55) may have possibly included some of the Ajo miners.

    Therrien (1945:39) gives the date of the ending of the active phase of this mining venture as 1856 rather than the 1859 date given by Rose, which probably marks the date when the property was finally sold at a sheriff's sale to satisfy a lien against it.

5. Clotts(1915a:l) writes that the village of Quitovaquito in 1914 had four resident families who represented "the remnants" of about 150 families of Arenenos or Sand Papagoes, who used to inhabit the country farther west toward Yuma in the sand dunes, and were devastated by some disease about 40 years ago, the survivors moving to Quitovaquito." This quotation seems to add some additional confirmation to the common belief that Childs' wife was a "Sand Papago". It is also interesting to note that Childs lived for a while at Bates Well where Daniels had settled down, also with a Papago wife.

6. In an earlier account of this same story it is stated that although Hovey settled with his laborers by paying them in the form of both groceries and whiskey it was "chiefly whiskey" that he gave them (A.C.N. July 4, 1919:1).

7. Barnes (1960:257) records that there were only four "Americans" living at the site later to be called "Old Ajo" in 1911 and Therrien (1945:78) reports that the ethnic balance for that year was "approximately twenty Mexicans to one American." Faulty memories or counts taken during different months of 1911 may account for these inconsistencies.

8. However, from several informants I learned that even today, small veins of very rich ore are sometimes found in the mine (e.g., see F.N. February 21, 1968).

9. As in Cornelia, strict racial segregation in housing was also practiced in Clarkston.

10. See Chapter Note #1.

11. It is interesting to note that on July 16, 1968 in an interview with the local company employment agent that total employment at this time was only about 1300, a somewhat inflated figure since the company had opened up some additional summer jobs for local students (college, mainly) (F.N. 7/16/68).

12. In terms of the theoretical model developed earlier, "strikers", from the viewpoint of company officials can be considered to be subsystems of the company that are in a temporary state of disorder (i.e., not

producing the "proper" output) even though from the unions' point of view, the workers are producing the "correct" output to achieve the system transformations desired by union officials.

13. In later testimony before a Federal Commission investigating the affair it was revealed that "the orders for the deportation by railroad were issued by Walter Douglas, then president of Phelps-Dodge" (A.R. July 9, 1967 :C-1).

14. This control mechanism is really that described earlier of a total system's movement to a new environment. The system in this case being a company official.

15. This obviously refers to the "three or four I.W.W.'s in the camp" who were labeled by the "Property Holders Protective Association, etc. as disturbers" and "agitators

16. However, it should be added that in August, three local "German" workers were arrested and sent to Nogales for internment during the war, being held there "under the President's warrant" (A.C.N. August 17, 1917:1). One of them, born in Switzerland, was arrested for making "derogatory remarks" about this country and an army officer from Ajo.

17. In an interview with the editor of the local paper (F.N. November 13, 1967) I learned that the paper is not directly controlled by the company but "merely" leases the office space and printing equipment from the company. She said that she did not believe in "crusading newspapers with the strong editorials" but rather liked to print the "facts" and let the people "decide for themselves" how to vote, etc. However, she went on to say that during the current labor dispute she had tried to get some statement concerning the strike from the local union officials, but they had refused to talk to her. She agrees with the comments heard from others that no one wants to "rock the boat" and that most townsmen fear "reprisals" from the company. She feels that "no one would be gunned down in an alley" but other things such as the loss of a job in a company town could be quite disastrous.

18. In the Ajo strike when the strike was almost over, three-fourths of the remaining 200 strikers were Mexicans (A.C.N. December 16, 1916:1). However, in the Bisbee strike although it was true that many of the men deported were foreign born, many were also United States citizens and registered for the draft (Cox 1938:177,183). Also very few of these men were from Germany or Austria.

19. However, in the infamous Bisbee deportation, 433 of the 1,186 men abducted were married (Cox 1938:182-183).

20. Evidence for company support for and domination of this 4th of July holiday can be seen in the fact that Superintendent M. Curley had been "elected" to serve as president of the "4th of July celebration committee" (A.C.N. June 29, 1917:1).

21. See (A.R. December 24, 1967:Arizona 6-9) for a fairly complete description of the modern ceremony.

22. The special case of the one black company employee will be discussed later in this chapter. The term "American" to refer to the white man was still in common usage in the 60's among certain Ajo Indians (e.g., see F.N. May 28, 1968).

23. Probably the children that had one Mexican or "American" parent, such as Tom Childs, would be more likely to attend school than the local "fullbloods".

24. Just earlier the local truant officer reported that there were "at least thirty Papago Indian children not in school" (A.C.N. May 1, 1926:1). Also, see (A.C.N. October 13, 1923:1) for a comment similar to Johnson's remarks.

25. The increase in average school attendance lagged behind the enrollment figures which jumped to 546 in October 1923 (A.C.N. October 13, 1923:1) and then rose gradually until an enrollment peak of 617 students was reached in December, 1925 (A.C.N. April 26, 1924:8; A.C.N. December 12, 1925:6) (dropping to 604 in February, 1926) (A.C.N. May 1, 1926:1),

26. She did, however, add that the "other kids bothered him" (i.e., this black student) all the time.

27. My informant's mother who was born in 1921 was old enough to be sent away to boarding school but her uncle who was born in 1927 was still too young so he "escaped" this fate. Therefore, this event must have occurred between the years 1927 and 1932 or 1933. Also an "Indian mission school" was established in Ajo by at least the fall of 1929 (A.C.N. November 14, 1929:1) so this roundup probably occurred between the years 1927 and 1929, although more data is needed on this point since the roundup could have occurred even after the mission school was established.

28. My informant who was born in 1935 began her education at the age of six under one of these "special teachers".

29. Several glaring inconsistencies in the information this informant gave me about the events of his younger days make this statement unreliable. He may not even have attended school in Ajo very much.

30. This school teacher (F.N. February 25, 1968) said that after World War II, the first break came in this very rigid pattern of segregation when a fair-skinned Mexican boy was put in an "American" first grade classroom by mistake. By the time the error was discovered a few weeks later, he was doing so well that the school authorities permitted him to remain with the "American" group throughout his school career. Two Papago miners who entered the school system at the end of World War II said that at that time, rigid segregation was only maintained in the first two grades for Indian students, and had been dropped entirely for Mexican students (L.I.48; L.I.50).

31. The extent of this continuing informal pattern of segregation can be seen in the comments of one father (L.I.50) who said that in 1961 when his daughter was in the 3rd grade, her class was "mostly Indians but included a few Mexicans and whites". He added that, although at this time in the "2nd grade they started to mix them with the others" (i.e., other races) in the lower grades the Indians were kept together pretty much until they reached the 7th grade or higher."

32. One mother (L.I. 30) said that her third son had "learned English better and faster" than her other children because in 1959 he had

been enrolled "by mistake" in a racially mixed class because the school personnel had thought that he was a Mexican rather than an Indian.

33. Actually this attack had begun the previous year. In an earlier article in the Ajo Copper News (September 19, 1919:1) it was stated that the American Legion was "after alien slackers".

34. As mentioned briefly in connection with the earlier discussion of patterns of school segregation, often for segregation purposes, Indians were put in the same "slot" as the Mexicans. However, from interview data to be discussed later, it is somewhat doubtful that many Papago Indians ever visited the pool and learned how to swim.

35. The bilingual person occasionally does deliberately carry on conversations with fellow bilinguals in the language not understandable to a monolingual bystander to safeguard the "privacy" of the conversation. However, the reason given the bystander for the use of the native tongue over the language understood by the bystander would probably be merely to state that it was "easier" to discuss things in the native tongue or that someone present in the discussion group didn't really understand much English, etc.

36. The location of this building was probably somewhere within the boundaries of the 1960's Indian Village.

37. On December 18, the week before, it was also announced that prices were being generally reduced on food items at the company store (A.C.M. December 18, 1920:1). However, upon a close analysis of the food prices both before and after the so-called price reductions went into effect, I discovered that out of a total list of 39 major food items, only thirteen items had lower prices after the "price-cut" while eleven items had higher prices and fifteen items remained unchanged.

38. Here again we are referring to those men who are the decision makers in this instance and not to a reified entity.

39. Therrien (1945:101) gives the lowest employment figure in 1922 as 320 using a different reference.

40. An editorial on December 3 (A.C.N. December 3, 1921:12) praised the company for this "generous" gift from the store's reserve funds, even though the store had lost money the preceding year due to reductions in prices charged for its goods. It should be noted, however, that most of these price reductions were not really cuts planned by the company since many prices were depressed, merely, to match competitors' prices during the general business depression that was sweeping over the entire country during this period.

41. Apparently many people were still around at the beginning of the summer since the 4th of July committee was planning the biggest and best celebration ever (A.C.N. June 4, 1921:1).

42. Actually the good news started even earlier in the summer with the first hint being published that the copper market was beginning to improve (A.C.N. June 4, 1921:4).

43. Unfortunately, as mentioned previously, no figures were given for the December, 1921, $7^1/_2$ per cent rebate in the Ajo Copper News (A.C.N. December 3, 1921:1).

44. In more recent times another attempt by the company to stabilize "the ethnic composition of the labor force at a controlled 65 per cent Anglo, 25 per cent Mexican and 10 per cent Indian proportion" was reported by Waddell (1969:55).

45. Apparently any "overflow" people banded together in tent towns erected near the established townsites (A.C.N. September 6, 1924:1).

46. This was the last major challenge they were ever able to mount against the Company

47. This is a classic example of "frequency interpretation" (See Erasmus 1961:22-23) and vividly illustrates the point being made by Rindos(1984).

48. Apparently there was at this time a separate Negro section of Mexican town which is mentioned specifically in a death notice two years later (A.C.N. November 21, 1925:6).

49. Greenway, himself was a Southerner (A.C.N. June 6, 1925:1).

50. However, it should be made clear that a significant number of Ajo Papagos voted in elections by the late 60's, probably partly due to the extreme social pressure associated with the various get-out-the-vote campaigns supported by both the company and the unions. Indian voting behavior in Ajo will be discussed again in greater detail in the next chapter.

51. Apparently many Ajo people had worked in the Great Lakes region before migrating to Ajo. Also, many individuals owned stocks in the companies in both areas of the country. Therefore, communication took place on a frequent basis between the two regions.

52. If this distance is accurate; it would put the location of the Indian village somewhat closer to the center of town than it is at the present time.

53. The opening of this route meant that Ajo was no longer on a main transcontinental motor route.

54. This may be a rounded figure since later in the same article the number is given as 966 plus "about 280" giving a total of "about" 1,246.

55. This is a good example of control action #35 where to insure system survival two systems enter into an obligate mutual relationship.

56. It was reported later in the Ajo Copper News (September 27, 1935:1) that the low point was 4.75 cents per pound during this depression period. This conflict in figures is probably not too significant since very few sales of copper at even 4.75¢ per pound were ever made by American producers, most of whom preferred to keep their copper off the market than sell at such a loss.

57. This figure includes an estimate that 19 adults represent 9 families since comparable data were not given for the two different types of aid programs assisting Mexican families in Ajo.

58. This represents a combined total for both ethnic groups of 167 adults and 201 children or a grand total of 368 people.

59. Waddell (1968:6) states that: "In the pre-depression years Papago individuals entered into patron-like dyads with permanent Anglo

residents of the town who were primarily responsible for the founding and organizing interests in the mining operation. Anglos befriended certain Indian families, showed interests in their welfare, and built up informal obligatory relationships which operated to insure perpetual family connections with the mining operation." However, from the evidence I have gathered and presented earlier in this book, most of these "dyads" involved actual marriage ties, usually between one of the early white male settlers in the Ajo region and his Papago wife and her relatives.

60. In January 1933, after these layoffs had been completed, only 28 men were still employed, and the company payroll for that month was only $3,500 (Therrien 1945:104).

61. There is again obviously a functional relationship between these latter two variables.

62. It is also not clear from the written account whether or not the second group of eighty men included any members that were also in the first group of fifty-four.

63. Negentropy =negative entropy (i.e., a measure of order and control over environment)

64. There were probably very few single men who would "qualify" for this type of relief in Ajo given the company's continuing bias in favor of married men.

65. A somewhat shaky assumption I must admit. However in 1923, an article in the local paper (A.C.N. October 13, 1923:1) stated that "The ratio of 5 to 1 is usually figured in estimating population from school census," but the article then added that the ratio was usually a little higher in the Ajo camp due at least in part to the non-attendance of Papago Indian children. Thus from a school enrollment of 546 a total population of "over 3,500" was estimated giving a ratio of 6.41 to 1.

Rose (1936:65) writing during the 1935-1936 school year estimated the population of Ajo at about 6,000 people while Leonard (1954:82) records that there were 917 school children enrolled that year, thus giving a ratio of 6.54 to 1.

For the year 1940 Leonard (1954:31) estimated the population of Ajo as being 5,795 stating that the population of Ajo was not tabulated in the 1940 United States census. However, an exact count using census data was made for 1940 and published in 1941 (A.C.N. February 27, 1941:1) showing a population of 4,678 for Ajo and the surrounding townsites and ranches. (For some strange reason Leonard overlooked this count, even though it was published both in the Ajo Copper News on the front page in a prominent article and by Therrien in her 1945 study.) Using the school enrollment figures of 945 in the school year 1939-1940 (Leonard 1954:82) we can calculate a ratio of 4.95 residents to I student for that year (This, of course, assumes that both census figures were collected at nearly the same point in time, which may not be true).

Finally, using census data from 1950, Ajo's population was listed at 6,588 while the school population in the school year 1949-1950 was 1,498 (Leonard 1954:31,82,24), thus giving a ratio of 4.40 to 1. A partial explanation for the lower ratios in 1940 and 1950 is that by then almost all Papago and Mexican children were attending school.

66. The fishing business at the nearby port of Rocky Point in Mexico was apparently thriving during this period, thus also generating store income in Ajo (A.C.N. January 12, 1933:1).

67. This last supposition is based upon patterns of behavior observed during the course of the 1967-68 strike.

68. Although data other than the school enrollment figures presented earlier are scarce in attempting to document this assertion, several interesting bits of information concerning the Clarkston townsite during this period are pertinent. Thus, in 1930 the population of Clarkston including the government townsite of Rowood was given as being 351 (A.C.N. May 15, 1930:1) while in October, 1933 (A.C.N. October 5, 1933:4) the Rowood-Clarkston population was estimated to be back up to 200 to 300 people, even though the mine was still closed.

69. The figures given by Leonard (1954:82) for total grade school enrollment for the years 1930 to 1953 do not agree with the figures given in a shorter list by Therrien (1945:5) for the years 1936 to 1944, differing by as little as one in the school year 1942-43 to as much as 87 in the school year 1940-41. Furthermore, in all but two years the Leonard figures are higher indicating possibly that these figures were tabulated later in the school year than the Therrien figures.

70. There seems to be some conflict between this figure and the following figures given by the local newspaper (A.C.N. March 2, 1933:1; January 11, 1934:1):

Date	Total Number of Students Enrolled
September 1932	About 250
March 1933	352
January 1934	397

71. This figure must apply to the period just before the mine reopened when large numbers of men were rehired to do repair work, etc. in preparation for the July reopening of the mine (A.C.N. May 31, 1934:1).

72. Although most men did not normally work on Sunday, July 4 was to be a holiday so that work done on this one Sunday would "make up" for the lost time of the day off three days later. Evidently, everyone wanted a full paycheck that first week.

73. The report of a Salt Lake City, Utah, paper that 1,400 men had returned to work at New Cornelia on July 1 appears to have been a highly exaggerated figure (A.C.N. July 2, 1934:1; September 20, 1935:7).

74. Waddell (1969:54) was told that the company "sent trucks out to the reservation villages to round up the Papagos and bring them in to work in the mine" at this time.

75. School enrollment figures also indicate that more men were leaving Ajo during 1944-45 than families, thus indicating that the draft was probably responsible for much if not most of this decline (See Stucki 1970 figure 5).

76. The next chapter will discuss in greater detail, further extensions of company control over the lives of Indian workers and their families which also during the course of the recent strike aided in binding the Indian miner and his family to Ajo.

77. On July 16, 1968 the company's employment agent said that there were "about 1,300" employees at that time working for the company in Ajo, although this figure was "somewhat inflated" since a few local college students had been hired on a temporary basis for the summer only. Also on this day, as near as I could determine, 108 of these employees were "Indians", although six of these men had been given other ethnic identifications by the company's employment agent and some of their fellow co-workers leaving only 102 who were clearly identified by all as being "Indians". Therefore, to approximate the definition of "Indian" as used by the company's employment agent and thus make my figures somewhat comparable to Waddell's, I have used the figure 102 in calculating this percentage.

78. In terms of the model developed earlier, the systemic status set replacement index (ratio) (i.e., the number of incoming individuals to systemic status set "r" over the number of outgoing individuals from systemic status set "r" during the time interval T2-T1) has dropped to and remained at a value well below one since 1960 and in fact appeared in 1968 to be rapidly approaching a value near zero. However, the role replacement index in 1968 remained at a value near one for the total Indian population of Ajo as seen also from the data given in figure 2. The explanation for this seeming paradox will be given in the following pages.

79. According to one local union official, the aptitude test was really the unions' idea in their continuing attempt to "fight job discrimination in Ajo" (L.I.47).

80. Waddell (1969:60) indicates that the percentage of unskilled Papago employees at the mine dropped from 74 percent of the 142 employed in 1940 to 43 percent of the 101 employed in 1965. My figure of 32.6 percent remaining in the unskilled job category of the 95 Papagos employed at the mine in July 1967 shows that this general trend toward higher job levels for those Papagos remaining on the payroll was continuing; however, the results of a survey in which I interviewed 40 Indian employees and/or their wives indicated that although the majority of these miners (21) have shown a steady progression from lower to higher job levels during their Ajo career, seven have remained at the same level and twelve actually have poorer jobs today than they had at one time in their work career at the mine, although all 12 had at one time or other been moving upward from their starting position at the mine. (Nine of the 12 reported the downturn came when automation was first introduced at the mine and workers above them displaced them from their better jobs and three reported that after the end of the 1967-68 strike they were shifted downward).

Also, it is interesting to note in terms of the discussion in the next chapter that 25 of the 31 Papago miners with unskilled jobs at the mine in July, 1967, live in the Indian village (i.e., 42.4 percent of the Papago miners living there had unskilled jobs) while only one Papago miner living in "Upper Mexican Town" was still in the unskilled job category (13 other Papago miners (93%) living there had skilled or semiskilled jobs). Possibilities for advancement to higher job categories for many of the remaining unskilled miners were now very limited, since many lacked the high school diploma and the other basic skills that were now required for any of the on-the-job training courses being offered by the company.

81. This is somewhat ironic, since the employment agent told me of several instances where the company had recently given special job opportunities to carefully selected Indian employees, but added that most Indians really did not try very hard to pass the employment test, or to advance in their job skills (F.N. April 29, 1968). Also, a company official, who preferred to remain anonymous, said that

Phelps Dodge had chosen the Indian as its "official minority" which meant that Indians still did not have to have as high qualifications as "Americans" or "Mexicans" to get a job at the mine.

Waddell (1974: 182-183) adds that the company's "rather rigid and well-defined" absenteeism rules "are bent a bit if certain Indians with good work records exceed the absentee limit"

82. By 1968, only three Yavapais still worked for the company in Ajo and only one of these still worked at the smelter. (One works in the mine and the other in the mill).

83. The Christmas celebration was carried on as usual every year throughout the war.

84. The rapid conclusion of this war after the two atomic bomb attacks in August on Japan could not have been anticipated by the Ajoites in July of that year.

85. This was evidently a company-sponsored union

86. See Chapter 9 for a discussion of why this relationship changed during the 1983 strike.

CHAPTER 7:

The End of the Last Remaining Flaw: the "Systematized" Indian

> High labor turnover is indeed endemic wherever
> modern economic enterprise relies on the native social
> structure to provide the worker's security, or has at least
> not offered sufficient inducement to capture the worker's
> whole loyalty.
> ... the ties of the reluctant recruit to his native village and
> kinsmen have often been assumed to be so fundamental
> that no attempt has been made to provide housing,
> opportunities for social discourse, or many other
> amenities that match even the meager standards of the
> pre-existing modes of life (Moore 1951:116, 309,311)

There is a commonly believed "truism" accepted without question
by many engaged in programs of directed culture change, that change
without breakdown can only occur through compatible substitutions
into existing native frameworks.[1] Moore (1951:116, 309,311), in
commenting on this, states that:

Despite all that may properly be said about incompatibilities between nonindustrial societies and the industrial way of life, the modern industrial system has a rather overwhelming record of penetration into and even conversion of these societies. It carries in its train, and in direct proportion to its success, many unifying cultural characteristics that cut across former differences.

High labor turnover is indeed endemic wherever modern economic enterprise relies on the native social structure to provide the worker's security, or has at least not offered sufficient inducement to capture the worker's whole loyalty.

... the ties of the reluctant recruit to his native village and kinsmen have often been assumed to be so fundamental that no attempt has been made to provide housing, opportunities for social discourse, or many other amenities that match even the meager standards of the pre-existing modes of life.

Also, Nash (1958:14,23-25) in his discussion of the cotton textile mill in the municipio of Cantel in Guatemala found that absenteeism, worker discontent, and a fairly extensive turnover were chronic features of the factory until the factory management gradually began to add services and make concessions to the workers which had the effect of reducing the attrition in the labor force and apparently helped stabilize it. The factory built houses for the workers and electrified the main streets of the factory settlement, the public buildings, and many of the factory-owned workers' houses. A health clinic and other health services were provided for the employees and a factory school, superior to those provided by the national government, was established for their children. Also, land was loaned to the workers without charge.

If the conclusions of Nash and Moore are valid, then one of the most basic assumptions in many of our early attempts at directed culture change was false. Thus, the Indian Bureau, the Peace Corps and most applied anthropologists for many years attempted to lead backward peoples into the modern industrial world by first making them into good farmers. The Vicos and the Fox projects (Holmberg 1957; Gearing et al. 1960) are prime examples of this attempt by anthropologists.

Although the Vicos project has been hailed by many as the most spectacular success of applied anthropology, the innovations in agriculture (e.g., the new potato) may actually have retarded, rather than facilitated, further modernization. Perhaps the Fox Indians, in spite of the failure of the agricultural program planned by the anthropologists, were in the 60's more quickly becoming completely integrated into the modern world.

Returning now to Ajo, the Papago mining community there has also provided data to verify further the conclusions of Nash and Moore and to illustrate the processes involved in the transition between two largely incompatible systems. Preliminary data from Ajo fails to reveal much societal breakdown. In fact, there are many indications of great stability in the Ajo Indian community. If Nash and Moore are correct, then the apparent low turnover rate among Indian mine workers at Ajo at the time of my study in the 1960's indicated that by then these Native Americans relied more heavily on the company than upon native social structure for security. That this is a correct assumption will now be demonstrated in the following pages.

As was stated previously, the Papago Indian miner with his often undependable work record and "poor" living habits had frequently been a source of great concern to local company officials who viewed the Indian community as being the last remaining major flaw in the otherwise near-perfect (from the company's viewpoint) social order that characterized

Ajo. We have already seen that, through the years, there had been many attempts to partially control the Indian community, and therefore decrease the entropy of (i.e., decrease the degree of "disorder" in) the company's environment through such mechanisms as the differential retention and promotion of carefully selected Indian employees chosen because of their "desirable"[2] personal characteristics, and the building of some company housing for them beginning in 1936. However, most other attempts at control were of a more sporadic nature, such as the time during the 1930's when one trusted Indian employee was encouraged by company officials to take a leadership role in the Indian community and "persuade" the local Indians to sign the papers needed for the newly inaugurated Social Security program (L. I. 27).

However, "officials of the U.S. Indian Service", "the Phelps Dodge Corporation", "social workers", and Father Daniel Matson, Franciscan missionary to the Indians"[3] as the number of Indians in Ajo had increased from 100 in prewar 1941 to 800 by September 1943, were reported to be "behind the problem of getting the Indians to organize their own self-governing group in Ajo" (A.C.N. September 23, 1943:1,4). A "tipping point" had obviously been reached and in a "special meeting of the tribesmen" where a "first" and a "second" "chief" were elected to lead a "self-governing committee":

> ... the 800 Papagos ratified the constitution and by-laws
> of the committee. These last set forth that the committee
> will be devoted to the "protection of the public health
> and morals of the Papago people and provide for public
> welfare; provide for the maintenance of law and order
> through cooperation with county authorities and
> officials of the Phelps Dodge Corporation; and will
> have administration of the recreation hall[4] in the Papago
> village and any other facilities which may be provided by

the Phelps Dodge Corporation for the social betterment of the Papago people. (A.C.N. September 23, 1943:1)

However, Henry A. Throssel, "chairman of the All-Papago Council" (i.e., the Reservation governing body of the Papago people) and the vice chairman, Manuel Puella, :

> ... brought out that the council's constitution does not permit an off-reservation group to organize nor do (sic) any Indian Service regulation. However, the tribal constitution does permit the organization of special committees to handle special problems.... (A.C.N. September 23, 1943:4)

This committee would be allowed to:

> ... send a delegate to the Tribal Council at Sells on the reservation, but he will be given no vote. He will, however, be able to keep in touch with reservation matters and receive advice from the council on Ajo problems. He will also be given contact with Sells Indian Service officials and cooperation on all matters. (A.C.N. September 23, 1943:4)

Given these restrictions on its independence from control by the nearby reservation's Tribal leaders, it is not totally surprising that this first major attempt to deal with poor school attendance, "a law and order problem" and "other health, sanitary and welfare problems" while trying to, keep up tribal traditions and maintain contact with tribal life on the reservation so the Indians do not become alienated from their own culture" quickly failed although, as will later be discussed in this chapter, this experiment was given new life in the 1960s.

This is not meant to imply that the Indians in the village in the 1940s were living in a state of chaos (i.e., of maximum entropy), although some of the "Americans" may have thought this to be the case. In reality, the "disordered" facade of the village hid an amazing complexity of highly structured social relationships (i.e., relationships characterized by a high degree of negentropy[5]). Also, although initially most of these relationships were kinship-based, by the 1940s, various sodalities had begun to arise, based upon such common interests as sports activity, church affiliation, and even place of origin. Thus, as early as the pre-World War II days, at least several Indians were playing softball and baseball with the "Ajo Miners" (an integrated team) in league play against different schools and colleges (A.C.N October 24, 1963:6; L.I.52) and at least one of these Indians continued playing with this team after he returned from the military service in 1945 (L.I. 52).

An all-Indian sports team was formed in 1950 by the Catholic priest in the Indian village and played basketball, football, and baseball on the nearby reservations (L.I. 48). At about the same time, or possibly a few years later, two men who were subsequently instrumental in the formation of the Intertribal Village Council (to be discussed later) helped form a racially mixed (Mexican and Indian) sports team (L.I.28; L.I.48; L.I.49) and several other all-Indian sports teams were formed in the next few years (L.I. 37). These early teams played baseball, football, or basketball, depending upon the season, using the same team name and same players for all three sports (L. I. 28). Often the teams were divided along ethnic lines such as the "Redskins", a largely Papago team, the "Braves", which was "mainly a Pima team" with most team members coming from the Sacaton area, and the "Indians", a team composed mainly of Indians who had originally come from the Ajo area and Mexico (i.e., the "Sand" Papago) (L.I. 37; A.C.N. April 4, 1963:6). However, the division along ethnic lines was usually not absolute.

There was much friction and rivalry between these teams which extended to the wives and families of the players during the games. However, according to one informant, there were "no hard feelings" after the games were over (L.I. 37). These teams used to hold dances, raffles, and dinners, as fund-raising activities for uniforms, travel, etc. (e.g., see A.C.N. June 7, 1962:6; April 29, 1965:2), but by the1960's most fund-raising activities in the Indian village were sponsored by the "Parents' Club" (to be discussed later) "to raise money" for the local village priest and activities sponsored by the local village Catholic Church (L. I. 28).

Membership in the teams was somewhat fluid and occasionally teams combined for postseason tournament play (e.g., see A.C.N. September 12, l968:5; L. I. 37). Also, after a while, most teams began to specialize in one particular sport with baseball being the most popular choice, followed by basketball, while football because of fear by the company of the injuries it might cause to workers was not played at all by the late 60's.[6] And in the 1960's, this widespread interest in sports, among Ajo's Indians, led to the creation of men's and women's bowling teams, and of basketball and baseball teams for Indian girls and baseball teams for young boys (e.g., see A.C.N. February 6, 1964:8; October 22, 1964:5; December 31, 1964:1,9; May 6, 1965:10; L.I. 31; L.I. 49; L.I. 54).

Although at times certain of these teams played in local leagues, (e.g., see L.I. 21) except for the men's and women's bowling teams, for the most part, they played each other, and such outside teams as the Papago team from Sells, a Mexican team from Sonoita, a Pima team from Sacaton, an Indian village team from Gila Bend, a racially-mixed team from Gila Bend, a mixed-Indian (Papagos, Pimas, Apaches and Navajos) team from Phoenix (L.I.8; L.I.17), a Papago team from San Xavier, and a white V.F.W. team from Tucson (e.g., see L.I.8; L.I. 17; A.C.N. April 27, 1961:8; August 3, 1961:8).

It has often been said that minority group members put so much effort into sports activities because "here… is a means by which they may compete on equal terms with the white man and often beat him" (Stucki 1967:309). The data from Ajo also tends to support this proposition since a local Indian boy had, at one time, signed a contract with a professional baseball team and, as the local Indians take pride in pointing out, only an unfortunate leg injury prevented him from becoming a professional major league ballplayer (e.g., see A.C.N. December 27, 1962:6).

The most important church sodality in terms of its influence in village affairs in the 1960s, was the very powerful "Parents' Club". An earlier social club connected with the village Catholic Church and similar in many respects to the present-day Parents' Club, had been formed in the late 30's or early 40's (L.I. 41; L.I.37), under the direction and leadership of the village priest. One of the main purposes of this early club was to sponsor the village fiesta in honor of St. Catherine, and one informant (L.I. 37) said that his parents, who were active members of this club, "put on the dance in 1943." However, membership in the club dwindled as many of the original members of the club died, and no new members were recruited. . Finally, only two of the original members of the club remained, and so, for a time, the club ceased to function (i.e., a systemic collapse occurred, as the number of members in the membership systemic status set dropped below a lower critical limit which in this case was apparently 3 members) (L.I. 41). A main factor in explaining this decline was probably the transfer of the priest who was instrumental in organizing and operating this club. With his departure, membership in the systemic status set that he had occupied which had the important role of membership recruitment and overall club leadership dropped from one to zero which insured that a systemic collapse of the first or second type described in Chapter 5 would be inevitable.[7]

A few years past, then, at some point in the late 40's or early 50's, a very energetic half-Papago, half-Cherokee lady, who was also later one of the key leaders in the creation of the Intertribal Village Council, organized an Indian Village community club to "sew clothes and make quilts" (L.I. 28; F.N. June 1, 1967; L.I. 37; L.I.39) and sponsor such events as birthday parties, bridal showers (A.C.N. September 19, 1962:8); and baby showers (e.g., see A.C.N. January 19, 1961:6). However, this newly formed club's activities soon expanded into other areas of community affairs such as the collection of funds for charities (e.g., the Red Cross) CLI. 39), the sponsoring of square and folk dancing (A.C.N. November 17, 1960:6), and the support of the kindergarten program for village children that began in the late 50's under the sponsorship of the local Catholic priest. Enrollment in the club at this point swelled as many parents joined what then became known as the "St. Catherine's Kindergarten Parents' Club" (F.N. June 1, 1967; L.I. 30; L.I.37). However, at this time the nature and goals of the club changed dramatically, as the local priests that were assigned to the village increasingly began to use the club to further other church activities than the kindergarten through various money-making projects. Thus, although it was reported in the fall of 1960 (A.C.N. September 29, 1960:6) that "The Parents' Club held a food sale at St. Catherine's Mission, September 25, and are planning to have it every two weeks to help run the Kindergarten school", it was also reported somewhat earlier (A.C.N. September 1, 1960:5) that the Parents' Club had sponsored a vacation fishing trip for the local Catholic priest and the "St. Catherine's Choir and Altar Boys, Boy Scout Troop 154" to a popular nearby Mexican fishing village on the Gulf of California. Also, other Parents' Club donations were announced later for such purposes as the local priest's "expenses" (A.C.N. March 2, 1961:6), medical treatment for a former Ajo priest, now staying at the Papago Mission near Tucson (A.C.N. March 2, 1961:6), the local priest's summer vacation (A.C.N. June 20, 1963:6), and repair of the nuns' convent on the Papago reservation near Tucson, which had been damaged by a freak tornado (A.C.N. November 5, 1964:5). It is also interesting to note that by at least September, 1961, a major share of the cost of supporting the kindergarten program had been shifted from the Parents' Club and the Catholic Church to the parents of the kindergarten children who were now required to pay $5.00 per month per child for "tuition" (A.C.N. September 14, 1961:3).[8]

However, this decline in the revenues donated by the Parents' Club to the kindergarten program was not paralleled by a decrease in fund-raising activities by the group. In fact, the opposite seems to be true, as the club not only sponsored raffles (e.g., see A.C.N. April 8, 1965:2) and combined food sales and dances in the village (e.g., see A.C.N. August 1, 1963:6), but also went to other locations such as Sells on the Papago reservation to sponsor similar activities (e.g., see A.C.N. July 18, 1963:6) as well as increasing the frequency of local food sales after mass on Sunday mornings (e.g., see A.C.N. February 21, 1963:8) and at town celebrations, such as the one held in downtown Ajo on the 4th of July (e.g., see A.C.N. July 4, 1963:6). Also, beginning at least as early as February 24, 1961 (A.C.N. February 23, 1961) and probably even earlier, the Parents' Club began sponsoring a series of Bingo games, giving out "different cuts of meat and cash" as prizes, and by September of 1961 (A.C.N. September 7, 1961:4), these began to be held on a regular weekly basis. Food sales and/or light refreshment sales (e.g., coffee and cookies) brought in added income on these nights (e.g., see A.C.N. December 12, 1963 :8)

Most of the money from this increased fund raising activity was used to support the activities of the Catholic Church, such as the repair of the parish in the fall of 1961 (A.C.N. September 14, 1961:3), the support of the local priest, and the staging of the massive annual feast and dance in honor of St. Catherine, which was first begun again in the post-World War II period in 1957 (A.C.N. May 10, 1962:2), by members of the Parents' Club[9]. As one of the active members of the Parents' Club told me, the club "sometimes" collects "50 to 60 dollars" at the weekly Bingo games which then all "goes to the church". This is not really too surprising, since, according to several informants (e.g., see F.N. October 30, 1967; November 3, 1967), most villagers contribute very little, if any, money voluntarily to the local priest and attempts to collect funds by direct personal contacts have, in the words of one village leader, "led to religious disputes" (F.N. October 30, 1967). Therefore, the Bingo game income is viewed by the Parents' Club members and village priest as being essential for the successful operation of local church programs. It is also interesting to note that at least one woman views the Bingo games as a pleasant way to donate her money to the church[10] (L.I.41).

In terms of the theory represented in Chapter 5, the system here faced with a possible loss of ultra-adaptability or systemic collapse in the late 50's was the local Catholic church, and the variable approaching a lower critical limit was its net income variable as voluntary contributions from the miners began to decline. Obviously, as discussed in Chapter 5, several different outcomes were possible at this point, including such far-reaching ones as the complete closure of the local mission. However, with the creation of the Parents' Club, an ideal opportunity arose for the village priest to expand his control over the distribution of this new source of income. This control was easily achieved, since most of the members of the club were Catholics (L. I. 28) and several of these people were extremely devout believers in the power and authority of the church over their lives (e.g., see A.C.N. December 19, 1963:12). Thus, it is not too surprising that more and more of the club's funds found their way into church coffers as the years passed by. (As a younger "do-gooder" while studying anthropology at U.C.L.A., I had learned of a similar increasing diversion of funds into the coffers of the Catholic Church at the Pala Mission in Southern California.[11])

Essentially, then, the Parents' Club was by now being used to generate an output (i.e., money) to prevent the net income variable of the local Catholic church from exceeding its lower critical limit (the control vector in this case is the village priest's increasing involvement in the club's fundraising activities and decision making about how the money generated should be spent.

One of the early systemic status set casualties of this "manipulative" process was none other than the original founder of what had by now become known as the "Parents' Club" and to make matters worse, according to one of the local priests (F.N. June 1, 1967), she had not only "deserted" the club but now she was trying to "undermine" it through the creation of a rival social organization early in 1961 (A.C.N. February 2, 1961:6) called the "Indian Community Benefit Fund." That at least some antagonism existed between the two organizations is vividly illustrated when after it was originally announced that the "Indian Committee (Community) Benefit Fund" was a subsidiary committee by the Parents' Club, (A.C.N. February 2, 1961:6), members of the new organization published the following statement, "to clarify questions that have arisen concerning the 'Indian Community Benefit Fund'" (A.C.N. February 9, 1961:6):

> The announcement of the fund was made at a Parents' Club meeting recently. Parents' Club is a subsidiary of St. Catherine's Mission, but the Benefit Fund is not under the jurisdiction of any religion or organization. It is a fund designed to channel charitable funds to the proper organizations and to eliminate needless giving. This Benefit Fund is definitely for our whole community: It is not a club but is comprised of a committee of five.

All monies collected for this fund are immediately banked and records are kept of charitable donations taken from the account.

And in spite of the statement to the effect that this "committee" was "not a club," in practice it functioned for several years much in the same manner as its rival, Parents' Club, holding dances (e.g., see A.C.N. April 13, 1961:6), raffles (e.g., see A.C.N. February 2, 1961:6; February 9, 1961:6), and Bingo games (e.g., see A.C.N. November 15, 1962:2) and selling food (e.g., see A.C.N. July 13, 1961:1). However, members of this new club continued to make sure that it was known to all, that the purpose of the club was to help all the people of the village and not just a specific church. Thus, it was later announced in the local newspaper that:

> Few of the people know the activities of the club. It is a charitable club for the Indian people. It helps people in distress, at the death of a family, occasionally paying for school lunches. As of now they are trying to build a scholarship for an Indian student of Ajo (A.C.N. November 15, 1962:2).

And that in connection with a food sale sponsored by the "fund" that:

> The proceeds will go to the Community Benefit Fund to be distributed to each community drive or when needed to help out a needy family or at the death in a family. The club is always willing to help out in any way when it has the money (A.C.N. January 31, 1963:6).

However, several years after it was formed, in spite of strong support from another rival group to the Parents' Club, the "Intertribal Village

Council,"[12] (e.g., see A.C.N. October 4,1962:8; C.M.M. February 13, 1964) to be discussed later in this chapter, the club's membership dwindled (O.M. January 17, 1963) and the final systemic collapse came as the same scandal and gossip rocked this club that later led to the drastic upheaval in the Village Council leadership and membership in 1966[13]. (L. I. 28; L. I. 50). In contrast, the Parents' Club, backed by the local village priest and the powerful Catholic Church, had greatly increased its influence in village affairs in the late 60's. The membership of this group, while remaining small in size since the transformation of in the club's financial objectives occurred, nevertheless continued to remain a very stable and dedicated body[14], exerting an influence in village affairs far greater than its mere size would lead one to believe possible.

Other sodalities have also existed for brief periods of time in the village with little lasting impact, but these have been usually either such potentially unstable groups as the "Pisinimo Ladies Club" (e.g., see A.C.N. November 24, 1960:3) and several sewing "classes"[15] or groups that have been sponsored directly by either the Parents' Club (and the local village Catholic Priest), or the Village Intertribal Council. For example, one particular local village priest who was remembered by one informant to have been "pretty active and quite an organizer"[16] (L.I.44) was instrumental in the creation of a Newman Club, a youth choir and a Parents' Club supported Boy Scout Troop whose initial members served also as the "St. Catherine's Choir and Altar Boys" (A.C.N. September 1, 1960:5; L.I.ll; L.I.28; L.I.39; L.I.44; L.I.49), but none of these groups survived by the late 60's. Also, the local "Mission" (i.e., priest) and the Parents' Club were the sponsors of a Cub Scout Pack (A.C.N. October 25, 1962:6), a Girl Scout Troop (A.C.N. December 6, 1962:8), an Explorer Scout Post (A.C.N. February 14, 1963:6), and an adult ladies' church choir (A.C.N. September27, 1962:8; L.I. 26), but only two of the three girl scout age groups (L.I.26)[17] and the church choir survived by 1968, and the church choir itself did not escape temporary systemic collapse during portions of the 1967-68 copper strike.

The Intertribal Council to be discussed in the next section of this chapter also sponsored several other sodalities, such as a men's bowling team (A.C.N. September 17, 1964:3) and one for the ladies (A.C.N. December 10, 1964:2), and cooperated closely with the "Community Fund Committee" as mentioned previously (e.g., see A.C.N. July 13, 1961:1; October 4, 1962:8; OM. January 17, 1963).

However, it is important to realize for the purposes of this analysis that none of these voluntary associations (e.g., the Parents Club and the Community Benefit Club) were under direct company control. Therefore, while some of the behavior channeled and controlled by these organizations would tend to reinforce company values and goals, this would not be true of all the behavior encouraged by such associations (e.g., attendance at an all night dance would hardly help a man perform his job well the next day at the mine.) Thus, when one understands the underlying reasons, it is not completely surprising that in 1961, a unique event occurred in Ajo when certain individuals from the local Indian enclave were allowed to assume rather broad powers over the lives of their fellow Indian employees. For, it was in that year that the old Ajo "Indian village" was given official company recognition as semiautonomous political unit with an "Intertribal Community Council" as its official governing body, operating under the provision of a formal company-approved constitution (A.C.N. May 14, 1964:2).

For many years prior to 1950, the "ugliness and filth" of the Indian village had remained fairly hidden from the view of most Ajoites because of its spatial isolation behind a large hill from the rest of the town. However, with the building of the new smelter in 1950 with its largely Mexican-American workforce (Waddell 1969:54) there was much pressure generated for the expansion of the "Mexican" section of racially segregated Ajo. Due to Ajo's natural topology and the position of the mine, its supporting buildings, and the "American" town the only direction that this expansion was possible was toward the Indian village. Since the new houses being built were superior to the houses in old "Mexican town," the company carefully chose those individuals who would be permitted to move into this new section of the community, usually on the basis of "desirable" personality characteristics and "clean-living" habits. Since this new section of town geographically bridged the gap between the "Mexican" and Indian sections of Ajo, "Indian town" had now, by default, become spatially integrated into "greater" Ajo. No longer could the "dirt", "filth", and rising juvenile crime of the village be ignored.

Also, at this time the forces of racial desegregation were gaining power in Ajo, adding further woes to the minds of the local mine officials as a bitter dispute arose in Ajo between the "Mexicans" and "Americans" over segregation in housing, jobs, and recreational facilities.[18] The local Indians, although not directly participating in the integration battle were also being affected by the spirit of the times. Many of them maintained close ties to the Pima or Papago reservations and were well aware of the rising success of the tribal councils on these reservations in modifying the decisions of the B.I.A. and in determining many local policies. Therefore, it is not too surprising that at this time, a small group of the more educated Ajo Indians, who felt reasonably secure in their company jobs, approached the local mine officials to complain about housing conditions[19] and to see about the possibility of forming an Indian village Intertribal council which unlike the earlier failed attempt in the 1940s would not be under the control of the Tribal leaders of the nearby Papago Reservation (A.C.N. September 23, 1943:1,4; L.I.28; L.I.55; A.C.N. April 20, 1961:1).

It is also not surprising that the company officials immediately endorsed this proposal gladly since as one later admitted:

... before the council was organized ... the company used to have a great deal of trouble at the village because of the destruction of property. If the company tried to find out who was the guilty party, no one would speak up. Things were so bad that it made the company feel that if the people at the village would not help themselves, then the company would not help them either. Now that this council is formed, we feel that we can work with this council. It has improved matters quite a bit. It is easier to work through an organization than it is to try to work with individuals (C.M. December 2, 1964).

Thus, the company viewed the creation of the council as a way to cheaply gain control of the still chaotic and now highly visible Indian village so they gladly gave the favored Indians a constitution that at least in writing granted the proposed council the authority to "promote and protect the health, peace, morals, company property, and general welfare of the community and its members."

Probably with the hope of maintaining control over the actions of the council, the company then began to grant certain privileges to council members in the form of access to better housing and jobs than their fellow Indians could obtain. This also eased the possibility of a legal attack on the company for its segregation policies as these favored Indians were given houses in the new addition to Mexican town on the fringe area nearest the Indian village.[20] Thus, from the company's viewpoint through the mechanism of the council, order could now hopefully be maximized in the structure of the newly enlarged social community under its control, which for the first time included the Indian village as an integral part.

The first election for membership on this new council was held on March 1, 1961[21] (A.C.N. March 9, 1961:4) and ninety-three voters cast ballots for their favorite candidates. In this first election an attempt was made to represent the tribal minorities in Ajo on the council so that although the council chairman, vice-chairman, and two councilmen were Papagos, two of the elected councilmen were Pimas, one was a Yavapai,[22] and one represented the "Spanish-speaking" or "Mexican" Papagos.

The Pima representation on the council, initially, was even more important than these numbers indicate even though the Pimas then, as in 1968, formed a very small minority of the total number of Ajo Indians. In terms of influence, their small numbers were more than compensated for by their generally superior educational backgrounds, and relatively higher job classifications at the mine (i.e., the Pimas were in general more "acculturated" in terms of the white Ajo value system). Even the constitution of the new Ajo Intertribal Council was "patterned after the Pima Constitution" (L.I.50).

However, in later elections Papago control over all council positions and activities became so absolute that one Yavapai lady complained that she had stopped coming to community meetings because she "could not understand what was being said because it was in Papago" rather than in earlier years when English had been the official common language used at community meetings with interpretation to and from Papago, if necessary, being provided for those present.[23] (C.M. December 2, 1964).

All seemed to be going well during the first year of council operation and shortly after the time of the next election held on February 22, 1962, two new and eight[24] returning council members proudly posed for a large picture accompanying a glowing article outlining the major achievements of the council during this initial period of operation (A.C.N. February 22, 1962:1). The council had, indeed, been able to obtain numerous company-derived benefits for the Indian village, such as improvements for the village community hall and new recreation facilities, as well as minor improvements for the average villager's house. The company appeared at this point to be solidly behind the actions of the council members so that their control at this time seemed to be nearly absolute over the lives of the local Indians.

However, a few cracks began to appear in the foundation of this power structure before long when the council proved to be less successful than company officials had originally anticipated in solving such problems as the curbing of juvenile crime among teenage Indians in the community and the maintenance and improvement of the outward appearance of the village. Probably as a result of what the company officials now perceived to be a poor return for their investment, fewer Indian village improvement promises were made and fewer yet kept in the years that followed the initial year of "success" for the council.

This is not to imply that the council members had not really tried to curb the rising crime rate nor attempted to improve the physical appearance of the village. Indeed, on January 12, 1962, a local Papago Indian had been sworn in as a "Special Deputy - Inter Tribal Council" by the Pima County Sheriff (A.C.N. January 18, 1962:6). Also, one of the council members had been appointed by his fellow councilmen to "go around and inspect the yards in the Indian Village" (C.M. December 29, 1963).

In order to put some authority and power behind the actions of these two men, the council started holding monthly meetings to "discuss any problems that arise pertaining to the Villagers" (A.C.N. February 22, 1962:1) and later these were supplemented by semiformal court "hearings" held in the community hall (e.g., Hearing October 28, 1964). At first, the company, the county sheriff's office, and the local county judge all seemed to be completely behind the actions of the council, even in matters that would normally be handled by the police and court systems in most other American communities. However, it was probably not long before at least some of the villagers began to realize that the council did not really have as much power to control their lives as they had earlier been led to believe.

Several factors in particular were especially important in creating this doubt in the council's omnipotency, one of the most important of these being the problem of funding council activities. It had been initially suggested that all miners in the village should contribute $1.00 a month to the council for the support of council activities or preferably $12.00 for the entire year to be collected on the first payday of the year (C.M. January 22, 1963), and at one point during the initial period of council operation it was reported in the Ajo Copper News (June 1, 1961:6) that at a community meeting held on May 25, 1961, "the people who attended were all in favor of continuing their donation to the councilmen each payday". However, it soon became evident to the villagers that the council had no way of enforcing the collection of these dues and at the beginning of 1963, a crucial test of the council's power arose as some of the individuals who had been paying dues on a regular basis demanded that something be done to force the other villagers to pay also (C.M. January 22, 1963).

The councilmen yielded to this pressure and on the next payday went around the village, visiting each delinquent miner in an attempt to collect the money owed, but this technique failed whenever miners said they "didn't have any money." Next the council went to the company to try to get the mine officials to withhold the assessed amount of dues from the miners' paychecks, but the company turned down this request after some complaints were heard from a few of the Indians, probably because such a withholding "tax" to support council activities could not legally be made under the laws of the state of Arizona against the will of the individual worker.(C.M.M. January 30, 1963). Failing in this attempt, the council leaders next tried to rally community support against the nonpayers by saying that in a public community meeting, cards would be passed out to each person to "let them know how much each person has donated" (C.M.M. January 30, 1963). Also, the names of those who had paid were frequently announced in many of the public meetings held by the council at this time, apparently in an attempt to shame others into paying. And late in the year 1963 (C.M. December 18, 1963) the council lowered the dues requested from each miner for the year 1964 to just $6.00 for the entire year, probably hoping that the number of dues paying miners would increase if the amount of the contribution asked for was reduced. However, these methods again failed to bring in any money except from those individuals who wanted to remain active for various personal reasons in council affairs.[25] Thus, the council was forced to continue to operate as it had since its creation on a very tight budget, using income coming mainly from a faithful few and from special fund raising activities such as dances, food booths, income tax preparation assistance, and drawings for prizes. (e.g., A.C.N. February 15, 1962:7; A.C.N. November 8, 1962:2; C.M.M. November 11, 1964; A.C.N. January 14, 1965:9; C.M. April 21, 1966), However, they often had to compete for the miners' money with several other powerful special interest groups, some of which were described earlier, such as the Catholic Church-dominated "Parents Club" and the various sports clubs who also sponsored many fund-raising activities.

Also adding to the troubles of the council during this period was a complaint from the councilman who had been given the job of inspecting yards in the village. He had by now begun to feel somewhat uneasy about continuing these inspections as he sensed that the villagers were becoming increasingly hostile toward him as he went around the village looking at their yards (CM. December 29, 1963).

There was perhaps some justification for this feeling of ill will on the part of some of the villagers toward him since the yard inspection report was commonly used by the company as an important factor in judging the "fitness" of a man to receive a promotion or of a family to receive a better house (L.I.54). Therefore, in an attempt to ease some of the pressure on this councilman, the council in December agreed that henceforth all villagers should be notified in advance before any of these inspections would begin, but apparently the pressure was still felt so strongly by the unfortunate councilman that he resigned from this duty and was not replaced by another councilman. With the company still demanding that this inspection be performed, it is not surprising that within a space of two months (C.M.M. February 13, 1964) the company's housing agent had again taken over from the council, the job of inspecting houses in the village. Thus, through fear of personal criticism, the council members had now lost one of their most effective mechanisms of control over village life.

Another major problem that the council was never able to solve satisfactorily was the control of juvenile crime in the village. Not only did this failure create hard feelings between certain villagers and the council leadership, but it was also probably the major factor in the rapid "drying-up" of company interest and funds for Indian village improvements after the initial year of council operation (i.e., the council had not produced the degree of order in village affairs that the company had originally expected for its initial investment)

Again, this failure to control the crime problem was not due to a lack of diligence on the part of the leading council members. Indeed, some villagers accused the council of unjust harassment of their children (e.g., C.M.M. November 11, 1964; L.I.50, March 14, 1968). Many "hearings" were scheduled each month and the "guilty" persons were summoned to appear before the council to answer the charges brought against them. A persistent problem concerned children who were continually creating "disturbances" around the Community Hall when groups were meeting there (e.g., C.M. December 11, 1963) or who were often driving or walking around the village late at night causing mischief (e.g., CM. May 15, 1963; A.C.N. October 15, 1964:13). Other "crimes" tried in these "hearings" in the community hall ranged from such minor offenses as breaking clothes lines, spilling trash barrels, and getting newly washed clothes dirty (e.g., Hearing March 1, 1966) through the more serious crimes of adultery (e.g., Hearing January 1, 1967) and burglary (Hearing n.d.1) to such very serious felonies as an attempted rape (Hearing October 28, 1964) and a stabbing (Hearing n.d.2). In all of these cases restitution was made wherever possible, moral lectures were given, and sometimes small fines were assessed the guilty (e.g., Hearing November 28, 1964; A.C.N. November 8, 1962:2). This system of "primitive" justice was probably in most cases more effective than our present day court system, but trouble began to develop in this system of community justice when a few individuals apparently chose to defy the decisions of the council handed down at several of these hearings and later refused to even appear at a subsequent hearing that had been scheduled (C.M. March 6, 1963; CM. May 20, 1963).

To solve this new crisis, the council members turned first to the company, seeking a statement that any Indian if he was a company employee would be fired if he did not heed the advice of the council about his own behavior or that of his children (C.M. March 6, 1963 A.M.). However, the company was unwilling to go this far in backing the actions of the council but instead agreed that "any person that does not obey the Council will be removed from the Indian Village, not fired, but will be moved to some other place" (C.M. March 6, 1963 P.M.). However, as far as I know, this threat was never carried out, although the company's housing agent did send at least one warning letter to the mother of a boy that was constantly getting into trouble in the village (C.M. December 2, 1964).

Even with this small degree of aid from the company, the council was still unable to control completely the nighttime behavior of certain village young people who, while often not doing anything illegal, would drive around in the village "at all hours of the night ... making a lot of noise" (C.M. May 15, 1963). Since, as one council member noted they were living "in the state and not on the reservation", the council sought aid concerning this problem from the local judge, juvenile officer, and police lieutenant but found out to their great disappointment that a state curfew law had not been passed and that a county or local one would be "hard to enforce" (C.M. May 20, 1963; C.M. May 23, 1963). However, when the council members met with the lieutenant from the county sheriff's office they did come up with a plan to force compliance with their "brand" of primitive justice as the following passage indicates:

> The (council) Chairman brought up the matter of juvenile trouble in the village. "We call children that get into trouble for a hearing and we have this last case where the boys did not show up. What do we do in a case like that? Should we call the Police to come and get him?" The Lieutenant said that when an officer is called he must do his duty to the Police Department, and therefore take the offender to the juvenile authorities.
> The decision that was made on this question was to warn the boy or boy's parents that if he does not show up at the hearing, he will be turned over to the juvenile authorities. This way they may be held to answer to the council (CM. May 20, 1963).

In a meeting a few days later with the local judge, the council members also heard him say that "it might be a good idea to warn the parents that if they will not show up at the hearing, they will be turned over to the sheriff's office" (CM. May 23, 1936). Here then, at least in theory, was the support the council needed for compelling villagers to attend the hearings and to comply with the council decisions.

This seemingly very effective control mechanism for enforcing council decisions was, however, somewhat blunted by the fact that the threat of turning an offender over to the sheriff's office was qualified by the council chairman's statement that this would be usually only be done after the person had committed the act for the fourth time (i.e., after three hearings had been held) unless a "serious" crime had been committed (C.M. May 23, 1963; see also F.N. October 30, 1967) and by another councilman's observation that "in some cases people do not want to sign a complaint against another person" (C.M. May 20, 1963). Therefore, it is not too surprising that law enforcement in the village still continued to be less than ideal. In practice, in spite of what the council chairman had said about turning those who had committed serious acts over to the sheriff's office, this was not done even for crimes as serious as attempted rape (Hearings October 28, 1964 and October 30, 1964) which would normally involve severe penalties under Arizona law.

Perhaps even this relative lack of strictness in applying the penal codes of Arizona to offenders in the village would have been tolerated by the company had the crime problem not spread beyond the boundaries of the village. However, the company and the sheriff's office had to act after serious trouble began late in 1964, when a group of young Indian boys was caught by the sheriff's department breaking into a bar on the main road through Ajo (C.M. November 17, 1964). Also, at about this same time the company's patrol car was stoned, breaking one of its windows, while the vehicle was passing through the village on a "security check". Everywhere the young people of the village seemed to be growing bolder (CM. October 8, 1964). The local Baptist church was broken into, robbed, and defaced. Firecrackers were thrown at adults and the men from the sheriff's office driving through the village were often openly taunted by village teenagers (L.I. 26, February 27, 1968; A.C.N. October 15, 1964:13). It was by now obvious to everyone that the council was rapidly becoming powerless in its attempts to curb the actions of certain of the youth of the village, so it is not surprising that in November of that year both the sheriff's office and the company again took upon themselves the direct responsibility for the enforcement of "law and order" in the village (C.M. November 17, 1964).[26] Strong measures were soon taken, resulting in the sending of the boys who had broken into the bar to Fort Grant, an Arizona reform school, and in the stringent enforcement of the curfew law that earlier the judge had said would be "hard to enforce" whereby all village young people caught "loafing" anywhere in Ajo after 12:00 midnight would be picked up and after the third such offense, the parents of the youth would be arrested and fined (C.M. November 17, 1964; A.C.N. December 10, 1964:2).

In looking for a scapegoat both the village council and the county juvenile officer turned on the village Indian policeman. The Council complained that he was the one responsible for much of the trouble in the village because he was not doing his job and the juvenile officer accused him of deliberately shielding law breakers from prosecution (C.M.M. November 11, 1964; C.M. November 17, 1964). This scapegoating during these emotional confrontations between the company and the county officers on one side and the council on the other was made easier since the poor village policeman was not present to defend himself from these, at least partially, unjustified criticisms.

The impact of this important change in company and county support for council actions greatly affected the attitudes of the average villager as more and more people began to bypass the council in their dealings with the company and the sheriff's office.[27] Thus, the council had by now become almost completely impotent in village affairs after having lost the last major hold it had over the villagers as individuals (i.e., the semiofficial criminal and civil village court hearings),[28] although it continued to exert some control over the various organized special interest groups in the village, such as the Parent's Club, the various scout groups, and the village sports teams, by still holding, at least in theory, control over the use of the community building which had been erected at company expense.

However, this was not really control in the absolute meaning of the word but rather in the sense that the council functioned in most instances as the arbitrator between spokesmen for the various groups with their often conflicting demands for usage of the building's facilities on a regular or single event basis. Also, the fact that often either the council members themselves or members of their immediate families or friendship circles were members of these competing groups greatly weakened the power of the council in making these decisions. This conflict of interest was not so noticeable during the early years of council operation when the many special interest groups in the village were all somewhat equally active in village affairs and all had more or less direct ties to at least one or two of the council members (e.g., see A.C.N. December 14, 1961:2; O.M. January 17, 1963 for examples of how conflicts were resolved during this early period). However, as the council came to be increasingly under the control of the Catholic Papagos through the years and as many of the village sodalities ceased to function (i.e., suffered systemic collapses due primarily to decreases in certain systemic status set population variables past lower critical limits), the powerful Parents' Club backed by the local Catholic priest began to assume increasingly more control over how the community building was to be used so that by1966 this club was able to ask for and receive permission by a unanimous council vote to exclude all other users of the building for a period of two weeks prior to the annual St. Catherine's Day celebration so that they could "clean up the yard and hall" (Letter - Parents Club to Village Council April 17, 1966; C.M. April 21, 1966).

Also, late in 1966 or early in 1967 (L.I.8, L.I.21) the non-Catholic leader of the girls' basketball team had to answer in one of the informal "court" hearings held by the council, charges leveled at "her girls" to the effect that her basketball team had been making so much noise during its practice that the numbers being called out during the weekly Bingo games could not be heard. She answered these charges by saying that she had always cautioned her girls to go home before the Bingo games began and that it was the "smaller kids" who were really causing the trouble by hitting the walls of the community center in their play.

This last problem was finally resolved when one of the council officers, who is also a member of the Parents' Club, agreed to patrol the area around the Community Hall each week during the Bingo games (a job he was still continuing to do while I remained in Ajo) (F.N. October 30, 1967; November 6, 1967). From this evidence and from my own personal observations it seemed obvious that by 1967 no one dared "cross" the Parents' Club and the local Catholic priest with respect to the scheduling of events at the Community Center. Thus the power of the council to regulate group affairs through this mechanism of control was by this time more symbolic than real.

The council had, however, by now found a new way to gain support for some of its goals from the company since they knew that the one thing almost as sacred in Ajo as motherhood is the protection and care of the youth of the town. So, to protect the school children of Ajo, a safety council was formed under the domination of the local judge and various local school personnel. Both the company and the village council send representatives to the meetings of this organization (e.g., see C.M.M. January 30, 1963) and at one time the village council chairman was actually voted in as the head of this "Community Safety Council"

(A.C.N. January 27, 1966:11). (However, in October of this same year, the company succeeded in electing its men to the top three Council offices as well as several lesser executive positions on the Safety Council (A.C.N. October 6, 1966:11).)

Now, anytime an improvement such as better night lighting in the village is desired, if the request could be tied in with the safety of school children and if it was acted upon by the Safety Council members, then the company usually did not dare resist the suggestion, not only because of its strong continual lectures to the men on mine safety but also, more importantly, due to the certainty that to resist such a recommendation would be almost as serious a "crime" as attacking "motherhood or apple pie" (F.N. November 10, 1967).

One of the most white-oriented and accepted Ajo Indians suggested that this same technique could have been used (but, unfortunately was not) in an attempt to get better housing for the Ajo Indians by pointing out to the company that certain state health codes were being violated in Indian village housing, thereby forcing the company to take action or risk having these violations reported to a state agency (C.M.M. March 18, 1964). Here then is positive proof that at least a few of the Ajo Indians have become highly sophisticated system manipulators in recent years.

It should be made clear at this point that the loss of village support for the council had not just begun with the advent of the 1964 crisis over juvenile crime since as early as October, 1961, the councilmen had expressed their concern over "the lack of response from the Indian people when they are called to monthly community meetings ..." (A.C.N. October 19, 1961:6) and by 1963 the council leadership was having trouble filling vacancies on the council (i.e., they were having trouble maintaining a systemic status set population variable above a lower critical limit), leading one man to suggest that "women should be interested in council membership"[29] (C.M.M. March 13, 1963) and another to state that if any candidate is nominated to run for a seat on the council he:

> ... shouldn't be asked if he wants to run ... because if the people want him for councilman they will elect him, regardless if he wants to or not. He is the people's choice (C.M.M. January 16, 1963).

This latter suggestion was followed and a number of candidates without consultation were put on the ballot[30] (C.M.M. February 13, 1963; C.M.M. February 20, 1963 A.M.; C.M.M. February 20, 1963 P.M.; C.M. February 18, 1963).

It is, therefore, not too surprising that some of the new council members elected a few weeks later were not motivated by their unasked for election to become active participants in council affairs in spite of some prodding by the older officers of the group. In fact, by March of that year (C.M. March 6, 1963) there was talk of calling up an old councilman to fill the place of a man who had recently been elected but who had shown absolutely no interest in the council.

Adherence to the democratic process had further added to the woes of the council when three of those most active in council affairs had been nominated for the single job of vice-chairman, thus after the election eliminating from the council two of the three, although all had been willing to serve on it (C.M. February 18, 1963; C.M.M. February 20, 1963 P.M.). This democratic procedure had been opposed by a minority at the earlier nominating meetings (C.M.M. February 20, 1963) and after the election they busily reminded the council officers of their correct prediction of the trouble that had by now developed (C.M.M. March 13, 1963).

Things got worse in 1964 when another councilman tried to resign (C.M. February 11, 1964) and the elections for that year were cancelled because "the people did not show up" for the nominating meeting[31] (CM. February 5, 1964; C.M.M. March 18, 1964). Again, a year later, in February 1965, no nominations for councilmen were made, even though meetings for this purpose were held (A.C.N. February 25, 1965:11). After this second failure in two years to stir up interest for an election, the council abandoned temporarily their faith in the democratic process and decided instead to choose twelve "young" ("young" relative to some of the older council officers) village men to become council trainees with approval of the people of the village and the "young" men themselves (C.M. March 4, 1965). This new plan was, not surprisingly, also a failure for at the time of the crime crisis in the village just a few months earlier the minutes of a community meeting held in November record that (C.M.M. November 11, 1964):

> It was expressed to the people about the importance of this council ... when it started it started out very good, but after a while it started going down hill. Now it seems that the people have no community spirit. The Council have to help themselves by selling different things, candy, pop and so forth.

During the following year a scandal involving the council chairman and a prominent village lady was brought to the attention of the council members, some of whom including the vice-chairman forced the chairman to resign (L.I.50, March 14, 1968). The vice-chairman was then elected by the council to serve as chairman until the next regular election was to be held and three other councilmen remained to serve with him (A.C.N. January 27, 1966:1,11) and in April other officers and council members were elected in a special village election (C.M. April 21, 1966) to fill the gaps that at this time existed on the council. However, in 1967, the "disgraced" former chairman, a generally well-liked individual, fought back in a surprise move and won re-election as council chairman in a campaign that brought out much bitterness on both sides. At this point the losing candidate for this office (the former vice-chairman recently elevated to the chairman's position) resigned rather than accept the job of vice-chairman again, which by now was again being automatically offered to the losing candidate in the race for chairman[32] (L.I. 50, March 14, 1968). Unfortunately, the regained glory of the old council chairman was short-lived since he was soon crippled by a stroke less than six months later (just after the 1967-68 long copper strike had begun). He never recovered from the complications arising from this stroke and later died, so that the leadership of the council passed into the hands of a man whom many of the villagers felt to be a much less capable leader (e.g., see L.I. 10; L.I. 21; L.I. 22; L.I. 27; L.I. 31; L.I. 32; L.I. 33; L.I. 38; L.I. 41; L.I. 50). Thus, at the end of my field experience, the council had almost ceased to exist as an effective organizational force in village affairs.

The extent to which the power of the council had already disappeared, even as early as March, 1964, was vividly illustrated when a major fund raising project that the council had been planning for several months was cancelled at the last minute when one of the councilmen casually announced that he would be holding a wedding dance on the same day as the planned bazaar, adding in a somewhat condescending afterthought that he would be willing to let the council "sell some things at this dance" (C.M. March 16, 1964).

Probably, the major factor in the general lack of village enthusiasm for the council and its leaders through the years was its increasing inability to deliver tangible benefits to the average villager. This cessation of benefits hastened the alienation of many Indians from the council as they accused the council members of forgetting the average Indian and his or her problems (C.M.M. January 30, 1963). Much jealousy had through the years developed among many villagers over the special treatment they felt that the council members had received from the company with respect to better housing and job opportunities[33] (e.g., see L.I. 50, March 14, 1968; L.I. 14, February 15, 1968).

Finally, the very fact that many of the Ajo Indians in the 1950's and 1960's were becoming individually more fully integrated into "greater Ajo" spelled disaster for the maintenance of an effective council as a middleman or "cultural broker" between the village and the larger community.[34] As many of the Indians found that they were no longer forced to remain within the confines of the village, some moved out to escape the "filth and disease" generated there by poor housing and sanitary facilities (e.g., see comments in C.M.M. March 18, 1964) and others moved to escape the rising crime problem in the village or as one lady expressed it, "the bad environment" for her children, one of whom had already been involved in an ugly knifing incident (L.I. 30, March 1, 1968).[35] Even those remaining in the village found that they could often get better service for house repairs, etc. and be more likely to obtain one of the new houses in "tortilla flats" (a somewhat derogatory term used by villagers to refer to the new part of Mexican town (e.g., see L.I. 14, February 15, 1968) by going directly to company officials, rather than by trying to work through the council (e.g., see L.I. 50, March 14, 1968; L.I. 21, February 21, 1968). Even with respect to the problems of crime, drunkenness, and fights in the village, many women quickly learned that the newly installed telephone was as useful for summoning police aid as it was for gossiping and that the trouble ended much faster using this new technique than using the older village council court system (e.g., see L.I. 25).[36]

Looking back on the demise of the council, one can easily discover that similar sequences of events have often occurred in the history of humankind. I was especially startled when, as I read an account of a people far removed from the hot, dusty deserts of Southern Arizona, I came upon the following passage:

> When I visited the village, I didn't know about the midnight curfew for young people. I went out until about three in the morning with a local girl. I went out again late the next night, and on the following day a council member spoke to me at the post office about the curfew. I told him I was a visitor from Barrow and I shouldn't have to obey the curfew. He said I did, but I kept going out late anyway. Finally, the whole council called me in and told me I could not go out after twelve o'clock any more, and I said, "This is America, not Russia and I can go out as much as I like". The council didn't like that, but there was nothing they could do . ... (Chance 1966:66)

Other passages also confirm this striking parallel. Thus Chance (1966:67-68) states that:

> It is in the area of law enforcement that the councils face their greatest dilemma. Having established regulations the members have no way to enforce their ruling ...
> When an individual disregards a local regulation, he usually is approached by the president or another council member, reminded of the ruling, and told to conform. If he persists, he is brought before the council and asked to account for his behavior. This practice is most effective with village youth, but is pursued with adults as well. Occasionally, council members take direct action against young people for minor infractions ...
> For more serious offences like minor theft, a combination of council and family pressures may be applied to the offender, who is usually a child or teenager ...
> Most teenagers and many children ignore curfews and few parents are inclined to assist in enforcing this

regulation. The young people are well aware that the council has little or no legal power to enforce its ruling, and therefore they disregard prohibitions unpleasant to them. ...

Here then, except for a change in location and cast, is Ajo. Today, the informal mechanisms of social control that were sufficient to regulate individual behavior in an earlier and simpler form of society no longer can adequately deal with the problems inherent in any modern urban setting. Therefore, all such artificially created organizations as the council discussed in this chapter seem doomed to failure, even before they are created, unless they are given or can seize sufficient economic and/or political power to enforce their decisions. However, one should not make the mistake of assuming that the level of chaos has increased in the Ajo Indian community because of the failure of the council to effectively control the actions of the villagers. Indeed, there is much evidence that the level of entropy among the Ajo Indians had actually decreased by the late 60's (from the company's viewpoint). Thus, as shall now be shown, the average Indian miner at that time seemed to be even more tightly bound by the various economic and social control mechanisms, described earlier, to the Ajo complex of systems than the typical white miner, judging from data collected during the 1967-68 strike when at a point near the end of the strike only about 17 out of 113 (i.e., about 15%) Indian miners were out of town while it was estimated that 40 per cent of the town's total population was elsewhere (A.D.S. March 4, 1968:1).

Many of the Ajo Indians by then, especially those who had already moved from the village, were beginning to experience intensive social contacts with the other ethnic groups in Ajo as the barriers imposed by the earlier rigid patterns of racial segregation rapidly began to topple in the 50's and 60's. However, much of the initial contact with other races was of a rather guarded impersonal nature and often occurred in rather formal settings, such as those found at the mine or on the sports field. Also in this category should be included such events as the participation of the St. Catherine's Boy Scouts in a "Scout-O-Rama" held in Tucson (A.C.N. April 25, 1963:6) where they exhibited various items of Indian bead and art work and performed several Indian dances and the performance of local Indian dance teams at such events as the Ajo Mexican "Cinco de Mayo" celebration (e.g., see A.C.N. May 16, 1963:6; April 28, 1966:1). Here the Indian was interacting with whites and Mexicans much as our actor does with an audience.[37]

Another accepted role of this type for the local Indian was as a member of a dance band and during this post World War II period many such groups were formed and played not only for Indian and Mexican audiences in Ajo and on nearby reservations but also for such "local waterholes" as the Hotel Cornelia Cocktail Lounge (e.g., see A.C.N. November 26, 1964:11) and for the local Ajo Teen Association (e.g., see A.C.N. May 2, 1963:6; April 15, 1965:6). But, in extremely few of these relationships was there much hint of any close social bond being formed between the typical Indian and members of the dominant Ajo society.[38] However, other events were occurring after 1940 that would later prove to be more effective in breaking down the barriers that socially isolated the Indian from the "Americans" and "Mexicans" of Ajo, one of the most important of these being several years of service in the military forces of our country by many young local Indians.

Many of these young returning veterans, after having experienced almost full racial equality in the military service during World War II and the Korean War, joined the local chapter of the V.F.W. (Veterans of Foreign Wars) at least partially motivated by the fact that as "veterans" they could legally buy drinks through the club, but as "Indians" they could not legally be served alcoholic beverages in local bars (L.I. 30; L.I. 31; L.I. 54). That this was largely a manipulative device to secure equal drinking rights can be seen from the comments of the wife of the only remaining Indian V.F.W. member[39] at the time of my fieldwork who stated, when referring to those Indian men who had at one time belonged to the organization, that "after they legally could get drinks in the local bars[40] they all quit." (L.I. 54).

Also, the "winds of change" could be seen in 1948 when the "disenfranchising interpretations of the Arizona and New Mexico constitutions were declared unconstitutional by judicial decrees, and Indians were permitted to vote in these states as they had been in other states" (U.S. Department of the Interior: Bureau of Indian Affairs, May 1968:7) and in 1954 when the Supreme Court decision, striking down the separate-but-equal doctrine with respect to education, was pronounced.

No longer could the local politicians and school boards ignore the Indian so that it is not at all surprising to see such events soon occurring as the presentation of a flag ceremony, complete with the singing of the "Star Spangled Banner" by the St. Catherine's girl scouts at a meeting of the Ajo "Women's Business Club" (A.C.N. October 25, 1962:6). Also, the local P.T.A. sponsored several special "Indian programs" complete with speeches by important individuals in both the Indian and non-Indian communities (e.g., see A.C.N. February 1, 1962:4; January 24, 1963:8; February 4, 1965) and many parents of Indian school children not only were encouraged to join both the P.T.A. and the "Home and School Organization" (the equivalent of the P.T.A. at the local Catholic grade school) but in several cases were made officers in these organizations (e.g., see L.I. 3; L.I. 26; L.I. 28; L.I. 29; L.I. 44; L.I. 50, L.I. 52; L.I. 54).

Such groups as the formerly all-white local Presbyterian Church also began to take an active interest in the local Indians, and it was not long before several Indian families were singing with the integrated church choir[41] and taking leadership roles in various church activities[42], most of which were fully integrated.[43] Another Indian lady and her family became active in the Mormon Church in the 1960's and became quite active in their Cub Scout program where she served as a den mother (L.I. 30). Her children performed Indian dances for various church functions and participated on an integrated basis in all church activities. Several of these children also participated in the church's "placement program" for Indian school children where each lived during the school year in the home of a white Mormon family in California, returning to Ajo only during the summer vacation period.[44] Also, although not exactly being a religious group, a Village chapter of "Alcoholics Anonymous" was formed under the guidance of local white organization officials and a prominent local Indian leader (Waddell 1969:114) and held meetings for a brief period of time in the "kindergarten room" at the local Catholic mission. (e.g., see A.C.N. January 5, 1961:1; February 23, 1961:6; March 9, 1961:4)

Other more secular groups from the outside world also began taking an active interest in the Indians during this period. Thus the Village council was invited to participate in the local "Cinco de Mayo" Mexican celebration, each year supplying both a food booth and entertainment in the form of several Indian dancers (e.g., see C.M. May 1, 1963; May 15, 1963; April 21, 1966; A.C.N. May 16, 1963:6; April 28, 1966:1). Also, a few individual Indians became members of such diversified social and religious groups as the "Knights of Columbus" (L.I. 37), the Mexican-American "American Citizens' Social Club" (L.I. 52), the "Catholic Youth Organization" (L.I. 52), the local "Roping Club"[45] (L.I. 37), the integrated "Newman's Club"[46], and even the local Lion's Club (F.N. March 18, 1968), although most Ajo Indians did not seek membership in such groups and would probably have been refused membership to many of the more exclusive of these groups, even if they had sought such membership.[47] It is interesting to note that those who were admitted to the more restrictive of these clubs were not viewed by those prominent Ajo citizens that I interviewed as being typical Indians but as exceptions to the usual stereotype and lavish praise was often heaped upon these individuals for having "overcome the handicap of their Indian past through their own personal ambition, education, and industry" (e.g., see F.N. June 18, 1967; May 18, 1968). This prestige also carried over to the children of these individuals, one of whom was elected student body treasurer at the local high school and Junior Rotarian for the month of November in 1965 (A.C.N. November 4, 1965:2) and another who was named as "one of two eligible for the (college) scholarship from the Desert Music Club" (a very elite local social organization) (A.C.N. June 22, 1961:1)[48]

Both the company and the unions also began to take an active interest in the "more promising" Indians at this time. Thus, it is not surprising that one Pima miner became the president of his union in 1958[49] (L.I. 47) and that he and several other Indians were promoted to high positions in the company (e.g., see S.I. 338; Waddell 1969:120,121; F.N. March 18, 1968; April 29, 1968). Also, several local establishments, a bar and a billiard parlor, with obvious interests in the local Indian community, proudly announced that they had "picked up the tab for the new uniforms and equipment to be used by the (Ajo Chiefs baseball) team" (A.C.N. April 29, 1965:2).

The ultimate sign that the Indians of Ajo had finally been accepted as an integral part of the community came in 1960 when the editor of the local newspaper announced that an Indian village social column would be published on a continuous weekly basis from then on (A.C.N. September 1, 1960:1). But, the complete social "arrival" of a few Indian ladies was signaled when news concerning such activities as baby showers was published independently of this Indian village social column in the local paper (e.g., see A.C.N. October 29, 1964:7).

These events should not, however, be interpreted as meaning that complete social integration among all residents of Ajo had occurred by the late 60's. On the contrary, as table XV indicates, just about half of all Indians living in the Ajo area (i.e., 432 out of 824), were still residing within the confines of the Indian village in the fall of 1967, including 65 of the 113 male Indians employed by the company at that time. Also, it can be easily seen from tables IV, V, VI and VII that very little social integration, as measured by the degree of ethnic group intermarriage had by this time taken place in the Indian populations of either "the Village" or "Upper Mexican Town", except between Indians originally from different tribes. However, there is little evidence to support the extreme position taken by Waddell following his June, 1963 to December, 1965 field work among the Papagos, when he states (1969:152) that:

> In Ajo, although socioeconomic statuses may be shared by the separate ethnic communities, stratification and social status indicators operate largely in the three separate social contexts. Yet the entire Ajo community is a hierarchy of the three stratified ethnic communities, with Anglos at the top, Mexicans in the middle, and Indians at the base. This feature prevails even when a Papago occupies the highest stratum in the Indian community, while an Anglo occupies the lowest stratum in the Anglo community. There is only negligible movement from one ethnic community to another.

But, Waddell should not be criticized too harshly, though, since in Ajo, his major Papago informant, "Raymond Victor"[50] (Waddell 1969: 90-92, 101-103, 108-109, 113-114, 120-122, 128-129) was a good example of one of the very few Ajo Papagos who continued to maintain close ties to the reservation by returning there as frequently as the work schedule at the mine would allow and who even when offered more responsible positions at the mine often refused them (e.g., see Waddell 1969:120-121, 129, 150; F.N. April 22, 1968; F.N. April 29, 1968; F.N. May 8, 1968) since they saw occupational mobility in the Ajo mine structure as a threat to their cultural identity as part of the greater Indian community.[51] These are the same people who sometimes decline, as Waddell (1969:129, 150) pointed out, "company offers to move into bigger and better houses" since their own acceptance of their 'inadequacy' helps to confirm that Indians are different and functions to preserve a kind of cultural identity".

However, there were few "Raymond Victors" remaining in Ajo in 1967. Instead, most Indians of Ajo were more firmly bound to the community than their Mexican or "American" counterparts. And even in the case of "Raymond Victor," despite his strongly voiced intension of returning to the reservation, he ended up dying in Ajo.

Finally, even long after the 1984 shutdown of the Ajo mine, the 2000 census still lists the American Indian population of Ajo as still being 255 out of a total population of 3705 with 167 of them being over the age of 18 (Localcensus.com 2008). And, if as I expect, there has been an increase in interethnic marriages in the past few decades, an even larger remnant Indian population remains in Ajo.[52]

Chapter Notes

1. I, too, was guilty of arguing for this position in an earlier paper on the "Fox Project" (Stucki 1967).

2. Again, from the company's viewpoint.

3. The Catholic Church with the help of the company had completed the construction of a new building for the local Indians one year prior to this time as a "tipping point" in local membership was reached. The priest's motivation for his support for the creation of a council is revealed in the following words:

Over 700 people are now living in this neighborhood, although not all of them are Catholics as yet by any means. But they are getting into the habit of coming to me frequently with their troubles and asking for advice. They seem to expect me to be here. If I am visiting one of the smaller missions and they fail to find me, they will say to me (A.C.N. November 5, 1942:1)

4. This new recreation center together with a children's playground "including a wading pool" had just been built one month prior to this time thus this proposed new "council" would be given the responsibility for the care of these new facilities (A.C.N. September 23, 1943:4).

5. Negentropy = negative entropy = the degree of order in a system

6. One local Indian said that "P.D." (the company) had actually "stopped" them from playing football since the company was afraid that the men might be so seriously injured that their work would be affected at the mine (F.N. November 3, 1967).

7. (Also see Miller 1960:154-155; Stucki 1967:309-310; and the later comments in this chapter on the village Boy Scout troop).

8. While I was not able to learn the exact salary of the different Indian ladies who taught this kindergarten class in successive years, the fact that only a high school education was needed for the job (e.g., see A.C.N. October 11, 1962:6) and that the turnover in teachers seemed to be fairly rapid, indicated that the money paid the lone teacher for the class probably exceeded the money collected from the parents of the students by little, if any (enrollment in the classes was 18 in the fall of 1961 (A.C.N. September 14, 1961:3) and 24 in October 1962 (A.C.N. October 11, 1962:6), and by June 1964, 31 students were listed as being kindergarten graduates that year (A.C.N. June 4, 1964:6)). However, to be fair to the Parents' Club, it should be noted that in 1964 they and several other Catholic men from the village donated all the labor and materials needed to construct "restroom facilities" for the St. Catherine's kindergarten school (A.C.N. October 8, 1964:11). But even here, a cynic might point out that this action mainly benefited the local Catholic Church, since the

kindergarten room and facilities were located in the church complex of buildings and were used for many other activities sponsored by the church when classes were not in session.

9. However, even by 1965, (e.g., see A.C.N. April 15, 1965:6) and possibly later, token amounts of money were still being given to drives sponsored by such groups as the Red Cross.

10. She said that she plays Bingo "all the time" but that she "never win(s) anything." Her husband "gets after (her)" saying, "all that money and you never win anything. Why don't you just give it to the priest? That's gambling." She answers him by saying that it all "goes for the church anyway."

11. I and a small group of fellow students volunteered to help the nearby Pala Mission Indians prepare the fundraising booths for an annual festival to raise money for their local Catholic grade school. However, as we set about building booths we were dismayed to discover that the only local Native American who was willing to help us was the paid assistant to the mission priest. Many of the other Indians merely watched us work from the comfort of the nearby front porches of the houses that surrounded the central town plaza. Mystified, I asked the paid assistant for an explanation for this perceived "ungrateful slothfulness." He explained by saying that in past years when the Indians were allowed to keep half of their individual booth profits, they had worked hard to make the annual festival a success but that in recent years when the priest felt that the school needed all of the festival's generated profit, the local Indians felt no need to support the event even though their own children would receive the educational benefits of the money.

12. The husband of the founder of this club was for many years the chairman of the Intertribal Village Council.

13. However, the lady who had organized this club continued to be active in fundraising activities for various charities, as was demonstrated in the spring of 1965 when she headed a group of 7 volunteer ladies in a Red Cross fund drive (A.C.N. March 25, 1965:2; April 8, 1965:2). None of the members of this transitory group were members of the

by now defunct "Indian Community Benefit Fund" except the leader herself.

14. Tight integration of this group was maintained by such devices as the celebration of birthday parties, bridal showers, and baby showers, discussed earlier, and such events as the "potluck" dinner, held just prior to Christmas Day in 1963 by the Club for its members and their families, after which gifts were exchanged among the members and their families, and everyone present was given a "Christmas bag" (A.C.N. December 26, 1963:5). In addition to the money they provided, the dedication of the members of the club and of the other Catholic villagers who closely supported their activities for the local Catholic Church and priest was also shown by the large number of hours of voluntary labor that was performed by these people in behalf of the church (e.g., see L.I. 5; L.I.8; L.I. 26; L.I.27; L.I. 43; L.I. 44; L.I. 50; A.C.N. June 21, 1962:6; December 19, 1963:12; October 8, 1964:11).

In terms of the theory presented in Chapter 5, it is interesting to note that one man told me (L.I. 43) that he began to do voluntary work for the local priest after he had been suspected of starting a major fire that destroyed much of the church building in 1966 (A.C.N. June 16, 1966:1). By this activity, he probably hoped to prove his innocence to the other villagers, or perhaps atone for his guilt, if he had indeed been guilty for the fire (he denied this guilt and was supported in this denial by a spokesman for the local firemen who had fought the blaze, who blamed the fire on a dog, who was heard howling inside the burning building, and who was believed to have overturned an altar, bearing many burning candles (A.C.N. June 16, 1966:1; L.I. 43)). In either case, the activity for the church functioned to reduce the level of the "anxiety variable" in his own mind.

15. One of these was organized by a "lady from the University of Arizona" who also taught sewing skills at Sells (the capitol city on the nearby Papago Reservation) (C.M. April 21, 1966) and another was started (November 1966) by a white Baptist lady missionary who noticed that there were "many kids but few adults" attending the Baptist services in the village, so she started the sewing class to get to know

the mothers of the children who were attending church services (L.I.48). The former group may not in the strictest sense possibly be called a club, but the Baptist "class" certainly would qualify under this heading since they had "potluck dinners" in connection with their all-day sewing activity each Thursday and sometimes went together "on picnics". Although this latter group increased in size from eight original members to twelve (including one Catholic, a "Mexican lady") at the time of my study, it is doubtful that the group survived the transfer of the missionary lady from Ajo, unless someone with equal interests replaced her (i.e., if the population variable of the crucial systemic status set she alone occupied dropped from one to zero, ultra-adaptability would have been lost for such a group).

16. After having met this priest on the Papago reservation, myself, in the summer of 1967, I can also verify his great talents in organizing young people. Both the Newman Club and the youth choir "stopped" when this priest was transferred out of Ajo (L.I.44) (i.e., the population of the systemic status set occupied by this priest dropped from one to zero when he left Ajo, thus dropping the value of this variable below its lower critical limit, one, which then precipitated the subsequent systemic collapse in both systems). The Boy Scout troop survived somewhat longer (L.I.39) since the systemic status set which can be labeled "leader(s)" contained more members than just this priest, so that this particular systemic status set population variable didn't drop to zero immediately upon his departure from Ajo (e.g., see A.C.N. December 27, 1962:6 where three other active adult leaders, one of whom was a white man from Phoenix (L.I.30; L.I.45), are named.) Here again, the lower critical limit with respect to this systemic status set is one.

Actually, according to the Indian leader who was the last scoutmaster in the village, the troop finally ceased meeting as the boys "gradually lost interest" and "quit coming one by one" (L.I.8). Therefore, the lower critical limit exceeded here appears to have been one in connection with the systemic status set which can be labeled "follower(s)" (i.e., Boy Scouts), even though in looking for reasons why this decline possibly occurred, one might suspect that there had been a qualitative or quantitative change in the output of one or more of the communications variables from the role set, "leader(s)" (one of the strongest of whom left Ajo shortly after the departure of the priest (F.N. October 30, 1967)), so that at least one lower critical limit had been exceeded in each of the boys that now one by one dropped out of activity.

17. The leader of the oldest age group in the Girl Scouts, the "Cadets" ceased to hold meetings during the strike, and even after the strike was over no resurrection of this organization immediately occurred (i.e., the population variable connected with the systemic status set, "leader(s)", for the oldest age group dropped from one to zero during the strike and remained at zero after the strike.).

18. (e.g., as mentioned previously at the local swimming pool, the Americans swam on Tuesdays, Thursdays, Saturdays, and Sundays and the Mexicans and other races on Mondays, Wednesdays, and Fridays (A.C.N. August 21, 1920:1; see also L.I. 52; F.N. March 5, 1968; March 27, 1968). Also, seating at the local movie theater was at one time segregated by ethnic group (F.N. December 3, 1967; March 5, 1968).)

19. Not only was the housing substandard in many ways, but also rocks and other debris from blasting operations in the mine occasionally broke through the roofs of the houses near the pit, at one time narrowly missing a sleeping baby (L.I.55; A.C.N. April 20, 1961:1).

20. One informant states that, "the Mexicans didn't like the Indians moving in at first but accept them now" (L.I.55).

21. Some Ajo Indians still remembered the earlier 1943 "Council" election (A.C.N. March 9, 1961:4; L.I.28).

22. The Yavapais were transferred to Ajo with the opening of the new smelter here in 1950 from Clarkdale where a Phelps Dodge smelter was shut down at that time (L.I.9; A.C.N. July 22, 1965:2; L.I.19).

23. The reason for this shift will be discussed at a later point.

24. All of the original eight won re-election to the council.

25. For example, one man who had had some trouble with the company's housing agent said that he "(wouldn't) mind paying $6.00 a year to help out the council", probably hoping that in return the council would assist him in his difficulties with the company's agent (C.M.M. February 13, 1964).

26. It is interesting to note that as late as October 15th of 1964, a spokesman for the Council was quoted as saying with respect to the growing disorder in the village that, "anyone doubting the council's authority to act on these cases, just keep it up" (A.C.N. October 15, 1964:13) (See also Chapter Note 28).

27. As one lady told me, "the Council is nothing ... the Company controls everything" (L.I.22, February 21, 1968).

28. This is not meant to imply that the council at this point stopped holding "hearings". In fact, there is evidence that they now tried to more rigorously enforce this form of "primitive" justice on their fellow villagers (e.g., Hearing November 28, 1964). Even as late as January of 1967 there is recorded evidence of a hearing having taken place (Hearing January 1, 1967). However, the power of the council to enforce any of its "court" decisions after this series of events in 1964 was largely nonexistent.

29. This advice was heeded partially (e.g., in 1966 a woman was elected secretary of the council - C.M. April 21, 1966), but other women of the village generally expressed no interest in becoming "councilmen."

30. The nominating meetings were held on February 20, 1963. Eight individuals, including the council officers, attended the morning meeting and sixteen the evening meeting. It is interesting to note that at this very same time one of the original founders of the council was successful in his attempt to resign from the council before the nominations were made (C.M.M. February 13, 1963; C.M.M. February 20, 1963).

31. Nobody at all except the councilmen came to the January community meeting.

32. There were also other changes in the election procedure to protect the council seats of those whom the councilmen did not want to

see eliminated from the council by an unfavorable vote, such as the change in the 1966 election (C.M. April 21, 1966) where the person receiving the second highest total in the race for council secretary automatically became the council treasurer. These modifications in the democratic process were designed to insure that the 1963 election disaster would not be repeated. In many respects, these changes were similar to the procedures followed originally in the 1961 ballot where only two men were running for the office of chairman with the loser automatically being given the vice-chairman's job. Also, in that election the men running for the special positions of secretary, treasurer, representatives for the Ajo Pimas, representative for the Ajo Yavapais, and representative for the Spanish speaking Ajo Papagos ran unopposed. (Here again is a prime example of an attempt to prevent certain systemic status set variables from exceeding lower critical limits.)

Where there were more men willing to serve in one particular systemic status set (e.g., that of the two councilmen representing the Ajo Papagos), a more "democratic" choice was presented to the Indian Village voter (e.g., five candidates were running for the two open positions in 1961) (A.C.N. March 9, 1961:4; a copy of the 1961 ballot). However, such "opponents" were almost impossible to find by 1967 (F.N. November 3, 1967) and, in fact, in the 1967 election it was impossible to find even the minimum number of ten men to run unopposed for the council offices available. Thus, it was the council itself, not the Indian voters, who decided who was to be put into each executive office (F.N. October 30, 1967).

33. By 1968, it was obvious to any observer that a deep rift existed between the council members (both present and past) and the "commoners" and that fairly sharp social class differences had already begun to emerge in the Ajo Indian community.In fact, several Indians appear to have used council membership to gain access to upper class benefits and then had abandoned this membership and most village ties when they had achieved the desired goal in terms of a better house and/or job and social acceptance in the white or Mexican community (e.g., see C.M. March 6, 1963).

34. Most Pimas because of their generally high level of acceptance into white society abandoned the council as an effective bargaining tool in Indian-company affairs at a much earlier date than did most Papagos, thus leading to the Papago dominance of the council and its activities by the late 60's. However, the most accepted family of Indians in Ajo in terms of the dominant white "value system" is headed by a highly educated Papago man and his talented wife.

35. This net out-migration from the village (i.e., net loss from the systemic status set, villager) has further eroded the power of the council since an Indian family living in any part of Ajo other than the village, seldom, if ever, paid much attention to the council and its actions, and the council itself failed to maintain adequate communication links to non-village dwelling Ajo Papagos in most cases, even when an Indian specifically requested to be notified of events occurring in the village (e.g., see L.I. 30). This breakdown in communication was greatly intensified when a weekly (at least at times) social column in the local Ajo newspaper that had begun in September, 1960, (A.C.N. September 1, 1960:1) finally ceased to be published in 1965 after no replacement was found for the last in a series of three Indian columnists.

36. Although most village Indians in 1968 did not yet have a telephone, there were now enough "spread" around the village to effectively "control" many potentially dangerous situations. The informal "sharing" of these phones that I observed on several occasions also served to increase the effective coverage density of telephone service in the village more than one might suspect on the basis of the actual number of installed units.

37. Activities of this type are in high demand in our society today when performed by "authentic" Indians (e.g., the top headline on the first page of the Ajo Copper News on April 2, 1970 reads, "Real Papago Dancers to Perform for Public in 'Annie Get Your Gun'").

38. The major exceptions to this generalization were certain "Sand Papagos" who had intermarried with many of the early Ajo miners. Also, various "informal, asymmetrical dyads between Anglo and Papago individuals" (Waddell 1968:10) had been formed through

the years, at times involving a type of joking relationship between two individuals who worked together at the mine (e.g., see F.N. March 19, 1968; May 27, 1968). By 1968, some intermarriage had occurred between Indians and "Americans" or "Mexicans" although such unions were often "frowned upon" by many of the friends and relatives of such a couple and the marriage partners themselves often have trouble adapting to each other's lifestyle and relatives (e.g., see F.N. February 25, 1968).

39. She herself was still an active member of the V.F.W. auxiliary at the time of the interview in 1967.

40. This legal change occurred in 1953 (United States Department of the Interior: Bureau of Indian Affairs, May 1968:9).

41. However, at least for a time there was a separate all-Indian Presbyterian choir formed in Ajo that sang at Presbyterian camp meetings in Sells (e.g., see A.C.N. September 21, 1961:1; September 19, 1963:6). The life span of this group must have been fairly short.

42. One Indian was elected to the position of deacon in this church and his wife was placed at the head of the "Help the Children Committee," a program designed to help children who were having trouble in school with their lessons (L.I. 47; L.I. 50).   T h i s committee is cosponsored by the local school board and the church's "United Women's Association".   Also, another local Indian lady was at one time put in as the head of the statewide Presbyterian Women's Association (L.I. 50).

43. The only major exception to this integrated participation in all activities by both local white and Papago Presbyterians that came to my attention was the attendance of several families of local Papagos at the annual Presbyterian Indian camp meetings held at Sells and Fort McDowell (e.g., see A.C.N. September 20, 1960:3; September 21, 1961:1; March 16, 1961:6; May 10, 1962:2; September 19, 1963:6) during the early 60's. (See also Chapter Note 44.)

44. Special missionaries from the Mormon Church have carried out a vigorous campaign in the past few years to proselytize the local Indians but by 1968 had only converted a total of three Indian women and

their families to their faith, including the woman mentioned here and one Yaqui woman who is married to a white man. In a personal interview with several of these young missionaries, I learned that they blamed their relative lack of success on bitter attacks against them led "from the pulpit" by the local Catholic priest. However, the missionaries have at times received Council permission to show several films in the Indian Village community including one on the harmful effects of alcohol on the body (A.C.N. October 15, 1964:13) and one on the "placement program."

No two members of the same family were ever put in homes near each other, since one of the main purposes of the program was to force the child into intimate social contact with members of the dominant white society. It is also for this reason that "placements" were never made in places like Ajo where the Indian population was relatively large. The effects of this massive program were felt on most reservations in the southwest and were the subject of much controversy as witnessed by me at an Indian conference held in Pomona in the spring of 1970, and in arguments appearing in such papers as the Navajo Times (e.g., see N.T. December 25, 1969:2; January 22, 1970:2; April 16, 1970:2).

45. This was a group sponsored by the local Junior Chamber of Commerce.

46. This organization was sponsored by the Catholic Church congregation in downtown Ajo, which was comprised mostly of whites and Mexican-Americans and is not the same organization that was formed in the Indian village.

47. One informant mentioned that the local Mexicans "complain that they can not get into Ajo social organizations" but that the Indians "don't want to join" these groups, even if the "whites" wanted them to join, which they "don't" (L.I. 50). Another man added that, "Indian people would feel out of place if they tried to join a social group." (L.I. 48).

48. Several of these individuals went away to college (e.g., see A.C.N. June 22, 1961:1; November 4, 1965:2; 5.1. 338), including one

who attended a special summer program at Yale University (A.C.N. August 11, 1966:4).

49. He still remained a union trustee" in 1968 and was succeeded in office as president in 1959 by a prominent local Papago who was also a member of the Village Intertribal Council at that time (Waddell 1969:113, 120).

50. This is merely a pseudonym for an Ajo miner, now dead.

51. Here I differ somewhat from Waddell (1969:150) who states this motive in terms of shared group goals rather than individual ones (i.e., he states that, "Papagos see occupational mobility in the Ajo mine structure as a threat to the cultural identity of the Indian community".) This difference in the interpretation of this type of behavior although superficially appearing perhaps to be quite small is, I believe, highly significant.

Another reason for refusing a higher job at the mine for those wishing to maintain their ties to the reservation is that most unskilled labor at the mine is performed during the day shift, thereby leaving time in the evening for quick return trips to nearby villages on the reservation to attend dances, etc. However, many semi-skilled jobs require that a miner often has to work on either the night or "graveyard" shift at least part of the time (e.g., see F.N. March 20, 1968).

52. An interesting follow-up study by some future researcher would be to try to document how many of the Indians stayed in Ajo after the closure of the mine in 1984 and how many of those departing chose to return to life on the reservation, a decision I would predict, based upon my interviews, would be made by very few.

CHAPTER 8:

New Ajos

Modern-day Morenci ... has no city government, no elected officials, and no police force. All municipal functions are in the hands of the Phelps Dodge Corporation, as are the town's only shopping plaza, bowling alley, and snack bar; even the books in the library are subject to approval by P.D. management. The high school football field, the water and electricity, the houses and the land under them, the cacti, the stones and the dust belong to Phelps Dodge. An old-timer in Morenci once told me, "This town only has two laws." He led me by the elbow into the street where we could get a clear view of the twin stacks of the Phelps Dodge smelter, and he pointed: There they are." (Kingsolver 1989: 23).

The days rolled on and the 1967-68 strike was soon almost forgotten in the hum of activity that abounded in Ajo by 1969. Rumors that had swept Ajo during the strike hinting at the exhaustion of the copper ore within a few years seemed ungrounded with the announcement by the

President of Phelps-Dodge that copper production in Ajo should remain at its present level "well into the 1980's" (A.C.N. January 30, 1969:1-2). However, still troubling were the fears that began on November 16, 1967 (A.C.N :1) about four months after the smelter had been shut down due to the strike, when it was announced that "new weather station and air pollution measurement equipment" had been installed the previous week at the Pima County Sheriff's substation in Ajo, including a device to measure "heavy particles" and "a high volume air sample[r] to check gases and lighter particles." Nothing more was published about this installation for many months, but by December 5, 1968, almost 9 months after the smelter had been put back into operation, it was obvious that officials from Pima County didn't like the readings they were getting on their air monitoring equipment in Ajo, for it was announced on that day in the local paper (A.C.N. December 5, 1968:1) that a public hearing on a controversial package of proposals to control air pollution in Pima County" was to be held in Tucson on December 23rd of that year, and the paper then added that:

> Supervisor Thomas S. Jay has said that he is particularly concerned about the proposed sulphur dioxide standards because Phelps-Dodge Corporation has already claimed that it would have to shut down its smelter in Ajo if the proposal is enacted by the board.
> County officials have said that if the regulations are not adopted by January 1, 1969, the County's air pollution control program will no longer be eligible for federal financial assistance.

Nothing was said in the local paper about the outcome of this hearing, but "miraculously" on March 5, 1970 (A.C.N. :1) the Ajo Copper News announced that the General Manager of the Western Division of the company had sent a letter to Governor Williams, promising him that a

400-ton sulfuric acid plant would be put in operation "as fast as we can", at the Ajo mine to eliminate the sulphur dioxide problem due to the smelter, and that an electrostatic precipitator would be also installed to "greatly increase the efficiency of the present system of removing solid particles" from the smelter's fumes. However, he did complain in his letter to the governor that:

> While sulfuric acid plants remove the sulfur dioxide from the air, a problem remains in disposing of the acid once it is made. ...even if the acid were given away without charge only about 18 per cent of the acid which would be produced by Arizona smelters could be disposed of. Unless outlets for very large quantities of sulfuric acid can be created ... we believe the matter of acid disposal would create hazards and potential pollution dangers far in excess of the present air pollution problem.

One has to admire the company officials for their persistent efforts to win this battle, even though there is considerable doubt about the facts and figures they present. Certainly, Governor Williams probably was not too much impressed by the company's logic at this point, since a new, more economical, and entirely smokeless way of processing copper ores had been already demonstrated by this time on a pilot basis at the Arizona State Fair held in the fall of 1967 (Arizona Republic November 8, 1967:Bl), with an actual 4 million dollar processing plant scheduled to begin operation in 1968.

Although this new commitment to environmental pollution research and control was not voluntarily undertaken by the company, its officials were quick to jump on the ecology "bandwagon" with an outward, if not inner, degree of enthusiasm, and in June, 1970 publicized its first action to help "fight the battle" against air pollution in the form of the awarding of contracts for "a total of $23,000,000 for the construction at Ajo of a sulfuric acid plant to remove sulfur dioxide from smoke from its copper smelter and for the installation of two new electrostatic precipitators to remove particulate matter from the smoke" (A.C.N. June 11, 1970:1). And quickly followed this by announcing the creation of a new "Environmental Research Department" to be headed by a man who, until this time, had been the Dean of the College of Mines at the University of Arizona, and also Director of the Arizona Bureau of Mines (A.C.N. July 2, 1970:1).

The vigor of this new commitment was not altogether unexpected in terms of the theory presented in Chapter 5, and can be viewed as being just one further step toward complete control over both the physical and social environment surrounding the company. Thus, by undertaking this control action over the pollutants being emitted by the smelter, not only could company officials placate such people as the governor and the worried citizens living in what was now often referred to as "the valley of the smog", but they could also obtain a salable byproduct, sulfuric acid, while greatly improving the health of many employees and their families who had long been suffering from the highly irritating and toxic gases which periodically inundated the town when the wind blew the "wrong" direction.[1]

Even the announcement of the final closing of the nearby radar base, which was to be completed by December 31, 1969 (A.C.N. October 30, 1969:1) must have been viewed by local company officials as being a blessing in disguise, since some of the military personnel stationed at the Ajo base had long been the most vocal critics of the company and its policies (e.g., see F.N. June 18, 1967). Also, the loss of income from the men and their families who had been stationed at the base almost certainly affected the "independent" businessmen in Ajo more than the company, thus increasing the company's relative control over its local social and economic environment. As one person told me a short time after the 1967-68 strike was over, "The company always wins" (F.N. March, 1968).

As pointed out earlier in this book, no individual or business in Ajo can be totally independent of some form of company control. Even I was once warned by a prominent townsman who was also the "bishop"(i.e., appointed, ordained lay leader) of the local "Ward"(i.e., congregation) of the Mormon church to be careful what I did in Ajo, and to avoid "stirring up trouble", since the company officials were carefully "watching" my actions and anything I did "wrong" might not only embarrass me but also the church as well (F.N. January 11, 1968; see also chapter #10). I also heard many reports of individuals and businesses that had been "driven out" of Ajo by the company (e.g., see F.N. July 25, 1967), although I was never able to verify any of these rumors. However, even if these tales were groundless, the point remains that most people I interviewed acted as if they believed that the company had always made, and would continue to make, life in Ajo unbearable for any "undesirable" individual or business. Here again, it is not a matter of what the company had actually done, or was willing to do, in any given situation, but rather what the people suspected that the company had done, or would do, that really mattered in explaining why only a "foolhardy" local person, even if he were not employed by the company, would ever dare to publicly criticize the company concerning any of its policies or actions. This was especially evident in my interviews with the local Indians, several of whom in statements given to me right after the start of the 1967-68 strike, while they still believed that the unions were stronger than the company, vigorously denounced the company and its "discrimination" in employment and housing against the Indian, but who in later statements, as the strike wore on, were very careful to avoid any major criticism of the company. Personally, I also felt the need to exercise great caution in what I did and said in Ajo, although I must admit that the high company officials I met on several occasions always treated me very kindly and were most cooperative toward my requests for information concerning Indian employees at the mine. Also, in spite of what many of the miners thought, I am convinced that these officials truly felt that total company control of Ajo's social and physical environment not only helped the company itself, but also furthered the welfare of all of the ordinary townspeople of Ajo as well.

In terms of the theory presented in Chapter 5, it was interesting, on one occasion, to listen to one of the top local company officials present new charters to several of the Cub Scout packs and Boy Scout troops in Ajo (F.N. February 15, 1968). Here, the company official enhanced his own image as a person vitally concerned with the well-being of the community and of the youth, especially. (It should be added that his own son was a Boy Scout at this time). Furthermore, since everyone was well aware of the fact that this man was a top official of the company, his performance conveyed the idea to everyone present that the company was also vitally interested in the young people of Ajo, and tended to "humanize" the company and reinforce its image as sort of a "Kindly Parent", the apex of kindness, generosity and benevolence, providing and caring for its own, as does the ideal mother for her children.

The Boy Scout District Council leaders, on the other hand, by their selection of this official for this important role in the meeting, were seeking to legitimatize their organization and elevate it in the social structure of the community and in the eyes of those spectators (parents and scouts) watching the performance. (An interesting parallel to this event was the attempt, on several occasions, by the local Indian Village Intertribal Council to legitimatize its role in the eyes of the local Indians and increase its power and respect by getting several high officials, both B.I.A. and tribal, from Sells, to speak at meetings in Ajo sponsored by the Council.)

In the many years that have intervened since my initial stay in Ajo I have often thought about the statement that "The company always wins" and have asked myself many times why it is that the company "always wins". We have heard so much about giant data banks, computers, and the invasion of personal privacy that most of us have come to believe that increased control over our physical and social environment can only come through greater and greater knowledge about each and every portion of the physical and social universe that surrounds us (i.e., we search after the statistics of the individual to gain control over the individual). However, this does little to explain how such an organization as "the company" can so totally control the lives of its employees that even without an exact knowledge of the thoughts, actions, or even whereabouts of many of its employees, within one day after the recent strike was settled, production of copper was already up to 90 per cent of normal (A.C.N. March 28, 1968) and within a two week period, virtually every miner[2] had returned to Ajo, even those who had been as far away as Pennsylvania or California (e.g., see F.N. March 15, 1968; May 28, 1968), and had, in many cases, obtained other permanent employment during the strike. Obviously, the company was not capable of keeping track of the actions and locations of all of its employees during the long 8-month strike, nor did it even try. Also, when one examines the control vectors utilized by the company during the strike, they appear to differ only slightly from those used during periods of normal operation at the mine, and included such things as the extension of credit at the company store, the continued maintenance of the town's basic utilities, hospital, social calendar (e.g., the annual Christmas celebration), and school system, the payment of the miners' group insurance premiums, and the return of the annual company store rebate to the striking miners just before Christmas.

However, the formerly tolerated practice of allowing miners to trade or sell a ten dollar company store coupon book for eight dollars cash, or merchandise from other stores in the area and in Mexico, was stopped during the strike when the company store manager insisted that proper identification was needed whenever a coupon was offered as payment for a purchase at the store. In particular, Indian miners in Ajo had in the past often used this method to get a quick cash loan. Many people and merchants were willing to buy these books, since they could then get what amounted to a 20 per cent discount on purchases at the company store. The Indian, on the other hand, was freed of the red tape of getting a loan from the local finance company or bank, even if his credit rating was good enough to get such a loan. Also, since the company charged no interest on credit purchases and since every year just before Christmas the company store gave each miner back a rebate on his credit purchases which at times amounted to as much as 13 per cent of the total amount spent, the miner was, in reality, only paying as little as 7 per cent annual interest for such a "loan".) (F.N. July 18, 1967; March 27, 1968; April 26, 1968).

The only other major change that occurred during the strike was that instead of a paycheck, the miner and his family received credit, not only at the company store, but also for his medical plan dues and group insurance premiums and for all of his utilities and rent if living in a company house. Also, just before Christmas the miner was given the complete[3] sum of money that was to have been paid him during his summer vacation in 1967 (A.C.N. November 30, 1967:1). And, other organizations, to some extent, also supplied some of the money or items that the missing paycheck would have provided. Thus, the unions handed out small weekly checks to the strikers (or credit at an independent grocery store in Ajo in the case of several of the smaller unions) and such items as turkeys at Thanksgiving time and held Christmas parties for the men and for their children; the federal government provided them with "food surplus" packages, temporary employment opportunities (e.g., fire fighting work for the Indians in the summer of 1967), and income tax refund checks just after Christmas; and the private local finance company extended them additional credit during the strike, as did some other local merchants. What, then, was the "secret weapon" used by the company and other organizations that also had vested interests in binding the miner to Ajo during the long 8 month strike?

I came to the answer slowly, but now realize that there are actually two different ways in which a system can increase the predictability of its immediate environment and the control it exercises over it. The first of these approaches to this problem where the system's leaders attempt to gain total knowledge of all aspects of both the social and physical environment that surrounds them (i.e., they attempt to gain a total knowledge of the environment's microstate) has already been discussed and is the "Big Brother" approach that we have often read about and feared. The second way is at the same time more familiar to us in practice, but less obvious to us in theory, than is the "Big Brother" approach to the problem of environmental control. Thus, through a process of natural selection, an organization such as the company in Ajo retains closely only those elements of the total universe which surrounds it, that can be ordered by the control vectors which the system is capable of producing and "discards" those elements of the surrounding universe that can't be "usefully" controlled by it (i.e., a certain portion of the universe surrounding each system at some distance is permitted to remain in a state of high entropy so that a state of low entropy can be maintained in the regions of the environment nearer to and closely interacting with the system. (The most important limitations on the usefulness of this second approach are, of course, that: (1) not all systems are free to either completely accept or reject each portion of their nearby universe and: (2) given a certain set of potential control vectors, there may be an "insufficient" supply of elements in the universe that can be "ordered" by the system.)

Therefore, the "secret weapon" that the company used during the long strike to maintain its control over its workers was almost exactly the same set of control vectors that it used successfully for many years previous to the strike to "weed out" from its work force those men who had "undesirable" work habits or "bad" personal characteristics, and retain tightly those men with "good" work habits and "desirable" personal traits. Obviously, then, all that the company, with the aid of the other interested local organizations, had to do during the strike was to supply certain minimum inputs to the very same set of control vectors that had been successful in binding the by-now-carefully-selected individual workers and their families to Ajo in the first place. In this effort they were remarkably successful, since, as I have shown, they had over a period of many years, learned precisely which control vectors were needed to successfully retain the needed workers Whether or not this success would continue into the future seemed, then, to rest mainly upon the assumption that the company's universe would continue to be able to supply the "desired" individuals and their families and on the supposition that the control vectors attracting and then binding the miners and their families tightly to the company town would be continuously maintained by the company and other cooperating systems above certain lower critical limits.

Thus, shortly after the end of the 1967-68 strike, the company continued to show its faith in the highly developed and very successful methods of social and physical control over its local surrounding environment that were fully perfected in Ajo as it created new "Ajos" in 1968 at Morenci, Arizona (A.R. May 5, 1968: F-1,6) and Tyrone, New Mexico (A.R. October 2, 1967:15; March 8, 1968:57), each complete with "curvy streets, carports, front lawns and a shopping center' (A.R.

October 2, 1967:15), and in the statement by the mining superintendent at "New Morenci" who said, a short time after the end of the 1967-68 strike, (A.R. May 5, 1968: F-6) that the return of 99 per cent of all Phelps-Dodge employees after the end of the strike was a major factor in the decision to create a "New Morenci", adding that:

> I honestly don't know whether a lot of them returned because of the money they owed the company.....1 guess a lot of them just said, "Well, this is home.
> We're a company town and we make no bones about it.
> We also know that we're bucking a trend against company towns, but the people seem to want it this way.

He then added, in the old company tradition:

> We have complete control over which businesses will rent in the shopping center.....We don't want anyone detrimental in the community.

And as late as 1995, Crawford (1995: 211) reports that "the impulses that generated company towns during the early decades of the twentieth century have not completely vanished" giving the following example:

> In 1980 Charles Crowder, a Texas real-estate developer, began planning an ambitious new industrial town, Santa Teresa, to be built on the border near El Paso, half in Mexico, half in the United States. Santa Teresa's industrial base was to be based on *maquiladoras*, American and Japanese-owned assembly planes that locate just across the Mexican border to take advantage of low-wage Mexican workers.... Santa Teresa resembles earlier company towns in many respects. Like those towns it attempts to improve efficiency and reduce labor turnover among low-wage, unskilled workers. ...

Santa Teresa's planning ... recalls western mining towns such as Tyrone and Ajo in its explicit provision of dual housing and services for Mexican and American workers. Management., mostly American, will live north of the harder, provided with suburban houses and golf courses. On the other side, Mexican workers will be housed in dense urban dwellings, organized around a central plaza. Significantly, like earlier capitalists, Crowder called on professionals to design the town. ...however, Sunwest Bank foreclosed on Charles Crowder's multi-million-dollar loans, making it unlikely that Santa Teresa will become the first of a new generation of company towns. (Crawford 1995: 211-212).

Chapter Notes

1. As far as I know, no comprehensive respiratory disease survey of Ajo had at this time ever been undertaken, or at least made public, but, judging from the data gathered by me from numerous informal interviews with many townspeople and from a carefully "guarded" statement that appeared in the local paper (A.C.N. July 23, 1970:11), the rate of such sickness had been extremely high. It is interesting that, although the article in the paper admits that there was a special problem in Ajo with respect to one form of such illness, (the exact figures were not revealed, however) the suggestion was made that the trouble was possibly due merely to the presence of large numbers of Indians and "Mexican-Americans" in the immediate vicinity of Ajo, a rather shaky assumption, I must say, since I have documented evidence of several employees who were shifted from one job to another because they became extremely ill breathing the fumes produced in certain areas of the smelting complex, and I remember very vividly attending a church service one Sunday morning when the words of the speakers were drowned out by the continual coughing of all members of the congregation.

On that particular morning, there was absolutely no wind blowing, so that thousands of feet of dense acrid smoke completely engulfed the town. Everyone I met in Ajo hated the fumes, but dared say little, since the discomforts of living next to a smelter were fatalistically viewed by most as being a necessary evil (i.e., a cross to be borne without complaint in the pursuit of the good life). Unfortunately, in spite of the fatalistic attitude I, too, was prepared to share, while living under the long shadow of "the great smokestack", I had to cut my field work in Ajo somewhat short, as I came down with a serious respiratory ailment just a few days after the smelter began pouring forth its noxious fumes at the end of the long strike. No recovery came until I moved a few months later to a location on the main reservation many miles distant from the mine, and thereafter held my return visits to Ajo for the remainder of the summer of 1968 to the barest minimum possible.

2. The final return figure for all Phelps-Dodge employees was given in May by a company official as being 99 per cent (A.R. May 5, 1968:F-6), a remarkable figure, considering the extreme length of the strike.

3. No deduction for the credit that had been extended to the striker was taken out of this check, although the annual rebate had, in most cases, been used to offset some of the credit extended the striker at the company store (A.C.N. November 16, 1967:1).

CHAPTER 9:

A Bitter Transformation

> ... The strikers lost everything: their jobs, their union, their homes and their community, where three generations of miners had toiled for Phelps Dodge Copper. (Bandzak 1991:1105)

In June of 1983, as a new labor negotiation deadline approached, workers in the Phelps Dodge copper mines of Arizona and New Mexico were expecting at most "a brief and conventional strike" (Kingsolver 1989: ix). But little did they realize how drastically their lives would be forever altered nor how much power would be lost by their unions in the following violent 18 months.

The contract settling the earlier 1967-68 strike had included perhaps the only major victory for the labor unions in that they had achieved their 1966 goal of industry wide "pattern bargaining" (Rosenblum 1995:38-44). Thus, despite the low demand and low price for copper in 1983, since every other major producer had already agreed to the "bare bones", "Strike-Free in '83" contract proposed by the coalition of unions led by the United Steelworkers of America, it was assumed by the Ajo and Morenci union members that a similar contract would quickly be signed and ratified by Phelps Dodge (Rosenblum 1995:4). Wages would be frozen but cost of living increases would be retained. However, to the surprise of the unions, the Phelps Dodge management team refused to sign such an agreement and instead "began permanently replacing strikers with outside hires" (Rosenblum 1995:4).

I, too, was taken by surprise by this change in company strategy since during my study of the 1967-68 strike the company had made life fairly pleasant for those men on the picket line and had extended fairly generous housing and food credits to the strikers. Thus, I had forgotten the long history of antagonism toward unions exhibited by Phelps Dodge beginning in the late 1890s and early 1900s with violent clashes between company guards, private police, state troopers, and striking mine workers in the company's Colorado copper mines and the infamous 1917 roundup and deportation of Bisbee union workers (Bruno 1994: 348).

Then, in contrast to the 1980s, the pool of potential workers swelled by large numbers of rapidly arriving immigrants from Europe and Mexico was enormous. However, the more restrictive immigration policies of the war years and the tremendous drain of manpower for the war effort created a massive labor shortage. And, by the 1940s, organized labor had gained through its vast political power much favorable backing from many "New Deal" politicians and other government officials in contrast to its extreme lack of political clout earlier in the century when most Americans associated the labor movement with the "evil, world-wide, treasonous communist conspiracy" which had seized power in Russia after World War I (Rosenblum 1995: 25-30). Thus, in 1941 the national unions backed by the National Labor Relations Act passed by Congress in 1935 won elections to replace company created and controlled unions such as the Bayway Employees Association in New Jersey and the Ajo Association of Copper Mine Employees in Ajo (Rosenblum 1995: 30; Therrien 1945: 106; Bruno 1994: 361). And, while as stated earlier in Chapter 4, in Ajo cooperation between the unions and the company was generally quite friendly during and long after World War II, continuing confrontation between the two was the rule in New Jersey (Leonard 1954: 28; Bruno 1994: 362-363). Thus, several short strikes occurred during the war years over such grievances as low pay to female workers and lack of winter heat in the plant while the company through its allies on the local draft board threatened to end the defense industry draft deferments that had been given to the men who were on strike (Bruno 1994: 362-363). And with the end of the war in 1945, worker unrest over "heavy handed" treatment by management and poor, often unsafe, working conditions peaked, culminating in the violent 1946 New Jersey strike (Bruno 1994: 348, 363)

Most of the other post World War II strikes that were taking place during 1946 were settled in the first three months but not the one that year against Phelps Dodge where the company attempted to break the long strike at its New Jersey fabrication plant by hiring many armed guards and offering "$20 a day to anyone who would enter the plant" (Bruno 1994: 367). At this point, the unions reacted by accusing the company of also hiring a mafia figure to "recruit 'thugs and murderers' from Brooklyn to break the strike" (Bruno 1994: 368).

During the seventh month, on July 30th, the dispute quickly escalated into the following violent confrontation between 100 strikers and hired company agents and scabs who were being brought into the waterfront plant by boat to avoid the land-based picket lines (Bruno 1994: 368-369):

> ...Before sunrise on July 30th, 100 workers climbed into three light barges ... and motored into Elizabeth Bay. ...

At 6:00 a.m. Phelps-Dodge "gangster" tugboats appeared right on schedule. In a matter of minutes the two naval forces were engaged in warfare. Fighting from the deck of the boats consisted of throwing bricks, bottles, spikes and an assortment of other deadly projectiles. Eventually, the Phelps-Dodge scabs reached the dock and climbed onto the wharf. The striking workers quickly followed and after circumventing a gauntlet of company men "invaded" the plant by climbing a maze of external scaffolding which extended from the wharf's edge to an opening onto the production floor. Once inside ... "vicious hand to hand combat" ensued with the "scabs." ... Outside of the plant demonstrators pushed violently against the main entrance gate, but 50 [police] officers and seven police cars prevented the crowd from entering the storage yard. ...

About 100 people received injuries in this battle and, unfortunately for Phelps-Dodge's public image, one of the two union members who were shot by company guards died ten days later leaving a wife and four children (Bruno 1994: 369). No one from the company was ever arrested for this killing thus giving it a new nickname, "Murder, Inc." as 10,000 angry workers from all over the northern New Jersey area poured into the city and staged multiple demonstrations at the company's plant (Bruno 1994: 369). Finally on September 14th the company capitulated to this pressure and gave the union a very generous new contract (Bruno 1994: 369-370). Why then did the similar violent confrontation in 1983 have such a different outcome for the union strikers?

The different outcome of the 1983 struggle between labor and management from that which had occurred in 1967-68 can be best explained by changes that had occurred in a few key environmental parameters. 1979 and 1980 had been good years for the copper producers as the price per pound rose to about $1.00 almost double the 1970 price

(Bandzak 1991:1117). However, in the following two years, rapid price declines to about 75¢ per pound by early 1982 led to the closure of all of Phelps Dodge's mines and three of its smelters on April 17 for "at least six weeks" (Chemical Marketing Reporter 1982:9; Fortune 1982:8) and to such headlines as that appearing in Business Week on May 3rd of that year (May 3, 1982:80) entitled "Why copper companies are running scared." Reasons given in this article for this scare were the following:

1) "Today's producer price of about 75¢ per lb ... is 15¢ to 20¢ below the breakeven level for most producers."

2) "... the trend to smaller cars and houses means long-term reduction in consumption."

3) "... copper is falling victim to heavy competition from plastic pipe and to cheaper and lighter aluminum in auto making."

4) "... in wiring ... copper will soon be running into growing competition from fiber optics."

5) With new contract negotiations with most unions coming in 1983, the threat of a long strike might "tempt... [companies] ... to make bargaining concessions, particularly if [as predicted by one industry spokesperson in the article] demand is on the upswing."

6) "... some 55% of all U.S. copper output is now controlled by oil companies. ... there is fear that many of these owners want to get out of copper and put their money into more profitable businesses ... [which] could mean rough times ahead for producers cast out on their own."

Phelps Dodge, in particular, was pictured as running scared since it had neither diversified its noncopper activities as much as other companies nor followed the lead of most other major copper producers that had "found shelter in the arms of rich oil companies" (Business Week July 26, 1982:58; Magnet 1983: 107). Even its few "timid" attempts to diversify into such metals as aluminum and uranium had proven to be disastrous and the prices for such refining byproducts as silver, zinc, molybdenum, lead and zinc had also fallen to new lows. (Business Week July 26, 1982:58; Chemical Marketing Reporter 1982:26; Rosenblum 1995: 52).

To attempt to cope with this crisis, a total of 3,800 blue-collar and salaried workers had been laid off with the April 17 mine and smelter shutdown, stock dividends were "slashed" by 75%, salaried jobs were "trimmed" by 12% and the remaining 4,500 such employees had their pay reduced by 4 percent on the first $40,000 of income and by 8 percent on any amount over $40,000 (Business Week July 26, 1982:58; Chemical Marketing Reporter 1982:9). Even the 5 members of the company's senior management team announced that they had "taken an additional cut of 12% on salary in excess of $150,000 and that the directors' yearly retainer [had] been cut from $12,000 to $9,000 and the fee for board meeting attendance [had] been reduced from $600 per meeting to $450 (Chemical Marketing Reporter 1982:9). They also submitted a request to the Environmental Protection Agency to permit them to have an additional eighteen months to complete the installation of an $185 million dollar pollution control project at the company's Morenci smelter (Chemical Marketing Reporter 1982:26).

The mine shutdown lasted longer than initially predicted as the price of copper fell by August 1982 to "just under 60¢/lb, a 25% decline" from the previous year (Chemical Week 1982:14). Thus, the newly elected president of Phelps Dodge, Richard T. Moolick, remained pessimistic about company earnings for the remainder of the year saying, "You have to look back to June 1932 to find hard times to match what we're going through now" (Chemical Week 1982:14). And though he was hopeful that one of the company's mines might be able to resume production "sometime in the next few months," he complained that in contrast to the 1930s when all copper producers cooperated to reduce worldwide production by 20% of capacity, foreign state-owned companies had "succeeded in driving world prices down ... because they [had] kept their production rates up" (Chemical Week 1982:14). And to make matters worse, Phelps Dodge was the only domestic producer to entirely shut down its mines in 1982 from April to October (Langley and Collier 1983:53), thus some other industry analysts said that U.S. copper producers had "only themselves to blame for low prices" since despite declining demand in 1981 they had increased production that year to 1.5 million m.t., about 342,000 m.t. more than in 1980. (Chemical Week 1982:14).

Although the previous company president, George Munroe, had during a series of "town meetings" held in Ajo, Bisbee, and Morenci shortly after the April 17, 1982 shutdown denied that the shutdown was intended to "send a message to the unions," in his Ajo speech he is quoted as having said (Rosenblum 1995: 53-54; Rosta 1984:46):

> The copper you produce here has to compete with copper produced in Canada, South America, Africa, Asia, Europe and Australia. Essentially the price for copper is the same all over the world. And no U.S. producer can continue operating for very long when its cost of producing a pound of copper approaches or exceeds the price for which it can be sold. It's as simple as that....
> The same eight dollars that Phelps Dodge pays for forty minutes of work would buy more than a full shift of work from the average mining employee at a large South American copper operation.... What will we be asking for? Our minds are open, but we know we need a substantial and immediate decrease.

He then went on to point out the unfairness to the company of the annual cost-of-living raise especially in Ajo where most employees live in company housing "at rents the company deliberately keeps low" and where the company "provides low cost medical care for both workers and their families despite rising costs" (Rosta 1984:46). And to show that the company was really serious about the need for all of its employees, both union and nonunion, to share the cuts needed to survive this industry crisis, he announced that the company had eliminated all COLAs to salaried personnel on April 1, 1982 (Rosta 1984:46).

However, the company's chief financial officer from 1977 to 1982, William Seidman, in a later 1991 interview (Rosenblum 1995:51, 55), admitted that although the high cost of labor in the U.S. was "certainly a part" of the 1982 shutdown decision: "The major part was that [the shutdown] gave us a chance to get rid of our inventories, enhance our cash position, and hopefully have some effect on market price -- and hopefully have some effect on the upcoming union problems." And in stark contrast to Munroe who in a later 1990 interview (Rosenblum 1995:50) called himself "very strongly pro-union," his July 1982 replacement[1] as the new president of Phelps Dodge, Richard Moolick, with a long anti-union reputation was quoted in a 1990s interview as saying (Rosenblum 1995:59):

> You're naive if you think it's good to operate with a union. It's no way to work for a company, for the employees, or for anyone. Mine-Mill [the original Morenci union] was an old and militant union. The first time I sat at a bargaining table there were some card-carrying commies on their side. To me it was an affront to sit across from a goddamned commie. ....

Moolick had first shown his anti-union hatred when crossing picket lines while working as a part-time printer during his college years (Rosenblum 1995:59). And in his first move against the copper miners' unions, claiming that a Morenci transportation workers' strike in 1959 was illegal, he fired the workers and hired new replacements (Rosenblum 1995:59). He then "precipitated a strike" in New Mexico, by hiring nonunion construction workers, gaining much support from local and state political leaders since, in contrast to most union employees, most of these nonunion workers were Mexican-Americans (Rosenblum 1995:59-60). Winning this battle, he then increased the number of nonunion contracts and employees in the New Mexico branch of the company under his control using at times an ex-FBI agent to inform him about "telephone conversations" of union leaders (Rosenblum 1995:60)

Moolick, who was out of the country when Munroe held his series of town meetings to try to convince the union workers that everyone in the company from the top down needed to sacrifice to save the company and their jobs, later ridiculed his former boss's efforts saying (Rosenblum 1995:56, 64) that Munroe's efforts were:

> ...dumb -- a very embarrassing thing. Why make yourself appear weak in front of the labor force?

Instead, under Moolick's direction as the new replacement in 1982 for Munroe as company president, the company authorized the hiring of a psychologist to train supervisors to conduct sessions "to bring to an end to all this grandfather to father to son stuff" and instead stress the importance of obedience to orders (Rosenblum 1995:56). And Rosenblum from a series of interviews he held with Moolick in the early 1990s states that (1995:56):

> ...Moolick felt that some of the young workers from Clifton and Morenci families were no longer seeking to work hard and advance; he believed that they had come to see work at the mine as an entitlement. When the company hired these workers ... it was getting only 'generations of sorriness.'"

Strong support for Moolicks anti-union, anti-paternalistic stand was now appearing at the national level following the election of President Reagan in 1980. Thus his firing of 12,000 striking air traffic controllers in 1981, was "widely believed [to have] sent a strong message to business leaders concerning how labor relations should be managed in the future"(Bandzak 1991:1116). Also, his appointees to the National Labor Relations Board had little sympathy for unions and generally favored company rather than union interpretations of labor laws (Bandzak 1991:1116). And the Republican obsession at this time to give top priority to the control of "runaway" inflation led to the imposition of such tight money policies as high federal reserve interest rates which greatly reduced the copper consuming demand for cars and houses (Bandzak 1991:1116) while at the same time the World Bank was increasing its loans to such countries as Peru, Chile, Zambia, and Zaire to help fund new copper mining projects whose exports to the U.S. also gained an additional advantage over domestic production because of the increasing strength of the "tight money" dollar (Rosenblum 1995:50; Hamilton 1983:H4-H5; Bandzak 1991:1116). Thus the foreign share of the U.S. market climbed from 7 percent in the early 1970s to nearly 20 percent at the end of the decade (Rosenblum 1995:50) and in 1982 Chile displaced the U.S. as the world's largest copper producer (Hamilton 1983:H1, H4). And despite such rosy predictions by such individuals as William Siedenburg, a vice president of Smith Barney, Harris Upham & Co. in May 1982 that the price of copper might rise to as much as $1.20 a lb. by the end of 1983 and maybe even $1.40 by 1984 (Business Week May 3, 1982:80), it fell to a new low of just over 60¢ a lb. in 1984 and remained there until 1987 (Bandzak 1991:1117). Nor did President Reagan, an avowed free-trader heed the recommendation of the International Trade commission which in June 1984 "found that U.S. copper producers were being seriously hurt by the surge in imports and should receive protection" (Bandzak 1991:1117). Thus, during his administration, the Trade Adjustment Assistance program for workers who were displaced because of foreign imports "was, for all practical purposes, abolished" (Bandzak 1991:1117).

However, about five months after Munroe's series of town meetings, union leaders began to suspect that the many stories circulating about Phelps Dodge's possible financial collapse were greatly exaggerated when more than half the laid off workers were called back despite the continued low world price for copper (Rosenblum 1995:55). And it was announced that on May 2,1983 with the scheduled reopening of the Tyrone, New Mexico mine and smelter, all of the company's mines and concentrators and all but one of its smelters would again be in production and that the company had been able to make a little money ("although not much") in Morenci (Hamilton 1983:H1, H4).

These union suspicions were confirmed when to the surprise of the union negotiating teams, Phelps Dodge, rejected a new contract proposal in which the unions would agree to a three-year wage freeze but keep the existing cost-of-living adjustment provision (Business Week July 18, 1983:58). This was initially puzzling to some analysts since the other major domestic copper producers, all who had higher production costs per pound than Phelps Dodge, had earlier accepted almost identical contracts (Business Week July 18, 1983:58). However, Phelps Dodge was merely following the earlier lead of many smaller, less unionized companies that had begun fights to "[force] concessions from workers even to the point of eliminating the union" (Business Week June 14, 1982: 66). Thus it became quickly obvious that Phelps Dodge under the leadership of its new president was intent on breaking the industry wide bargaining pattern that had been established at the end of the 1967-68 strike. And to aid them in that effort they turned to the strategies outlined in the book, <u>Operating during Strikes</u>, written by a Wharton School of Business (University of Pennsylvania) professor and two private lawyers and funded by Phelps Dodge, other large corporations, and some conservative think tanks (Rosenblum 1995:60-61).

Moolick, having failed in his attempts earlier that year to persuade the C.E.O.s of the other major American copper firms to take a united stand against the cost-of-living adjustment (COLA), felt that conditions were now right to enable him to fight the battle alone (Rosenblum 1995:60). Gone was the friendliness of the 1967-68 strike when the company deferred rent for company-owned houses and gave strikers credit for food, clothing, etc. in the company stores (Magnet 1983:106: Langley and Collier 1983:53).

Having rejected the final company offer, the union miners walked off their jobs at Morenci, Ajo, Bisbee, and Douglas and the first pickets appeared at the mine gates one minute after the midnight June 30, 1983 expiration of the old contract (Kingsolver 1989: 15). At Morenci the company immediately drafted office workers and foremen into service and along with 600 nonunion personnel in a convoy of more than 150 vehicles rolled up to the mine gate in time for the 5:30 a.m. shift change vowing to keep the mine and smelter operating at a 40 percent level (Kingsolver 1989: 25-26). As the cars continued to pass through the gate, the level of verbal abuse rose and a few car hoods were pounded but no major flare-up occurred (Kingsolver 1989: 26). But Phelps Dodge sought and a few days later won a court injunction limiting picket lines to ten union members at Morenci (Rosenblum 1995: 85-86).

A more restrictive restraining order was soon obtained for Ajo not only limiting the number of gate pickets but also prohibiting the setting up of a "gauntlet of persons or automobiles" along all roads to the mine's gates (Kingsolver 1989: 26). And the order further stated that "unless defendants' illegal or nonpeaceful acts are restrained, inhabitants of Ajo may be deprived of electrical energy or water" (Kingsolver 1989: 15).

In addition to this legally backed coercion, the company began a massive newspaper and letter war against the union "alternatively coaxing and threatening strikers" (Rosenblum 1995: 85). Thus replacement workers were told that even if a settlement was reached with the unions, they would have a right to retain their jobs while strikers were reminded that their wages "were higher than just about anywhere else" and that they should not "squander a good thing" (Rosenblum 1995: 85). This threat was made especially clear in a series of letters sent to the strikers by the Morenci mine manager, John Bolles, which included such chilling messages as:

> Too many people for too few jobs is like a game of musical chairs. Have you thought about what it means to you and your family if you don't have a chair when the music stops? (Rosenblum 1995:86)

Support for the company's position also quickly came from the Arizona Republic, the states largest newspaper, which five days after the strike began, in an editorial which blasted "bloated" labor agreements that "merely passed along the costs of lower productivity, higher wages and golden fringe benefits to the captive and unquestioning U.S. market," went on to assert that, "Jobless Butte [Montana] miners undoubtedly would be very happy to accept what Phelps Dodge's miners have refused" (Kingsolver 1989: 16).

The coalition of 13 unions led by the United Steel Workers retaliated by telling crowds of as many as 1600 strikers and supporters that they were already offering concessions (Langley and Collier 1983:53) and that, in the quarter just prior to the strike, Phelps Dodge, in contrast to the other copper companies that had agreed to the pattern contract, had made a profit(Rosenblum 1995: 87). And to counter the picket line restraining orders, the miners' wives "began holding mass pickets of their own" (Kingsolver 1989: 15).

On July 3rd, in Morenci, a strikebreaker was knocked in the face after work, followed on July 10th by the burning of a railroad trestle and on July 12th by the smashing of eight windows at the smelter (Rosenblum 1995: 86-87). but the most disastrous public relations nightmare for the unions occurred four weeks after the start of the strike when a bullet slammed through the wall of a house occupied by a man known as Ajo's first strikebreaker, hitting his sleeping three-year-old daughter in the head (Rosenblum 1995: 88). And though she miraculously survived this shooting, Arizona's leading newspaper, the Arizona Republic in a July 29, 1983 anti-union editorial, "A Child Lies Wounded," stated (Rosenblum 1995: 89):

> What did the child do to deserve a bullet? She has a
> father working to support her while other kids' dads are
> on strike against the copper mines.[2]

However, despite its month long "carrots and sticks" media campaign and the rapidly increasing public disapproval of the copper unions following this shooting, the company had persuaded fewer than five hundred[3] out of a total of twenty-four hundred[4] current and former employees to cross the picket lines (Rosenblum 1995: 92). And the company's claim that it was now running the mines at 83% of pre-strike levels (Magnet 1983:110) was misleading since those people crossing picket lines were working exhausting 12-hour shifts (Magnet 1983:110); the mines in the immediate prestrike period had not been operating at full capacity; and the Tyrone, New Mexico mine was still in full operation since its union contract would not expire until 1987 (Bandzak 1992:647). Thus, seven days after the shooting, in a secret meeting, the company under the leadership of President Moolick, made the decision to begin to hire permanent replacement workers for those men on strike even though he knew full well that this would escalate and dramatically change the nature of the confrontation between the company and the striking unions since as Rosenblum (1995: 90-93) suggests:

> ...Unions generally maintain at least a veneer of control over a strike when the replacements are crossovers and furloughed employees. Strikers can look their ex-colleagues in the eye and cuss them out; they can impose a measure of shame. These are neighbors, friends, family. But outside replacements are a declaration of war on unionism. They have just one role -- to take union jobs -- and they are virtually immune to pressure from unions.
> ...

A hastily arranged news conference was called after the August 5, 1983 secret company meeting to announce that on Monday, the 8th, employment offices in Morenci, Tucson, and Phoenix would begin hiring outside replacement workers (Rosenblum 1995: 93). Tension mounted by Sunday as one five-year employee was quoted as saying (Arizona Daily Star August 7, 1983):

> There's going to have to be some violence here -- you just can't let people take over your job, your home. It's just going to be one hell of a mess if they bring in people off the street. It's going to be a battle.

And a union spokesman was quoted as saying that the company was "inviting trouble" adding prophetically that, "It would take an army to protect the mines." (Arizona Daily Star August 7, 1983: ; Rosenblum 1995: 93).

On Monday the 8th in Morenci, an angry crowd of two thousand men and women gathered near the mine, one third of the combined population of Morenci and nearby Clifton (Rosenblum 1995: 94; Kingsolver 1989: 28). Two potential new hires that had entered the local employment office had their motorcycles kicked to the ground by an angry mob of two hundred union workers and had to be escorted to safety by two state troopers (Rosenblum 1995: 94-95). The crowd then demanded that the company employment director, Dick Boland, shut the employment office down and not let the two newly hired men enter the mine (Rosenblum 1995: 95). He agreed to these demands but "within minutes, a rumor spread that the men had been allowed in a back entrance of the ... mine" (Rosenblum 1995: 95). The mob armed with "sticks, clubs, and baseball bats" in a half mile "human chain" then "surged" toward the main entrance of the mine just before the scheduled 3:00 p.m. shift change (Rosenblum 1995: 95-96).

Even though he had the backing of 60 state troopers, the mine manager, John Bolles, agreed to cancel the shift changes for 24 hours and announced that Arizona governor, Bruce Babbit, accompanied by top union and company negotiators, would be arriving shortly to seek a peaceful end to this crisis (Rosenblum 1995: 95-96). But only the intervention of a local six-foot six-inch union spokesman, Rick Melton, prevented the angry strikers from overturning a busload of departing strikebreakers, urging them instead to air their grievances to the incoming governor and bargaining committee at the Clifton courthouse (Rosenblum 1995: 95). Fearing for their lives, most of the 300 or so remaining strikebreakers elected to spend the night on cots in the mine and with no more workers attempting to leave the mine and the help of falling rain, the crowd slowly dispersed for the night (Rosenblum 1995: 95; Kingsolver 1989: 30).

News of the events at Morenci on the 8th spread quickly to Ajo which had remained fairly peaceful during the strike, except for the tragic shooting of three year old Chandra Tallant on July 27 (which, as stated earlier, had become a public relations nightmare for the unions); some Ajo businesses refusing to serve "scabs"; and small acts of violence and some threatening phone calls (e.g., see A.C.N. August 11, 1983:6, 8). Among those angered upon hearing of the events at Morenci was Ajo's first woman miner, Janie Ramon, who was now the reporting secretary for her union, the International Chemical Workers Union Local 703 (Kingsolver 1989: 31). She claimed credit for trying to "stir up some resistance to Phelps Dodge in Ajo" to counter the charge by the Morenci strikers that the Ajo miners had no "courage" but instead were "meek little mice" (Kingsolver 1989: 31). She and her friends got into a fight with some scabs at a local bar the night of the 8th and on the morning of the 9th she joined other angry men and women trying to stop cars from entering the mine (Kingsolver 1989: 31). And though she claimed that bats were not used that day, the local paper reported that (A.C.N. August 11, 1983:1):

> Non-striking Phelps Dodge workers and supervisory personnel were met by an angry mob as they tried to go to work early Tuesday morning, August 9.
> The crowd attacked vehicles with rocks and baseball bats, severely damaging one vehicle and damaging others to a lesser extent. No serious injuries to people were reported and those bound for work turned back.
> The local sheriff's department quickly called in reinforcements and soon the town "resembled an army camp as dozens of uniformed sheriff's deputies and highway patrol officers arrived in town to maintain law and order" (A.C.N. August 18, 1983a:1) with an additional "32 more officers ... on call in Tucson [who]

could be in Ajo within two hours" ,(A.C.N. August 11, 1983:1).

Janie later recalled that the next day six vehicles with armed state troopers showed up at the mine gate and the drivers jumped out and aimed "machine guns" (i.e., M-16s) at her and two other women's heads only putting them down when according to one of the other two women, Gloria Blase, a nearby striker "grabbed a camera and started taking pictures" (Kingsolver 1989: 31). Later that day, four police vehicles again returned to investigate the breaking of a window on a "scab" vehicle at the plant gate (Kingsolver 1989: 32) which led the next day to the arrest of Natalie Munoz "in her home, [who] in front of her daughter [was] dragged away in her nightgown." (Kingsolver 1989:193; A.C.N. August 18, 1983b:1) Three men were also arrested that week for strike related acts (A.C.N. August 18, 1983b:1) and:

> Elsewhere in town there were several incidents of window breaking, tire slashing, and general vandalism. A house ... was flooded when someone put a water hose through the window and turned the water on. The PD employment office was also flooded with water (A.C.N. August 18, 1983b:1).

By the end of the month the number of those arrested specifically for the violence at the plant gate on August 9, totaled 11 (Kingsolver 1989:193). Janie, herself, although never identified in the local paper as having been arrested for a strike related activity (e.g., see A.C.N. February 2, 1984:1 for the names of the eleven individuals arrested) told of her arrest for the earlier barroom fight and claimed that the local judge, a former PD security division employee, offered her and other arrested strikers a choice between "crossing the picket line or staying behind bars" (Kingsolver 1989: 32).

Finally, using filmed documentation, since the company could not legally fire strikers without cause, during the next few weeks, she and seventy-four other Ajo strikers "were fired and ordered to vacate their company owned homes," (Kingsolver 1989: 32-33; A.C.N. August 18, 1983c:1).

The chief company negotiator, Pat Scanlon, commenting later on these and other Arizona strikers fired for "misconduct" during the strike, felt that the 188 firings were good for the company since:

> Our perception of that group is that in general it included a lot of the less desirable employees that were working, either because they were general troublemakers, or unreliable, or drunks, or whatever. So it had the effect of purging the work force of a lot of people who were not really on the company's side ... so in that respect, we upgraded the workforce" (Kingsolver 1989: 33).

By August 15, 220 workers felt safe enough to cross the picket lines at Ajo and the number grew to 285 on August 23 (A.C.N. August 18, 1983c:1; A.C.N. August 25, 1983a:1). These included not only new hires but also many men who had been laid off since the 1982 shutdown and some strikers, despite the union announcement that striking and laid off employees who were "honoring the picket line may be eligible for emergency financial aid" (A.C.N. August 18, 1983d:1). And with the resumption of high level talks between union and management officials in Phoenix; the identification of three suspects in the shooting of the three year old; her release from the hospital; and the warning from the sheriff's department that if needed "we can have additional people in Ajo in a very short time"(A.C.N. August 18, 1983c:1; A.C.N. August 25, 1983b:1); the August 25 local paper reported that "not a great deal of excitement showed up in the sheriff's log for the past week" (A.C.N.

August 25, 1983c:1)[5] although, as was soon to be demonstrated, one striker who asked not to be identified accurately warned that:

> As long as they're meeting, we'll keep quiet and not cause trouble. If they stop talking -- watch out! (A.C.N. August 18, 1983c:1)

Meanwhile in Morenci, with governor Babitt acting as a "peace negotiator" between the company and the unions, a ten-day moratorium on hiring replacements was agreed upon during which time a federal mediator would attempt to resolve the contract dispute. However, this agreement which still allowed the mine to operate during this ten-day period did little to satisfy the angry crowd that was back at the mine gate on the morning of the 9th "waving bats," "lengths of pipe," and "chains," "demanding a shutdown by noon" (Rosenblum 1995: 98-99). The "solemn" Steelworkers local president, Angel Rodriguez, warned Scanlon, the company negotiator, that he and the other union officials had "completely lost control" of their workers and that:

> The people at the gate say if the company does not agree by twelve noon to shut down production, they will rush the gate and the DPS officers [i.e., the state troopers]. They say they will go inside the plant and drag everyone out. If that means killing them, they say they will kill them (Rosenblum 1995: 99).

Scanlon, taking this threat very seriously, attempted to reach company president Moolick for a decision but failing this reached instead company chairman Munroe who told him to do "whatever" he felt was "proper" (Rosenblum 1995: 100). A written agreement promising that the company would immediately stop hiring replacement workers and shut down the Morenci mine and smelter for a ten-day negotiating period was then quickly drafted and signed (Rosenblum 1995: 100; Business Week August 29, 1983:18).

Union president Rodriguez, just a few minutes prior to the noon deadline, using a bullhorn, read the company's statement to the crowd at the Morenci mine entrance adding:

> We've got a victory here. Let's don't blow it. You've got it in writing. [The strikebreakers] are going to come out peacefully. Don't punch the cars -- don't throw anything. Just watch 'em (Rosenblum 1995: 100-101).

Temporarily satisfied, despite the failure of the company to promise similar shutdowns at Ajo, Bisbee, Douglas or El Paso, the strikers marched down the highway toward their homes chanting "Union! Union! Union!" (Rosenblum 1995: 101).

Moolick, initially displeased upon hearing of the agreement, nevertheless wasted little time using the ten-day "cooling off" period to his advantage (Rosenblum 1995: 101). Thus in a secret meeting, he authorized the continued payment of hourly wages to those workers who had been brave enough to cross the picket lines and told the management team of his intent to "smuggle" twenty shotguns and ammunition into the mine (Rosenblum 1995: 102). John Boland, Phelps Dodge's Western Operations legal advisor and labor negotiator, and his son, Dick Boland, the Morenci personnel manager, advised Moolick privately that it would wiser to continue to shut down the Morenci operations for the duration of the strike while keeping open the Ajo property which now seemed to be totally under control thanks to the vigorous action of the Tucson-based sheriff's department but this suggestion "infuriated" Moolick who vowed that that the Morenci mine and smelter would reopen at the end of the ten-day "cooling off" period (Rosenblum 1995: 102-103).

Even though the governor of Arizona, Bruce Babbitt, was a democrat, there was a strong anti-union Republican majority in the state legislature that threatened to pass new legislation to strengthen the extant "right to work" law to give actual physical protection to workers not choosing union membership (Rosenblum 1995: 104). The company, seizing upon this strong political backing, refused to back down from its industry-pattern-breaking demands of "wage cuts for new hires, reduced medical and vacation benefits across-the-board, and termination of cost-of-living increases" while the unions insisted upon limiting their concessions to those agreed upon in the contracts already negotiated with the other major copper producers (Rosenblum 1995: 105: Iron Age 1983:70).

Babbitt at this point faced a difficult decision: should he or should he not send in the National Guard to keep the peace in Morenci when the company reopened the mine and smelter at the end of the ten-day "cooling off" period (Rosenblum 1995: 107)? On the one hand, sending in the guard would alienate his organized labor political support and perhaps doom any future political aspirations. However, having received secret intelligence reports from ACISA ("Arizona's own CIA") undercover agents that very violent union activities were being planned should the mine and smelter reopen and knowing that the small number of Department of Public Safety state troopers were no match against the strikers who, in addition to baseball bats, dynamite, and many concealed weapons, almost all had hunting rifles, Babbitt made the politically painful decision to send in the National Guard (Rosenblum 1995: 109-115).

Early on the morning of August 19, 1983, the several mile long "Operation Copper Nugget" convoy arrived in Morenci guarded by Huey combat helicopters flying overhead and armed riflemen stationed on the hilltops overlooking the main road to the mine (Rosenblum 1995: 116, 119-120; Kingsolver 1989: 34-35). In addition to 325 National

Guardsmen, their trucks, amphibious carriers, jeeps, M-16s, and armored personnel carriers, came 426 DPS state troopers (Rosenblum 1995: 119). Given this level of protection, 450 workers crossed the picket lines two days later as the mine and smelter reopened (Langway and Collier 1983:53).

This overwhelming show of force and the ensuing six-day stay of the Guard near the gate totally intimidated the strikers while hundreds of unemployed workers from nearby towns came to Morenci seeking employment having now no fear of violent confrontations with angry strikers and having the written promise from the company that they would not be terminated in case of a strike settlement (Rosenblum 1995: 121-122). This non-termination promise had been made possible by a new Supreme Court decision in the case of Belnap v. Hale which not only allowed companies to make such promises but also allowed newly hired people the right to sue companies if they were later laid off to make room for returning strikers (Rosenblum 1995: 123).

With the help of this legal decision and the powerful presence of the Arizona National Guard and DPS officers, the company's earlier dream that by making the decision to hire permanent replacement workers, the number of workers crossing picket lines would reach a "critical mass, leading to a flood of returning employees fearful of losing their jobs permanently" (Magnet 1983:110) soon became a reality. Thus, only a few weeks later on September 26, 1983, the company reported that 2,400 workers including 1,500 union members (800 strikers and 700 previously furloughed union members) were now crossing the picket lines (Business Week September 26, 1983:39). By now the united front of the 13 unions was unraveling as clearly seen when the representative for the Machinists, the second largest union in the coalition, in a strategy meeting on August 26th told Frank McKee, the leader of the Steelworkers Union and the union coalition:

You can't win 'em all Frank. Let's cut our losses and fight another day (Rosenblum 1995: 123).

Fulfillment of the company's dream was also helped by a major law enforcement assault on strikers in Ajo the very next day, August 27th (Rosenblum 1995: 124) when ten Ajo strikers were arrested, handcuffed and jailed on charges of "rioting, obstructing traffic, or interfering with the judicial process" although one defendant claimed that her only crime had been using her telephone to tell a former friend that she now considered him a "scab" (Kingsolver 1989: 33). Bail for those arrested was set as high as $20,000 ($175,000 for all ten), bankrupting the local union coffers overnight, and most were later taken in handcuffs in the back of a van without air conditioning or water on a hot day to Tucson, a three-hour drive to the east (Kingsolver 1989: 33; Rosenblum 1995: 124). And though the unions were finally able to raise the bail money and six years later win a court decision against the company for those arrested (Rosenblum 1995: 124-125), the damage to the unions' Ajo struggle by the fall of 1983 was irreversible. Thus, the company feeling its increasing strength, in September announced that "it had filled all jobs at its plants and [had] sent termination notices to workers who remained on strike" (A.C.N. December 29, 1983a:1)

In desperation, Union leaders met with Governor Bruce Babbitt and Senator Dennis DeConcini to protest the treatment of strikers by law enforcement agencies, charging that the Department of Public Safety had created a police state. (A.C.N. October 20, 1983a:1)

Additionally, the unions sought help from such groups and individuals as the retired union workers of Sun City (A.C.N. October 27, 1983:1) and Cesaer Chavez (A.C.N. November 24, 1983:3) who "vowed to help start a boycott of PD products and to expose the company to adverse publicity" adding that "those now working for PD would be joining the strike when they found out how PD was using them" (A.C.N. December 1, 1983a:1). An appeal to the National Labor Relations Board by the unions to obtain the names and addresses of newly hired workers failed although the unions won a partial victory when the board dismissed claims by the corporation that "unions were engaging in unfair labor practices with their pattern bargaining techniques" (A.C.N. October 27, 1983a:1).

By the first week in November 1983, following threats to end their medical benefits (A.C.N. October 20, 1983a:1), strikers who lived in PD housing were told that they were no longer company employees and that as "ex-employees" those who were behind in their rent payments would be evicted (A.C.N. November 3, 1983a:1). And though the unions won an important victory when the arbitrator chosen by both sides reinstated the strikers' medical benefits providing that the strikers continue to pay their share of the monthly insurance premiums (A.C.N. December 22, 1983:3), they lost the important battle, in a 3-2 Arizona Supreme Court decision, to avoid eviction from company owned housing (A.C.N. December 22, 1983:3).

However, the unions did at this time receive some encouragement from the House Education and Labor Subcommittee that in a preliminary report to Congress accused Phelps Dodge of never seriously attempting to reach an agreement with the unions and deliberately choosing to provoke a strike against it (A.C.N. December 22, 1983:6). However the futility of this minor union victory had been obvious as early as the end of September when Matthew P. Scanlon, a vice president and the company's chief negotiator, reported that the corporation was operating at nearly normal levels despite the walkout by 2,600 mine and smelter workers on July 1 (Business Week September 26, 1983:39). Thus, by the end of September, "800 strikers and 700 previously furloughed union members" were crossing the picket lines along with 900 new employees (Business Week September 26, 1983:39).

The returning workers gave up cost-of-living increases and accepted a three-year freeze of their old wage of $12.65 an hour (Business Week September 26, 1983:39). One holiday and a fifth week of vacation were lost; new employee payments for health benefits were added; and altered "productivity raising" work rules were instigated (Business Week September 26, 1983:39). Also, the newly hired replacement workers earned as little as $7.00 per hour although gradual pay raises were promised.(Business Week September 26, 1983:39).

This erosion of union power in Arizona by the fall of 1983 was, however, highly predictable given the continuing national decline in jobs for blue-collar workers and the earlier crushing defeat of the Air Traffic Controllers' 1981 strike by Ronald Reagan which "dramatically stiffen[ed]" the resistance of most companies to union demands (Anderson et al. 1983:50). Thus in 1981, unions "won only 30.3 percent of all certification elections" and "were ousted in 74.9 percent of the cases" in which decertification elections were held (Anderson et al. 1983:52).

While Moolick was wining the battle against the unions and had by the end of September 1983 achieved about a 10% reduction in labor costs as an added immediate bonus (Business Week September 26, 1983:39), Munroe continued his crusade against American private and government subsidies to competing "uneconomic" foreign mines giving as an example the state-owned Cobriza mine in Peru which he claimed was losing 60¢ a pound on every pound they produced but which continued to flood the market with copper "because they need[ed] the foreign exchange" (Dorfman 1983:140).

The optimistic forecast that the Ajo smelter might reopen sometime in 1984 (A.C.N. October 20, 1983c:1) was countered by PD's announcement of a 28.4 million third quarter 1983 loss (A.C.N.

October 27, 1983b:1) and a gloomy Arizona Department of Economic Security forecast for copper industry recovery during 1984 (A.C.N. December 29, 1983c:4).

By the start of November, weakened by massive worker defections, the strikers were no longer able to put much pressure on those crossing the picket lines; thus, only a few incidents at these lines , "none serious," were still appearing in the Ajo Sheriff's weekly log (A.C.N. November 3, 1983b:1). And as the strike entered its seventh month in January with no new talks scheduled between the unions and the company (A.C.N. January 5, 1984:1), the company sensing complete victory on January 9, 1984 watched sheriff's deputies, "peacefully" evict two fired Ajo strikers from their company-owned homes although one of these men, Art Galvez, felt that the eviction was unfair since "...some [of the other accused] strikers who had used baseball bats [on August 9, 1983] had had the charges against them dropped when they crossed picket lines and went to work..."(A.C.N. January 12, 1984:1). And on January 27, both of these evicted strikers and seven others of the 11 Ajo strikers and supporters, who had been arrested on felony rioting charges for their August 9, 1983 actions at the plant gate, pled guilty to the lesser misdemeanor charge of disorderly conduct while charges against the final two were dismissed "for lack of evidence" (A.C.N. February 2, 1984:1).

Munroe in a long luncheon speech on January 18, 1984 "hosted by Phelps Dodge in Tucson[6], Arizona for Tucson business, government, and community leaders" strongly denied "the Steelworkers' charge" that the company's conduct during the strike "was an attempt to break the unions" (A.C.N. January 26, 1984a:10). Instead, he stated that

> Our battle is not with the principle of unionism, but with socialized foreign competition, subsidized by international lending agencies.... to which the United States taxpayer is the largest contributor.....

This subsidization comes in two basic forms: one, compensatory financing by the IMF to buffer our competitors from damage caused to the copper markets by their destructive production policies; the other, the financing of new or expanded mines by multilateral development banks." (A.C.N. January 26, 1984a:10-11).

Citing a disastrous drop of 28% in the price of copper in 1981 and 1982 while wages under the 1972 COLA (cost of living adjustment) agreement during these two years rose 30%[7], Munroe said "the elimination of COLA was our principal objective in 1983's contract bargaining" (A.C.N. January 26, 1984a:10). He then went on to state that when the 1983 strike deadline neared, the company was faced with three choices, they could: one, accept the pattern agreement that retained COLA that other companies had agreed to; two, reject the pattern agreement and shut down operations during a strike; and three, continue to operate during a strike (A.C.N. January 26, 1984a:10). Option two was viewed by Munroe as being even worse than option one since historically "the operations just stayed shut down until the company was ready to cave in" leaving option three as the only viable one (A.C.N. January 26, 1984a:10). And he seemed pleased to announce that the company's completed hiring program to replace the 42% of its workforce which still supported the strike had been very successful adding that, "Productivity is high, turnover is low, and we are experiencing an important improvement in our labor costs." (A.C.N. January 26, 1984a:11). Thus, it is not surprising that the first talks between the company and the unions in two months on January 23 lasted only ninety minutes (A.C.N. January 26, 1984b:1)

As the strike entered its eighth month the copper industry made a "last-ditch plea" to Washington to impose strict import quotas on foreign copper (Business Week February 13, 1984a:37-38) and more union members had crossed the picket lines than those who remained on strike (i.e., 1300 versus 1140) (Business Week February 13, 1984b:38). By now the company referred to the current 947 "new hires" as "permanent replacements" which meant that the company had no intension of reaching any agreement with the unions since such an agreement would require the rehiring of strikers and firing of the "new hires", an action that the Supreme Court in 1983 had ruled would allow the "permanent replacements" to sue the company in state court for damages (Business Week February 13, 1984b:38).

Further adding to the despair of the strikers at this time was the news that the Ajo Food Bank after one year of operation was "struggling to survive" (A.C.N. February 16, 1984:1). However, on March 12, 1984 they did win a U.S. District Court decision to continue receiving company medical benefits (A.C.N. March 15, 1984:1) although the company planned to appeal the ruling (March 29, 1984a:1). And plans to evict, as early as March 19, an estimated 100 strikers still living in company housing were put on hold until the end of the school year (A.C.N. March 22, 1984:1; March 29, 1984b:1).

Meanwhile, Senator Dennis DeConcini introduced in the Senate a series of measures "designed to help alleviate the copper crisis" (A.C.N. March 8, 1984:8). These included an act to place a quota limit on copper imports, a maximum tariff of 15 cents per pound on copper imported from countries not meeting America's clean air standards, a resolution calling upon the international trade community to "develop a method for stabilizing worldwide copper production and recommend initiatives to restrict subsidized overproduction," a request that the President should "support the purchase of 200,000 short tons of copper for the national defense stockpile" during the coming year, and the use of copper "as a canister material to store radioactive waste"

News continued to be bad for the unions that spring as the National Labor Relations Board released a ruling on April 4, 1984 that rejected evidence provided by the unions that the company had "failed to bargain in good faith" (A.C.N. April 12, 1984:1). And on April 20, 1984 U.S. District Court Judge Alfredo C. Marquez ruled that company officials had "acted properly in giving the unions sixty day notice of its intent to evict strikers" (A.C.N. April 26, 1984:1).

After this ruling, the company immediately sent eviction notices to 18 strikers in Ajo and 25 in Morenci[8], targeting those strikers it "charged ... with picket line violations" giving them the possibility of a 5 day extension past the May 31 deadline if they had children in school (A.C.N. May 3, 1984:1). However, the company decided to delay making an eviction decision in the case of five other Ajo strikers who were merely "delinquent" in paying their rent (A.C.N. May 3, 1984:1).

A possible clue as to why the company delayed evicting these and the other remaining strikers can be found in the May 15, 1984 announcement that the Ajo smelter which had been closed since April 17, 1982 would be reopening (A.C.N. May 17, 1984:1) following the optimistic report by Board Chairman Munroe that, in addition to the labor cost savings that had been implemented, there had been "substantial decreases in the free world's copper inventories" and that the company's overall operating costs would be reduced because of the very low cost copper now being produced at the Tyrone, New Mexico mine using a new solvent extraction-electrowining process (A.C.N. May 10, 1984:8). However it appears that none of the remaining strikers took advantage of these new job opportunities since the local paper reports, "Of the 115 workers at the smelter, 72 are new hires and the remaining 43, including supervisors, are transferring from other departments." (A.C.N. May 17, 1984:1).

Seeing the success of Phelps Dodge in resisting union demands, Kennecott, at that time the nation's largest copper producer, citing "poor copper markets," asked its unions to go back to the bargaining table" to renegotiate a new contract (A.C.N. May 24, 1984:11). And the local Ajo paper reported that "a move [was] made to decertify the electricians' union at Phelps Dodge's plant in Tyrone, New Mexico" even though the union contracts there were not yet up for renewal (A.C.N. May 24, 1984:11).

This decertification movement succeeded by a vote of 15 to 11 and on May 22 in Morenci and May 23 in Ajo, security guards voted to decertify their union. (A.C.N. May 31, 1984:1). At this point two of the remaining three certified unions in Tyrone voted to accept the new contract terms offered them by Phelps Dodge while Magna Copper Company and Inspiration Consolidated Copper Co. joined Kennecott in initially unsuccessful attempts to press their unions for contract renegotiations (A.C.N. May 31, 1984:1; June 7, 1984:1).

By mid-June, the owners of the Duval mine, whose employees had voted to continue working during contract negotiations, now following the lead of Phelps Dodge to seek better union concessions, withdrew their contract offer that had already been accepted by two of their three unions (A.C.N. June 14, 1984:1). while Kennecott warned its workers that continuing bad economic conditions could "force" it to lay off 2000 Utah workers (A.C.N. June 21, 1984:1)

Adding to the copper industry's gloom was news that the Internal Revenue Service had proposed regulations to retroactively tax "compounds formed in the production of copper"[9] while Phelps Dodge received the bad news that it had been denied a renewal of the Department of Health Services' operating permit for the Morenci smelter and that most strikers were legally fighting eviction notices (A.C.N. June 21, 1984:1). And, despite the continuing fall in the price of copper to 66¢ per pound, another copper mine[10] which had been shutdown since June 26, 1982, resumed full production (A.C.N. June 28, 1984:1). However, new hope came to the industry when it was announced that the International Trade Commission, by a unanimous vote, had ruled that imports had "damaged" the domestic copper industry (A.C.N. June 28, 1984:1). Four of the five members of this commission then urged President Reagan to take action to give relief to United States copper producers although they were divided over what specific action he should take with two wanting him to impose tariffs, two preferring import quotas, and one recommending no presidential action but if one be taken that it be in the form of a tariff rather than a quota (A.C.N. July 5, 1984:3). Also encouraging to PD executives was the news that "several Phelps Dodge workers" had requested desertification petitions from the National Labor Relations Board since after the end of one year, workers on strike would no longer be allowed to vote in desertification elections (A.C.N. June 28, 1984:1).

Although Morenci "saw some violence" on the first anniversary of the strike, the other PD towns, including Ajo, remained relatively calm despite a ruling by the National Labor Relations Board that a union "may not restrict its members' right to resign" (A.C.N. July 5, 1984:3). Instead, switching targets with almost half of U.S. copper workers laid off or on strike, labor leaders led a rally of an estimated 200,000 union supporters in San Francisco at the start of the Democratic convention calling for the defeat of President Reagan who was widely perceived to be both anti-labor and indifferent to the plight of the U.S. copper industry (A.C.N. July 19, 1984:8). And on July 12, the television program 20/20 examined the continuing crisis facing the domestic copper industry repeating many of the charges made earlier by Munroe against the support of foreign mining companies by U.S. taxpayer-supported international lending agencies while American producers were "hampered by high labor costs, pollution restrictions, and a dwindling ore supply" (A.C.N. July 19, 1984:8).

But despite these troubles and a 20.7 million dollar second quarter loss (A.C.N. August 2, 1984a:1), Phelps Dodge was reported to be nearly ready with the work needed to enable the Ajo smelter to be the second Arizona smelter to meet the new federal and state standards limiting sulfur dioxide smokestack emissions (A.C.N. July 19, 1984:8).

In contrast, Standard Oil decided against reopening its Cyprus-Bagdad mine but Anamax Mining corporation following the lead of Phelps Dodge, on the one year anniversary of the August 1, 1983 walkout of its workers, having continued to operate its Twin Buttes mine with management personnel, broke off all talks with its five unions (A.C.N. August 2, 1984b:1). And despite a decision by a top union official to stage the next massive rally of strikers and supporters in Clinton on Labor Day, things continued to look ever bleaker for them when the National Labor Relations Board handed down a decision stating that "unions must show majority support of a company's workers to gain bargaining rights; even if the company has engaged in unlawful conduct to prevent the union from organizing workers" (A.C.N. August 2, 1984b:1).

The shocking announcement by Phelps Dodge on August 5, 1984 that although the Ajo smelter would continue to operate treating concentrates from the Morenci and Tyrone mines, the Ajo mine and concentrator would be shut down on August 12 for "at least three months," caught both strikers and "scabs" by surprise (A.C.N. August 9, 1984:1). Of the approximately 680 Ajo employees only about 180 would remain on the payroll (A.C.N. August 9, 1984:1). Laid off workers were promised health benefits for ninety days and would be given rehiring preference over strikers although, if there were still any vacancies when the mine and concentrator reopened, a striker would be considered for reemployment if he "abandoned" the strike (A.C.N. August 9, 1984:1).

That the company was still hopeful that this shutdown would merely be temporary was indicated by its subsequent decision to give each of the laid-off workers a supplementary unemployment weekly benefit of $60 in addition to the government supplied benefit and to continue to pay dental and vision benefits (A.C.N. August 16, 1984:1). Also, the company promised to defer one half of the monthly rent for company housing until the laid-off worker either returned to work for the company or made over $240 per week from some other employment (A.C.N. August 16, 1984:1).

However, some "community leaders" soon began expressing doubt that the mining crisis would soon end as seen in this statement by Enrique Celaya on what must be done to prevent Ajo from "becoming a ghost town":

> Ajo still has a lot of potential that is just sitting there with no one doing anything about it. We've got to work together, stress the positive points of our town, and attract new industry and business. Ajo is ideal for retirement and winter living, and a small industry couldn't find a better location. (A.C.N. August 23, 1984:5)

Final defeat for all the PD unions at El Paso, Bisbee, Ajo, Morenci, and Douglas came with a decertification vote held in early October 1984 (Rosenblum 1995: 195). Success for the company by that time was assured since, as stated earlier, after a strike had lasted for one year, replacement workers were allowed to vote in such an election while those still out on strike were not (Rosenblum 1995:195).

The first vote from El Paso, 372 votes against the union and 4 votes in favor, to the dismay of the unions was released in the middle of the three-day voting period in Arizona (Rosenblum 1995:196). This led to charges of National Labor Relations Board bias and a legal challenge which delayed the Arizona vote count for three months but on January 24, 1985 the final vote count was tabulated and released (Rosenblum 1995: 196). All thirty union locals at these locations were abolished by a vote of 1,908 to 87. And on February 19, 1986 came the legal end of the strike as the unions' final legal appeals were rejected (Rosenblum 1995:198).

To this day the Ajo mine has not reopened even though the high price of copper in recent years has occasionally led to rumors of a possible future reopening. However, the optimists were right in their prediction that Ajo instead of becoming a "ghost town" would survive and prosper for the very reasons they enumerated in 1984. Thus Crawford (1995: 210) reports that, "After the Phelps-Dodge mine closed, Ajo, Arizona became a popular destination for "snowbirds," retirees seeking inexpensive winter lodging."

Chapter Notes

1. Munroe at this time was "promoted" to the less demanding position of company chairman and while, in theory, he was still Moolick's boss, in practice, Moolick's power now exceeded Munroe's.

2. Ironically, although the girl recovered from the wound (A.C.N. , August 25, 1983b:1) and a suspect was arrested (A.C.N. October 20, 1983b:1), her father was killed in a tragic car accident only a few months later (A.C.N. December 1, 1983b:1).

3. The company's claim at the time was 635 (Magnet 1983: 110).

4. On September 26, 1983 Newsweek (page 39) reported that the total number of strikers had been 2,600.

5. Even the Pima County Parks and Recreation department decided to aid this peacekeeping effort by reopening the town swimming pool "in an attempt to provide an added activity for the people of Ajo" (A.C.N. August 25, 1983d:1)

6. The headline mistakenly gives Phoenix as the location where he gave this speech.

7. Wage raises averaged 12% a year since the 1972 COLA (cost of living adjustment) agreement while copper prices rose only an average of 3.5% a year according to Munroe (A.C.N. January 26, 1984a:10-11).

8. On June 7, the Ajo Copper News reported that that the actual number of eviction court actions filed was 16 against strikers in Ajo and 27 against strikers in Morenci (A,C.N. June 7, 1984:1).

9. Senator DeConcini quickly "introduced an amendment which would forbid any IRS appropriated funds to be used to implement or enforce the proposed tax" (A.C.N. June 21, 1984:1)

10. This was the Pinto Valley mine formerly owned and operated by the Miami Operations division of Cities Services Company but now a new subsidiary of the Newmont Mining Corporation.

CHAPTER 10:

Exporting Order, Control, and Centralized Power Far Beyond Salt Lake City: the Example of the Mormon Church as a Highly-Successful Ultra-Adaptable System

... that cultural system which more effectively exploits the energy resources of a given environment will tend to spread in that environment at the expense of less effective systems. ... (Sahlins and Service 1960:75)

...it is clear that Mormon financial and political power is exerted in Washington to a degree far beyond what one would expect from one voter in fifty.... The nation will not always be only two percent Mormon. The Saints outlive the rest of us, have more children than all but a few American groups, and convert on a grand scale, both here and abroad.... ...my own guess is that by the year 2020 ... they could well form at least ten percent of our population, and probably rather more than that. Their future is immense: the Mormon people consistently are the hardest-working, most cohesive bloc in our society; only Asian-Americans rival them in zeal, ambition, and intensity. Salt Lake City may yet become the religious capital of the United States. (Bloom1992: 112-113)

As we have seen, environmental parameters, "viral" agents, the "laundering" of past realities, and the control of the communication of goods and services are some of the key factors in explaining the persistence of certain systems in Ajo, Arizona. The extension of this type of analysis to the wider world offers a possible new paradigm to assist planners in predicting the probable outcome of their efforts.

In expanding the type of analysis and prediction in this book beyond Ajo, it is often quite easy to identify the key environmental and historic reasons why certain systems thrive and urban nuclei develop at particular points in the space/time continuum. Thus Price (1972:19) citing the earlier similar approach to urban analysis by Arensberg (1968) and Gulick (1967, 1968) starts his critique of his own study of Reno, Nevada with the hypothesis that:

> Reno's special character can best be explained in terms of its geographical and historical adaptations in a symbiotic cultural network. It is an important link in an interdependent relationship between Nevada and California. Nevada is a resource-poor area with vast reaches of almost useless arid land. Over 85% of Nevada belongs to the federal government, for such purposes as atomic and military testing ranges. ... These resource-poor, large space, low population and convenient location factors have pressured Nevada into earning a living by supplying what are usually illegal services: gambling, quick divorce, quick marriage, risqué shows, and prostitution. Nevada is culturally symbiotic with the other Western States and with America generally, so much so that Nevada could not feed its own population on its agricultural production

And though the low population comment is no longer true in the Las Vegas region, the other named parameters remain today. Here, it is interesting to note the rise of the gambling industry on many Indian reservations as a similar "solution" to an almost identical environmental problem.

This same type of approach to urban analysis is also taken by the journalists, Wiley and Gottlieb (1982), who in their detailed study of the "six great power centers" of the Western Sunbelt (i.e., Los Angeles, San Francisco, Las Vegas, Phoenix, Salt Lake City, and Denver) saw the power brokers of these centers now triumphing over those in the East in terms of their ability to influence national and at times international events. And it is to one of these important power centers, Salt Lake City, that I now turn to test the analytical and predictive power of the new general systems model that I have outlined in the preceding pages of this book. But before proceeding let me briefly discuss the following dilemma I faced in choosing this particular test.

It has become more difficult for many anthropologists to do research in recent years as the traditional groups that they studied have either denied them permission to conduct studies or have demanded censorship privileges over anything to be published. Thus, starting with people like Barbara Meyerhoff (1978) who studied the residents of a Jewish rest home in Santa Monica, California, some anthropologists have begun to study their own ethnic groups. This type of research presents its own special problems, however, even though it is politically correct to support the common but often false belief that an inside member of a particular group is the person best able to fully and objectively understand and explain the dynamics of his or her group to the outside world.

In particular, it is especially hard for an insider to avoid heavy pressure from friends, relatives, and other members of the group to always promote a positive image of the group while suppressing any negative comments or revealing any "skeletons in the closet." This has been an extremely difficult task for me since "the Church of Jesus Christ of Latter-day Saints" or as it is more commonly known "the Mormon Church" is ultra-sensitive to any negative comments coming from any of its members more than from such "friendly" outsiders as Jan Shipps. However, in the following expansion of my analysis of why some systems succeed while most others fail, I, as an insider, have tried to remain as scientifically objective as possible in examining this remarkably successful system.

Looking back at my first arrival in the remote, small mining town of Ajo, I vividly remember how amazed I was to find a large Mormon church congregation there since beginning with Brigham Young during the California 1849 gold rush, Mormon prophets for many years discouraged church members from seeking the earth's mineral treasures. Thus, even in the Church's Utah home base, to this very day, many non-Mormons continue to work in the mines, a legacy of this 19th century counsel from Brigham Young and the antagonism that often developed in Utah's mining towns toward the leaders of the Mormon Church.

However, the Ajo mystery was quickly solved when I learned more about the company's initial decision about how the religious needs of its workers should be met in its carefully planned new town. Thus, two church buildings were constructed, one for the Catholics and one for the Protestants. However, just as the company hospital often had trouble attracting and retaining doctors in such a remote rural location so sometimes did the local churches especially during World War II. Thus, during a brief period in this war period when there was no resident protestant minister in Ajo, members of the congregation asked a local company official and prominent civic leader, Malin Lewis, who happened to be an active Mormon to give a few Sunday sermons. This request he quickly accepted and by the time that a new protestant minister finally arrived in town, it was reported to me that this "lay"[1] Mormon preacher had converted about half the protestant congregation to the Mormon faith (a classic example of control action #37).

Looking now at the system that greatly motivated not only this remarkable lay preacher but also a local Ajo Native American boy who would later in the Bush administration become the head of the Bureau of Indian Affairs, let us begin our story in the central core area of this amazing Church, one state to the north.

No one living in the state of Utah now would deny that of all the "controlling" systems present locally, none is more powerful than the Mormon Church. However, as my model would predict and as Wiley and Gottlieb (1982:141-142) confirm, there are other influential "power brokers" present today in Utah, many of whom have long ago ceased trying to "out compete" the power of the Mormon Church and have instead entered into various other types of noncompetitive interaction (e.g., "neutralism" or "facultative mutualism") with the system that is locally referred to as "the L.D.S. Church" or more often simply "the Church" by both members and non-members. Especially important have been the massive cooperative humanitarian aid efforts to rush relief supplies to victims of natural disasters throughout the world with the LDS Church supplying the needed items that are often then distributed by other cooperating organizations including such former rivals as the Catholic Church.

This is not to say that all other systems, especially the Gay Community which by its increasing influx of members and supporters into the inner city's "gayborhoods" has helped elect "gay friendly" city council members and the last two Salt Lake City mayors, have ceased their efforts to limit or diminish the Church's sphere of environmental control. Thus, these last two mayors have made the center city "gay friendly" with their vigorous support of "gay pride parades" and "equal rights for domestic partners" of city employees. Other powerful foes of the Church surfaced, a few years ago, after the city sold to the Church, part of Main Street between the LDS temple and the main Church Office building, blocking traffic on this major north-south downtown road. And this opposition intensified when the Church tried to limit the behavior of pedestrians on this former public street, especially the ubiquitous, very-vocal, "anti-Mormon" demonstrators.

Still, the Church finally won the Main Street battle and the Gay Community has had only very limited success in its efforts elsewhere in Utah although, as will be discussed later in greater detail, they, in 2008, intensified their efforts to fight Church leaders after a letter from the new Mormon Prophet, Thomas S. Monson, and his two Counselors was read to members in California Mormon chapels urging members to do all they could to help pass the fall 2008 "anti-gay" marriage amendment. Thus, even though many competing systems have at times been able to persuade certain "black boxes" (i.e., individual members) to leave the LDS Church or openly criticize its leaders, the Church has always through both its massive missionary program and its highly successful efforts to keep the members' birthrate well above the national average been able to more than compensate for any such "black box" defections and greatly limit the power of those systems still opposed to it. Therefore, all who have ever seriously attempted a study of Utah have had as their first assignment, the often-difficult task of determining the source and nature of the power that emanates from one of the most successful ultra-adaptable systems that has ever been created on the face of the earth.

However, at its time of formal birth in 1830 in the state of New York, few would have guessed that "the Church of Jesus Christ of Latter-day Saints" would ever achieve such enormous regional, national, and international political and economic power that it is now viewed by certain non-Mormon scholars as being the first major new world religion to have arisen since the time of Mohammed (e.g., Stark 1984). What then are the reasons for the success of this remarkable system?

The average Mormon that you would meet on a street in Salt Lake City or elsewhere would answer this question by saying: "God is directing this work!" However, the more secular Mormon or observant non-Mormon, could also supply additional, more scientifically acceptable, reasons for this enormous success. Thus, turning now to the new model proposed in this book, secular scholars would argue that the "creation" (or according to the Mormons, the "restoration") of a very powerful core of central doctrines by Joseph Smith and other early leaders proved to be irresistibly attractive to large numbers of "black boxes" seeking more satisfactory "answers" than they had been given by other belief systems as they faced the daily realities of sickness, death, accident, and injustice. As Stack(1992: D-1) points out in her article on "LDS Lingo" and can be seen in the previous few sentences, it is often easy to identify Mormons in Utah and elsewhere by the ecclesiastically-"correct" key words and phrases they use when discussing religion, politics, morality, etc. (i.e., control action #24)[2] Thus, in the following discussion, to give the non-Mormon reader a taste of this boundary-maintaining "lingo," I shall put many of these words and phrases in quotation marks followed by (LDS). Rival words in quotation marks often used by opponents of the Church and by outside scholars will be followed by (non-LDS). And it should be pointed out that such words are often very "emotionally-charged."

To the true believer, the rise of Mormonism is the fulfillment of the prophecy in Daniel (Chapter 2) which states that in the "last days" (LDS) the God of heaven will set up a kingdom which will destroy all secular kingdoms and eventually "fill the whole earth." (LDS) And to him/her, such events as the Protestant Reformation, the discovery of the New World, the defeat of the various Indian tribes, the American Revolution and the return of the Jews to their old homeland were not just chance events but instead were integral parts of God's plan to restore the "true" (LDS) church to the earth. (e.g., see I Nephi 13 in the Book of Mormon) And such a divinely directed view of destiny is further enhanced, when the individual is told through a "patriarch" (LDS) that he is a literal[3] (or sometimes now "adopted") descendant of one of the tribes of Israel (usually Ephraim or in the case of American Indians, Manasseh) and was chosen by God in "the preexistence" (LDS) to come to earth in "these latter days" (LDS) to prepare the way for the "Second Coming of Jesus Christ" (LDS) and to rule with Him and the other Israelites over the inhabitants of the earth. And still further, when he or she is assured that if he and his wife or she and her husband are "eternally sealed" (LDS) to each other (and to their dead ancestors) in the Mormons' "sacred"[4] (LDS) ("secret" (non-LDS)) temple rituals and if they remain "faithful to the covenants" (LDS) they make there, they will themselves become "Gods and Goddesses" (LDS) of other worlds peopled by their own "spirit children" (LDS) (or as Church members often state: "As man is, God once was and as God is, man may become." (LDS))

Many people in the past and present have tried without much success to block the progress of the Church by attempting to show that the Church's founder, Joseph Smith did not really receive any revelations from God but instead created out of his own mind and the culture of his time, the "scripture-like" (non-LDS) stories and "racial myths" (non-LDS) that are contained in the Book of Mormon and the Pearl of Great Price. However, what these critics fail to realize is that the strength of the Church against outside criticism of these two books comes basically not from the members' knowledge (in the scientific sense) that these latter-day scriptures are true, but rather from what they strongly believe has been an "answer" (LDS) to a promise contained in the Book of Mormon that:

... when ye shall receive these things, I would exhort you that ye would ask God, the Eternal Father, in the name of Christ, if these things are not true; and if ye shall ask with a sincere heart, with real intent, having faith in Christ, he will manifest the truth of it unto you , by the power of the Holy Ghost (Book of Mormon, Moroni 10:4).

Although not all members have received the promised answer to their prayers about these two books, even many who doubt their historical accuracy continue to be bound tightly to the Church by the intense social unity and psychological security that the Church offers its members. However, it would be wrong to imply that such strong security features were always present in the Church. Thus, it is of value to examine how the rather fragile system that was officially formed in 1830 was able to maintain its ultra-adaptability and continual high growth rate through time while many hundreds of similar competing religious systems failed in achieving one or both of these objectives. And, from a careful analysis of the types of individual and collective "control actions" initiated through the years by the occupants of the controlling systemic status sets of this remarkable church, it should be possible to make fairly accurate predictions about certain future developments not only in Utah but also in other areas heavily influenced by the rising power of this rapidly emerging new world religion, even though many of these past "choices" were severely limited given the nature of the "core" doctrines of Mormonism as they developed and certain powerful environmental parameters over which the Church had little or no control.

For example:

1) The early heavy emphasis on the doctrine of the gathering of the "Saints" (LDS) to "Zion" (LDS) and on their oaths of unquestioned

obedience to religious leaders "who daily received direct guidance from God" (LDS) rather than to secular ones often created alarm among other residents of the frontier regions in which large gatherings of the Saints were occurring. Thus, until the Church was finally able to strengthen its transducing power over such often violent "environmental" opposition, systemic collapse was usually prevented by the strategic moves of the central core of the system (and most members) from New York to Ohio to Missouri to Illinois and finally to Utah (control action #1).

2) The introduction of the doctrine of "polygamy" (LDS) (i.e., polygyny) as a variable "essential" (LDS) to "exaltation" (LDS) into the Church (control action # 24) was one of the key events that led to the death of the first Mormon prophet, Joseph Smith and to the power struggle for control of the top leadership systemic status sets in the Church after his death. At first Joseph and the other leaders tried to hide this new doctrine from ordinary church members and the outside world (control action #12) but when this failed, the Church leaders publicly denied the existence of this new "revelation" (LDS) and practice (control action #25) and finally went so far as to destroy the printing press of a local independent newspaper that had revealed this secret (control action #28).

This event led to the jailing and murder of Joseph Smith and his brother by an angry mob (again control action #28) which then led to a bitter battle within the Church over who should take the dead prophet's place (control action #10).

The majority of the members chose to follow the senior member of the "quorum of the twelve apostles" (LDS), Brigham Young, thus laying the precedent for the selection process that has been followed ever since for the single occupant of the highest systemic role set in the Church when the reigning "president" (LDS) (i.e., "prophet" (again LDS)) of the Church dies (control action #13). And rather than give up "polygamy", the doctrine of the gathering, and unquestioned obedience to "God-directed" (LDS) leaders over secular ones as "core" religious beliefs, this group again chose control action #1 and began preparing for the move to Utah.

Many of those who opposed Brigham Young eventually created a new ultra-adaptable system the Community of Christ (formerly known as the Reorganized Church of Jesus Christ of Latter-day Saints from 1872 to 2001) which by giving up an "essential core belief" (i.e., the belief in and practice of "polygamy" (control action #7) retained by the Utah Mormons, allowed its members to remain in peace in Illinois. (Also given up by the leaders of this new system were the "sacred" (LDS) ("secret" (non-LDS)) temple rituals probably because of their, by now, close association with the newly introduced "core" principle of ""polygamy"".) Stabilization of the leadership succession issue (control action #13) also occurred in this new system with the decision to always appoint as Prophet, a direct descendent of Joseph Smith, a choice welcomed by Joseph's widow, Emma.[5]

3) Several other crucial decisions by Brigham Young greatly helped preserve the ultra-adaptability of the main body of the Church as it moved westward following the death of Joseph Smith. For example:

a) Instead of taking either offensive or defensive action against the Church's perceived enemies, he urged the Church members to abandon their homes and flee across the Mississippi in mid-winter (control actions #1 and #4).

b) As the main body of the Church prepared to move farther west he entered into a facultative mutual relationship (control action #34) with the U.S. government to supply a battalion of soldiers to help defeat the Mexican government in the war between the two which began in 1846. In return for this help he arranged to have all the military pay for this assistance forwarded to him to help the "Saints" (LDS) in their move to Utah. (Individual "saints" (LDS) also entered into similar agreements with people in neighboring towns to earn money and supplies for the move westward.)

c) Instead of proceeding on to the much more desirable lands in California and Oregon, Brigham Young had the Saints stop and take control of the less desirable but also less coveted desert regions of Utah and the surrounding states (control action #1). (The remarkable geographical similarity of this region's Great Salt Lake fed by a river coming from a higher elevation large fresh water lake to the Dead Sea, Jordan River, and Sea of Galilee in the Jewish homeland probably did much to entice his followers to settle here rather than pursue their neighbors to the richer lands to the west since it served to reinforce their "literal" identification with the House of Israel (control action #24).)

d) He forbade the Saints to get personally involved in the frantic search for gold and silver (control action #21). Instead they profited greatly (and much more predictably and in a more "controlled" fashion) through trade links with both the miners passing through to California and those who established mining camps in Utah and the surrounding states. (Local food and animals were exchanged for gold and imported goods) (control actions #34 and #35).

e) He was able to persuade the incoming U.S. army that had been sent to put down the so-called "Mormon rebellion" (non-LDS) to settle in a valley distant to most of the Saints to better limit the quality and quantity of interaction between the Saints and the soldiers (control actions #12, and #26). And with the withdrawal of all of these soldiers as the Civil War began, the Church obtained most of the large amount of material wealth left behind (control action #27).

4) As the federal government consolidated its control over its western territories, "polygamy" was chosen as the excuse needed to break the tremendous secular power that the Church held over much of the intermountain region. And though Church leaders again tried such earlier unsuccessful control actions as #25, and #26 and for a time confined the performing of new plural marriages to colonies in Mexico

and Canada (control actions #2, and #4), since by now there were no more new "Utahs" to which the main body of the Church could relocate itself, eventually control action #7 was reluctantly taken even though "polygamy" was by now providing for many system needs for which even today the modern church has not yet found as successful a substitute. Thus, under "polygamy", the unbalanced sex ratio of females to males in the Church (caused by the stronger power that the vectors (control action #16) of the Church have always had in attracting and retaining female converts over male and the higher early death rate of males) was never a problem. Also, "polygamy" insured that a disproportionately high percentage of the new generation of Church members would be raised ("programmed" (non-LDS)) (control action #23)) in the homes of the "strongest" (LDS) Church patriarchs.

Since the abandonment of this practice, it has become obvious to many Mormon authors (e.g., Barker 1987:27; Wahlquist 2005:11-12) that enforcement of certain aspects of a revelation "given" (LDS) to Joseph Smith as a "Word of Wisdom" (LDS) has now replaced the practice of "polygamy" as a quick outward sign to both believers and non-believers alike of the level of faithfulness of an individual to the teachings of the Church (control actions #7 and #24). Thus, especially since World War II, Church members have been commanded to abstain from the common worldly vices of coffee, tea, tobacco, and alcoholic beverages. (The penalty for nonobservance of this commandment includes not only a denial of access to the "sacred" (LDS) ("secret" non-LDS) temple rituals (control action # 21) but also often to an informal "shunning" by many active members of the Church who are quick to detect the odor of alcohol or tobacco on a person's breath.)

5) Like many of the other religious systems begun in the 19th century, the Church had not only introduced an alternative sexual arrangement to the traditional monogamous one but had also engaged in several forms

of communal living experiments (control actions #7 and #24). These, too, were abandoned for the "present time" (LDS) (control actions #4 and #5) and like "polygamy" were placed in a category of principles to be practiced again in the next life or "when the Savior returns again." (LDS) And, though strict obedience to Church leaders in "religious matters" (LDS) continues to be stressed to this very day, Church leaders began during the crisis over "polygamy" to emphasize the need for Church members to submit themselves (until the return of Christ) in all other matters to rule by secular authorities. Thus, to show their loyalty to the government and constitution of the United States, Church leaders began emphasizing passages in the Church's modern day scriptures that tell of the divine origin and destiny of the U.S. government and constitution and then deliberately assigned Church members to different political parties to make it appear to outsiders that the Church was now fully able to accept the American notion of separation of church and state (control actions #5 and #7).

6) Church leaders now embraced the free enterprise system with such enthusiasm that soon the message of Mormonism to the "oppressed" of any ethnic background was nothing less than the ultimate extension of the highly traditional American "rags-to-riches-through-self-discipline-and-hard-work" dream. And, though Mormonism puts great financial burdens on its members, they were promised that if they met these commitments which in many cases exceeded 20 percent of their take-home pay before deductions, the Lord would "pour...out a blessing that there shall not be room enough to receive it" (LDS) (Malachi Chapter 4).

To make certain that this last prophecy would not fail in the secular sense, the Church in the 1930's began the establishment of an enormous welfare system to provide for the needs of the poor in the Church and to "combat the evils of the government dole" (LDS) for which members of the Church were often cautioned to avoid applying.[6] (Until recent years, the Church required all who received church aid to work for it if they could, doing various tasks in the program itself or at such assignments as the maintenance of Church buildings and grounds.)

Also, the highest church officials on the local, regional, and Salt Lake levels of organization began to be almost entirely chosen from the ranks of successful business leaders or highly trained professionals who not surprisingly sought continually to try to upgrade the skill and income levels of the ordinary church members under their control by "developing" (LDS) their "hidden talents." (LDS) Thus, today, almost every active member has at least one job in the Church and (especially in areas outside of the western U.S.) often many more, the fulfilling of which usually involves the expenditure of much time and effort, attendance at seemingly endless numbers of meetings, and heavy personal cash outlays for such items as automobile expenses, telephone calls, teaching materials, and food items. But even here, the rewards for such efforts are frequently secular in that the "talents" (LDS) one develops as a teacher, speaker, and leader in the Church are often precisely the same personal skills highly prized by the business and professional world. Thus it is not surprising that Howard Hughes surrounded himself with the "Mormon Mafia" (non-LDS) or that, as the New York Times (Johnson 2009) recently reported, many sales organizations eagerly hire returned young Mormon missionaries who can usually sell cars etc. with as much enthusiasm as they earlier "sold" (non-LDS) salvation.

7) The Church prides itself on its policy of lay leadership and indeed on the local level only the custodian is paid for his work. (Even at the highest Salt Lake level, the "general authorities" were for many years, until their recent release from these positions, believed (all church financial records are currently closely guarded secrets (control action # 12)) to have derived much of their income through memberships on the

boards of directorship of the many large secular business corporations that the Church owns or controls rather than directly from the tithing receipts of the Church.) However, many people are now paid by the Church for their work in the central offices in Salt Lake or throughout the world in the educational, welfare, and "social services" (LDS) programs of the Church[7] and some are accused by their fellow employees as being "kingdom builders." Nevertheless, the enormous worldwide church missionary and welfare programs are staffed by full time leaders, older retired couples, and thousands of young men and women who either pay their own expenses or, in the case of most of the younger missionaries, receive support from their parents or other members of their local church congregations. Also, many local and regional leaders such as bishops, branch presidents, relief society presidents, high council members, and stake presidents frequently spend 40 or more hours per week doing church work for no pay in addition to performing their daily secular activities.

8)   To better prepare its young people to be willing to assume these enormous burdens and to develop their leadership potential in the Church, in recent years, Mormon officials have devised several ingenious programs that effectively integrate "fun activities" (LDS) and heavy doses of parental and peer pressures so that the average young "Latter-day Saint" (LDS) today spends endless hours attending meetings, studying the scriptures, developing his/her "talents" (LDS), overcoming his/her "weaknesses" (LDS), and praying. Older people, too, have in recent years been coming under greater pressure to "lengthen their stride" (LDS) in doing missionary work among their neighbors and to "better fulfill" (LDS) their other numerous assignments in the Church. In fact, as more than one member has observed, if you attended all the meetings you were expected to attend and did all the other tasks demanded of you by church leaders, you would never have time to sin and fall away from the

Church. Here again, peer pressure operates as local congregations are compared statistically to each other on a monthly basis which can be very embarrassing to the leaders of the units at the bottom of the list in such matters as attendance at meetings, "home teaching visits"(LDS), or financial contributions. And the ordinary member too, feels this pressure when he/she fails to complete such tasks as doing "home teaching," (LDS) "missionary work," (LDS) and "temple work" (LDS) for his/her dead ancestors.

9) Church members are encouraged to "be in the world but not of the world"(LDS). Hopefully, this "worldly contact" (LDS) will not only produce an improved social and political environment for the Church, but will also lead to the "finding of golden contacts" (LDS) who then can be "fellowshipped" (LDS) into the Church. However, to insure that such interaction will produce the desired results, members are continually cautioned to avoid intermarriage with nonmembers ("gentiles"[8] (LDS)) and to shun such common "worldly sins" (LDS) as smoking and the drinking of alcoholic and caffeine containing beverages[9] (especially coffee and tea) (control action #24). Also, further isolation from the world is achieved by participation in the "sacred" (LDS) ("secret" non-LDS) temple rituals, a reminder of which the initiate wears as "garments" (LDS) (i.e., an officially-sanctioned type underwear) on his/her body day and night throughout the remainder of his/her life (control action #24).

Outside observers often fail to realize the power of these rituals in the maintenance of unity in the Mormon Church. Critics of the Church claim that these rituals are merely modified versions of Masonic rituals since in the past there were many similarities between the two and most of the early Mormon leaders including Joseph Smith were avid Masons. Church leaders counter that their rituals are a restored version of the original ones practiced by the ancient Israelites while those practiced by the Masons are corrupted versions of these early Hebrew rituals.

Only "worthy" (LDS) members of the Church are allowed to enter the temple after it is "dedicated" (LDS), to participate in these ritual activities, the successful performance of which is believed to be absolutely essential to the achievement of "exaltation" (LDS) (i.e., godhood) by both the "living" (LDS) and their dead ancestors.

10) Though the Church continually stresses the doctrine of "free agency" (LDS) and is a strong advocate of the American free enterprise system, there is no more tightly controlled and standardized religious system of this size in the entire world. Indeed, no change in church doctrine by local officials is ever permitted and such matters as finances, teaching manuals, meeting formats, and access to temple rituals and leadership positions is regulated through strict guidelines given to each local leader and enforced through very frequent letters and phone calls between local leaders and the Church headquarters in Salt Lake and by frequent meetings with and surveillance by intermediate level leaders (e.g., "regional representatives" (LDS), "stake" (LDS) or "mission" (LDS) leaders, etc.). Still, a semblance of democracy exists in many local and regional meetings since relatively free debate about various decisions is permitted in leadership meetings and the ordinary member is allowed to vote by the raising of his or her right hand as to whether or not he or she approves of decisions made by the local leaders and whether or not he or she approves of those who are chosen for leadership and other church callings, but even this freedom is limited by the Church edict that after the discussion has ended, it is always the leader in charge at the local, regional, or Salt Lake level who makes the final decision. Thus, it is an extremely rare occasion to observe any member in a public meeting actually vote against a leader's decision. And church members are well aware that they belong to a theocracy rather than a democracy for as was

stated in an official church publication, "When the Prophet speaks, the debate is over."

Furthermore, deviance from church doctrine and moral principles is ultimately controlled through a very formal system of church courts which offer the accused few of the "normal" (non-LDS) protective rights that most secular criminals in our society now take for granted (e.g., the accused is usually not allowed to confront his/her accuser or, frequently, even find out who he/she is). Smaller sins such as smoking or the drinking of alcoholic beverages or coffee are never grounds for court action but larger sins such as adultery, having an abortion, or openly living a gay lifestyle almost always lead to excommunication especially if such sins are committed by persons in church leadership roles or who are in the full time missionary program. Likewise, committing murder (unless during wartime or in self defense) and other serious crimes, advocating "polygamy", or preaching openly against the Church leaders or their programs are usually grounds for excommunication. However, there are also a host of other lesser sins which may or may not lead to excommunication or lesser punishments such as being "disfellowshiped" (LDS) or the taking away of a "temple recommend" (LDS) (i.e., the worthiness document that must be renewed every two years[10] to gain admittance to the temples and their ritual activities) depending on the circumstances under which the sin was committed and the "degree of repentance" (LDS) (as determined by local church leaders) which the person accused, exhibits at the trial. And recently there was an unusual punishment given to a member who had created a calendar "featuring shirtless returned missionaries" (Dobner 2008a:A11). Thus, in addition to being excommunicated "for conduct unbecoming a member," after he had completed the requirements for his degree at the Church owned BYU, the school refused to award him his degree until he had been reinstated as a "member of the church in good standing" (Dobner 2008:A11).

Appeals to higher courts are permitted but because there is great reluctance on the part of leaders higher in the Church's hierarchy to overturn decisions which local leaders feel were "inspired" (LDS), lower court rulings are rarely overturned. However, after a suitable time period which varies with the nature of the sin and the Church position of the person who committed it (i.e., the higher the position, the longer the period of repentance must usually be), a person may be rebaptized into the Church and have his "temple blessings restored" (LDS). But, the crime of murder is viewed as being an "unforgivable sin" (LDS) and no amount of repentance will lead to forgiveness in this life.

Since certain local leaders are more tolerant than others of what behavior of a member necessitates the convening of a court, members often exhibit a high level of self-censorship. For example, Dr. Omer Stewart, one of my professors at the University of Colorado, was very bitter about his excommunication for telling students that he didn't believe in the historical accuracy of the Book of Mormon while other members having the same doubts openly, are never brought before a court. Thus, never sure whether a disbelief in the historicity of the Book of Mormon or the Pearl of Great Price might lead to a loss of Church membership or a lesser punishment, an unknown number of members have become "closet doubters." Here, there is a striking parallel to Ajo where without any evidence that I could find to back the many stories about the awful things that the Company had done in the past and was still capable of doing in the present to local "trouble makers", self-censorship made many local people hesitant to criticize the Company openly. Also, since I was an active member of the local Mormon congregation, I was once told by the local bishop that the Company was "watching me" and that he hoped that I would not do or write anything that would embarrass the Church.

The belief that God personally leads the Church at all times through "continuous revelation" (LDS) to His "chosen prophet" (LDS) leads to the important conclusion that even though each prophet may have minor personal weaknesses, "God will never permit him to lead the Church astray" (LDS). Thus, even in those cases where a person feels through "personal prayer and revelation" (LDS) that a local or regional authority has made the wrong decision, he/she has been taught that by obeying such an authority, the punishment for any sin committed will then be transferred to the erring leader. Here again rather than open opposition to the authority, self-censorship often occurs or silent withdrawal from further Church activity.

11) In spite of the growth of the large, paid, somewhat protected business, social work, and educational bureaucracy that has developed (especially in the Utah area), the occupants of the top systemic status sets in the Church have in recent years instigated a new series of control actions that have helped them consolidate their almost absolute controlling power over this enormous worldwide system. Thus to discourage potential rivals for power in this system:

a) The systemic status set occupied by the "Church Patriarch" (LDS), a position which had usually been passed from father to son and had always been occupied by a descendant of Hyrum Smith, Joseph's brother, was eliminated and its last occupant given "emeritus" status (control actions #8 and #10).

b) Occupants of the powerful "First Quorum of the Seventy" (LDS) were either retired or told that they would no longer have lifetime tenure in their positions but instead would only serve for a period of three to five years. Thus only the President of Church and the members of the "Quorum of the Twelve Apostles" (LDS) still have lifetime tenure in their positions and even this tenure in the case of the apostles is not unconditional as was demonstrated when one of them, Richard M. Lyman[11] was excommunicated for adultery. (At any given time there are always twelve active apostles in the Quorum of the

Twelve plus two or three others who serve as counselors to the President of the Church but who if they return to the Quorum after the death of a president because they have not been chosen to serve as counselors to the new president, nevertheless retain their seniority rights in the Quorum) (control action #10).

c) There was instigated the requirement that all general authorities submit their general conference speeches in advance to obtain approval and "corrective" advice (control action #25).

d) "Errors" in conference speeches are now "corrected" before they are distributed in their final version to the Church membership as a whole (control action #25). The controversial rerecording of Ronald E. Poelman's October 1984 "General Conference" (LDS) speech to be further discussed in Chapter 10 is a prime example of this control action. (See Fletcher 1985:44 for a list of the changes made and a discussion of the "concerns" which led to these changes.)

e) There is a more rapid release and rotation of authorities at all levels with the "best" of these "black boxes" receiving promotions. "Poorer" "black boxes" may be released from any position at any time without being given a reason for their release (control actions #9, #10, and #13). And Church members employed as faculty or staff at BYU, or in other Church positions elsewhere, lose their jobs if they fail such "worthiness" interviews as the one required for obtaining a "temple recommend" (LDS).

f) Leaders in foreign countries are encouraged to master the English language and as a few of them rise to the rank of a "general authority" in the Church, they are seldom assigned duties in their own country, probably to minimize the possibility that such an individual could become the pivotal figure in an ethnic or national split in the Church. (This assignment policy was also seen in the case of one American Indian, Dr. George P. Lee, who while having been elevated to one of the lesser general authority systemic role sets in the Church and while occasionally being allowed to speak to Indian audiences was never given a "line-authority" position over any American Indian reservation or special American Indian program[12], control of which still resided firmly in the hands of non-Indians. In 1989, Dr. Lee was excommunicated from the Church for apostasy after he accused the General Authorities of the Church of shutting down many of their special programs for "Lamanites" (LDS) (the special term used by Mormons for Native Americans) and "slowly causing a silent, subtle scriptural and spiritual slaughter of the Indians and other Lamanites."[13] (Lee 1989: 55)) (control actions #9 and 10)

g) All tithing money is immediately transferred by computer to a central Church account and much of the money is spent and invested in the Salt Lake area even for items that are shipped to distant locations which at times could be purchased for less money locally at those locations[14] (control action #12). Any "improper" handling of tithing funds is dealt with swiftly and severely (control actions #9, #20, and #26).

h) The design and construction of church buildings and the control of janitorial services for these buildings which had formerly not been completely standardized throughout the U.S. and other countries have now been brought under rigid centralized control as have also all "official" church manuals and publications (control actions #11 and #26).

i) There is now a worldwide emphasis on simple uniform lessons with warnings to teachers to not allow open class discussions about the "mysteries"(LDS) (control action #11, #12, #21, and #26)

j) The Corporation of the First Presidency of the Church of Jesus Christ of Latter-day Saints alone holds title to all of the worldwide church buildings, businesses, farms, and all other assets of the Church (i.e., local congregations have no legal control over buildings and only very limited control over certain minor local Church donations) (control actions #10 and #26).

These control actions insure that only the most time-tested and loyal members often linked by close family or other personal ties ever reach the very few remaining lifetime "tenured" positions in the Church (control actions # 10, #13, and #26). And though it is tempting to compare the selection process for leadership roles in the Church to that occurring in other large bureaucratic structures such as those in many large corporations, certain other churches (e.g., Catholicism), the non-democratic governments of China, North Korea, Cuba, and the one that until recently ruled the U.S.S.R., the occupants of the highest role sets in such bureaucracies usually have far less absolute power to alter long term goals than do their L.D.S. counterparts since in these other organizations lower ranking bureaucrats usually have created and maintained powerful alliances to prevent their easy removal from office, a luxury denied most people in the Mormon hierarchy. In fact, perhaps the closest parallel in the modern world to the almost absolute power that the top 15 L.D.S. leaders possess is found in the U.S. supreme court which also confers an extremely powerful lifetime tenure position on an individual without the usual ponderous bureaucratic restraints which prevent top executives from drastically altering the course and/or mission of an organization. Thus, the enormous concentration of both secular and (at least in the opinion of most Mormons) "divine" power in the top few systemic status sets of the Church give the Mormon leaders a tremendous advantage over their corporation, church, or government counterparts in their ability to rapidly change policies, practices, doctrines, scriptural interpretations and "official" church history that earlier generations of Church leaders and followers had believed were "eternal truths."(LDS)

This was illustrated most dramatically recently when some major parts of the temple ritual were eliminated and when a few years ago the Prophet Spencer W. Kimball received a "revelation from God" (LDS) that the Church's long standing policy denying the "priesthood" (LDS) to the male "descendants of Cain" (LDS) (i.e., the black race) would no longer be pursued even though many previous prophets had on numerous occasions justified this denial of priesthood rights on the basis that black people had been "less valiant"(LDS) in the "war"(LDS) in the "preexistence"(LDS) adding that a reversal of this prohibition would not occur until the end of the millennium by which time all other "more worthy"(LDS) males would have been first given the opportunity to be ordained to the priesthood. And even in such superficially appearing "trivial" matters as the choice of songs to be sung in the local meetings, this power of the top general authorities to force quick arbitrary change was seen in 1986 as individual bishops were strongly instructed to quickly replace the old song books with new ones even though there was often much local criticism of the elimination of some of the favorite old songs and of the many anonymous, undocumented, and seemingly capricious changes in music and words in those old, favorite songs that were retained and the fact that the new songbook was available in only one color-- green.

The past is often the key to understanding why certain controversial decisions are made by top Church leaders. Thus the choice by Church leaders to bow to the wishes of secular authorities when systemic collapse was occurring during the final years of the "polygamy" struggle helps explain the Church's later support of Hitler's government in pre-World War II Germany to the extent that one young anti-Nazi underground fighter was excommunicated from the Church. And, though Mormons in the United States take great pride in their displays of super patriotism as seen in such events as the massive "Freedom Festival" (LDS) held every summer in Provo, Utah, in countries where many of the traditional American freedoms are suppressed, the "saints"(LDS) are cautioned to obey their leaders and "turn the other cheek." Thus, in spite of the "right wing" (non-LDS), strongly anticommunist bias of the majority of the Church's present members, who firmly believe that the Mormon scriptures declare that systems that deprive humans of their "free agency" (LDS) are inspired by Satan rather than God, the Church gained permission long before the collapse of communism in Eastern Europe to build a temple in East Germany and to begin missionary work there and in Poland. And when the Church encountered strong opposition to its planned construction of a satellite campus of BYU in Jerusalem from a group of militant orthodox Jews, it was not altogether surprising that the Mormon leaders publicly promised that no missionary activities would be allowed at this new center, despite the fact that missionary effort has always been one of the core essential variables of the Church with every member being constantly reminded about his/her missionary obligations. Thus such core doctrines as the practice of "polygamy", the right of every person to exercise "free agency" (LDS), and the obligation of every member to "warn his neighbor" (LDS) are "temporarily" allowed to be suspended if their continued practice would hinder the spread of the Church's programs or influence in any given country. And in the case of other former key doctrines that hurt the spread of the Church in certain areas of the world such as the equation of the modern Catholic Church with "the great and abominable church "described in the Bible's Book of Revelations, Church leaders have now suggested that statements by earlier prophets and other general authorities, in support of this belief were in error. (One former apostle who put a passage suggesting such an equation in his book, Mormon Doctrine (McConkie 1958:108), quickly deleted it when the book was reprinted with the following explanation:" In publishing this Second Edition, as is common with major encyclopedic-type works, experience has shown the wisdom of making some changes, clarifications, and additions." (McConkie 1966:Preface).)

Also, scriptural passages such as those in the Book of Mormon emphasizing how God, at times, curses "wicked" (LDS) people by giving them dark skins or that appearing in Joseph Smith's official history in the Pearl of Great Price where he states that the Lord told him to join none of the existing Christian sects since "they were all wrong" having creeds that were "an abomination in his sight" being led by individuals who were "all corrupt", are no longer widely quoted as Church leaders often stress the universal brotherhood of humankind and praise the good being done by other churches and their leaders in Utah and in other parts of the world. And following a special day of fasting, Church leaders even donated a considerable amount of money to support the work of charitable agencies supported by certain of these other churches in the drought-plagued areas of Northern Africa (control action #34). (Not surprisingly, this ecumenical approach by Church leaders has often been reciprocated especially in the Wasatch Front area where other churches are usually very supportive of Mormon sponsored projects and concerns.)

Other former rivals including certain mining and business interests which in the 19th century began publishing the formerly strongly anti-Mormon Salt Lake Tribune have long ago made a partial peace with the Church as illustrated by the recent merger of the printing and advertising operations of the Salt Lake Tribune with the "rival" Church-owned Deseret News and the great reluctance of the Salt Lake Tribune to now accept advertisements for "anti-Mormon" books as told to me when I recently had a chance to briefly talk to one of the Church's long time nemeses, Sandra Tanner[15]. And though the Church is often accused of using a heavy hand in controlling what is taught in the state's public school system, Jarvik (1982:13) in an article about higher education in Utah states:

> Except at its own private school--Brigham Young University in Provo--the Church seems to take pains to stay clear of outright maneuvering and control. Its influence is largely indirect, the result of it being the shaper of basic beliefs of a majority of the state's residents and sometimes as much as 90 percent of the state legislature.

This same strategy is extended to almost all other aspects of life in Utah. Thus control action 37 is by far the most frequently favored Church control option since when "something goes wrong" it is the individually-involved Church member who becomes the target of outside criticism rather than the Church itself which in most cases tries to portray itself as a "neutral" bystander although when the actions of individuals win "worldly praise" the influence of the Church in "shaping" their lives and values is given prominent notice in the press releases of the Church. Even in such controversial issues as abortion, the ERA movement and Utah's liquor laws, the Church in recent years has preferred to encourage individual members to launch their own private and at times collective (but unofficial) actions in support of the "understood" Church position, which is only officially released to the world at large for issues which the Church leaders feel are "moral" rather than "political." (e.g., the vigorous effort by Church leaders to persuade voters to reject the 1992 proposal to allow gambling on horse races in Utah, and the recent letter to California members to do all they could to support passage of their state's 2008 "anti-gay" amendment.) However, when many business people in the Church failed to understand the threat to the continued control by the Church of much of its now existing core area if the huge MX missile complex proposed by the Carter administration were to be built in the Utah and Nevada deserts, Church leaders issued a strongly-worded statement condemning the proposed location. (Most local and some national observers feel that this strong stand by the Church leadership was the key to this proposal's defeat.)

Mormons believe that man's spirit is eternal and that we all lived as "God's spirit children" (LDS) before we came to this earth. Thus, Mormons are encouraged to have large families and to oppose abortion except in the case of rape or incest (and until recent years birth control techniques) so that a larger percentage of these "spirit children"(LDS) will receive mortal bodies in the "homes of the righteous" (LDS). Even the Church's strong opposition to the E.R.A. amendment was inspired in part by this wish of church leaders that mothers have and personally raise as many children as possible to accommodate "those spirits still waiting for bodies"(LDS) and "to help the missionary work go forward"(LDS). (The remarkable success of this persuasive argument is seen in the crude birth rate statistics for church members which even though they have fallen in the last few years are still far above the national average. (e.g., see Mayorga 2008:B6))

Not surprisingly, schools are very crowded and underfunded[16] in Utah but despite the talk of many Church and secular leaders in Utah about the need to provide better and more numerous employment openings for the state's bumper crop of children, the annual export of thousands of young Mormons from Utah, as nannies, college graduates, etc. serves to spread the influence of the Church not only into the nearby western states but also into much more distant areas of the country and the world (control action #37). (In Ajo, as stated earlier, one such active Mormon working for the Phelps Dodge company gained many converts to the Mormon faith by volunteering to give some sermons when the minister of the combined Protestant congregation left town.) And helping prepare (or at times enticing) the young person to make such an exodus is often that person's "missionary experience" (LDS) in some distant state or country. However, as predicted by the model, not all change in this particular system and its surrounding environment is of the type foreseen (or desired) by the occupants of its controlling systemic status sets. Thus the infamous "scandal" in the French mission in 1958 when certain young missionaries were converted to polygamous teachings by the assistant to the mission president who was secretly a member of an "apostate" (LDS) group (control action #37), resulted from the indoctrination the missionaries had received from childhood that they were always to obey their Church leaders without question. And it is not by accident that Utah is now known as the fraud capitol of the United States since, as was stated in Business Week (Atchison 1985:70), the promoter of a fraudulent investment scheme "need only drop the names of Mormon officials on his board or his own church activities to disarm investors." Also, the pressure on members to have large numbers of children while at the same time donating much of their income and "free time" to the Church has encouraged many of them to flock to various get-rich-quick schemes especially since the large surplus of children produced and the continual immigration of Saints seeking a "better place" to raise their children have created such a heavy labor surplus (especially in places like the Provo-Orem area) that average wages have often been driven very low. And critics of the Church suggest that even the F.B.I. agent, Richard Miller, who was arrested in October 1984 (Office of Counter Intelligence 2008) in Southern California, was apparently at least in part motivated to hand over secrets to the Russians because he felt he needed the extra money to support his very large, eight children, family and other financial obligations (including those to the Church). Thus, even in such seemingly unrelated areas as criminal activity, some non-Mormon scholars have theorized that it is wrong to completely discount the indirect influence of the Church that they claim is demonstrated by the extremely high rates of theft, embezzlement, and other crimes involving money and property in a state where violent crime rates are very low. And, even some of the more violent crimes such as the ritual throat slashing murder of a woman and her child by two excommunicated Mormons in 1984 and the 1988 police shoot out with a polygamist family after the bombing of a Mormon Stake Center, some authors have suggested (e.g., Krakauer 2003; LeBaron Jr. 2008), were an unforeseen consequence of certain past Church beliefs and practices even though Church officials would strongly deny any action of theirs, either present or past, was either directly or indirectly responsible for such brutal murders. Instead, such acts would appear to them to be further proof of the power of the Devil over the minds of those who had chosen to distort Church doctrine and disobey Church leaders. Also, many individuals, both Mormon and non-Mormon, have suggested that the relatively high rate of teenage suicide in the state can be better understood if one realizes the extreme guilt which can develop in gay individuals or others who fail to maintain the extremely high standards of "sexual purity" (LDS) demanded by Church leaders. And young Church members rebelling against the pressures to serve as missionaries and/or to "marry in the temple" (LDS) often drop out of church activity and visibly indicate to their families, friends, and other church members by such outward signs as hair length, beard growth, the type of clothing worn, breaking of the "Word of Wisdom" (LDS) (i.e., by using tobacco products or drinking coffee, tea, or alcoholic beverages) and/or the sexual standards of the Church, etc. that they have broken their ties to the Church and wish to be relieved of its many direct and indirect pressures. (Although in theory, Church leaders are supposed to work even harder with such rebellious young people, this strategy often works since most members of the Church find it very difficult to develop close ties to people who are openly disobeying Church standards.)

Although the women's liberation movement has won some sympathy among certain of the more educated Mormon women, such women tend to marry rather late in life and have fewer children than their "less liberated sisters" (non-LDS). Thus, one could argue that in a long-term evolutionary sense, this movement is a self-defeating one not only within Mormonism but also outside of it (as is also the homosexual one). However, many church programs have now been geared more to the working wife (control actions #6, #7, #11 and #14). Here, often insurmountable, environmental pressures abound (e.g., see Harris

1981). Thus, relatively few male members of the Church now have sufficient income to provide for the needs of their families especially given the Church pressures to have large numbers of children and to donate relatively large sums of money and time to the Church. Also, with the abolishment of "polygamy" and the rural to urban shift of the Church membership, widowed and divorced females are in most cases now forced to enter the outside-the-home labor market.

As more women enter the workforce in Utah, this further adds to the local oversupply of workers, creating a positive feedback loop that drives the average wage for male workers down even more, thus putting pressure on the few remaining full-time housewives to also return to the work force. The resulting falling birthrates and rising delinquency and Church inactivity rates among unsupervised children and teenagers, created, in the mid-80s, such concern in the mind of the "newly anointed Prophet" (LDS), Ezra Taft Benson, that in one of his first, very strongly-worded messages, he told the women of the Church to leave the work place and return to the home to bear and properly raise their children even if this meant that their families would have to sharply reduce their standard of living (i.e., control action #6)

Some working mothers have heeded this advice but most have not, trusting their own calculations rather than relying on faith that through some miracle (e.g., the husband getting a better job, etc.), their family's basic needs can be met with only one breadwinner in the family. Adding to this widespread lack of faith in this particular Prophet's counsel are the generally low wages paid to male workers in many Church owned or controlled businesses and institutions such as Brigham Young University. (In fact when I was an adjunct professor at BYU, it was often easier for a male worker's wife to find more stable work with greater benefits at B.Y.U. than men such as I could obtain.)

The feminist movement has not been able to mount a successful attack on the Church's policy of only giving "the priesthood" (LDS) to males even though many such individuals (e.g., Sonia Johnson) have campaigned for this change for many years. The Church has, however, now allowed women to offer prayers in Sacrament meetings and has given them their own special semiannual church-wide meetings as counterparts to the semiannual church-wide meetings that still are open only to male "priesthood holders" (LDS).

Future Trends

What then does all this mean to anyone seeking to predict the future of the urban area known locally as "The Wasatch Front"?:

1. Even though the birth rate among Mormons is now falling due to the same financial, etc. pressures affecting most Americans, it will continue to remain much above the national average and though many members for sometimes long periods of time leave the area in search of better employment opportunities, large numbers of these ultimately decide to return to the "safety of Zion."(LDS) even though this sometimes requires tremendous financial sacrifices. Also, despite strong efforts by the top leadership of the Church since World War II to convince members in other parts of the United States and other nations that no longer should they all come to Utah but instead create their own "Zions" (LDS) in their own locations, many eventually decide to migrate to Utah. Non-Mormons are coming to Utah in increasing numbers often attracted by the many outdoor recreational activities this state offers but many of these "outsiders" choose to live in neighborhoods and cities with fewer Mormons where their political influence has been increasing in recent years (e.g., Salt Lake City's "gayborhoods"). In turn, Mormons, especially those with school age children, have increasingly moved from Salt Lake City to its many nearby suburbs (e.g., see Stack 2008a). Still, overall in the state as a whole, I predict, that for the above

reasons, Mormons will in the foreseeable future never lose their political and social dominance over their rivals.

2. Although some past researchers mistakenly predicted that the final closing of such major relatively high paying companies as Geneva Steel Corporation in Utah County, would have disastrous consequences on the economy of the region and might drastically slow the population growth of the area, its mid 1980's long-term shutdown and later final shutdown made little if any negative impact on the area. Instead, many new, relatively low-paying service and manufacturing jobs replaced those lost and most displaced workers either reduced their living standards or sent their wives to work to remain in Utah. And in recent years as could now be predicted from this analysis, it is the non-Mormon "black box" rather than the Mormon worker who is more likely to leave the state as individual wages fail to match those found in other areas of the country. Also, even among the non-Mormons who choose to remain in the state, there is a selection process occurring which also increases the Church's control of the area leading one critic of the Church at the University of Utah to state that "There aren't many people [at the U.] on the fringes like me" (Jarvik 1982:18). This selection process even affects members of the Church who are more likely to leave the area if they feel "uncomfortable" about the level of control they feel the Church either indirectly or directly exercises over their lives. (This was especially evident during my years at BYU where many students openly complained about the restrictions placed upon such things as the hairstyles, clothing, housing, entertainment, and speakers allowed.)

3. Ever since yielding on the "polygamy" issue, the Church has been extremely conscious about its public image and in many instances this has proven to be the key essential variable to examine in making successful predictions about the actions of top Church leaders in the modern world. Thus, as we discussed earlier, the public support of the

Church by the "power brokers" of ruling governments has been sought even at the expense (at least temporary) of other variables normally viewed as being part of the essential core of system variables which will remain essential "throughout all eternity."(LDS) The extreme nature of certain of the dress standards at BYU and for the full-time missionaries (e.g., forbidding male missionaries and BYU students and faculty members from growing beards) is part of this attempt at portraying a "squeaky-clean" (non-LDS) Mormon image to the world as is also the famous Mormon Tabernacle Choir. The heavy emphasis on the "Word of Wisdom" (LDS) in the past half-century has also often been used to increase the positive image of the typical Mormon in the eyes of the world, especially as the dangers associated with smoking have been verified by scientists. And the removal of the "curse of Cain" (LDS) from the blacks must have also brought many sighs of relief from the General Authorities of the Church and their public relations people. Famous people (e.g., politicians, athletes, entertainers, beauty queens, astronauts, businessmen) are often heavily promoted in the official Church press and its releases to the other media as long as their public image is positive but are quickly downplayed as their fame slips or when they fail to live up to the "squeaky-clean" image sought by Church leaders (e.g., Marie Osmond's temporary fall from grace because of marital problems). And the massive commitment of both time and money to make the football and basketball teams at BYU "the best in the nation" are also certainly motivated by this same desire to instill in every nonmember a positive image of the Mormons.

However, this extreme desire to project this flawless public image to the world has in recent years eroded the level of control the Church exercises over both members and non-members, especially in the Wasatch Front area. Thus, though Church leaders quickly excommunicate members who become polygamists or who commit adultery, they move much more slowly and cautiously against their own scholars who in the name of the traditional American values of science, free speech, and scholarship make speeches and publish papers and books which "mar" (non-LDS) the "perfect image" (non-LDS) of the Church. This then helps explain why the Church refused to take open action[17] against such ultraliberal Mormons as Sterling McMurrin who, until his death, on many occasions publicly attacked the historical accuracy and divinely revealed nature of the Book of Mormon, a "crime" (non-LDS) that as mentioned earlier had brought almost instant excommunication to one of my professors at the University of Colorado, Dr. Omar Stewart, who lacked McMurrin's high visibility and strong social ties to high Church leaders. Also, I'm sure that certain Church leaders winced every time Michael Quinn, a former history professor at BYU wrote another paper or book (e.g., see Quinn 1987) that revealed more embarrassing aspects of the Mormon past before finally deciding to excommunicate him. And in 2003, Church leaders backed off in attempts to excommunicate Thomas W. Murphy, the Chairperson of the Department of Anthropology at Edmonds College in Washington State, who, on the basis of DNA evidence, attacked the historical accuracy of the Book of Mormon.

In commenting on this restraint by the Church hierarchy by the 1980s in avoiding intervention in the affairs of the University of Utah, President Gardner in 1982 (Jarvik 1982:15) stated:

> I've been here eight years and I can honestly say there have been only two occasions where an effort was made to influence the University. These were mere probes and I quickly snuffed them out.

And McMurrin adds that in the twenty years he was in the university's administration (Jarvik 1982:15):

I never knew of any [Church] pressure to hire or fire anyone... In recent years, the Church has been remarkably well-behaved regarding the university. It could use all kinds of pressure; it could exert a remarkable influence; but it doesn't.

This is not to imply, however, that no action is taken against members who for various reasons publicly do something which mars the desired positive image since as Fletcher, a past editor of Sunstone, notes (1985:6-7), there is still a list of books that can never be mentioned in Church-sponsored publications and people who are released from their church positions on the basis of unproven accusations often from unknown accusers. And in the case of the banning of the independent student newspaper, the Seventh East Press, from the Brigham Young University bookstore after "a single phone call to the manager," Fletcher (1985:7) states:

The editors and writers had no chance to defend themselves; once again they had no idea which was the offending article, if any, what their crime had been, or the identity of the authority.

(It was, however, widely believed by most that a published interview with Sterling McMurrin in which he tells of his doubts about the Book of Mormon, etc. was the final "straw that broke the back" of this particular "camel".)

Still, Michael Quinn, the most controversial former BYU historian, while at BYU dared challenge two of the general authorities who publicly rebuked his type of scholarship, compounding his "crime" by openly ridiculing the demands of these apostles in a strongly-worded speech to BYU's student history association, the text of which was released to the local and national news media (e.g., see Woodward 1982:77).

This erosion of control was also seen in other seemingly insignificant news events such as a decision some years ago to lift the ban on the appearance of the Budweiser Beer wagon and horses and also allow large numbers of marching Shriners in the "Days of 47" parade which honors the arrival of the Mormon pioneers in the Salt Lake Valley and in the sudden bravery of the Provo City building inspectors (after having silently tolerated numerous similar past violations) to try to shut down several BYU campus construction projects which were being undertaken without the securing of the proper city building permits (Wright 1985:1). However, such toleration has been greatly curtailed the last few years in the case of the "Days of 47" parade which no longer permits the Budweiser Wagon nor the Shriners to participate although it still permits a float featuring a singing black choir from a non-LDS church.

Also, attempts by Church leaders to change the officially released version of a "too liberal" conference address by one of the general authorities and to ban the writers of a book about the wife of Joseph Smith from speaking about the book in church meetings have been widely revealed and ridiculed in the local and state news media (e.g., see Nelson 1985:3; Utah Holiday Staff 1985:34). And probably to avoid FCC license and national network disputes, the Church-owned KSL TV and radio stations have very secular programming during most of the Sunday hours with only a small amount of time (except for such events as the twice a year, general conference sessions or the death of a prominent Church leader (e.g., the 2008 death of the Mormon Prophet, Gordon B. Hinckley)) in non-prime hours for LDS programming. Even the long-running Sunday Morning broadcast of the Mormon Tabernacle Choir has at times lost out to secular programming now that the station has changed its affiliation from CBS to NBC, at the time of the change, a more popular network, ironically, with fewer "family friendly" programs. However, with 4 channels of digital programs now on its BYU TV station and the May 18, 2009 launching of a new 24/7 "church-related content" (Horiuchi 2009: B1) radio station (following the earlier decision of the Utah Catholic Church to begin broadcasting "Catholic-based content" (Horiuchi 2009: B2) on a station it had recently purchased), the surrendering of much of the on-air time to secular programming on its other stations is now a much less important compromise with the outside world.

And, until the1990s, BYU had gone out of its way to recruit black athletes and hire "compatible" non-Mormon faculty members even though some of these people openly ridiculed certain cherished Mormon beliefs and practices as exemplified by a female BYU Chemistry professor who in an interview published in the student newspaper is quoted as having responded with the epithet, "Hogwash," to the often cherished Mormon idea that if a woman with children had to work, it was better that she choose work that could be done in the home (Lewis 1985:6). She then went on to state that:

> Women who work in the home doing something they are not required to concentrate on are probably doing something not worth doing, and those who have children and work in the home on something they are required to concentrate on are probably neglecting their children. (Lewis 1985:6)

She is then reported as saying that one of the reasons "Utah is five years behind" the rest of the nation is because LDS church programs for boys emphasize Boy Scout activities and learning about computers while they encourage girls to learn how to cook, sew, and take care of children (Lewis 1985:6).

Other Mormon and non-Mormon faculty and students during the 1980s gained enough "courage" (non-LDS) to publicly attack the traditional Mormon feminine role. Thus a student, Karen Hawbecker, is quoted in this same article (Lewis 1985:6) as having stated:

> The image of women at BYU really bothers me... Only 30 percent of the women who enter as freshmen ever graduate... A lot of women don't consider all of the options that are open for them.

And even stories about such successful reversals of traditional male-female roles as "househusbands," "male nurses" and lady "astronauts" appeared during this time period in the BYU student newspaper.

However, this period of tolerated criticism of Church doctrines and traditional beliefs did not last when the Church leaders in 1996 replaced the outgoing BYU president, Rex E. Lee with Elder[18](LDS) Merrill J. Bateman one of the general authorities of the Church and with the firing of such critics as anthropology professor, David Knowlton in 1993 (Smith 2001). Also, in recent years there has been an increasing emphasis for all instructors in various church organizations throughout the world to refrain from using any source materials other than those contained in the official scriptures, publications, and yearly-issued manuals. (control action # 12)

The enormous wealth of the Church has recently been used to good advantage to revitalize the downtown area of Salt Lake City (much of which it owns) to counter the common type of inner city decay which was creeping dangerously close to the famed temple square area. But the need of the Church to divert most of its funds to support such enormously expensive programs as the worldwide building of churches and temples and the support of BYU has at times in past years forced the Church to welcome as allies in this revitalization attempt such unlikely partners as the wealthy Arab, Khashoggi, who backed his promises with the money needed to begin the construction of a 600 million dollar downtown office-shopping complex which among other clients now houses the Church-owned radio and TV stations. (However, to the embarrassment of both the Church and other local investors, this turned out to be a giant scam when Khashoggi pulled more money out of the project than he had originally invested, leaving behind many unpaid creditors (e.g., see Isikoff 1987:A1).) And more recently, in cooperation with several major national retailers, a massive redevelopment of the two large city blocks just south of the adjacent blocks occupied by the Mormon equivalent of "Vatican City" is now being undertaken. Other big corporate spenders such as Delta Airlines have also recently found the Salt Lake atmosphere congenial as have the ski resort interests backed by such wealthy individuals as Robert Redford, the founder of the Sundance resort near Provo. And according to Wiley & Gottlieb (1982:164):

> ...on the outside, looking in, are the big energy companies and their corporate counterparts. They are ready to make their move, potentially capable of overwhelming the region in their search for new sources of energy and other investments.

Still, the greatest danger to the Church's continuing control over the future development of its intermountain empire is its increasing reluctance to publicly "flex its considerable economic and political power" if there is any risk of massive unfavorable public publicity which could conceivably damage the favorable national and international public image which present church leaders seem to so desperately want to protect. Thus, in terms of long-term survival in the evolutionary sense (i.e., the ability to remain in the ultra-adaptable state) the Church shares this same "fatal" flaw that has on many occasions since World War II led to numerous defeats for the leaders of the United States government (and other systems overly concerned with their public images) in diplomacy, military actions, etc. This vulnerability was especially visible in the 1985 Mark Hoffman scam where several high ranking church leaders and their friends bought a series of documents apparently initially with the intent of hiding them away before the "blemishes" they contained about certain aspects of early Church history would be revealed to the general public.

This attempt utterly failed and in a sensational double murder investigation it was revealed that all of the documents were forgeries. However, similar genuine potentially embarrassing documents revealed by Michael Quinn, the Tanners, and others both before and after this scam (e.g., see Quinn 1987 and Foster 1984) have proven to have had little impact upon the "testimonies of the faithful."(LDS). Why not? Perhaps, as some have suggested, one could argue that just as the "Big Mac" has conquered most of its "ethnic" rivals in the world of cuisine (e.g., see Kottak 1978), Mormonism has also often triumphed over its own cultural foes for the very same reason, that both offer the "customer" (non-LDS) a highly standardized "slice" of an "improved" version of the traditional "American pie." Thus in this age of cynicism where many adherents of the doctrine of cultural relativity have openly ridiculed those individuals who speak of patriotism and America's "Manifest destiny," the Church of Jesus Christ of Latter-day Saints embraces and nurtures such beliefs. Serving as a refuge for all those of any ethnic background who still pursue the traditional protestant ethic, Mormons like the earlier Puritans, still believe strongly that hard work, self-discipline, and loyalty to God and Country will bring the individual great secular as well as spiritual rewards.

However, an even stronger reason for its continuing success was proposed by Lowie (1963:532, 542) when he writes:

One day it occurred to me that both the Indians and the hardy souls who were trying to convert them to Christianity had some inner strength I lacked. ...

The Catholic priest, the Mormon missionary, the Eskimo shaman, the African witch-doctor, and the Protestant clergyman were all alike in their sense of inner conviction, in their intense desire to help others, and in their dependence upon some force outside themselves that gave them courage....

... through my reading I discovered that no group of people had ever been found who did not have a religion of some kind....

... What an average man wants above everything else is security. But does science supply this? The answer is "No." ... In this perilous universe he is forever beset with dangers beyond his control. ... so long as the enormous chasm yawns between man's rational control of nature and his biologico-psychological drives, there will still be room for belief in a Providence that grants not mere comfort, but security – not mere probability, but certainty....

Whatever one believes about the source of Joseph Smith's "revelations" (LDS), no honest researcher can deny the power of his assurance that if we remain faithful members of his "true" (LDS) Church not only will we live again in perfected physical bodies after death but also that we will be reunited with our husbands or wives, our children, our friends, and, through the performance of certain "sacred" (LDS) "secret" (non-LDS) temple rituals, our ancestors and all others who would have accepted the "true gospel" (LDS) had they had the chance to learn about it in this life.

Added to this is the physical security given in this life by the Church's massive welfare program and the social and emotional security offered by caring fellow members. This perhaps explain why the Church has seen conversion rates decline in recent years in much of Western Europe's welfare states as well as why here in the United States conversion rates have been much higher among the urban poor than among better off Americans. A good example of this was in the city of Reading, Pennsylvania where I taught at a local college for 16 years. The last few years I was there, at times there were as many as seven pairs of missionaries who were told to restrict almost all of their efforts to the inner-city, mostly minority populations. This effort paid off in quantity of converts (almost always 2 to 5 new baptisms per week) but not usually in quality, since extremely few of these new converts stayed "active" (LDS) for more than one or two weeks. In seeking a reason for this apparent "failure," it became obvious to me that the weekly influx of so many new members greatly overtaxed the social, emotional, and physical security that the local "Ward" (LDS) members could provide for these new converts to fill the loss of the intense contact they had had with the young missionaries who by now had turned most of their attention to new potential converts. And, from reports I have heard from Church leaders and many returned missionaries, this same problem appears to exist in many parts of Latin America and elsewhere in the World where large numbers of incoming poor people have overwhelmed the ability of local leaders and their congregations to "fully fellowship" (LDS) them.

F. Reed Johnson in an extremely important paper entitled "The Mormon Church as a Central Command System" (1979) drawing upon "some recent developments in comparative economics" observes that "many of the coordination problems of this type of organization (i.e., the Mormon Church) are remarkably similar to those encountered in socialist or centrally planned economies..." (p. 80). And though many members of the Church might take offence at the comparison that he and other outside observers have made between the Church and such "command societies" as the 1905 German Army, the Jesuits, and Maoist communism, he states that:

> However dissimilar the Mormon Church is to these organizations in other important respects, it does seem to share the four characteristics of a command society: (1) The church is a self-acknowledged theocracy, the prophet (with title of President of the Church) occupying the pinnacle of a hierarchic pyramid of authority· (2) Obedience to the principles of the gospel is defined as adherence to administrative rules and behavioral instructions issued by the leadership. Apart from disfellowshipping or excommunication on grounds of sexual immorality. heretical activity, and certain other serious offenses, costs of disobedience are denial of temple recommends or relatively weak, informal social sanctions. (3) There is a very strong emphasis on obedience to priesthood authority and "sustaining the brethren" as measures of worthiness. (4) Institutional rewards for conformance to religious standards and demonstrated loyalty to priesthood authority take primarily the form of promotion in the hierarchy. Despite disclaimers that any officer holds more authority or is more important to the operation of the Kingdom than any other, considerable social prestige is associated with appointment to a bishopric, stake presidency, or other "calling" as a regional or general authority. Such callings clearly endow the holder with ever increasing decision-making authority. (page 83).

In a hierarchical nonmarket organization like the Mormon Church, almost all information flows vertically (between levels of the hierarchy). Information regarding goal-related decisions and administrative rules flows fairly efficiently from Salt Lake: down to local leadership via leadership conferences and policy letters. Performance information is communicated upward in the form of detailed monthly reports on many aspects of ward activity. This information is presumably processed at the center and used to determine technological and organizational constraints and to formulate future goals and administrative rules. (page 87).

The central leadership of [he church has therefore become a gerontocracy, with its associated virtue of long-range perspective and defect of strong conservatism.

Although some conflicts may persist simply because information flows are inadequate for communicating the problem to the appropriate decision-maker, obvious inconsistencies are usually resolved on the basis of authority rather than consensus. Nevertheless. a minimum degree of consensus is necessary in a noncoercive system in order for decisions to be effective. The need to stress obedience to instructions in an organization of this type is obvious. (page 91).

Chapter Notes

1. Although he had no formal ministerial degree both he and his new bride had spent several years as young missionaries for the Church (A.C.N. December 30, 1943:4). The church also sent other young missionaries and older couples to Ajo during and after this time to help bring in new converts to the local "Branch" (LDS) which he now headed as a "Branch President" (LDS) and then later as "Bishop" (LDS) as the "Branch" increased in size to become a "Ward" (LDS) (e.g., see A.C.N. September 30, 1943:1; A.C.N. July 31, 1947:1)

2. See also, "The language of the Mormons: A sociocultural perspective" in Sorenson 1997: 137-148.

3. The literalness of this belief is now often being modified (e.g., see Mauss 2003:32-36, 40).

4. Mormon leaders insist that the temple rituals are "sacred" not "secret" even though they strongly warn members that "have taken out their own endowments" (LDS), that they have made a "sacred" (LDS) promise to never to discuss the details of the rituals outside of the

temple even to other members of the Church who have also made this same promise.

5. This decision has now been reversed.

6. In more recent times this is no longer always true. Thus, in the 1980s, I was in a leadership meeting in North Carolina where LDS Bishops were told to encourage people in financial need to apply for government welfare programs.

7. Thus Stack (2009: B1) in reporting on a "hiring freeze" by "Utah's largest employer" (i.e., the LDS CHURCH) (apparently unable to obtain more recent employment statistics) gives the following employment figures for the year 2002: "about 3,760 employees … at the church's 28-story worldwide headquarters," "[a]bout 400 … on Temple Square and at the Administration Building," "a faculty and staff of 18,000" at BYU," "an estimated 2,035 instructors and staff" at LDS high school "seminaries" (LDS) and college and university "institutes of religion" (LDS), "about 1,500" custodians for its "thousands of meeting houses and facilities throughout the state," an "estimated 75" at the "church's catastrophe-proof [record storage] vault carved into [a nearby] granite mountain side," and "an estimated 1,705…[including "hundreds of disabled people"] engaged in collecting, refurbishing and reselling second-hand furniture, appliances, clothes and other merchandise … with the goal of preparing trainees for and placing them in other private-sector jobs.""

8. In Utah any non-Mormons including Jews are often called "Gentiles."

9. The drinking of caffeinated soft drinks although not specifically forbidden is "frowned upon."

10. Until a few years ago it needed to be renewed annually. The change was made to lesson the workload that these lengthy interviews placed on "ward" (LDS) and "stake" (LDS) leaders.

11. He was a nearby neighbor of mine as I was growing up. He often hired me to cut his lawn and shovel snow off his sidewalks. For many years after his excommunication even though he had fully repented

from his adulterous act and attended the weekly Sacrament Meeting (LDS) (although not being allowed to partake of the Sacrament), he was not allowed to be "rebaptized" (LDS) and have his "temple blessings" (LDS) restored.

12. While I was an adjunct professor at BYU, I was encouraged by the Chairman of the Anthropology Department, Dr. John Sorenson, to submit a copy of a paper about the Church's Indian Programs, that I had presented at a meeting of the American Anthropological Association, to "Elder" (LDS) Lee for his comment but in his reply to me he said that he had been given no authority over any Church Indian program and advised me to submit it to those who had been given this responsibility.

13. See Mauss (2003) for a detailed account of many of the events (that I, too, will briefly discuss in the next chapter) that led up to the two angry, hand written letters that Lee (1989:50-55) delivered to the Church's top leaders.

14. An example of this occurred while I was serving as one of the leaders of a small congregation ("Branch" (LDS)) in North Carolina. When we ordered a piano, we were not allowed to purchase it locally but had to order it from a dealer in Salt Lake City. This created many problems for us since it arrived in a damaged condition which we were never able to get repaired and the newly-baptized local leader in charge of signing a release of payment for the piano to the Salt Lake City supplier was threatened with excommunication if he didn't sign the release even though no repairs were promised or ever received. However, the "Branch President" (LDS) of a nearby community who was a long-time member of the Church and a very successful businessman when confronted by a similar problem of being asked to approve payment for a shipment of damaged furniture, instead, on a trip he had already planned to Salt Lake City, went to Church Headquarters to complain directly to the Church employees who had demanded his "signoff." And when they at first refused to back down on their demand, he left their office saying that he was going upstairs to talk directly to the "Prophet" (LDS). At this point they

immediately called him back and agreed to replace the damaged furniture.

15. She said that she has given up trying to place ads in the "supposedly neutral" Salt Lake Tribune since the marketing executives either reject them outright or heavily censor each ad's wording. However, she feels that these acts are motivated more by fear of offending other advertisers and thus losing vital advertising revenue than by any direct pressure from Church leaders.

16. The percapita funding for schools is now the lowest in the nation (Henslin 2007:498) as it has also been for many past years (e.g., see Online NewsHour 2008)

17. When Sterling McMurrin once came to speak to the students and faculty of the Anthropology Department at BYU while I was employed there as an adjunct professor, he was not allowed to speak in a building on the main campus even though he was allowed to meet with us in the off-campus Anthropology Museum.

18. "Elder" is the title Mormons use when introducing or writing about both their young missionaries and their top "General Authorities."

CHAPTER 11:

The Search for "Eternal Truth"

It is important ... to know the difference between eternal
gospel principles which are unchanging, universally
applicable and cultural norms which may vary with time
and circumstance. (From a speech by "Elder" (LDS)
Ronald E. Poelman as quoted in Fletcher 1985: 45)
What are the underlying characteristics of Mormonism
which contribute to its modern day attraction? Some
... have emphasized Mormonism's flexibility, its ability
to accommodate a wide range of personalized religious
meanings. Mormonism has indeed demonstrated an
ability to change, and it has done so while adapting
to the use of modern administrative methods. But
we would argue that perhaps the primary appeals of
Mormonism in the modern world are not so different
from what was offered by the vision of the Mormon
kingdom in the nineteenth century: authoritative
centralized leadership, moral certitude, a strong sense
of community identification and active involvement in
a transcendent cause. Like other conservative religions

in modern society, Mormonism functions largely as an alternative to the confusing diversity and moral ambiguity of modern secular life. (Stark 1984:40)

As Peggy Fletcher writes in her January 1985 <u>Sunstone</u> article: " To many American Saints, Elder Ronald E. Poelman's Sunday morning address, "The Gospel and the Church," at October conference was "the best they heard" since it seemed to ease the conflict in their minds concerning several major changes that have occurred in recent years in key doctrines and rituals in the Church. Although often welcoming such changes as the lifting of the ban forbidding the giving of the "priesthood" (LDS) to males and "endowment"(LDS), "eternal marriage"(LDS) and "sealing"(LDS) ceremonies to both men and women having any degree of African descent, this particular change undercut the statements of such earlier Mormon prophets as Brigham Young who taught that this denial of "priesthood blessings"(LDS) was a result of their "less valiant"(LDS) behavior in a pre-birth existence; therefore their turn to "obtain these blessings" would not occur until the end of the prophesied millennium after all other humans had first been given this opportunity. Also, the elimination of certain portions of the "sacred" (LDS) "secret" (non-LDS) temple ceremony that had often troubled first time ceremonial initiates, although welcomed by most, was also troubling to many lifelong members who had been taught from childhood that Joseph Smith was guided directly by God to restore the "true order"(LDS) of temple worship restoring key elements that had been lost or altered in the rituals passed down through time from the temple of Solomon by the Masons.[1] Thus, Poelman seems to suggest that even the founding prophets of Mormonism were, at times, being influenced more by "cultural norms" than by "eternal gospel principles which are unchanging, universally applicable."

However it was sad to many members that immediately after his speech, Fletcher (1985:44) reports that:

> ... those Apostles who regularly deal with Mormon apostate groups "pointed out" to Elder Poelman that his remarks might (be) misinterpreted. He was told that such apostate groups might use his remarks to argue that "those fully versed in and converted to the gospel do not need the Church," according to his brother, Stuart, a Salt Lake City attorney. Elder Poelman then revised his speech with those concerns in mind.
>
> ... In order to make the edited version as printed consistent with the video version that is sent to the foreign missions and for the historical archives, Elder Poelman returned to the tabernacle a few days after conference and retaped the speech with the changes. This tape was then spliced into the original conference tape replacing the previous address. In addition a "cough-track" was provided to make it sound more like an audience was present.
>
> According to L. Don LeFevre, a story in the Salt Lake Tribune on November 16, 1984, said, "The most obvious place to retape his talk was from the pulpit." When asked if that would give a false impression that Elder Poelman was actually speaking to an audience, LeFevre said, "it could."
>
> Although a number of talks have been edited after presentation for publication in the Ensign in the past, no speech has ever been retaped in this manner.

Especially saddening to those who had been troubled by abrupt changes in what they had been taught were "eternal gospel principles" was the elimination of the quotation that began this chapter. Still, the very fact that Elder Poelman had been allowed to include this passage in his original broadcast speech gave some comfort to those troubled by such "doctrinal" changes as has also, a recent message by Dieter F. Uchtdorf, Second Counselor to the current Prophet, who in an official Ensign article states:

> The Church, with all its organizational structure and programs, offers many important activities for its members aimed at helping families and individuals to serve God and each other. Sometimes, however, it can appear that these programs and activities are closer to the center of our heart and soul than the core doctrines and principles of the gospel. Procedures, programs, policies, and patterns of organization are helpful for our spiritual progress here on earth, but let's not forget that they are subject to change.
> In contrast, the core of the gospel--- the doctrines and the principles--- will never change....(Uchtdorf 2008:5)

Thus, few active members of the Church remain troubled for long by such changes especially those that have vastly increased favorable national and international publicity about Church programs and individuals.

And, in contrast to the days of my youth when I vividly remember being shown an anti-LDS pamphlet published by the Catholic Church with a map of the United States on the cover with only the state of Utah being shown in solid black and the later publication of the first edition of Apostle McConkie's book, Mormon Doctrine (1958:108) where he equated the Catholic Church to the "great and abominable church" mentioned in the Bible's "Book of Revelation"[2], on many moral issues and humanitarian efforts, both churches are now the best of allies. Also, no longer is the passage from Joseph Smith's History in The Pearl of Great Price (1:19) often quoted that states that, when Joseph seeking to know which church he should join in a vision where he saw God the Father and His Son, Jesus Christ, was told that he:

... must join none of them, for they were all wrong; and the Personage who addressed me said that all their creeds were an abomination in his sight; that those professors were all corrupt; that: "they draw near to me with their lips, but their hearts are far from me, they teach for doctrines the commandments of men, having a form of godliness, but they deny the power thereof."

Instead, the recently deceased Mormon Prophet, Gordon B. Hinckley:

> ... highlighted Mormon commonality with other Christians, forging alliances with other faith groups while scolding LDS Church members for being too clannish, self-righteous and unfriendly to their neighbors. ...
> ... He built goodwill by opening the Tabernacle on Temple Square to interfaith groups, by creating an Inner City Mission to help people find their way out of poverty, illness and addiction, and by contributing to the restoration of the Catholic Cathedral of the Madeleine and Westminster College of Salt Lake City. (Stack 2008b:H2,H5)

Thus it was not surprising that upon Hinckley's death "... current and former non-Mormon religious leaders... collectively praised LDS Church President Gordon B. Hinckley...." (Ravitz 2008a:A4)

Other scriptures that are seldom openly discussed in Church meetings now that the "priesthood" (LDS) is given to all "worthy" (LDS) males and "temple blessings" (LDS) to all "worthy" males and females regardless of ancestry include:

> [Verse 6] And again the Lord said unto me: Look; and I looked towards the north, and I beheld the people of Canaan, which dwelt in tents. [Verse 7] And the Lord said unto me: Prophesy; and I prophesied, saying:

Behold the people of Canaan, which are numerous, shall go forth in battle array against the people of Shum, and shall slay them that they shall utterly be destroyed; and the people of Canaan shall divide themselves in the land, and the land shall be barren and unfruitful, and none other people shall dwell there but the people of Canaan; [Verse 8] For behold, the Lord shall curse the land with much heat, and the barrenness thereof shall go forth forever; and there was a blackness came upon all the children of Canaan, that they were despised among all people. (Pearl of Great Price, Moses 7:6-8)

[Verse 21] Now this king of Egypt was a descendant from the loins of Ham, and was a partaker of the blood of the Canaanites by birth. [Verse 22] From this descent sprang all the Egyptians, and thus the blood of the Canaanites was preserved in the land. [Verse 23] The land of Egypt being first discovered by a woman, who was the daughter of Ham, and the daughter of Egyptus, which in the Chaldean signifies Egypt, which signifies that which is forbidden; [Verse 24] When this woman discovered the land it was under water, who afterward settled her sons in it; and thus, from Ham, sprang that race which preserved the curse in the land. [Verse 25] Now the first government of Egypt was established by Pharaoh, the eldest son of Egyptus, the daughter of Ham, and it was after the manner of the government of Ham, which was patriarchal. [Verse 26] Pharaoh, being a righteous man, established his kingdom and judged his people wisely and justly all his days, seeking earnestly to imitate that order established by the fathers in the first generations, in the days of the first patriarchal reign, even in the reign of Adam, and also of Noah, his father, who blessed him with the blessings of the earth, and with the blessings of wisdom, but cursed him as pertaining to the Priesthood. [Verse 27] Now, Pharaoh being of that lineage by which he could not have the right of Priesthood, notwithstanding the Pharaohs would fain claim it from Noah, through Ham, therefore my father was led away by their idolatry; (<u>Pearl of Great Price</u>, Abraham Chapter 1: Verses 21 – 27)

[Verse 21] And he had caused the cursing to come upon them, yea, even a sore cursing, because of their iniquity. For behold, they had hardened their hearts against him, that they had become like unto a flint; wherefore, as they were white, and exceedingly fair and delightsome, that they might not be enticing unto my people the Lord God did cause a skin of blackness_to come upon them. (<u>Book of Mormon</u>, 2 Nephi 5: Verse 21)

[Verse 14] And it came to pass that those Lamanites who had united with the Nephites were numbered among the Nephites; [Verse 15] And their curse was taken from them, and their skin became white like unto the Nephites; [Verse 16] And their young men and their daughters became exceedingly fair, and they were numbered among the Nephites, and were called Nephites. And thus ended the thirteenth year. (<u>Book of Mormon</u>, 3Nephi 2: Verses 14-16)

[Verse 6] And then shall they rejoice; for they shall know that it is a blessing unto them from the hand of God; and their scales of darkness shall begin to fall from their eyes; and many generations shall not pass away among them, save they shall be a pure and a delightsome people. (<u>Book of Mormon</u>, 2 Nephi 30: Verse 6)

In many ways this doctrinal transformation is similar to that which occurred in the early Christian Church when Peter had a vision where he was commanded to eat "unclean" food (Acts 10:9-15) as Paul brought the gospel message to the gentile nations where converts were no longer required to observe Jewish food restrictions and the law of male circumcision (Acts 11:1-10).

Further evidence of this more recent dramatic change was seen in the following quotation from a speech of President Hinckley's Second Councilor, President James E. Faust, entitled "The Healing Power of Forgiveness" in which he tells the story of how the Amish reacted to the family of a man who had killed five of their young school girls and seriously wounded five others:

> This shocking violence caused great anguish among the Amish but no anger. There was hurt but no hate. Their forgiveness was immediate. Collectively they began to reach out to the milkman's suffering family. As the milkman's family gathered in his home the day after the shootings, an Amish neighbor came over, wrapped his arms around the father of the dead gunman, and said, "We will forgive you." Amish leaders visited the milkman's wife and children to extend their sympathy, their forgiveness, their help, and their love. About half of the mourners at the milkman's funeral were Amish. In turn, the Amish invited the milkman's family to attend the funeral services of the girls who had been killed. A remarkable peace settled on the Amish as their faith sustained them during this crisis.... How could the whole Amish group manifest such an expression of forgiveness? It was because of their faith in God and trust in His word, which is part of their inner beings. They see themselves as disciples of Christ and want to follow His example. (Faust 2007:67-69).

And in the Sunday February 24, 2008 broadcast of the Mormon Tabernacle Choir on KSL TV, the brief sermon extolled the courage of Rosa Parks as she defied the command to give up her seat on the bus she was riding. Also, the final musical number was not a traditional sacred Mormon hymn but instead an extremely lively version complete with a normally forbidden (in Sunday worship services) clarinet solo of "When the Saints Go Marching In" in a style that many African Americans would remind them of versions sung by their own church choirs. This friendly "outreach" to other Christian churches apparently did not stop with the death of President Hinckley but continues under the leadership of the new Mormon Prophet, President Monson, as demonstrated by the inclusion in recent Sunday Choir broadcasts of other "forbidden" hymns never permitted in any other of its regular world-wide Sunday worship services (e.g., "Amazing Grace" in the May 25, 2008 broadcast and "Old Time Religion" in the June 1, 2008 broadcast.) And the ultimate proof of the end of the former "racist" (non-LDS) denial of "priesthood" and "temple" "blessings" (LDS) was vividly demonstrated with the creation of the "LDS Swahili Branch" in January 2009 in Salt Lake City (Stack 2009b:C1) and the later April 2009 "ordination" (LDS) of the first black African "general authority" (LDS) who became a member of the "First Quorum of the Seventy" (LDS), "the church's second most important tier of leaders" (Stack 2009c:C2).

But the hope by "feminists" in the church that they will be given the "priesthood" (LDS) and "equal treatment" (as defined by them) to males in the Church still appears to be a lost battle ever since Lavina Fielding Anderson in September of 1993 was excommunicated from the LDS church "for documenting and publishing instances of the church's punishing treatment of Mormon intellectuals and feminists, as well as other instances of ecclesiastical abuse." (Maloney 2003:27). Earlier attempts in the late 1970s and 1980s by others such as Sonia Johnson to counter the Church's large-scale efforts to block the passage of the Equal Rights Amendment to the US Constitution had also failed, as had the feminist efforts by several BYU faculty members who ended up losing their positions at that Church-controlled institution.

However, equating the denial of ordination of female members to the priesthood to the past denial to members with African heritage would be a serious mistake since non-African women have always had access to leadership roles in such Church organizations as the adult women's "Relief Society" (LDS) and the children's "Primary" (LDS) as well as in certain "sacred" (LDS) "secret" (non-LDS) temple rituals. Also, the Church now allows female members to say the opening and closing prayers in "Sacrament Meetings" (LDS) (a practice previously forbidden) and, as stated earlier, has created a women's counterpart to the traditional male-only "Saturday Night General Priesthood Meeting" (LDS) that is held twice a year as part of the "Semi-Annual World Conference" (LDS). Also, in recent years, local leaders have been told to not automatically disbelieve women's complaints about abuse from husbands or other "priesthood holders" (LDS) and to stress the importance and "sacredness" (LDS) of "motherhood" (LDS) as in this admonition by President Gordon B. Hinckley the recently deceased Mormon Prophet who states:

> Woman is God's supreme creation….
> Of all the creations of the Almighty, there is none more
> beautiful, none more inspiring than a lovely daughter of
> God who walks in virtue with an understanding of why
> should do so….
> God will hold us accountable if we neglect His daughters.
> (Scott 2008:3)

Potentially even more threatening to the very survival of the Church are the attempts by some scholars both in and out of the Church to use historical and scientific evidence to attack Joseph Smith's accounts of visions and the historicity of the sacred Mormon scriptures, especially the "Book of Mormon." Just how serious do I feel these threats have become, not very, for the following two reasons:

1. Although no non-Mormon archeologists to my knowledge support the historical accuracy of the Book of Mormon, a Church support group of Mormon scholars (using the acronym F.A.R.M.S.[3]) at BYU publishes many articles and books on possible supporting evidence for the book's historicity. They are quick to point out that even non-Mormon scientists are examining the evidence that is now appearing that some ancestors of American Indians may have arrived in the New World by boat rather than by foot over the Bering Straits ice age land bridge. Also they have been quick to counter negative DNA evidence that American Indians are most closely related to Asiatic populations not the ancient Israelite voyageurs chronicled in the Book of Mormon. Thus, Dr. John Sorenson's thesis (1985) building upon the earlier work of M. Wells Jakeman and Thomas Stuart Ferguson (Larson 2004:12-13) that all the events described after the arrival of the seafarers in the New World took place in a relatively small region of Central America has gained the support of most Church leaders especially when combined with the supposition that these boat people mingled with much larger numbers of earlier arriving Asiatic populations.[4] And, it is argued, since few of the seafaring Israelites survived their final battles, their contribution to the gene pool of today's Native Americans would be minimal. This, in turn, helps Church leaders and members who have long been troubled by the very marginal "spiritual conversion" (LDS) success of such intense, special Native American conversion efforts as the now abandoned, Indian Student Placement Program, which as Mauss (2003: 95-96) clearly documents, were, however, highly successful in raising the secular educational, vocational and leadership skills of hundreds of Indian men and women. Thus, Church Leaders following the death of the Mormon Prophet, President Spencer W. Kimball who had spearheaded the many

post World War II efforts of Church to bring about the prophesized return of the "Lamanites" (LDS) to the "true religion" (LDS) of their ancestors, "had envisioned a different kind of yield from their investment in Indian education"(Mauss 2003:97). For these leaders, their "ultimate objective was clearly more spiritual than simply "a degree and the ability to make a living" desirable as these might be." (Mauss 2003:97). Instead, in discussing a talk given by Elder Packer, one of these leaders, to BYU Indian students, Mauss (2003:97-98) states that Packer and his colleagues were looking for "converted Indian youth who would attend their church meetings regularly and participate fully in church service, so that they would be prepared to take the gospel to the "countless millions of [their] people waiting for [their] ministry…"(a direct quote from Packer's speech)."

Thus, the many failures of these programs is now often being blamed on the selection of the wrong target population. Instead, many Church leaders and members now feel that the real Israelite remnant populations lie south of the U.S. border where conversion and retention rates have been much higher, although I personally would argue that a more convincing argument could be made for this relative failure on the "apartheid" conditions present on Indian reservations and reserves that exist in the U.S. and Canada but not in Latin America.[5]

It is therefore not surprising that the following sentence in the introduction to the Book of Mormon has been changed from: "After thousands of years, all were destroyed except the Lamanites, and they are the principal ancestors of the American Indians." to "After thousands of years, all were destroyed except the Lamanites, and they are among the ancestors of the American Indians." (Nicita 2008). Although some critics (e.g., Watson 2007, Long 2007) feel that this change contradicts Joseph Smith's "words" and "blows holes in the many references to the Lamanites in the Doctrine and Covenants…", most Church members show little concern about it (e.g., Black 2007). And for those still concerned about the problem of the pre-Columbian Old World animals named in the book, Sorenson (1985:288-299) suggests that Joseph Smith had used the names of animals commonly known to 19th Century Americans as approximations for the actual animals named in the "Golden Plates" (LDS). However, one prominent BYU professor told me, in private, that in contrast to Sorenson's possible explanation, he believes that the book's story really took place in Asia not America and another scholar (Olsen 2004:30-34) has suggested that most of the story took place on the Malaysian Peninsula with some survivors then sailing to America. Again, outside critics marvel that despite their relentless efforts to present massive historical and scientific evidence against the historicity of the book, most active members firmly believe that after they finished reading the <u>Book of Mormon</u>, they received a divine positive answer to the following promise made near the end of the book:

> [Verse 4] And when ye shall receive these things, I would exhort you that ye would ask God, the Eternal Father, in the name of Christ, if these things are not true; and if ye shall ask with a sincere heart, with real intent, having faith in Christ, he will manifest the truth of it unto you, by the power of the Holy Ghost. [Verse 5] And by the power of the Holy Ghost ye may know the truth of all things. (<u>Book of Mormon</u>, Moroni Chapter 10, Verses 4,5)

Thus, most Mormons rely on a "spiritual witness" (LDS) that the Book of Mormon and their other sacred scriptures are true rather than on any actual historical or scientific evidence. Many members have personal miracle stories and/or firmly believe the many other miracle stories told to them by other members and leaders regarding such things as missionary efforts, healings, misfortunes averted, temples, etc. to back up this faith not only in these scriptures but in the "divine guidance" (LDS) they receive through their present-day Church leaders. And some, such as I, have ancestors who have recorded miracle stories about the events that led to their conversion to Mormonism.[6]

2. Similar earlier attempts to discredit the "Book of Abraham" in the "Pearl of Great Price" seemed promising to the enemies of the Church especially when the actual papyrus fragments from which it was "translated" (LDS) by Joseph Smith were suddenly rediscovered in the library of the Metropolitan Museum of Art in New York City. Non-LDS scholars translating these fragments said that they contained excerpts from the "Book of the Dead", a common text found with many Egyptian mummies that bore almost no resemblance to Joseph Smith's Book of Abraham. Most Mormon scholars did not dispute the conclusion of these scholars but instead came to the conclusion that the text that became the "Book of Abraham" was given by direct revelation to Joseph Smith from God not from the fragments themselves which perhaps merely inspired him to seek a vision. Also, they pointed out many similarities between his text and other ancient sources. Again, most active Mormons rely on "the witness they receive from the Holy Ghost" (LDS) rather than that provided by skeptical Egyptian scholars although an active Mormon acquaintance of mine now feels he has evidence that modern translations of ancient Egyptian hieroglyphics based upon "the educated guesses" of the translators of the famous Rosetta Stone may not be reliable especially given the relatively recent creation of the engravings on this particular stone. And, I strongly suspect that Church scholars will eventually produce a counter-argument to a more recent, but not widely read or discussed, scientific attack (Anderson 2003: 75-118) on the "Book of Abraham's" astronomical statements.

Turning now to the recent raid on the "Yearning for Zion" ranch in Texas where 462 "children" [7] (Adams 2008c:A1) were taken away from their polygamist parents in this breakaway sect from the main Mormon Church, one critic (Nielsen 2008:A13) of the one remaining aspect of polygamy in the main Church was prompted to suggest that despite the "passionate rebuttal" of the main Church's leaders that "the LDS Church has nothing to do with polygamy or the FLDS" (i.e., the Fundamentalist Church of Jesus Christ of Latter-day Saints) and that any known polygamists are excommunicated, the main Church needs to:

> Develop a new understanding – a revelation, even – regarding Doctrine & Covenants 132, the section of Mormon scripture that forms the foundation for polygamy and celestial marriage. As part of this, discontinue the policy allowing men to be sealed to more than one woman. [This is now only allowed if the first wife has died.] Such a change would make it clearer than ever that polygamy is in the past. … That the current policy suggests parents are not only wed in eternity but sometimes even wed to more than one spouse, seriously undermines the claim that polygamy is in the past. Instead, it suggests that polygamy is in both the past and the future, and that current policy is the exception rather than the rule. (Nielsen 2008:A13)

And a prominent Mormon writer for the Salt Lake Tribune (Stack 2008e:A16) gives as an example of this polygamist remnant that three of the current apostles after their first wife died remarried and were "sealed" also to the new wife. Thus, "Each will have two wives in the eternities." (Stack 2008e:A16). However, Stack goes on to state that:

> These days many Mormons see polygamy of the past as a noble God-sanctioned venture, but the contemporary practice as not only illegal, but as debased, unhealthy and burdensome on society. [adding that in contrast to such currently practicing groups as the FLDS]...

Brigham Young did not arrange marriages unless asked and readily consented to a divorce, allowing any woman who wanted to get out. (Stack 2008e:A16)

And to further demonstrate how much further the main Church has distanced itself from modern-day of polygamists she states:

... the church's global missionaries cannot share the church's message with African polygamists.

Mormons do not live in isolated compounds, arrange marriages, dress in old-fashioned clothing or wear unusual hairstyles, LDS Apostle Quentin L. Cook said Friday in a video interview. Rather, they are participating members of the communities in which they live, get married at the average age of 23, and are well educated. (Stack 2008e:A16)

Thus, not understanding the desire of the main Church to distance itself from the modern-day polygamists, the Texas judge, Barbara Walther, who had ordered the removal of all the children from their polygamist parents while refusing to "make any ruling that would allow breast-feeding mothers to remain with their children in state custody" did "rule that the women currently staying at the San Angelo Coliseum could meet twice a day to pray without being monitored by state workers." (Adams 2008a:A4). And, she naively "asked Texas Child Protective Services to find a member of the mainstream LDS church or some other 'appropriate religious person' who would not be seen as 'making their service less sacred' to oversee the sessions." (Adams 2008a:A4). However, it was not long before she learned that the mainstream LDS church would not accept such a request (Adams 2008b:A4) and under heavy pressure from the Texas breastfeeding lobby she finally agreed to let the mothers of the youngest children continue to nurse them.

Still, Church leaders soon discovered to their horror that many members of the general United States public also share her belief of a continuing close connection between the LDS and FLDS churches. Thus they mounted an expensive media campaign to try to counter this perception. (Stack 2008f:A10)

However, instead of feminism, the historicity of the LDS scriptures, or the revival of the polygamy issue, the most recent major challenge to one of the most strongly held, supernaturally-sanctioned "core" beliefs of Mormons is coming from the practicing gay community. This conflict will not easily or perhaps ever be resolved since embracing homosexuality as a legitimate expression of sexuality is viewed by Church Leaders as a major threat to the survival of not only the traditional family but also of our nation. Thus, although the Church no longer endorses change therapies nor encourages gay males to marry women, as a member of the LDS Orchestra recently found out, they are not always tolerant of those criticizing Church Leaders for their efforts to oppose gay marriage proposals (Stack 2008c: A1, A9). Instead, the official Church position regarding same sex attraction was reiterated by LDS Apostle Jeffrey R. Holland in September 2007 who stated that "same sex attraction is not a sin; only acting on it is immoral" (Stack 2008b: A9). But following the death of President Hinckley, a gay Mormon support group, hoping that his successor would show "greater compassion" (non-LDS) toward their "sexual orientation" (non-LDS) sought in February 2008 to have a one on one meeting with Thomas S. Monson, the newly installed Church President.

Although declining this request, President Monson, instead, initially offered the gay support group a chance to meet with the director for LDS family Services and an August meeting was scheduled. But according to a Church spokesman, the meeting was postponed "indefinitely" in late July, "pending the appointment of a new director for LDS Family Services"

(Dobner 2008b:C5). However, many outside observers felt that the real reason for the indefinite postponement was the already negative media "heat" the Church was feeling from the release of a statement from the top three leaders of the Church to be read in California LDS churches on Sunday, June 29, 2008, "asking California Mormons to support a proposed constitutional amendment that would recognize only a marriage between a man and a women" thus nullifying California's recent Supreme Court Decision allowing gay couples the right to be legally married in that state. (Stack 2008d: A1, A4.)

Now, with the narrow passage of this amendment on November 4, 2008, Gays across the country are focusing more of their wraith upon the Mormon Church for its organizational and monetary support than upon any other amendment supporting sponsors.

In response to this anger of opponents to Proposition 8 after it passed, the Church issued a statement "calling for civility among its members and those who opposed same-sex marriage bans" (Hunsaker and Kinsey 2008) and, according to ABC 4 News, during a massive November 7th protest against the Church in downtown Salt Lake City except for a few Church members singing LDS hymns in front of the massive Church headquarters building:

> …The verbal confrontations were left to a couple of street preachers who carried signs condemning the gay lifestyle. One also carried a bull horn trying to out shout the multitude. Ironically, these are some of the same preachers who show up at every general conference of the LDS Church. On those occasions they have ridiculed Mormons, but on this night they found themselves in the odd position of defending the LDS Church's stand on marriage. Politics makes for strange bedfellows. (Hunsaker and Kinsey 2008)

Trying to calm down the situation, an official spokesman for the Church, Elder L. Whitney Clayton, "called ... for members to heal rifts caused by the emotional campaign by treating each other with civility and love" adding that the LDS Church does not object to domestic partnership or civil union legislation "as long as these do not infringe on the integrity of the traditional family or the constitutional rights of churches" (Adams 2008d:A1,A4). However a few days later, Stephanie Pappas, chairwoman for the gay-rights advocacy group, Equality Utah, challenged the Church's "civility" that was "promised" by asking for its support for 5 "gay-rights" bills to be introduced in the 2009 state legislative session (Ravitz 2008b:B2) followed by an even stronger challenge from Mike Thompson, Equity Utah's executive director who:

> ... asked the LDS Church, to continue "its willingness to engage in political issues" by stepping in to help.
> "Is the LDS Church willing to assign a member of its Presidency of the Seventy to lead church efforts to secure these rights, just as it did with Proposition 8?" he asked. And, he continued, "will the First Presidency draft a letter to Utah Latter-day Saints in support of rights and protections for gay couples ... [and] . ask for this letter to be read to all Utah congregations on a specified date," as it did in California? Ravitz (2008b:B2)

No immediate response to these demands was forthcoming, however, this reluctance to respond to such questions is obvious as the Church tries to avoid drawing even more unfavorable press attention toward its massive efforts to aid the passage of Proposition 8.

Church Leaders feel that they are being unfairly "singled out" (Hunsaker and Kinsey 2008) by thousands of demonstrators since the proposition would have gone down to defeat without support from other churches and Black and Hispanic voters. And protestors seem to have paid little attention to the fact that the largest single contributor to the effort to pass Proposition 8 was the Knights of Columbus "having given $1.4 million" (Leff 2008:A4) as opposed to the Church's $2,078.97 in-kind direct donation (Associated Press 2008a:B4) to the pro-amendment 8 campaign. However, as one opponent of Proposition 8 pointed out, by October 25th, "59,000 Mormons [had]…contributed more than $19.15 million" to the campaign which was "77 percent of the $24.89 million raised by the entire Yes on 8 campaign" (Stack 2008f:C1). And, as Stack(2008g:A12) earlier reported:

> The LDS Church's campaign to pass Proposition 8 represents its most vigorous and widespread political involvement since the late 1970s, when it helped defeat the Equal Rights Amendment. It even departs from earlier efforts on behalf of traditional marriage, in which members felt more free to decide their level of involvement.
>
> This time, LDS leaders have tapped every resource, including the church's built-in phone trees, e-mail lists and members' willingness to volunteer and donate money. Many California members consider it a directive from God and have pressured others to participate. Some leaders and members see it as a test of faith and loyalty.[8]
>
> Those who disagree with the campaign say they feel unwelcome in wards that have divided along political lines. Some are avoiding services until after the election; others have reluctantly resigned. Even some who favor the ballot measure are troubled by their church's zeal in the matter
>
> "I do expect the church to face a high cost – both externally and internally for its prominent part in the campaign said LDS sociologist and Proposition 8 supporter Armand Mauss of Irvine, Calif. He believes

church leaders feel a "prophetic, imperative" to speak out against gay marriage

The internal cost will consist of ruptured relationships between and among LDS members of opposing positions, sometime by friends of long standing and equally strong records of church activity, " Mauss said.

...

Robert Rees, a former LDS bishop in California, says he has not witnessed this much divisiveness in the church over a political issue in the last 50 years...."

And adding further "fuel to the fire" in the eyes of the gay community was the speech by M. Russell Ballard, an LDS apostle, in a videotaped conference shown in California LDS Chapels and at BYU Campuses in Utah, Idaho, and Hawaii where he urged young California Mormons including those attending out of state schools to "use texting, blogging, videos, podcasts, Twitter, and Facebook to "go viral" in support of Proposition 8, promising them that "God will bless you as you do your part" (Stack 2008g:B1).

And as in earlier times in other controversies, some of the strongest opposition to the Church's efforts to encourage its California members to back the passage of an anti-gay marriage amendment (Proposition 8), comes from some of its own members such as Ben Jarvis, a "seventh generation Mormon" who in a letter to the editor (July 5, 2008:A10) states:

> ...This directive undermines families with gay members, including my own, and places active Latter-day Saints in the position of choosing the church over loved ones. This is wrong.
> ...If LDS leaders do not like the way we do business in the Golden Sate, they should dissolve their stakes, close their temples and retreat back to Utah where they won't

have to deal with the realities of the modern world. In the meantime, Mormons like me, people who understand that civil marriage is a civil right, will fight the marriage ban with all our heart, mind and strength.

Like Ben there are sizable numbers of other Mormons who have gay children, siblings, or other close relatives or friends, who are openly coming out against the Mormon Prophet. These, in addition to ordinary members like Ben, include such prominent individuals as the wife of Steve Young, the former football star, who gave "nearly $50,000" (Tribune staff and wire services 2008) to the effort to defeat Proposition 8 and one of the two founders of WordPerfect who "donated $1milllion" (Winters 2008:A1) to fight it, leading to the breakup of a long standing friendship and business relationship with his partner who donated "the same amount" to fight for its passage (Walsh 2008:B:1).

As discussed earlier, such a strong attack on top LDS leaders in the past has usually led to excommunication since it implies that these leaders are no longer divinely inspired, an accusation that most Mormons would vigorously reject. However, if past practices are followed, as an official spokesman for the Church, Elder L. Whitney Clayton, states, "any action regarding members who spoke out against the measure would be left to local church leaders' discretion" (Adams 2008d:A4).

As this book is being finished, the full fury of many gay supporters both within and outside of the Church is being unleashed against the Church, important Mormons, and even Utah's tourist industry. The widened extent of this anger is documented in an article from the Los Angeles Times which reports that:

Activists who oppose Proposition 8 have targeted for boycotts businesses whose employees or owners contributed money toward its passage. They have pored through campaign contribution databases and then "outed" the donors online.

They also have gone onto a restaurant review Web site to give bad notices to eateries linked to the Yes on 8 movement. (Abdollah and DiMassa 2008:A6)

Thus, in addition to press releases and letters sent to editors demanding that the Church's tax exemption be revoked and strongly suggesting that people should cancel their planned vacations to Utah (e.g., Stack 2008h, Twohy 2008:A12) not only are large donors such as Robert Hoehn, the vice president of a California Honda dealership who gave $25,000 receiving "vitriolic messages and phone calls" and having his dealership picketed, but even a relatively small $100 donor, Marjorie Christoffersen, a manager of a popular Los Angeles Mexican restaurant, El Coyote, and a daughter of its owner who found herself facing:

Hundreds of protesters [who] converged on El Coyote west of downtown Los Angeles on Wednesday night, and the picketing got so heated that police officers in riot gear had to be called in. [She then] ... met with protesters, apologized for the contribution and at one point broke down in tears, said Arnalda Archila, another El Coyote manager. But the activists were not satisfied. "She had a chance to make nice and blew it. I was almost feeling a tiny bit of sympathy for her. Not no more!!" wrote one poster, who listed competing Mexican restaurants where diners should go instead of El Coyote. (Abdollah and DiMassa 2008:A6)

Christoffersen left town the next day but the remaining restaurant employees including some who were gay were:

...left staggered by the protests, including more than 50 calls a day criticizing the restaurant.

- 433 -

"We are all a family," [another manager] said. "If this is going to affect the business, it's going to affect them [i.e., even the gay employees]. There are people who have to feed children and pay mortgages." (Abdollah and DiMassa 2008:A6)

Similarly, in Sacramento, "protests over his donation to [the] campaign to ban gay marriage in the state" led to the resignation of the artistic director of California's largest non-profit musical theater company (Reitz 2008:A7). Then as the LDS targets spread across the nation, John Aravosis, an influential Washington, D.C. based blogger, told The Associated Press:

> The main focus is going to be going after the Utah brand....We're going to destroy the Utah brand. It is a hate state. (Stack 2008h)

And, one of the first targets of this group was the international Marriott hotel chain and its founder, Bill Marriott, who has been a leader in the LDS Church in the Washington, D.C. area. However, Stack (2008h) reports that:

> While acknowledging that he is a Mormon, Bill Marriott said that neither he, nor his company, Marriott International, contributed to the campaign to pass Proposition 8, a California ballot initiative that defines marriage a exclusively between a man and a woman. ...
> For the past 20 years, Marriott International has had domestic partner benefits, and has earned a perfect score on the Human Rights Campaign's Corporate Equality Index for two consecutive years, Marriott said in a statement earlier this week.
> Many of the hotels have hosted lesbian, gay, bisexual and transgender community functions and events for years.

"The Bible that I love teaches me about honesty, integrity and unconditional love for all people," Marriott said. "But beyond that, I am very careful about separating my personal faith and beliefs from how we run our business."

There were also some acts of vandalism on LDS wardhouses in Utah and some fake "anthrax" (i.e., white powder) letters sent to LDS temples in Salt Lake City and Los Angeles which were widely believed to be a direct outcome of the Church's involvement in the Proposition 8 battle although no gay group or individual supporter claimed credit for these acts (e.g., see Gehrke 2008:B4; Bergreen 2008:B2).

However, it was not only Mormon leaders who voiced their dismay over these events but also the leaders of Equality Utah, a gay rights group, who were quick to strongly condemn the acts of violence and intimidation as well as the suggested boycott of the Sundance Film Festival and the Utah ski resorts which they felt would be "counterproductive" to their efforts to achieve equal rights in Utah and elsewhere (Wharton 2008:A16; Stack 2008i:B1). And despite their past differences with the LDS Church, the leaders of other conservative churches also joined the Mormons in the defense of Proposition 8 (e.g., see Associated Press 2008b:B5, Maffly 2008:A19, Hodges 2008:C2).

Still, the combined forces against gay marriage are facing a battle that will continue to be fought vigorously state by state, courtroom by courtroom, and in the media backed by such powerful individuals and groups as Newsweek Editor, David J. Jefferson (2008:54-56), and what a writer for Time Magazine (Cloud (2008:52-55) calls the "Gay Mafia... seven wealthy, gay political donors who are quietly pouring money into races all over the country—and redefining liberal politics in the process." Still unanswered at the time this book is being written is the long-term effect that this controversy will have on the future "ultra-adaptability" of the Church. Is this a major "P. R. fiasco" for the Church as many observers both within and without the Church have proclaimed or will it instead "help it win friends among Evangelicals" as others have suggested (Stack 2008j)? As further evidence for the "fiasco" prediction, Peggy Fletcher Stack (2008j), a reporter for the Salt Lake Tribune, tells of a family whose daughter "has lost friends over the issue" and whose son, who is now a missionary for the Church in California, "has had a disproportionate number of potential converts cancel appointments" but then goes on to report that:

> Last week, [Rev. Jim] Garlow, of Skyline Church in San Diego, was so outraged by the protests against Mormons that he emailed 7,200 California pastors urging them to "speak boldly" in defense of the LDS role in passing Proposition 8. "We were not going to stand by and be silent while there was anti-Mormonism in the streets," Garlow said Friday. "Our theological differences with Mormonism are, frankly, unbridgeable, but these are our friends and neighbors and attacks on them are unacceptable."
> The Proposition 8 campaign deepened his relationship with Mormons, he said, and the protests have solidified it.

And Thomas Burr (2008:A5), another reporter for the same Salt Lake City paper, in speculating about the potential impact that the Church's Proposition 8 support will have on Mitt Romney's political future states:

> The LDS effort could give Romney a crucial boost among evangelicals who wield great power in choosing the Republican presidential nominee. But it might leave the former Massachusetts governor an even tougher slog among a broader electorate.

However, despite the negative impact that its pro-amendment 8 efforts will surely produce, I still predict that, as in the past when the highest Church leaders were under similar attacks over other "moral issues" (LDS), gay activists, either within or outside the Church, will fail to lure away large numbers of "temple-worthy" (LDS) members who cherish their leaders' promise of an afterlife where they will be still united with their spouses, children, parents, and other relatives. And, as Spence (1960:66) writes:

> Mormons rear large families the better to provide human bodies for ... children of God. Because Mormons hope to obtain divinity, it behooves them to live saintly lives on earth. Marriage in a Mormon Temple is the first step toward divinity....

Thus, it is extremely unlikely that the current intense opposition to the Church and other religious groups that consider gay sexual activity sinful will be resolved by another "revelation," since the homosexual lifestyle is viewed by most members as an important part of "Satan's efforts" (LDS) to attempt to thwart God's plan for the "salvation and exaltation" (LDS) of his children here on earth.

In conclusion, the present-day LDS Church is one of the most successful ultra-adaptable organizations that has ever existed in human history for the following reasons:

1. In contrast to most other large churches and corporations, by relying almost entirely on a lay leadership and by limiting the maximum time that almost all individuals in the Church can serve in any position of authority and often ending that service instantly without any prior warning, it is virtually impossible for lower level local or regional authorities to effectively oppose changes decreed from the Prophet

and the Twelve Apostles. The popular Mormon belief that "God will never permit the Church's Prophet to lead its members astray" is firmly supported by such superlative leaders as the current Prophet Thomas S. Monson and his long time predecessor Gordon B. Hinckley whose wit, wisdom, media savvy, and humanitarian efforts have not only endured them to Mormons but also to many outsiders. And, though, such absolute centralized power has spelled the downfall of many other "ultra-adaptable" religions in the past as less capable leaders have occupied this all-powerful "systemic set," most Mormons are convinced that God will never permit this to occur in these, "the last days before the second coming of Christ" (LDS).

2. Just as I pointed out in my paper about the rising political and economic power of the Navajo tribe versus other tribes and white neighbors due to its higher birthrate (Stucki 1971), the expansion of the Church's power and wealth is also greatly aided by its much higher than average birthrate which in Utah "during a 12-month period in 2005 and 2006" was 83.2 births per 1,000 women of child-bearing age, compared with the national average of just 54.9 births per 1,000 women,".... "the highest birthrate in the nation" (Mayorga 2008:B6). Thus, in contrast to the Israelis who often seem willing to give up control of conquered lands rather than integrate Palestinians into their state because of fear of the Palestinian much higher birthrate, the Mormons have welcomed outsiders but still control most state and national offices in Utah despite the influx of these outsiders. And as children in these larger than national average families seek better employment for their skills than is available in Utah, they expand the political and economic power of the Church not only in nearby Western States but also in such areas as Boston and Washington, D.C.

3. Most young active men and increasing numbers of young women serve as unpaid missionaries, the men for two years and the women for

18 months. This not only provides large numbers of new "black box" converts but also serves as a "boot camp" (non-LDS) to mold these young people into "faithful, prayerful, tithe-paying" (LDS) members prepared to become the next generation of Church leaders. And as Carstens (2001:6) points out in his discussion of my work in Ajo and his in Africa:

> This strategy of gaining control over people's lives included the weeding out from the workforce all those men who had "undesirable" work habits and "bad" personal characteristics, retaining only those who met the company's standards.

Young men who refuse this assignment or who are found to be "unworthy" (LDS) for sexual or other "sins" often become social outcasts and drop out of Church activity. And those who have difficulty obeying the rigid rules of behavior required of missionaries and "are sent home" (LDS) or voluntarily choose to leave their missions, are often viewed by their parents and others as failures. Thus, more than once, a parent has said that he would rather have his son come home in a coffin than with a "dishonorable" (LDS) discharge. In particular, an administrator at BYU upon learning that his son had been "sent home" from his mission expressed his anguish to me about the disgrace his son had brought to the family.

4. There is an extremely effective sorting mechanism of adult Church members into those who are "temple worthy" (LDS) and those who are not since new "worthiness" (LDS) two stage[9] interviews to obtain the coveted "temple recommend" (LDS) to be allowed to enter any of the many world-wide temples and participate in the "sacred" (LDS), "secret" (non-LDS), temple ceremonies are required every two[10] years. This creates great anxiety in members having trouble supporting

local or higher level leaders, paying tithing, keeping the Church's strict moral code, abstaining from coffee, tea, alcohol, or tobacco products, or wearing the "sacred temple garments" (LDS) ("Mormon underwear" (non-LDS)). Thus, only those who pass these interviews are ever considered to be completely "worthy" members who could also then be considered to be "called" (LDS) to top leadership positions in the local or higher level Church.

5. Although it would be difficult to remove "offending" (to non-Mormons) passages from the Church's sacred scriptures and completely repudiate certain past practices and historical events that are embarrassing to the modern Church, any possible damage to the faith of members, especially new converts and the youth of the Church, is greatly reduced by increasing efforts to limit teaching assignments to only those members who are willing to avoid prolonged discussions about controversial topics and "mysteries" (LDS). Instead, these lay teachers are told to stick to the lesson material in the officially-sanctioned manuals and cautioned against including any unauthorized outside sources into their lessons. Also, most speakers at meetings are given carefully chosen assigned topics. Thus, in addition to possibly offending scriptural passages, such topics as the past practice of polygamy and the infamous "Mountain Meadows Massacre"[11] are almost never discussed in classes or meetings or if introduced by a class member are quickly passed over. Also, the often-told story of European converts' difficulties in crossing the plains as "Handcart Pioneers", usually fails to mention that Brigham Young sent the last group of Swiss converts, including my father's ancestors, to Santa Clara in Southern Utah to grow grapes for the Sacramental Wine. Nor is it often told that coffee was on the list of provisions that the early pioneers were advised to bring with them. However, with the abandonment of polygamy, "The Word of Wisdom" started to replace polygamy as one of the most important boundary

maintaining mechanisms between Church members and outsiders and changed from being merely a "word of wisdom" to a commandment. Now, almost no Church members that I have met have ever heard of the "Wine Mission" or that in its earliest years in Utah, the Church used wine in its Sacrament Service instead of the presently used substitute, water.[12]

6.   Finally, the widespread exchange of miracle stories in the monthly "fast and testimony" (LDS) meeting where any member is allowed to freely speak, as well as such stories told in other Church meetings, and informal gatherings, greatly supports the faith that members have that any secular or theological changes made by their Prophet and Apostles are divinely directed. Although the emphasis in this chapter has been on secular reasons for the remarkable ability of this Church to be able to not only survive but also outcompete many of its rivals, the power of supernatural beliefs to motivate human behavior should not be neglected. Especially important is the strongly felt obligation of active Mormons to marry and raise much larger than average families despite the economic sacrifice that this often requires. Equally critical is an unquestioning belief in an after life where rewards and punishments are based upon our actions here in mortality. However, in sharp contrast to Islamic suicide bombers who believe that rewards in the anticipated next life can be gained by killing nonbelievers, Mormons, through their genealogical research and proxy baptisms and marriages, wish not to destroy their religious rivals but to offer them, here or in the next life, the opportunity to enter the highest level of heaven together with their extended families and friends.

Chapter Notes

1.   Joseph Smith and many other Church leaders were active Masons and many authors have pointed out certain similarities between

the two ritual systems although the number of similarities has now decreased.

2.	Under rumored pressure from other Church Leaders, in the revised 2nd edition of his book McConkie changed his definition of the "great and abominable church" from the Catholic Church to "… all churches or organizations of whatever name or nature – whether political, philosophical, educational, economic, social, fraternal, civic, or religious – which are designed to take men on a course that leads away from God and his laws and thus from salvation in the kingdom of God."

3.	F.A.R.M.S. stands for Foundation for Ancient Research and Mormon Studies

4.	Priddis's (1975) suggestion that a better fit for the many geographical features described in the Book of Mormon can be found in South America rather than in Central America has received little general attention probably because it would require massive geological changes in South America to have occurred at the time that Christ died.

5.	See (Stucki 1984:71), (Manners and Collier 1972), and (Brophy, Aberle, et al. 1966) for listings and analyses of the many historical events and changes in government programs and policies that have made efforts by the Mormon Church and multitudes of other "do-gooders" both in and out of government to fully integrate Native Americans as equal citizens into modern-day America, usually fail.

6.	In my own case, these stories are found in Stucki (1932) and Hafen (1983)

7.	The earlier first reported count was only 416 but it grew to this number on April 26, 2008 as the state officials also took into protective custody, as children, any mothers who they felt were under the age of 18 even if the mothers claimed to be older than 18. This number continued to fluctuate as children were born and legal challenges to the state's age determinations were pursued and was finally reported to be reduced to 439 (Adams 2008e) as Texas child welfare officials announced that they had ended their investigation

8. For a more detailed account of the Mormon Church's pro-Proposition 8 activities in California see the November 15, 2008 New York Times article by Jesse McKinley and Kirk Johnson and the June 22, 2009 Time article by David Van Biema.

9. The first interview asking a series of standardized questions is done by a member of the "Ward Bishopric" (LDS) and the second interview asking the same set of questions is conducted by a member of the "Stake Presidency" (LDS).

10. Until recently, new interviews were required on a yearly basis but was changed to ease the workload of local "ward" (LDS) and "stake" (LDS) leaders.

11. Many books and articles have been written about this tragic event, the first most critically acclaimed by Juanita Brooks (1950), my father's first cousin. Although she was never excommunicated for writing this account, both she and her husband were never offered major lay positions in the local ward after the book was published.

12. My grandfather felt he was responsible for the change from the use of wine to water since he wrote a letter to the Prophet of the Church, Lorenzo Snow, just prior to the change, complaining that many of his fellow wine growers and makers were "sampling too much" of the product and becoming "drunkards." And as proof of his input into the making of this change, he tells how when one of the apostles came to Southern Utah to announce the change, his letter was mentioned.

CHAPTER 12:

Is "Eternal" Ultra-adaptability Achievable: Mormons, Masons, McDonalds, Miners, Jews, Money, Navajos, Muslims, Wombs, and the March of Dimes

> This new goal displacement may guarantee the organization's existence forever; for it is a goal so elusive it can never be reached. (Henslin 2007:182)

The LDS Church shares many of the most important control practices of other highly successful organizations. Thus, like the Masons, they know the power of secret, shared rituals to create extremely strong in-group bonds. And like McDonalds the Church offers "the assurance that products will be the same … in all locales" (Ritzer 2004:14). Thus, no matter where in the world one attends a Mormon service, the same meeting format will be followed, the same songs sung, and the same lessons taught – only the language might differ. And like numerous other religions, the Church creates boundary-maintaining practices to partially separate its members from the outside world. Thus, members in good standing do not drink coffee, tea, or alcoholic beverages, the ubiquitously offered drinks at most social events. Nor does the "sacred temple garment" (LDS) permit them to wear many of today's "often-revealing" clothes. However, unlike many Muslims and other groups like the Amish or the FLDS whose outer garments set them apart from others even when seen at a distance, "temple garments" (LDS) are always to be hidden under whatever outer-clothing a person is otherwise free to choose as long as it completely covers the "garments" that are not to be modified in any way to permit the wearing of skimpier clothing.

Emphasis on the "law of tithing" (LDS) especially as a requirement for obtaining the coveted "temple recommend" (LDS) has given the Church a financial base that on a per capita basis far surpasses that of all other major world religions. Although the Church no longer gives its members a detailed description of how this money is spent, most active members have complete trust in those leaders making financial decisions especially given the constant news of hundreds of Church buildings being built each year, an enormous welfare system, the support of several large universities, and large quantities of relief supplies being sent to disaster victims not only in this country but also throughout the world. However, as mentioned earlier, there is apparently now enough left over to complete the recently begun massive revitalization of the area of downtown Salt Lake City south of the LDS Temple and other Church buildings, effectively creating an LDS equivalent of Vatican City.

Just as the mining companies of Ajo found a plentiful supply of "black box" minorities from the nearby reservation and Mexico so they were able to sort the "good" workers from the bad, as stated earlier, the LDS Church has in many areas of the world, as conversion rates among white populations have fallen, now increasingly turned to minority groups, immigrants, and other urban and rural poor for the bulk of its new converts even though relatively few of these new converts stay "active" (LDS) for more than a very brief period of time.

Furthermore, remaining ultra-adaptable has often exacted a price in membership numbers. Thus, the decision of most members, following the assassination of Joseph Smith and his brother, to follow Brigham Young from Nauvoo, Illinois to the Salt Lake Valley left many "black boxes" (including Joseph's wife and children) behind. Likewise, the decision to abandon polygamy and much later the "granting of the Priesthood" (LDS) to black males and "temple ordinances" (LDS) to black husbands, wives, and children caused more "black box" defections. The doctrinal effects of this latter decision still linger in the minds of many members since the earlier ban supported a comforting explanation for why inequality in birthplace and quality of life exists in today's world. Thus, God was not to blame if our birth circumstances were less than ideal, rather our misfortune was due instead to the fact that we were "less valiant" (LDS)[1] in following Jesus Christ in a "pre-mortal existence" (LDS).

Along with this change has been a de-emphasis on the old idea that most people who join the Church are literal descendants of one of the tribes of Israel and most missionary efforts specifically directed at Jewish populations have been cancelled. Specifically, when I was a graduate student at UCLA in the 1960s, our Mormon student group had regular social and religious exchanges with our Jewish counterparts. Also at that time, special missionary lessons had been developed for Jews and a highly-praised, touring Mormon youth Israeli dance group was created. However, it was not many years before the dance group was dissolved by Church leaders and special conversion efforts to Jews were abandoned. And though the Church received permission to build a BYU educational center on the Mount of Olives in Jerusalem, as mentioned earlier, Church leaders made the extraordinary promise to send home any faculty member or student who talks to a Jew about the LDS religion even if asked a specific religious question. This is especially remarkable, since, as stated earlier, every LDS member is constantly encouraged to "be a missionary." The pro-Palestinian, anti-Israeli outcome of this policy became clear to me in the comments I heard when I attended a social gathering of BYU faculty members who had taught at the Center where most of the local staff was Palestinian. Also, relations between the Church and certain Jewish groups worsened when the Jews learned that Mormons were performing proxy baptisms for Holocaust victims. And though Church leaders promised to stop this practice, this controversy is unlikely to completely stop since members having Jewish ancestors are not stopped from having proxy baptisms performed for them even if they or close family members were Holocaust victims.

Further adding to the difficulty of performing these proxy baptisms and other "sealing ordinances" (LDS)[2] is the recent directive from the Vatican to all Catholic Parishes to prevent the Mormons from having access to church genealogical records to prevent them from performing proxy baptisms for dead Catholics. Here, not only Mormons are affected by this reaction to a "core" religious practice that is unlikely to ever change, but all others who for whatever reason are seeking to identify their dead ancestors since the genealogical records of the Mormon Church are often used more by non-members than members.

Another "victim" of a reaction to a "core" Mormon belief is the Democratic Party. Thus, although in past years many members of the Church and their elected officials were Democrats, as the promotion of gay rights became a firm part of the party platform, this, even more than the feminism and pro-abortion rights agenda, has turned most Mormons against the party especially in Utah where gays and other vocal opponents of the Church increased their control over those selected as Democratic candidates for local or state elected offices. This is especially seen in Salt Lake City where, as many Mormon families fled to its nearby suburbs north and south, elected officials, running as Democrats, have become increasingly "gay friendly." The irony of this is that in many ways, Mormon scriptures and its massive welfare program are much more compatible with the goal of Democrats to reduce the increasing wealth gap between the super rich and the average or poorer American. For example, in the Book of Mormon, we read that, following the post-crucifixion visit of Jesus Christ to the Americas, in the land:

> [Verse 2] … there were no contentions and disputations among [the people] and every man did deal justly one with another.
> [Verse 3] And they had all things in common among them; therefore there were not rich and poor, bond and free, but they were all made free, and partakers of the heavenly gift. (Book of Mormon, 4 Nephi 1: Verses 2,3.)

The Mormon Church, militant Muslim sects, Jehovah's Witnesses, the FLDS and other religions whose members believe their leaders are divinely inspired often face potentially dangerous threats to their continued ultra-adaptability when non-believers seek to curtail or eliminate certain cherished beliefs and practices. One possible solution to these outside pressures was seen in an earlier chapter when the rationale for denying "the Priesthood" (LDS) to blacks was completely rejected by "divine revelation" (LDS) to the Church's Prophet even though many skeptics suggest that such factors as the many demonstrations against BYU sports teams or the difficulty of tracing the ancestry of mixed race converts in such places as Brazil had a major influence on this momentous decision. However, as I stated earlier, I strongly doubt that such a "revelation" giving gay LDS members "full equality" in the Church will ever be received even if the gay lobby ultimately wins the "marriage" battle and/or the Church experiences many "black box" defections and such negative sanctions as losing its tax exempt status.

However, in sharp contrast to the Mormon Church and militant Muslims, both of which are unlikely to compromise on the most strongly held, supernaturally-sanctioned "core" beliefs, are those systems such as Phelps Dodge and other corporations which remain ultra-adaptable by changing the assets they control and the products they produce. "Core beliefs" of such companies can suddenly and easily change as unprofitable products and assets (including skilled "black box" workers) are abandoned. Money, which long ago increasingly replaced the direct exchange of goods and services between individuals as human population densities grew, has often become a "curse" for the average individual "black box" since it always makes it easier for certain individuals, organizations, and countries to prosper at the expense of others. Thus, even before the rise of gas prices to over $4.00 a gallon in 2008 which has fueled such things as the more than $ 1 trillion of construction projects in the Dubai and other nearby Persian Gulf states (Whitelaw 2008:33-36, 38-39), for many years now, the inflation-adjusted income gap between the average worker in America and company CEOs and other "super-rich" individuals has dramatically increased. However, as was seen in the earlier chapters of this book, such increasing inequalities in wealth distribution often lead to bitter conflicts between the "haves" and the "have-nots" that the "haves" do not always win. This is especially true when the "have-nots" out-reproduce the "haves" as was pointed out in my 1971 paper (Stucki 1971) on the rising political and economic power of the Navajos in Arizona, New Mexico, and Utah. Thus as Navajos because of their fast rising numbers both on the reservation and in nearby border towns have begun to outnumber other voters in counties often originally gerrymandered (especially in Arizona) to minimize their voting power, angry border town residents frequently now complain when elected Navajo officials increase off-reservation property taxes to fund reservation schools, roads, and chapter houses on the reservation where property taxes are not levied.

A few years ago this led to a so-far unsuccessful attempt in Northern Arizona to redraw county lines to remove non-property tax paying reservation voters and recently caused one irate New Mexican to suggest that:

> Native nations are not part of New Mexico and Natives living on the reservations should not be allowed to vote in New Mexico, "nor be represented in New Mexico state and local government." (Yurth 2009:A1).

As stated earlier, Israelis fear being outbred by internal and external "have-not" Arab populations as does a "group of an estimated 10,000 believers [which] is attempting to reverse American Christianity's declining birthrate by shunning all contraception, in obedience to Psalm 127…." (News of the Weird 2009:A2). Thus, one spokesperson for the group states that in her own church the mothers have an average of 8.5 children adding that:

> The womb is such a powerful weapon … against the enemy. …The more children I have, the more ability I have to impact the world for God. (News of the Weird 2009:A2)

Although the writers of the "News of the Weird" column apparently found this story amusing, I seriously doubt that Muslims, Jews, Mormons, and Navajos would fail to underestimate the importance of its Darwinian message.

Finally, perhaps one of the best examples of an "eternal" ultra-adaptable system is the "March of Dimes". Thus as Henslin (2007:182) states:

> The March of Dimes was founded by President Franklin Roosevelt in the 1930s to fight polio. When a vaccine for polio was developed in the 1950s, the organization did not declare victory and disband. Instead, its leaders kept the organization intact by creating new goals – fighting birth defects....
>
> [Now] "Fighting birth defects" has been replaced by an even vaguer goal, "Breakthroughs for Babies." This new goal displacement may guarantee the organization's existence forever, for it is a goal so elusive it can never be reached,

Chapter Notes

1. Although this explanation has been officially rejected by Church leaders, it has been hard for many members to completely give it up.
2. Husbands and wives are "sealed" (LDS) to each other in an "eternal marriage bond" (LDS) and to their children.

Corrected Fall 1967 American Indian Census Data for Ajo, Arizona

(See Chapter 3, Chapter Note 2). Persons temporarily out of town during the strike have also been included in this count as if they were all in the Ajo area while the census was taken.

Key to Tables V through XV

First Letter

F = "full"   T = "three-quarters"

H = "half"   Q = "quarter"

N = "non-Papago"

Second Letter

P = "Papago"

I = member of an Indian tribe

N = "non-Indian" (but associated with at least one "Indian" in the same family)

Third Letter

M = "miner" (i.e., company employee)

W = "housewife"

S = "student"

C = "child below school age"

U = "unemployed adult, on welfare, pension, Social Security or obtaining support from parent(s) or relative(s)"

O = "steady employment at job other than for the company"

H = "female head of household" (unmarried, separated or divorced)

D = "female head of household--widowed"

A = "away at school"

L = "away in the military service"

Fourth or More Letter

(M) = "ex-miner"

(O) = "other" (See Third Letter "U")

(G) = "employed at the door factory in Gila Bend"

(F) = "farm laborer"

(D)="unmarried older daughter who is not attending school but who is still living with parent(s)"

(S) = "unmarried older son who is not attending school but who is still living with parent(s)"

(B) = "full time babysitter"

(I) = "kindergarten teacher"

(K) = "does housework in Ajo"

(N) = "nurse's aide in Ajo Hospital"

(U) = "Public Health Service survey interviewer in Gila Bend"

(V) = "in government training program to become a diamond cutter"

(R) = "does ranch work and odd jobs"

(T) = "hauls trash"

(E) = "works at radar base"

(P) = "operates heavy equipment for Pima County"

(A) = "bartender"

(L) = "motel housemaid"

TABLE V. - Fall 1967 census data for Ajo Indian Village in terms of fraction Papago "blood"

						Totals
FPM = 55	TPM = 1	HPM[1] = 3		NIM = 6		65
FPW = 61		HPW = 2	QPW = 1	NIW = 3		67
FPS = 127	TPS = 10	HPS = 6	QPS = 1	NIS = 7	NNS = 2	153
FPC = 54	TPC = 12	HPC = 13		NIC = 3		82
FPU(M) = 9		HPU(M) = 1				10
FPU(O) = 1		HPU(O) = 1				2
FPO(G) = 1						1
FPO(F) = 1						1
FPH = 10		HPH = 1				11
FPD = 9					NND = 2	11
FPU(D) = 7	TPU(D) = 2	HPU(D) = 2				11
FPU (S) = 11	TPU(S) = 2	HPU(S) = 2				15
FPO(D)[2] = 4						4
FPO(S)[3] = 1				NIO(S)[4]= 1		2
FPU(B) = 1						1
SubTotals 352	27	31	2	20	4	436
FPA = 34		HPA = 2		NIA = 2		38
FPL = 8						8
Totals 394	27	33	2	22	4	482

Additional Fourth Letter Kinship and Occupation Notes

1. Includes one (S)

2. Occupations = (I, I, K, N)

3. Occupation = (U)

4. Occupation = (V)

TABLE VI. - Fall 1967 census data for Ajo Indian Village in terms of fraction Indian "blood" from Papago and all other tribes

					Totals
FIM[1] = 64	TIM = 1				65
FIW = 66	TIW = 1				67
FIS = 145	TIS = 2	HIS = 4	NNS = 2		153
FIC = 74	TIC = 3	HIC = 5			82
FIU(M) = 10					10
FIU(O) = 1		HIU (0) = 1			2
FIO(G) = 1					1
FIO(F) = 1					1
FIH = 10		HIH = 1			11
FID = 9			NND = 2		11
FIU(D) = 11					11
FIU (S) = 14		HIU(S) = 1			15
FIO(D)[2] = 4					4
FIO(S)[3] = 2					2
FIU(B) = 1					1
Subtotals 413	7	12	4	436	
FIA = 38					38
FIL = 8					8
Totals 459	7	12	4	482	

Additional Fourth Letter Kinship and Occupation Notes

1. Includes one (S)

2. Occupations = (I, I, K, N)

3. Occupation = (U, V)

TABLE VII. - Fall 1967 census data for upper (New) Mexican town in terms of fraction Papago "blood"

					Totals
FPW* = 14			NIM = 6		20
FPW = 13		HPW = 1	NIW = 4	NNW = 3	21
FPS = 29	TPS = 1	HPS = 12	NIS = 6	NNS = 2	50
FPC = 5		HPC = 10	NIC = 2		17
FPU(D) = 1					1
			NIU(S) = 1		1
Subtotals 62	1	23	19	5	110
FPA = 1		HPA = 1			2
			NIL = 1		1
Totals 63	1	24	20	5	113

*includes a miner who had a serious stroke shortly after the strike began and later died

TABLE VIII. Fall 1967 census data for upper (new) Mexican town in terms of fraction total
      Indian "blood"

			Totals
FIM* = 20			20
FIW = 18		NNW = 3	21
FIS = 38	HIS = 10	NNS = 2	50
FIC = 14	HIC = 3		17
FIU(D) =			
FIU (S) =			
Subtotals 92	13	5	110
FIA = 1	HIA = 1		2
FIL = 1			1
Totals 94	14	5	113

* includes a miner who had a serious stroke shortly after the strike began and later died

TABLE IX. - Fall 1967 census data for lower (old) Mexican town in terms of fraction Papago "blood"

						Totals
FPM = 4		HPM = 3	QPM = 1	NIM = 2	NNM = 3	13
FPW = 8	TPW = 1	HPW = 2	QPW= 2		NNW = 2	15
FPS = 7	TPS = 12	HPS = 9	QPS = 9			37
FPC = 3	TPC = 7	HPC = 4	QPC= 2			16
FPU(M)= 2						2
					NNU(O) = 1	1
		HPO(G) = 2	QPO(G)*= 1		NNO(G) = 1	4
FPO(F) = 1						1
					NNH = 1	1
FPD = 7						7
FPU(D)= 2						2
Subtotals 34	20	20	15	2	8	99
FPA = 1						1
Totals 35	20	20	15	2	8	100

Fourth Letter Kinship Note

* (S)

TABLE X. - Fall 1967 census for lower (old) Mexican Town in terms of fraction total Indian "blood"

					Totals
FIM = 5		HIM = 3	QIM = 2	NNM = 3	13
FIW = 8	TIW = 1	HIW = 2	QIWF = 2	NNW = 2	15
FIS = 8	TIS = 17	HIS = 6	QIS = 6		37
FIC = 3	TIC = 8	HIC = 4	QIC = 1		16
FIU(M) = 2					2
				NNU(O) = 1	1
		HIO(G) = 2	QIO(G)*= 1	NNO(G) = 1	4
FIO (F) = 1				NNH = 1	2
FID = 7					7
FIU(D) = 2					2
Subtotals 36	26	17	12	8	99
FIA = 1					
Total 37	26	17	12	8	100

Fourth Letter Kinship Note

* (S)

- 458 -

TABLE XI. - Fall 1967 census for "integrated" Ajo (the main "white" part of town and its partially integrated suburbs (e.g., Gibson) in terms of fraction Papago "blood"

						Totals
FPM[1] = 7		HPM = 5		NIM = 4	NNM = 5	21
FPW = 8	TPW = 4	HPW = 5	QPW = 3	NIW = 4	NIW = 1	25
FPS = 14	TPS = 8	HPS = 15	QPS = 10	NIS = 7	NNS = 1	55
FPC = 11	TPC = 1	HPC = 8	QPC = 12	NIC = 3		35
FPU(O) = 1		HPU(0)= 3		NIU(O)= 1		5
		HPO(G)= 1				1
		HPO(R)[2]= 2	QPO(R)[3]= 1		NNO(E)[4] = 4	7
FPH = 2			QPH = 1	NIH = 1		4
FPD = 1		HPD = 1	QPD = 1		NND = 1	4
FPU(D) = 2	TPU(D)= 2		QPU(D) = 1			5
			QPU(S)= 1			
Subtotals 46	15	40	30	21	11	163
FPA = 1	TPA = 4	HPA = 3	QPA = 2	NIA = 2		12
	TPL = 1		QPL = 1			2
Totals 47	20	43	33	23	11	177

Additional Fourth Letter Kinship and Occupation Notes

1. Includes one (S)

2. Occupation = (T)

3. Also (S)

4. Occupations = (P,R,A)

TABLE XII. - Fall 1967 census for "integrated" Ajo (the main "white" part of town and its partially integrated suburbs (e.g., Gibson) in terms of fraction total Indian "blood"

					Totals
FIM[1] = 10	TIM = 1	HIM = 5		NNM = 5	21
FIW = 11	TIW = 4	HIW = 7	QIW = 2	NIW = 1	25
FIS = 28	TIS = 15	HIS = 4	QIS = 7	NNS = 1	55
FIC = 12	TIC = 2	HIC = 8	QIC = 13		35
FIU(O) = 1	TIU(O)= 1	HIU(0)= 3			5
		HIO(G)= 1			1
	TIO(R)[2]= 2		QIO(R)[3]= 1	NNO(E)[4] = 4	7
FIH = 3			QIH = 1		4
FID = 3		HID = 1			4
FIU(D) = 2	TIU(D)= 3				5
	TIU(S)= 1				1
Subtotals 70	29	29	24	11	163
FIA = 2	TIA = 5	HIA = 4	QIA = 1		12
	TIL = 2				2
Totals 72	36	33	25	11	177

Additional Fourth Letter Kinship and Occupation Notes

1. Includes one (S)
2. Occupation = (T)
3. Also (S)
4. Occupations = (P,R,A)

TABLE XIII. - Fall 1967 census for "rural" Ajo (Childs Ranch, Darby Wells, etc.) in terms of fraction Papago "blood"

					Totals
		HPM = 2			2
FPW = 1	TPW = 1	HPW = 2			4
FPS = 4	TPS = 3	HPS = 4	QPS = 6		17
			QPC = 4		4
FPU(O)= 1	TPU(O) = 1				2
FPO(R)= 1		HPO(R)= 1		NIO(P) = 1	3
		HPH = 1			1
FPD = 1					1
	TPU(D) = 1	HPU(D)=1	QPU (D)=1		3
FPU(S)= 1	TPU (S) = 2	HPU (S)=1	QPU(S) = 1		5
	TPO(D)¹ =1		QPO(D)²=1		2
Subtotals 9	9	12	13	1	44
			QPA = 1		1
Totals 9	9	12	14	1	45

Additional Fourth Letter Occupation Notes

1. Occupation = (K)

2. Occupations = (L)

TABLE XIV. - Fall 1967 census for "rural" Ajo (Childs Ranch, Darby Wells, etc.) in terms of fraction total Indian "blood"

					Totals
		HIM = 2			2
FIW = 1	TIW = 1	HIW = 2			4
FIS = 4	TIS = 4	HIS = 9			17
	TIC = 1	HIC = 2	QIC = 1		4
FIU(O)= 1	TIU(O) = 1				2
FIO(R)= 1		HIO(R, P) = 2			3
		HIH = 1			1
FID = 1					1
	TIU(D) = 1	HIU(D)= 2			3
FIU(S)= 1	TIU(S) = 2	HIU(S)= 2			5
	TIO(D)[1] =1	HIO(D)[2]= 1			2
Subtotals 9	9	12	13	1	44
			QIA = 1		1
Totals 9	9	12	14	1	45

Additional Fourth Letter Occupation Notes

1. Occupation = (K)

2. Occupation = (L)

TABLE XV. - Total number of Ajo Indians (and associated non-Indians)

	Indians In town	Indians away to school	Indians in military service	Associated non-Indians	Totals
Indian Village	432	38	8	4	482
Upper Mexican Town	105	2	1	5	113
Lower Mexican Town	91	1	0	8	100
"Integrated" Ajo	152	12	2	11	177
"Rural" Ajo	44	1	0	0	45
Totals	824	54	11	28	917

APPENDIX A:

CONSTITUTION AND BYLAWS OF THE AJO INDIAN COMMUNITY

PREAMBLE

We, the people of the Ajo Indian Community, in order to show our gratitude to almighty GOD, and to preserve in ourselves the Rights of self-government and to provide a means for the orderly transaction of community business and the free expression of the community will, do ordain and establish this Constitution and Bylaws for the Government of the People of this Village, hence forth to be known as the AJO Indian Community.

ARTICLE I - TERMS

Section 1 - For the convenience of brevity and unless otherwise specified, the following terms will be construed to have the meaning set forth in this paragraph:

A. Community - AJO Indian Community.

B. Council - Inter-tribal Community Council.

C. Manager - Manager of the Phelps Dodge Corporation, New Cornelia Branch, under which the community is placed for administrative purposes or his successor in office.

D. Chairman - Chairman of the inter-tribal community council.

E. Vice-chairman - Vice-chairman of the inter-tribal community council.

F. Treasurer - Treasurer of the inter-tribal community council.

G. Councilman - Male or Female member of the community council.

ARTICLE II - JURISDICTION

The jurisdiction of the community shall extend to all lands now comprised within the area of the Indian Village, and hereafter any land that may be acquired from the Company for the use and benefit of the community.

ARTICLE III - MEMBERSHIP

Section 1 - The membership of the community shall be determined as follows:

A. All persons of Indian blood who live in the Indian Village or in the townsites around the Phelps Dodge Corporation area shall be designated for membership.

B. All children of the members shall be entitled to membership if they are at least one-fourth Indian blood.

The Council shall have the authority to prescribe Rules in compiling a membership in accordance with provisions of this Article. The Council shall also have power to enact ordinances subject to review of the Manager governing present and future membership, loss of membership, and the adoption of members by the community.

ARTICLE IV - RIGHTS OF MEMBERS

All political power is inherent in the people. Governments derive their just powers from the consent of the governed and are thus established to protect and maintain individual rights. A frequent recurrence to fundamental principles is essential to the security of the individual rights and the perpetuity of the free government.

1.   No person shall be deprived of life, liberty, or property without due process of law.

2.   The right of petition and of people to assemble peaceably shall never be abridged.

3.   Every person may freely speak, write, and publish on all subjects - being responsible for the abuse of that right.

4.   No person shall be disturbed in his private affairs or shall his home be invaded without proper authority of the law.

5.   Justice in all cases shall be administered openly and without delay.

6.   All elections shall be free and equal. No power shall at anytime interfere to prevent the free exercise of the Right of Suffrage.

7.   Freedom of Religion or Conscience shall not be abridged.

ARTICLE V - GOVERNING BODY

Section 1 - The governing body of the community shall be known as the Inter-tribal Community Council. It shall consist of_____ members who shall be elected by the qualified voters of the community.

Section 2 - Each tribe shall be represented by ONE or MORE council men relative to the number in a tribe.

Section 3 - The Chairman or in his absence the Vice-chairman will be the presiding officer of the council. He shall take part in all discussions.

Section 4 - No person shall be elected or hold office unless he has reached the age of 21 and be of One-fourth Indian blood.

ARTICLE VI - POWERS OF THE COUNCIL

Section 1 - The council shall exercise the following powers which are subjected to any limitations impressed by the Company and subjected further to all expressed restrictions upon such powers as contained in this constitution.

1. To negotiate with the Manager and Company on behalf of the community.

2. To act for and on behalf of members of the community at the request of such members.

3. To provide for the manner of conducting elections.

4. To promote and protect the health, peace, morals, company property, and general welfare of the community and its members.

5. To help provide for law and order at all community and social gatherings.

6. To provide by ordinance for removal or exclusion from the territory of the community members and presently inducted members of those whose presence may be injurious to the peace, health, or welfare of the community and company property.

APPENDIX B:

TWO "COURT" HEARINGS

The "homey" type of "court" proceedings administered in the Indian Village is vividly illustrated by the following two hearings (Hearing September 24, 1964; Hearing October 28, 1964), the first involving a relatively minor offense and the second, what would normally be considered to be a major crime in the average American community (All names have been changed but all other wording in these hearings is exactly as it was recorded by the Indian who recorded the sequence of events in these "court" proceedings as they occurred):

1. Hearing, September 24, 1964, Thursday 6:10 p.m. Defendant - Charles Worsley

Jack Andrews (the council chairman): "On the night of September 17 at about 2:00 a.m. you were driving reckless in the Indian Village. You were driving a white 1959 Impala Chevrolet with red interior."

Charles: "I was not driving a gray car at that time."

Jack: "You were seen driving this car by him (indicating Jim Nelson who saw him that night) and someone else phoned Jed Joseph (the village policeman) complaining about your driving. We also found out from the police that the car belonged to your father and we know that your father would not be driving around in the Indian Village at that time of night."

Jack then went on to advise the offender (about) the reason for this hearing: "We are here not because we want to be mean to you but rather to try to help you."

Jim: "Do you admit that you were driving around the Indian Village at a reckless speed?"

Charles: "Yes, I admit it."

Jim: "I am glad that you are willing to tell the truth: otherwise if you had tried to lie, it would go in your record against you."

Jim explained to the boy about the danger that is present when some one is driving at that speed around the Village.

He told the boy to give this thing serious thought when he went from this hearing. Charles said he would.

The hearing adjourned at this time.

2. Hearing, October 28, 1964, 5:30 p.m.

Cindy Viril was walking home from the Joseph Jennings home to her home which is diagonally across the street about five houses when two boys, Sol Brainard and James Cleo, Jr. approached her and said they were going to walk her home. Instead of walking her home they grabbed her and started dragging her past her home toward the dead end of the street and the arroyo which is about 50 yards from her home. Some smaller children who were playing in the streets saw what was happening and ran and told Cleo's mother. Cindy's older brother came and scared the two boys away but he knew who they were.

Jack asked the boy what he had in mind when he was doing this thing. Sol said he had nothing in mind.

Jack said, "you must have (had) something in mind and we are going to look in the Arizona Code and see what is the penalty for what you had in mind."

Sol admitted that he had done this thing with James Cleo, Jr.

Jack talked to the boy about the seriousness of the offense of which he was accused. He (Jack) read from the Arizona Code (that) the penalty for this offense would be 10 to 15 years.

"We are only helping you when we call you so that you will know that it does not pay to do these things. It is also not good because you now have a record here in the files and if anything like that ever happens again you would probably be the first to be suspected even though you would have (had) nothing to do with it."

Jim spoke to him about thinking clean thoughts and the many things that (are) good for a boy of his age (to) think about and (that he should) not be thinking about doing the thing (of) which he was accused.

APPENDIX C:

THE SURVEY FORM

(**If the person had trouble** understanding a question, then it was usually rephrased. On several questions especially those soliciting sociometric data, answers were difficult to obtain and some reworking of this survey form is needed before being used again. Other minor flaws also appeared quickly in this questionnaire necessitating some oral modification in the way certain questions were asked although fairly complete forms were obtained from all those interviewed. In the actual form used, there were often longer blank spaces for many answers)

Answers to the following questions will be kept strictly confidential. Your name will not be used in any publication of the results. We are only interested in seeing why so many of the Papago people (and members of other tribes) have come to Ajo and why they continue to stay here. Also we are interested in how you are getting along here. We would be very happy to hear any additional comments you have about your life in Ajo. In return for your time and cooperation in this survey we have arranged for a small payment of $2.00 (to be paid in cash or in books) to be given you upon completion of the survey form. This survey is being conducted under the authorization of Dr. Robert A. Hackenberg of the University of Colorado. If you have any further questions about this survey, please contact Larry R. Stucki - 1211 Kilbright Avenue, Ajo.

If the head of the house does not work at the mine go directly to question 7.

1. Have you (has your husband) stayed in Ajo all the time since the strike began last July? (Did you (your husband) stay in Ajo all the time during the strike?)

If yes:

1A. Have you (has your husband) ever thought about leaving Ajo during the strike? (Did you (your husband) ever think about leaving Ajo during the strike?)

If no, go to question 2.
If yes:
Why have you (has your husband) stayed here? (Why did you (your husband) stay in Ajo?)

Go to question 2.

If no:

1B. Have you (has your husband) left Ajo more than once during the strike? (Did you (your husband) leave Ajo more than once during the strike?) (If yes, give the details of each stay away.)

1C. Where did you (your husband) go?

1D.   When did you (he) go?

_____

1E.   Who went with you (him)? (wife, (you), family, friends, other relatives, etc.)

1F.   How long did you (he) stay?

1G.   Did you (he) live with relatives? (If yes, give relation ship.)

1H.   Did you (your husband) try to get another job there?

If no, go to question 1I.
If yes:
Did you (your husband) get another job there?

_____

If no, what kind of work were you (was he) looking for?

If yes, what kind of work did you (he) get?

_____

1I.   Did your wife (you) or your children want to stay in Ajo during the strike?

If no, go to question 1I3.
If yes:
1I1. Who wanted to stay in Ajo?

_____

1I2.   Why did they (she) (you) want to stay?

1I3.　　Did they (she) (you) stay in Ajo?

_____

If yes, go to question 2.

If there are no school-age children in the family skip to question 2.

1I4.　　Did your wife (you) or your children return to Ajo to start school in September?

If no:
1I4A.　Which school did your children attend during the fall and winter?

If yes:
1I4B.　Who came back?

_____

1I4C.　Where did they (you) stay?

_____

2.　Did you (your husband) find part-time work in Ajo during the strike?

If no, go to question 3.
If yes:
2A.　　What kind of work?

_____

2B.　　How long did it last?

_____

3.　During the strike did you (your husband) make short visits to other places?

If no, go to question 4.

If yes:

3A.   Where did you (your husband) go?

_____

3B.   How often did you (he) go?

_____

3C.   Why did you (he) go?

3D.   Who went with you (him)?

_____

(Give the approximate period during which these visits were made.)

4. Did you (your husband) go with the men to fight fires this last summer?

5. Did you (your husband) do any work for the church or community during the strike? (e.g., help build the path for the school children)

6. Had you (your husband) ever seriously thought about leaving Ajo before the strike began, to look for work someplace else?

If no, go to question 7.

If yes:

6A.   Had you (your husband) ever actually left Ajo before this strike began?

If yes, go to question 6B.

If no, what held you (him) back?

Go directly to question 7.

6B.   Where did you (your husband) go?

_____

6C.   When did you (he) go?

_____

(Give the approximate year and season of the year)

6D.   How long did you (he) stay there?

_____

6E.   Why did you (he) go?

6F.   Did your wife (you) and your children want to go too?

If yes, go to question 6G.
If no, why did they (you) want to stay in Ajo?

6G.   Did they (you) leave Ajo to live with you (your husband)?

If no, go to question 6H.
If yes:
6G1.   Did your wife (you) and your children stay for a while in Ajo before leaving to join you (your husband)?

6G2.   Did they (you) return to Ajo before you (your husband) did?

If no, go to question 6H.
If yes, why did they come back early?

6H.   Why did you (your husband) return to Ajo?

The following question refers to the time in Ajo before the strike began.

7. When you have (your husband has) days off from work or vacations
(when you leave Ajo for short visits to other places) where do you (does he) usually go? (If the answer to this is to the reservation, record the village or villages visited and go directly to question 8B.)

8. Have you (has your husband) ever visited the reservation while you have (he has) lived in Ajo?

   If no, go to question 9.
   If yes:
   8A.   What village or villages do you (does he) visit?

   8B.   How often do you (does he) go to the reservation?

   8C.   Who goes with you (him)?
   _____

   8D.   Do you (does he) have your (his) own home on the reservation or do you (does he) stay with friends or relatives? (If relatives, give relationship.)

   8E.   Do you (does he) own any cattle or horses on the reservation? (If yes, how many of each do you (does he) own?)

8F. Do you (does he) have fields that you (he) still farm (farms)?

8G. Do you (does he) return for village fiestas and ceremonies?

8H. Do you (does he) return for deaths of relatives or marriages or births of children?

8I. When you are (he is) on the reservation do you (does he) speak English most of the time or Papago (Pima, etc.)?

_____

8J. When you visit (he visits) the reservation do you (does he) talk most about things happening in Ajo and other off-reservation places or do you (does he) talk most about what has happened on the reservation?

8K. Do you (does he) still collect cactus' fruit or other wild plants?

8L. Do you (does he) visit any relatives on the reservation? (Name them.) (e.g., brother, sister, parent, children, in-laws)

8M. What did you (he) talk about most on your (his) last few trips to the reservation?

8N. When you return (he returns) to the reservation do you (does he) take gifts for any of the people there? (If so, what kind?)

8O.   Have you (has he) gone to the reservation more often, less often, or about the same in the last few years as compared to when you (he) first came to Ajo?

8P.   Have you (has he) ever voted in district elections on the reservation while you have (he has) lived in Ajo? (If yes, which district and when?)

9.   Do you (does he) ever give or send money to friends or relatives on the reservation? (If yes, to whom?)

10. Does your wife (do you) or do any of your children ever return to the reservation without you (your husband)?

If no, go to question 11.
If yes:
10A.   Who goes?

_____

10B.   Why do they (you) (does she) go?

10C.   Where do they (you) (does she) stay?

_____

10D.   How long do they (you)(does she) stay?

_____

10E.   How often do they (you)(does she) go?

_____

10F.   What season or seasons of the year do they (you)(does she) go? (summer, fall, winter, spring)

10G.   Have they (you)(has she) gone to the reservation without you (your husband) more often, less often, or about the same in the last few years as compared to when you first lived in Ajo?

11. Have you or your wife (your husband) or your children ever returned to the reservation for medical care while you have lived in Ajo? (If yes, give approximate date or dates.)

12. Have you or your wife (your husband) or your children ever been treated by a medicine man? (If yes, was this before or after coming to Ajo?)

13. Do you (does your husband) usually read a daily newspaper?

_____

Ajo Copper News?

_____

14. Do you (or your husband) subscribe to or buy any magazines? (Name them.)

15. Do you (does your husband) ever watch news broadcasts on T.V. or listen to them on the radio? (If yes, how often?)

16. Do you (or your husband) subscribe to or buy the "Papago Bulletin" or the "Papago Indian News" or any other Indian newspaper or bulletin?

If head is a non-Papago skip to question 18.

17. Would you or your wife (husband) like to have a voting representative from Ajo on the Papago Tribal Council? (If yes, what do you feel that you could gain by this as an individual or group?)

18. Do you and your wife (husband) speak mostly English or mostly Papago (Pima, Spanish, etc.) to your children at home?

19. Have you or your wife (husband) ever told your children much about the reservation?

20. Have you or your wife (husband) ever taught any of your children any of the old Indian songs or dances or any skill such as basket weaving or making pottery?

21. Where were you (was your husband) born?

_____

22. Where were you (was he) raised as a young child?

23. Where were you (was he) when you were (he was) a teenager? (If answer is Ajo, skip to question 34)

24. When did you (your husband) first come to Ajo?

_____

25. What village or city did you (your husband) leave when you (he) first moved to Ajo?

26. Why did you (he) decide to leave there? (If the answer is to live with husband or to get married, skip to question 32.)

27. Did you (he) have a job there? (If yes, why did you (he) leave it?)

28. Where did you (he) hear about the work opportunities in Ajo? (Who told you (him)?)

29. Did you (he) have relatives or friends in Ajo when you (he) first came here? (Name them.)

30. Whom did you (he) stay with when you (he) first came to Ajo?

31. Were you (was he) married when you (he) first came to Ajo?

_____

32. Did you (he) come by yourself (himself) to Ajo? (If no, who came with you (him)?) (e.g., wife, children, friend, other relative)

33. After you (he) had lived in Ajo for a~hile, did you (he) send for -~anyone back home to come to live with you (him)? (e.g., wife, child ren, parent, other relative, friend)

34. Where did you meet your wife (husband)?

_____

35. If any of your children are married where did they meet their husbands or wives? (Give name of child and the husband or wife and indicate the tribe or race of the husband or wife).

36. List the jobs you have (your husband has) held in Ajo and the years you (he) worked at each one. (Give job titles for work for the company.)

37. Has your wife (have you) or any of your children ever worked in Ajo? (If yes, give names and list jobs and years worked at each.)

38. What do you (does your husband) like most about Ajo?

39 What does your wife (do you) like most?

_____

40. What do your children like most?

_____

41. What do you (does your husband) dislike most about Ajo?

42. What does your wife (do you) dislike most?

_____

43. What do your children dislike most?

_____

44. Where do you plan to go when you retire (your husband retires)?

45. Why do you (does he) plan to go there?

46. What schools have you (has your husband) attended?

47. Did you (he) graduate from high school or college?

_____

48. Do you feel that the Ajo public schools are better than BIA. schools? (Why?)

49. Have you ever thought about sending your children to the Immaculate Conception School in Ajo?

50. Do you have any idea why most Indian children do not attend the Immaculate Conception School in Ajo?

51. Do you feel that children get a better education in the Ajo public schools than in mission or church schools?

52. Do you or your wife (husband) participate actively in any community or church activities? (Name them.)

53. Do you or your wife (husband) attend community meetings called by the village council? (If yes, how often?)

54. Do you or your wife (husband) attend the St. Catherine's Day fiesta in the village in May?

55. Do you or your wife (husband) help out with the food or ceremony?

56. Do you or your wife (husband) play Bingo on Monday nights? (If yes, how often?)

57. Did you and your wife (husband) and children attend the community Christmas program this year?

58. Have all of you attended in past years?

---

59. Did your children attend the Christmas party at the Immaculate Conception Church or other union parties this year? (If other parties, name them.)

60. Do you or your wife (husband) or children take part in sporting activities at the present time? (e.g., swimming, bowling, baseball, football, basketball, track) (If yes, give name and activity.)

61. Have you or your wife (husband) or children ever participated in other sporting activities in past years? (If yes, give name, activity, and year or years.)

62. List all the organizations (voluntary associations) to which you or your wife (husband) or children belong. (Boy Scouts, Girl Scouts, Parents' Club, P.T.A., Elk, Moose, Lions' Club, Masons, Village Council, etc.)

63. Are there any organizations to which you or your wife (husband) or children belonged in past years but not now?

If head is not a miner skip to question 72.
64. Do you (does your husband) feel that you have (he has) enough time off from work with the 26 day-on-2 day-off work schedule?

If yes, go to question 65.
If no:
64A.　What work schedule would you (he) prefer?

64B.　What would you (he) do with the extra time off?

65.　What do your wife (you) and your children feel about this work schedule?

66.　Do you (does your husband) belong to a union? (If yes, write name of union.)

67.　What are your feelings about the strike?

68.	What are the feelings of your wife (husband) about the strike?

69.	Do (does, did) you (your husband) receive strike benefits from the union?

If no, go to question 70.
If yes:
69A.	Is (was) this in the form of credit at the Shopper's Market or do (did) they pay you (your husband) in cash?

69B.	How much do (did) they pay you (him) each week?

_____

70. Do (did) you receive any welfare aid or government surplus food during the strike?

71. List the names of those people whom you talk (he talks) to most at work.

72. Who are the most influential (most important) non-Indians in the community? (Name them and tell why each one is so important.)

73. Who are the most influential (most important) Indians in the community? (Name them and tell why each one is so important.)

74. List the names of those people whom you visit most during your free time? (Are they mostly relatives of yours?)

75. List the names of those people that your wife (husband) spends most of her (his) free time with.

76. List the names of the best friends of your older children.

77. When you or your wife (husband) need advice about a problem, whom do you usually go to?

If head lives outside of the Indian village skip to question 79.
78. Have you and your wife (husband) ever thought about moving out of Indian Village? (If yes, why have you stayed?)

Skip to question 81.
79. Why did you and your wife (husband) decide to live outside of the Indian Village?

80. Do you and your wife (husband) own your own home?

81. Are you and your wife (husband) planning to buy a home in Ajo in the future sometime?

82. What other houses have you and your wife (husband) lived in in Ajo? (Give dates, approximate location, and reasons for moving.)

If head is not a miner, skip to 89.
83. Do you (does your husband) usually get much Christmas Bonus money from the company store? (About how much each year?)

84. Do (did) you use the $35/week credit offered by the company store?

85. Did you use the $25/child credit on "back to school specials" at the company store last September?

86. Do (did) you have enough money each week to pay all your bills?

    If yes, go to question 87.

    If no:

    86A.   Have you had (did you have) any trouble with bill collectors or with letters demanding payment of debts?

    86B.   Have you had (did you have) to borrow money to pay your bills?

87. Were you in debt to anyone before the strike began? (If yes, to whom and about how much?) or did you have any savings?

88. Are you in debt to anyone now? (If yes, to whom and about how much?)

89. Do you and your wife (husband) vote in local or national elections?

90. Did you and your wife (husband vote in the last election for village councilmen? (If no, have you ever voted in the past?)

91. Do you or your wife (husband) feel that there is any discrimination against the Mexican or Indian in Ajo at work, in schools, in stores, or in housing?

    If no, end of survey.

If yes:

91A.   Have you noticed any change in the attitude of white people toward Indians and Mexicans in the years you have lived in Ajo? If yes, what kind of change?)

End of Survey

REFERENCES CITED

"A.R." stands for The Arizona Republic, a daily newspaper published in Phoenix, Arizona.

"A.D.S." stands for The Arizona Daily Star, a daily newspaper published in Tucson, Arizona.

"A.C.N." stands for Aio Copper News, a weekly newspaper published in Ajo, Arizona.

"N.T." stands for Navajo Times, a weekly newspaper published at Window Rock, Arizona, by the Navajo Tribe.

"C.M." stands for the minutes of the council meetings of the Ajo Indian Village Intertribal Council.

"C.M.M." stands for the minutes of the community meetings held by the Ajo Intertribal Council.

"O.M." stands for the minutes of the meetings attended by the officers of the various community sodalities (e.g., Girl Scouts, Parents Club) to work out schedules and solve intergroup problems.

"S.I.", "F.N." and "L.I." are code numbers for a series of interviews held in Ajo during the period July 1967 to June 1968. The names of those interviewed have been withheld for their protection.

"Hearing" stands for the minutes of the semiformal court trials that were staged in the village by the Ajo Intertribal Council.

References to the Mormon Scriptures are from a 1983 combined collection of the King James Bible with LDS headings and Chapter Notes, the Book of Mormon, the Doctrine and Covenants, and the Pearl of Great Price with an appendix that includes a Topical Guide, a Bible Dictionary, a Gazetteer, Maps, and a section containing excerpts from Joseph Smith's revised (i.e., "inspired" (LDS)) translation of certain bible verses. Although Joseph Smith is usually listed as the author of almost all of the Mormon portion of this collection, many mostly minor (but not always) changes have been made through the years in the later printed versions of the material he originally dictated to various scribes. Most of these are attempts by anonymous Church editors and leaders to correct spelling and grammatical errors but some do alter the perceived meaning of certain passages.

Adams, Brooke

2008a   Judge: LDS to watch as FLDS pray? The Salt Lake Tribune April 22:A1, A4.

2008b   LDS Church turns down request to watch over FLDS. The Salt Lake Tribune April 23:A4.

2008c   Pregnant teens: Fact or fiction? The Salt Lake Tribune April 26:A1, A4.

2008d   Gay-unions fight roars on. The Salt Lake Tribune November 6:A1, A4.

2008e   Child abuse, neglect said widespread in FLDS polygamous sect. The Salt Lake Tribune December 24,

2008.   Electronic   document,   http://www.sltrib.com/ci_11299207, accessed January 8, 2009.

Abdollah, Tami and Cara Mia DiMassa

>2008 Foes of California's Proposition 8 widen protest circles. The Salt Lake Tribune November 14:A6.

Addicott, John F.

>1984 Mutualistic Interactions in Population and Community Processes. *In* A New Ecology: Novel Approaches to Interactive Systems. Peter W. Price et al. eds. Pp. 437-455. New York: John Wiley & Sons.

Allen, James B.

>1966 The Company Town in the American West. Norman: University of Oklahoma Press.

Anderson, Duwayne R.

>2003 Farewell to Eden: Coming to terms with Mormonism and Science. (no city given): 1st Books Library.

Anderson, Robert

>1984 The Superorganic and its Environments in White's Science of Culture. Journal of Anthropological Research, Vol. 40, No. 1: 121-128.

Anderson, Harry, Richard Manning, James C. Jones, Howard Fineman, Rich Thomas, Diane Weathers, David Gonzalez, and Peter McAlevey

>1983 The Rise and Fall of Big Labor. Newsweek September 5: 50-54.

Anonymous

>1966 Letter from Parents Club to Village Intertribal Council April 17, 1966). (unpublished)

Arensberg, Conrad M.

>1968 The Urban in Crosscultural Perspective. In Urban Anthropology: Research Perspectives and Strategies, Elizabeth M. Eddy (ed.). Southern Anthropological Society Proceedings, No. 2.

Arizona Daily Citizen (The)
    1901   Article on Thomas Childs, Jr. February 1, 1901, 4:2.
Arizona Daily Star
    1983   Windows Smashed in Morenci; Tension Builds on
            Picket Lines. August 7, 1983.
Arizona Republic
    1983   A Child Lies Wounded. July 29, 1983.
Aronsen, Robert L.
    1961   Labour Commitment among Jamaican Bauxite
            Workers. Social and Economic Studies 10:156-182.
Ashby, W. Ross
    1956   An Introduction to Cybernetics. New York: John
            Wiley and Sons, Inc.
    1960   Design for a Brain. New York: John Wiley and Sons,
            Inc. (Revised Edition).
    1970   Analysis of the System to be Modeled. *In* The Process
            of Model-Building. Ralph M. Stogdill, editor. Ohio
            State University Press.
Arensberg, Conrad M.
    1968   The Urban in Crosscultural Perspective. *In* Urban
            Anthropology: Research Perspectives and Stratagies,
            Elizabeth M. Eddy (ed.) Southern Anthropological
            Society Proceedings, No. 2.
Associated Press, The
    2008a   LDS Church donates to back Proposition 8. The Salt
            Lake Tribune, October 29:B4
    2008b   Catholic bishop OK with LDS support. The Salt Lake
            Tribune, November 14:B5.
Atchison, Sandra D.

1985   The Wild West Days May Be Back for Utah Brokers.
        Business Week, July 1: 69-70.

Bandura, Albert
1969   Principles of Behavior Modification. New York: Holt,
        Rhinehart, and Winston.

Bandzak, Ruth A.
1991   A Productive Systems Analysis of the 1983 Phelps
        Dodge Strike. Journal of Economic Issues Vol. XXV,
        No. 4 (December):1105-1125
1992   The Strike as Management Strategy. Journal of
        Economic Issues Vol. XXVI, No. 2 (June):645-659

Bargatzky, Thomas
1984   Culture, Environment, and the Ills of Adaptationism.
        Current Anthropology Vol. 25, No. 4:399-415.

Barker, M.
1987   The Xenophobic Mormon. Sunstone, January:26-30.
        Barnes, Will C.
1960   Arizona Place Names. Tucson: University of Arizona
        Press.

Barth, Fredrik
1967   On the Study of Social Change. American
        Anthropologist 69:661-669.

Beals, Alan R.
1967   Culture in Process. New York: Holt, Rinehart and
        Winston.

Benfer, Robert A.
1967   A Design for the Study of Archeological
        Characteristics. American Anthropologist 69:719-730.

Bennett, John W.

1967   Microcosm - Macrocosm Relationships in North American Agrarian Society. American Anthropologist 69:441-454.

Bergreen, Jason

2008   FBI analyzing powder sent to LDS Temples in SLC, L.A. The Salt Lake Tribune, November 14:B2.

Biema, David Van

2009   The Storm Over the Mormons. Time, June 22, 2009:48-53.

Black, Pete

2007   LDS Church Offers welcome explanation. Faith Forum. The Salt Lake Tribune, November 10:E4.

Bloom, Harold

1992   The American Religion: the Emergence of the Post-Christian Nation. New York: Simon & Schuster (A Touchtone Book).

Bock, Philip K.

1969   Modern Cultural Anthropology. New York: Alfred A. Knopf.

Brady, Peter

1941   Reminiscences of Peter Brady. Tucson: Arizona State Historical Society. (Unpublished manuscript).

Brooks, Juanita

1950   The Mountain Meadows Massacre. Stanford: Stanford University Press.

Broom, Leonard, Bernard J Siegel, Evon Z. Vogt, and James B. Watson.

1954   Acculturation: an Exploratory Formulation. American Anthropologist 56:973-1000.

Brophy, William A. and Sophie D. Aberle et al.

1966　　The Indian: America's Unfinished Business. (Report of the Commission on the Rights, Liberties, and Responsibilities of the American Indian. Norman, University of Oklahoma Press.

Bruere, Robert W.

1918　　Copper Camp Patriotism; an Interpretation. Nation, February 21.

Bruno, Robert

1994　　The 1946 Union of Electrical, Radio and Machinist Workers' Strike against the Phelps-Dodge Copper Company of Elizabeth, New Jersey. Labor History Vol. 35, No. 3 Summer 1994.

Buckley, Walter

1968　　Society as a Complex Adaptive System. *In* Modern Systems Research for the Behavioral Scientist. W. Buckley, ed. Pp. 490-513. Chicago: Aldine.

Buechler, Judith-Maria

1978　　The Dynamics of the Market in LaPaz, Bolivia. Urban Anthropology 7, No. 4:344-359.

Burling, Robbins

1962　　Maximization Theories and the Study of Economic Anthropology. American Anthropologist 64:802-821.

Burr, Thomas

2008　　LDS Prop. 8 push may impact Romney future. The Salt Lake Tribune, November24:A5.

Business Week

1982　　Why copper companies are running scared. May 3:80.

1982　　Concessionary Bargaining: Will the New Cooperation Last? June 14: 66-69, 72, 77, 79, 81.

1982　　The crisis that endangers Phelps Dodge. July 26:58-60.

1983   Industrywide Wage Patterns Get a Test in Copper. July
        18:58.

1983   Labor: No More Mr. Nice Guy. August 29:18-19.

1983   Phelps Dodge May Have Tamed Its Unions.
        September 26:39-40.

1984   Copper's Last-Ditch Plea to Hold Back Imports.
        February 13, 1984a:37-38.

1984   The Strikers Start to Crack at Phelps Dodge. February
        13, 1984b:38.

Carneiro, Robert L.

1967   On the Relationship between Size of Population and
        Complexity of Social Organization. Southwestern
        Journal of Anthropology 23:234-243.

Carstens, Peter

2001   In the Company of Diamonds: De Beers, Kleinzee, and
        the Control of a Town. Athens: Ohio University Press.

Caudill, Edward

1997   Darwinian Myths: The Legends and Misuses of a
        Theory. Knoxville: The University of Tennessee Press.

Chance, Norman A.

1966   The Eskimo of North Alaska. New York: Holt,
        Rinehart and Winston.

Chemical Marketing Reporter

1982   Phelps Dodge Cuts Dividend, Applies Austerities. May
        10:9,26.

Chemical Week

1982   A New Chief at Phelps Maps the Road Back. August
        11:14.

Cleland, Robert Glass

1952   A History of Phelps Dodge 1834-1950. New York: Alfred A. Knopf, Inc.

Clotts, Herbert V.

1915a   Country West of the Ajo Mountains. Report submitted to Chief Engineer, U.S. Indian Service, March 15, 1915. Washington, D.C.

1915b   Nomadic Papago Surveys and Investigations, 1914-15. Report submitted to Chief Engineer, U.S. Indian Service, July 2, 1915. Washington, D.C.

Cloud, John

2008   A Gay Mafia. Time Vol. 172, No. 19 (November 10): 52-55.

Corle, Edwin

1941   Desert Country. New York: Duell, Sloan and Pearce.

Cox, Annie M.

1938   History of Bisbee 1877 to 1937. Tucson: Unpublished Master's thesis, Department of History, University of Arizona.

Crawford, Margaret

1995   Building the Workman's Paradise. London: Verso.

Dawkins, Richard

1976   The Selfish Gene. New York: Oxford University Press.

Depew, David J. and Bruce H. Weber

1995   Darwinism Evolving: System Dynamics and the Genealogy of Natural Selection. Cambridge: MIT Press.

Deutsch, Karl W.

1951   Mechanism, Organism and Society. Philosophy of Science, 18, 3:239-252.

Dobner, Jennifer

2008a   BYU yanks calendar maker's diploma. An Associated
         Press article *in* The Salt Lake Tribune, October
         18:A11.

2008b   Mormon agency delays meeting with Affirmation. An
         Associated Press article *in* The Salt Lake Tribune, July
         26:C5.

Dorfman, John R., editor

1983   Vicious Circle. Forbes August 29:140.

Ebeling, Heather

1985   Shuttle Astronaut Officiates at Reading Room
         Opening. BYU Daily Universe, Tuesday, June 4: 1.

Ekman, Anna

1926   Ajo from 1856 to 1926. Ajo Copper News, May 8:5.

Erasmus, Charles J.

1961   Man Takes Control. Minneapolis: University of
         Minnesota Press

Farnsworth, Becky

1985   Men's Roles in Society Moving to Encompass
         "Women's" Roles. BYU Daily Universe, Thursday June
         13: 5.

Faust, James E.

2007   The Healing Power of Forgiveness. Ensign, May:67-69.

Fermi, Enrico

1956   Thermodynamics. New York: Dover Publications, Inc.
         (republication of 1936 edition.).

Fletcher, Peggy

1985   Poelman Revises Conference Speech. <u>Sunstone</u> Issue
         45 (January): 44-45.

Fortune

1982   Copper Cutback. May 3:7-8.

Foster, Brian L. and Stephen B. Seidman

    1982   Urban Structures Derived from Collections of Overlapping Subsets. Urban Anthropology Vol. 11, No. 2:177-192.

Foster, Lawrence

    1984   Career Apostates: Reflections on the Works of Jerold and Sandra Tanner. Dialogue: A Journal of Mormon Thought. Vol. 17, No. 2 (Summer): 35-60.

Fox, Richard G.

    1972   Rationale and Romance in Urban Anthropology. Urban Anthropology Vol. 1, No. 2:205-233.

Friedl, John and Noel J. Chrisman

    1975   City Ways: A Selective Reader in Urban Anthropology. New York: Thomas Y. Crowell Co.

Gallagher, Maggie

    2008   Treated like racists The Salt Lake Tribune July 2:A12 (Letter to the Public Forum).

Gearing, Fred, Robert Mac Netting and Lisa R. Peattie, eds.

    1960   Documentary History of the Fox Project: a Program in Action Anthropology. Chicago: University of Chicago (Dept. of Anthropology).

Gladwin, Malcom

    2000   The Tipping Point. Boston: Little, Brown and Company.

Gould, Stephen Jay

    1997   Death by Social Darwinism (A Tale of Two Worksites). Natural History Vol. 1, No. 9 (October):18-20, 22, 29, 62-68

Gulick, John

1967   Tripoli: A Modern Arab City. Cambridge: Harvard
        University Press.

1968   The Outlook, Research Strategies, and Relevance
        of Urban Anthropology: A Commentary. In Urban
        Anthropology: Research Perspectives and Strategies.
        Elizabeth M. Eddy (ed.). Southern Anthropological
        Society Proceedings, No. 2.

Hackenberg, Robert A.

n.d.   Prediction and Control of Social Change: the
        Theoretical Basis of Applied Anthropology.
        (Mimeographed paper), 33 pp.

1964   Aboriginal Land Use and Occupancy of the Papago
        Indians. (Mimeographed report submitted to the
        Lands Division, U.S. Department of Justice.)

Hackenberg, Robert A. and C. Roderick Wilson

1969   Mobility and Modernization: the Migration Process in
        Papago Indian Adaptation. An unpublished report to
        the Health Program Systems Center, US-PHS-IHS.
        Boulder, Institute of Behavioral Science, University of
        Colorado.

Hafen, Mary Ann

1983   Recollections of a Handcart Pioneer. Lincoln :
        University of Nebraska Press. (Reprinted from a
        privately published 1938 first edition.)

Hall, A. D. and R. E. Fagen

1956   Definition of System. Reprinted in Modern Systems
        Research for the Behavioral Scientist. W. Buckley, ed.
        Chicago: Aldine (1968).

Hamilton, Martha M.

1983 Copper Starts its Recovery. Washington Post, May 1:H1, H4-H6.

Hardin, Garrett

1963 The Cybernetics of Competition: a Biologist's View of Society. Perspectives in Biology and Medicine 7:58-84.

Harris, Marvin

1981 America Now: The Anthropology of a Changing Culture. New York: Simon and Schuster (A Touchstone Book).

Henslin, James M.

2007 Sociology: A Down-To Earth Approach. Boston et al.: Pearson (eighth edition).

Hockett, Charles F.

1953 Book Review of the Mathematical Theory of Communication by Claude L. Shannon and Warren Weaver. Language 29, No. 1:69-93.

Hodges, Corey J.

2008 Better security is needed at churches. The Salt Lake Tribune, November 15: C2.

Hoebel, E. Adamson

1960 The Cheyennes: Indians of the Great Plains. New York: Holt, Rinehart and Winston.

Holmberg, Allan R.

1957 From Paternalism to Democracy: the Cornell Peru Project. Human Organization Vol. 15, No.3:15-18.

Horiuchi, Vince

2009 LDS radio station on the air. The Salt Lake Tribune, May19: B1-2.

Hunsaker, Brent and Kerry Kinsey

2008   Same-sex marriage protest held near Temple Square. ABC 4.com. Electronic document, http://www. abc4.com/content/news/top%20stories/story. aspx? content_id =ec9e6b02-c7f4-434a-be80- 0765733bfbaa, accessed November 8, 2008.

Iron Age

     1983   Copper Prices Holding Despite Limited Walkout. July 22:70.

Isikoff, Michael

     1987   Deals of Developer Khashoggi Building Frustration in Utah; Millions Sought From Arms Figure's Firm. The Washington Post, January 4: A1.

Jarvik, Elaine

     1982   Utah: Going against the Trends. Change, July/ August:12-19.

Jarvis, Ben

     2008   Fight LDS Marriage ban (Letter to the Public Forum). The Salt Lake Tribune, July 5:A10.

Jefferson, David J.

     2008   How Getting Married Made Me an Activist. Newsweek, November 24:54-56.

Johnson, Clarence Elbert

     n.d.   A Study of the Administrative Organization and Finance of a Small City School System. Tucson: Henry G. Engstrom Collection, Arizona Pioneers Historical Society, Manuscript Section. 152 pp.

Johnson, F. Reed

     1979   The Mormon Church as a Central Command System. Review of Social Economy Vol. 37, issue 1, 1979:79- 94.

Johnson, Kirk

    2009   Door to Door as Missionaries, Then as Salesmen. Electronic document, www.nytimes.com/2009/06/12/12coldcalls.html, accessed 6/12/09.

Jones, Delmos J.

    1972   Incipient Organizations and Organizational Failures in an Urban Ghetto. Urban Anthropology Vol. 1, No. 1:51-67.

Kaplan, David

    1965   The Superorganic: Science or Metaphysics. American Anthropologist, Volume 67:958-976.

Keesing, Roger M.

    1972   Paradigm Lost: The New Ethnography and the New Linguistics. Southwestern Journal of Anthropology, Vol. 28, No. 4 (Winter): 299-332.

Kingsolver, Barbara

    1989   Holding the Line: Women in the Great Arizona Mine Strike of 1983. Ithaca: ILR Press Cornell University.

Kottak, Conrad P.

    1978   Rituals at McDonald's. Natural History Vol. 87, No. 1 (Jan):74-83.

Krakauer, Jon

    2003   Under the Banner of Heaven: A Story of Violent Faith. New York, N.Y. :Doubleday.

Kroeber, A.L.

    1917   The Superorganic. American Anthropologist Vol. 19, No. 2:163-213.

    1948   Anthropology. New York: Harcourt, Brace.

Kunkel, John H.

1985   Comment, pp. 82-83. *In* Darwinian Selection,
        Symbolic Variation, and the Evolution of
        Culture, David Rindos with "Comments" by other
        scholars. Current Anthropology Vol. 26, No. 1
        (February):65-88.

Langway, Lynn and Randy Collier

1983   Standoff in the Copper Mines. Newsweek August
        29:53.

Laughlin, Charles D., Jr., and Eugene d'Aquili

1974   Biogenetic Structuralism. New York: Columbia
        University Press.

Larson, Stan

2004   Quest for the Gold Plates: Thomas Stuart Ferguson's
        Archaeological Search for the Book of Mormon. Salt
        Lake City: Freethinker Press.

LeBaron Jr., Garn

2008   Mormon Fundamentalism and Violence: A Historical
        Analysis. Electronic document, www.exmormon.org/
        violence.htm, accessed 2/8/08.

Lee, George P. Lee

1989   The Lee Letters. Sunstone Volume 13:4, Issue 72
        (August 1989):50-55.

Leeds, Anthony

1979   Forms of Urban Integration: "Social Urbanization" in
        Comparative Perspective. Urban Anthropology Vol. 8,
        No. 3 and 4:227-247.

Leff, Lisa

2008   Same-sex marriage ban nets big bucks. The Salt Lake
        Tribune, October 27:A1, A4.

Leonard, John Wallace

1954   The Economics of a One-Industry Town. M. A. Thesis, Department of Economics, University of Arizona.

Lesure, Thomas B.

1955   Ajo. Arizona Highways. January: 4-9.

Levi-Strauss, Claude

1953   Social Structure. *In* Anthropology Today A.L. Kroeber, Chairman. Pp. 524-553. Chicago: U of Chicago Press.

1962   Social Structure. *In* Anthropology today: selections, Sol Tax, ed. Pp. 321-350. Chicago: University of Chicago Press.

Lewin, Roger

1984   New Regulatory Mechanism of Parasitism: Parasites of Certain Red Algae Insert Nuclei into the Cells of their Hosts and Cause Dramatic Changes in Metabolism and Morphology. Science 226 (Oct. 26): 427.

Lewis, Kimberly

1985   BYU Women Slowly Integrating into Male-dominated Majors. BYU Daily Universe, Wed. June 26: 6.

Localcensus.com

2008   Ajo, Arizona – Census Information. Electronic document, http://www.localcensus.com/city/Ajo/Arizona, accessed 11/9/08.

Long, Norton E.

1966   The Local Community as an Ecology of Games. *In* Political Sociology. Lewis A. Coser, ed. Pp. 146-166. New York: Harper and Row.

Long, Phillip

2007   Change punches holes in Mormonism. Faith Forum. The Salt Lake Tribune November 10:E4.

Lowie, Robert H.

1963   Religion in Human Life. American Anthropologist Vol. 65:532-542

Lumholtz, Carl

1912   New Trails in Mexico. New York: Charles Scribner's Sons.

Lynch, Owen

1967   Rural Cities in India: Continuities and Discontinuities in India and Ceylon: *In* Unity and Diversity, Phillip Mason, ed. Pp. 142-158. Oxford: Oxford University Press.

Maffly, Brian

2008   Two groups join rally for traditional marriage, rail against gay unions. The Salt Lake Tribune, November 16:A19.

Magnet, Myron

1983   Phelps Dodge's Lonely Stand. Fortune August 22:106-107, 110.

McKinley, Jesse and Kirk Johnson

2008   Mormons Tipped Scale in Ban on Gay Marriage. The New York Times, November 15. Electronic document, http://www.nytimes.com/2008/11/15/us/politics/15marriage.html?th&emc=th, accessed November 15, 2008.

Moloney, Karen Marguerite

2003   Saints for All Seasons: Lavina Fielding Anderson and Bernard Shaw's Joan of Arc. Dialogue Volume 36, No. 3:27-39.

Manners, Robert A. and John Collier

1972   Pluralism and the American Indian. *In* The Emergent Native Americans, Deward E. Walker, Jr., ed. Pp. 124-143. Boston: Little, Brown.

Mauss, Armand L.

2003   All Abrahams Children: Changing Mormon Conceptions of Race and Lineage. Urbana, University of Illinois Press.

Mayorga, Carlos

2008   Utah still has the highest birthrate in U.S.. says the Census Bureau. The Salt Lake Tribune, August 19:B6.

McConkie, Bruce R.

1958   Mormon Doctrine. Salt Lake City: Bookcraft, Inc.

1966   Mormon Doctrine. Salt Lake City: Bookcraft, Inc. (Revised Second Edition).

McCormick, T. P.

1919   Letter to the Commissioner of Indian Affairs Concerning the 1918 Papago Census of Various Reservation and Off-Reservation Locations. March 8, Tucson, Arizona.

Meyerhoff, Barbara

1978   Number Our Days. New York: P. D. Dutton.

Miller, Walter B.

1960   Authority and Collective Action in Fox Society. *In* Documentary History of the Fox Project: a program in action anthropology. F. Gearing, et al., ed. Chicago: U. of Chicago (Dept. of Anthropology).

Moore, Kenneth

1975   The City as Context: Context as Process. Urban Anthropology. 4, No. 1:17-25.

Moore, Wilbert E.

1951   Industrialization and Labor: Social Aspects of Economic Development. New York: Russell and Russell (1965).

Moran, Emilio F.

1990   Ecosystem Ecology in Biology and Anthropology: a Critical Assessment. *In* The Ecosystem Approach in Anthropology: from concept to practice, Emilio F. Moran, ed. Pp. 3-40. Ann Arbor: U. of Michigan Press.

Nash, Manning

1958   Machine Age Maya: the Industrialization of a Guatemalan Community. American Anthropologist Vol. 60, No.2, pt.2 (Memoir No.87).

Nelson, Lee

1985   The Best and the Worst in Utah Valley. Central Utah Journal, Sunday August 4: 1,3, 4.

News of the Weird

2009   Womb as a weapon. The Salt Lake Tribune, April 22: A2.

Nielsen, Michael

2008   How the LDS Church could address the polygamy question. The Salt Lake Tribune, April 15: A13.

Nicita, Lisa

2008   1 new word in Book of Mormon stirs church-vs.-science debate. The Arizona Republic, January 17, 2008. Electronic document, www.azcentral.com/news/articles/0117mormonword0116.html, accessed March 5, 2008.

Odum, Eugene P.

1953   Fundamentals of Ecology. Philadelphia: W.B. Saunders Co.

Odum, Howard T.

    1971   Environment, Power and Society. New York: Wiley-Interscience.

Olsen, Ralph A.

    2004   A Malay Site for Book of Mormon Events. Sunstone, Issue 131, March:30-34. Office of Counterintelligence.

    2008   Richard William Miller. Electronic document, www. hanford.gov/oci/ci_spy.cfm? dossier=51 - 26k, accessed 9/22/08.

Online NewsHour

    2008   Education Backgrounder—School Funding. Electronic document, www.pbs.org/newshour/backgrounders/school_funding.html, accessed 8/22/08.

Ostow, Mortimer

    1951   The Entropy Concept and Psychic Function. American Scientist 39:140-144.

Pitt-Rivers, J. A.

    1961   The People of the Sierra. Chicago: The University of Chicago Press (Phoenix Edition).

Priddis, Venice

    1975   The Book and the Map: New Insights into Book of Mormon Geography. Salt Lake City: Bookcraft, Inc.

Price, John A.

    1972   Reno, Nevada: The City as a Unit of Study. Urban Anthropology 1, No. 1:14-28.

Quinn, D. Michael

    1987   Early Mormonism and the Magic World View. Salt Lake City: Signature Books.

Rapoport, Anatol

1953   What is Information: Etc.: A Review of General Semantics10:247-260.

1956   The Promise and Pitfalls of Information Theory. Behavioral Science 1:303-309.

Ravitz, Jessica

2008a   Leaders of Utah faiths praise LDS president. The Salt Lake Tribune, January 29:A4.

2008b   Equity Utah asks LDS Church for support on 5 bills. The Salt Lake Tribune, November 11:B1,B2.

Reitz, Stephanie

2008   LDS theater director resigns. An Associated Press article *in* The Salt Lake Tribune, November 13:A7.

Rindos, David

1984   The Origin of Agricultural Systems: An Evolutionary Perspective. New York: Academic Press.

1985   Darwinian Selection, Symbolic Variation, and the Evolution of Culture. Current Anthropology Vol. 26, No. 1:65-88.

Ritzer, George

2004   The McDonaldization of Society: Revised New Century Edition. Thousand Oaks, Pine Forge Press.

Robbins, Michael C., Anthony V. Williams, Philip L. Kilbride, and Richard B. Pollnac

1969   Factor Analysis and Case Selection in Complex Societies: a Buganda Example. Human Organization 28:227-234.

Rollwagen, Jack R.

1975   Introduction: The City as Context: a Symposium. Urban Anthropology Vol. 4 (1):1-4.

1979 Some Implications of the World System Approach for the Anthropological Study of Latin American Urbanization. Urban Anthropology Vol. 8, No. 3 and 4:249-265.

Rose, Dan

1936 The Ancient Mines of Ajo (Publisher unknown).

Rosenblueth, Arturo and Norbert Wiener

1945 The role of models in science. Philosophy of Science 12:316-321.

Rosenblum, Jonathan D.

1995 Copper Crucible: How the Arizona Miners' Strike of 1983. Recast Labor-Management Relations in America. Ithaca: ILR Press.

Rosta, Joseph

1984 Big Copper Busts the Unions. Business and Society Review, Winter: 45-48.

Rubin, Jeffrey Z.

1981 Psychological Traps. Psychology Today, Vol. 15, No. 3:52-54.

Rubinstein, Robert A.

1975 Reciprocity and Resource Deprivation among the Urban Poor in Mexico City, Urban Anthropology Vol. 4, No. 2:251-264.

Rund, Nadine H., Herman Siegel, and Ella G. Rumley

1968 Demographic and Socio-Cultural Characteristics: Papago Indian Reservations, Arizona. Tucson: Health Program Systems Center, Indian Health Service

Rund, Nadine H. and Ella G. Rumley

1968 Demographic and Socio-Cultural Characteristics: off- reservation service population Sells Service Unit,

Arizona. Tucson: Health Program Systems Center,
Indian Health Service.

Sahlens, M.D., and E.R. Service, eds.

1960   Evolution and Culture. Ann Arbor: University of
Michigan Press.

Schrodinger, E.

1944   What is Life?: the Physical Aspect of the Living Cell.
Cambridge: Cambridge University Press.

Scott, Richard G.

2008   The Sanctity of Womanhood. New Era,
November:2-5.

Shannon, Claude and Warren Weaver

1949   The Mathematical Theory of Communication. Urbana:
University of Illinois Press.

Shipps, Jan

1985   Mormonism: The Story of a New Religious Tradition.
Urbana: University of Illinois Press.

Singh, Jagjit

1966   Great Ideas in Information Theory, Language and
Cybernetics. New York: Dover Publications, Inc.

Sitter, Albert J.

1968   Mining Expert Debunks Maze of Copper Strike
Fallacies. Arizona Republic, January 28:BI-B2.

Sloan, Richard E. and Ward R. Adams

1930   History of Arizona, Vol. II. Phoenix: Record
Publishing Company.

Smith, Christopher

2001   Nation's Anthropologists Evaluate LDS Culture. The
Salt Lake Tribune, December 1. Electronic document,

http://www.rickross.com/reference/mormon/
mormon57.html, accessed October 1, 2008.

Smith, Joseph

See the note about the Mormon Scriptures at the beginning of
the References Cited Section of this book.

Smith, M. Estellie

1976   Questions of Urban Analysis. Urban Anthropology 5,
No. 3:253-269.

Sorenson, John L.

1985   An Ancient American Setting for the Book of
Mormon. Salt Lake City, Deseret Book.

1997   Mormon Culture: four decades of essays on Mormon
society and personality. Salt Lake City, Utah: New Sage
Books.

Spence, Hartzell

1960   The Story of America's Religions. New York: Holt,
Rinehart and Winston.

Stack, Peggy Fletcher

2008a   Mormon Exodus. The Salt Lake Tribune, June 19: A1-
A2.

2008b   Hinckley: A lifetime of faithful service. The Salt Lake
Tribune, January 28:H2-H5.

2008c   Debate on gays forces musician out of LDS. The Salt
Lake Tribune, February 24: A1, A9.

2008d   Mormons urged to block gay marriage. The Salt Lake
Tribune, June 24: A1, A4.

2008e   Modern-day Mormons disavow polygamy. The Salt
Lake Tribune, April 20: A16.

2008f   Accusations fly as battle over Prop. 8 nears finish. The
Salt Lake Tribune, October 25:C1, C5.

2008g   Church: "Go viral" with Prop 8 support. The Salt Lake Tribune, October 9:B1, B2.

2008h   Bill Marriott: Marriott International did not contribute to the campaign to pass Proposition 8. The Salt Lake Tribune November 14. Electronic document, http://www.sltrib.com/ci_10982563, accessed November 17, 2008.

2008i   Church and gays condemn attacks. The Salt Lake Tribune, November 15, 2008:B1.

2008j   Prop 8 involvement a P.R. fiasco for LDS Church. The Salt Lake Tribune November 22. Electronic document, http://www.sltrib.com/ci_11044660, accessed November 24, 2008.

2009a   LDS Church freezes hirings. The Salt Lake Tribune, January 8, 2009:B1, B2.

2009b   LDS Swahili Branch unites African Mormons who live from one end of the Salt Lake Valley to the other. The Salt Lake Tribune, April 18, 2009:C1, C2.

2009c   Africa's Mormon superstar is LDS Church's first black African general authority. The Salt Lake Tribune, April 18, 2009:C1, C2.

Stark, Rodney
    1984   The Rise of a New World Faith. Review of Religious Research, Vol. 26, No. 1 (September).

Steward, Julian H.
    1955   Theory of Culture Change: the Methodology of Multilinear Evolution. Urbana, University of Illinois Press.

Stucki, John

> 1932   Family History Journal of John S. Stucki. Salt Lake
> City: Privately Printed.

Stucki, Larry R.

> 1967   Anthropologists and Indians: a New Look at the Fox
> Project. Plains Anthropologist 12-37:300-317.

> 1969   Who Controls the Indians?: Social Manipulation in an
> Ethnic Enclave. Paper Read at the 68th Annual Meeting
> of the American Anthropological Association on
> November 22, 1969 at New Orleans, Louisiana.

> 1970   The Entropy Theory of Human Behavior: Indian
> Miners in Search of the Ultrastable State During
> a Prolonged Copper Strike Ph.D. Dissertation,
> University of Colorado. (December).

> 1971   The Case Against Population Control: The Probable
> Creation of the First American Indian State. Human
> Organization Vol. 30, No. 4, (Winter): 393-399. 1973
> Who Controls the Indians?: Social Manipulation in
> an Ethnic Enclave. In American Indian Urbanization:
> J.O. Waddell and O.M. Watson, editors. Pp. 28-50.
> Institute for the Study of Social Change, Purdue
> University,

> 1984   Will the "Real" Indian Survive?: Tourism and Affluence
> at Cherokee, North Carolina. In Affluence and Cultural
> Survival, R. Salisbury and E. Tooker, eds.Pp. 53-73.
> Washington, D.C.: American Ethnological Society.

Therrien, Corinne Rentfrow

> 1945   The Historical Background of the Ajo, Arizona,
> School System. Tucson: Unpublished Master's thesis,
> Department of Education, University of Arizona.

Tribune Staff and Wire Services

2008 Wife of Steve Young active in efforts against California proposition to ban gay marriage. The Salt Lake Tribune, November 4. Electronic document, http://www. sltrib.com/ci_10890609, accessed November 12, 2008.

Twohy, Patrick

2008 Won't be back. (The Public Forum) The Salt Lake Tribune, November 14:A12.

Uchtdorf, Dieter F.

2008 Developing Christlike Attributes. Ensign, Vol. 38, No. 10 (October 2008):5-7.

U.S.Department of the Interior: Bureau of Indian Affairs

1968 Answers to Your Questions about American Indians. Washington: U.S. Government Printing Office.

Utah Holiday Staff

1985 The Best and the Worst. Utah Holiday, Vol. 14, No. 11 (August 1985): 32-54.

Valley National Bank

1968 Arizona Progress (A monthly report on the economic "health" of the state of Arizona), February. Phoenix: Research Dept., Valley National Bank.

Van Valkenburgh, Richard

1945 Tom Childs of Ten-Mile Wash. Desert Magazine, December: 3-6.

Waddell, Jack 0.

1964 Unpublished June 1964 Census of Indian Heads of Households in Ajo, Arizona.

1966 Adaptation of Papago Workers to Off-reservation Occupations. Ann Arbor: University Microfilms (Authorized microfilm-xerography facsimile 1967).

(This is a copy of Waddell's Ph.D. dissertation which was later published with just a few deletions and other minor changes in 1969 by the University of Arizona Press under the title, Papago Indians at Work (see below). Most references in my book have been changed to indicate the corresponding pages in the 1969 printing of Waddell's thesis, except where deletions made this impossible.)

1968   From Patronage to Bureaucracy: Culture Change among the Papago Indians. A paper read at the 67th Annual Meeting of the American Anthropological Association, Seattle, Washington.

1969   Papago Indians at Work. Tucson: University of Arizona Press.

1974   Resurgent Patronage and Lagging Bureaucracy in a Papago Off-Reservation Community. *In* Anthropology and Community Action, Elizabeth Hegeman and Leonard Koopeman, eds., Pp. 176-186. Garden City, New York: Anchor Books.

Wahlquist, Reed

2005   My Adventures as a Coffee Abstainer. Sunstone, November: 11-12.

Walsh, Rebecca

2008   Prop 8 rips friendship asunder. The Salt Lake Tribune, November 9:B1, B4.

Wharton, Tom

2008   Gay-rights leaders oppose Utah boycott. The Salt Lake Tribune, November16:A16.

Watson, Blair

2007 Smith's words don't support the new "truth". Faith
   Forum, The Salt Lake Tribune, November 10:E4.

Weekly Phoenix Herald
  1890 A New Uncle Tom. December 18, 4:2.

White, Leslie A.
  1959 The Evolution of Culture: The Development of
     Civilization to the Fall of Rome. New York, McGraw
     Hill.
  1975 The Concept of Cultural Systems: A Key to
     Understanding Tribes and Nations. New York:
     Columbia University Press.

Whitelaw, Kevin
  2008 Riding the Oil Boom. U.S. News & World Report,
     June 16: 33-36, 38-39.

Wiley, Peter and Robert Gottlieb
  1982 Empires in the Sun: the Rise of the New American
     West. New York: G.P. Putnam's Sons.

Winderhalder, Bruce and Eric A. Smith
  1992 Evolutionary Ecology and the Social Sciences. *In*
     Evolutionary Ecology and Human Behavior, B.
     Winderhalder and E. A. Smith, eds. Pp. 3-33. New
     York: Aldine De Gruyter.

Winters, Rosemary
  2008 Ex-Mormon donates $1M to kill LDS-backed Prop. 8.
     The Salt Lake Tribune, September 18:A1

Wirth, Louis
  1956 Rural Urban Differences. *In* On Cities and Social
     Life, Albert J. Reiss, ed. Pp. 221-225. Chicago: The
     University of Chicago Press.

Woodward, Kenneth L.

1982   Apostles Vs. Historians. Newsweek, Feb. 15:77.

Woodward, Kenneth L. and Jack Goodman

1981   Thus Saith Ezra Benson. Newsweek, Oct. 19:109.

Wright, Ed

1985   Building Inspectors Question Renovations. The Daily Universe, Tuesday, July 30:1.

Yurth, Cindy

2009   Diné racist Anglo says. Navajo Times, April 16: